APPROACHES TO GROUP WORK

A HANDBOOK FOR PRACTITIONERS

David Capuzzi

Portland State University

Merrill
Prentice Hall

Upper Saddle River, New Jersey
Columbus, Ohio

Library of Congress Cataloging-in-Publication Data
Approaches to group work : a handbook for practitioners / [edited by] David Capuzzi.
   p. cm.
  Includes bibliographical references.
  ISBN 0-13-090760-X (pbk.)
   1. Group counseling. I. Capuzzi, Dave.

BF637.C 6.A65 2003
158'.35—dc21   2001059085

Vice President and Publisher: Jeffery W. Johnston
Executive Editor: Kevin M. Davis
Associate Editor: Christina Kalisch Tawney
Editorial Assistant: Autumn Crisp
Production Editor: Mary Harlan
Production Coordination: Lea Baranowski, Carlisle Publishers Services
Design Coordinator: Diane C. Lorenzo
Cover Design: Heather Miller
Cover Art: SuperStock
Text Design and Illustrations: Carlisle Publishers Services
Production Manager: Laura Messerly
Director of Marketing: Ann Castel Davis
Marketing Manager: Amy June
Marketing Coordinator: Tyra Cooper

This book was set in Garamond by Carlisle Communications, Ltd. It was printed and bound by Banta Book Group. The cover was printed by Phoenix Color Corp.

Pearson Education Ltd.
Pearson Education Australia Pty. Limited
Pearson Education Singapore Pte. Ltd.
Pearson Education North Asia Ltd.
Pearson Education Canada, Ltd.
Pearson Educación de Mexico, S.A. de C.V.
Pearson Education—Japan
Pearson Education Malaysia Pte. Ltd.
Pearson Education, *Upper Saddle River, New Jersey*

Merrill
Prentice Hall

10 9 8 7 6 5 4 3 2
ISBN: 0-13-090760-X

PREFACE

The role of a professional counselor calls for practitioners who have the knowledge and skills to assist clients as they strive to attain higher levels of self-understanding, problem solving, relationship building, and planning for the future. Counselors in school, community/mental health, hospital, private practice, rehabilitation, business and industry, and a variety of other agency settings are called upon to deliver a variety of services to a culturally diverse and challenging clientele comprising children, adolescents, and adults. In many instances, clients can be well served through the provision of task, psychoeducational, counseling, or psychotherapy groups. Counselors and therapists must master the basic knowledge and skill competencies needed to facilitate groups in order to meet the needs of a substantive segment of their clients served in particular settings and to obtain positions in those settings. Ability to do group work with clients is essential to beginning and experienced professionals committed to providing the constellation of services their clients deserve.

This handbook is unique in several ways. The 23 authors of the approaches to groups included in this resource are all residents of the Pacific Northwest. They represent a wide range of interests as well as expertise spanning a 40-year continuum from the beginning to the experienced professional. Except for one faculty contributor, all were members of a graduate student cohort in the counselor education program in the Graduate School of Education at Portland State University in Portland, Oregon.

The models for group facilitation presented in this handbook were created for implementation with specific age groups in either the work settings or proposed internship sites of the authors. Each author used the following paradigm to plan the group interventions described: statement of purpose, conceptual framework, goals for the group, plans for pre-group screening and orientation, descriptions for eight group sessions, evaluation of the group experience, and plans for referral and follow-up.

Even though no two professionals facilitate groups in exactly the same way, each author provides a thorough description of each of the eight sessions so that other practitioners can follow the same format. The purpose, theme, and materials needed for each session are addressed. In addition, each author described the "process" variables that should be taken into consideration to enhance the opportunity for participation by each member of the group and to focus the group experience in constructive and therapeutic ways. In all cases, it is also true that the interventions described probably exceed what could be accomplished in just eight sessions and that those using this resource will find that each group intervention could take considerably longer than eight sessions to complete. In part, this is based on a shared philosophy that it is better to "over plan and under use" so that the plan or format for the group does not begin to take precedence over the needs of group members during a given session.

Part 1 of this handbook describes approaches to group work with children, Part 2 describes approaches to group work with adolescents, and Part 3 describes approaches to group work with adults. This handbook can be used by graduate students in counselor education, psychology, and social work as a practical adjunct to a more theoretical text used in the process of preparing the group-work specialist.

In addition, *Approaches to Group Work: A Handbook for Practitioners* can also be helpful to professionals who have completed their graduate degrees and wish to continue developing the knowledge and skills base needed for the successful facilitation of groups.

Acknowledgments

I would like to thank the 23 authors who contributed their time and expertise and worked so diligently to develop this handbook. I would also like to thank my family, who provided the support to make this writing and editing effort possible, as well as the counselor education faculty at Portland State University. My thanks are also directed to Kevin Davis and other staff at Merrill/Prentice Hall for their encouragement. Special recognition is given to Melinda Haley and Jena Johnson, both graduate assistants and candidates for the Master's degree in the community specialization of the Counselor Education program at Portland State University. Both worked diligently and competently to make this handbook a reality. I am also grateful to those who reviewed this manuscript for their comments and suggestions: Adrian Blow, St. Louis University; Stacey Tantleff Dunn, University of Central Florida; Dana Edwards, Georgia State University; Jerry L. Johnson, Grand Valley State University; and Judith M. Unger, Western Illinois University.

DISCOVER THE COMPANION WEBSITE ACCOMPANYING THIS BOOK

THE PRENTICE HALL COMPANION WEBSITE: A VIRTUAL LEARNING ENVIRONMENT

Technology is a constantly growing and changing aspect of our field that is creating a need for content and resources. To address this emerging need, Prentice Hall has developed an online learning environment for students and professors alike—Companion Websites—to support our textbooks.

In creating a Companion Website, our goal is to build on and enhance what the textbook already offers. For this reason, the content for each user-friendly website is organized by topic and provides the professor and student with a variety of meaningful resources. Common features of a Companion Website include:

For the Professor—

Every Companion Website integrates **Syllabus Manager**™, an online syllabus creation and management utility.

- **Syllabus Manager**™ provides you, the instructor, with an easy, step-by-step process to create and revise syllabi, with direct links into the Companion Website and other online content without having to learn HTML.
- Students may log on to your syllabus during any study session. All they need to know is the web address for the Companion Website and the password you've assigned to your syllabus.
- After you have created a syllabus using **Syllabus Manager**™, students may enter the syllabus for their course section from any point in the Companion Website.
- Clicking on a date, the student is shown the list of activities for the assignment. The activities for each assignment are linked directly to actual content, saving time for students.
- Adding assignments consists of clicking on the desired due date, then filling in the details of the assignment—name of the assignment, instructions, and whether it is a one-time or repeating assignment.
- In addition, links to other activities can be created easily. If the activity is online, a URL can be entered in the space provided, and it will be linked automatically in the final syllabus.
- Your completed syllabus is hosted on our servers, allowing convenient updates from any computer on the Internet. Changes you make to your syllabus are immediately available to your students at their next logon.

For the Student—

- **Counseling Topics**—17 core counseling topics represent the diversity and scope of today's counseling field.

- **Annotated Bibliography**—includes seminal foundational works and key current works.
- **Web Destinations**—lists significant and up-to-date practitioner and client sites.
- **Professional Development**—provides helpful information regarding professional organizations and codes of ethics.
- **Electronic Bluebook**—send homework or essays directly to your instructor's e-mail with this paperless form.
- **Message Board**—serves as a virtual bulletin board to post—or respond to—questions or comments to/from a national audience.
- **Chat**—real-time chat with anyone who is using the text anywhere in the country—ideal for discussion and study groups, class projects, etc.

To take advantage of these and other resources, please visit the *Approaches to Group Work: A Handbook for Practitioners* Companion Website at

www.prenhall.com/capuzzi

MEET THE CONTRIBUTORS

David Capuzzi, Ph.D., N.C.C., L.P.C., is a past president of the American Counseling Association (formerly the American Association for Counseling and Development) and is professor and coordinator of Counselor Education in the Graduate School of Education at Portland State University in Portland, Oregon.

A former editor of *The School Counselor*, Dr. Capuzzi has authored a number of textbook chapters and monographs on the topic of preventing adolescent suicide and is coeditor and author, with Dr. Larry Golden, of *Helping Families Help Children: Family Interventions with School-Related Problems* and *Preventing Adolescent Suicide*. He co-authored and edited *Youth at Risk: A Prevention Resource for Counselors, Teachers, and Parents; Introduction to the Counseling Profession; Introduction to Group Counseling;* and *Counseling and Psychotherapy: Theories and Interventions* with Douglas R. Gross. He has authored or co-authored articles in a number of ACA-related journals.

A frequent speaker and keynoter at professional conferences and institutes, Dr. Capuzzi has also consulted with a variety of school districts and community agencies interested in initiating prevention and intervention strategies for adolescents at risk for suicide. He has facilitated the development of suicide prevention, crisis management, and post intervention programs in communities throughout the United States; provides training on the topics of "youth at risk" and "grief and loss"; and serves as an invited adjunct faculty member at other universities as time permits. He is the first recipient of ACA's Kitty Cole Human Rights Award.

Ann Strachan Bethune, B.A., is completing her Master's degree in counseling from Portland State University. She has spent many years working with chronically mentally ill adults and with the frail elderly population. Most recently, she has specialized in working with people who are suffering from Alzheimer's disease. For the last three years, she has facilitated support groups for family members of people with dementia. These experiences have contributed to a strong interest in grief work.

Anna Colleen Bourassa, B.A., received her Bachelor's in Management and Organizational Leadership from George Fox University. She is a Disability Benefits Analyst for Standard Insurance Company. Ms. Bourassa was on the founding committee of Yamhill County Mediators and served two terms on the board. She is a medication trainer and an ongoing facilitator/mediator. She is currently pursuing graduate studies in Vocational Rehabilitation Counseling at Portland State University.

Lori Butler, B.A., is currently a student in the School Counseling Specialization of the Counselor Education program at Portland State University. She has a Bachelor's degree in Linguistics from San Diego State University. Her previous experiences include teaching English to adults and children in Spain and several years as an elementary school teacher in California.

Cathleen Callaway, M.S., recently worked as a school counselor at Centennial High School in Gresham, Oregon. In her previous nine years as an educator, in addition to the development and implementation of Language Arts curriculum, she organized peer mediation teams, parent and youth communication groups, a credit recovery program, cultural diversity curriculum, drug and alcohol prevention programs, career education curriculum, and ninth-grade empowerment training. Her professional interests and expertise include issues related to drug, alcohol, and violence prevention, life-skills training, and building resiliency among youth.

Lisa M. Carbone, M.Ed., earned her Master's in Special Education: Deaf and Hard-of-Hearing at Lewis and Clark College in Portland, Oregon. After 10 years in education, she has realigned her interest in children from the classroom-sized group to the individual child, and is currently working on her Master's in Counselor Education at Portland State University. Her studies are concentrated in marriage and family counseling, and she intends to become a play therapist focusing on issues of grief and loss.

Christie L. Carlson, B.S., is an Oregon Laurels scholarship recipient and a Master's student in the Counselor Education program at Portland State University. She received her Bachelor's in psychology from Portland State University and has two adult children whom she credits with her ambition to learn and to serve. Ms. Carlson is interested in spiritual awareness, social mindfulness, and the individual as a unique and essential force. Her professional ambitions include psycho-educational counseling with expectant parents and work with grief sufferers.

Jonathan W. Carrier, B.S., completed his Bachelor's degree with a double major in Psychology and Sociology at East Tennessee State University in 1999. He is currently pursuing dual Master's degrees in Rehabilitation and Community Counseling at Portland State University and plans to pursue a Doctorate in Counseling Psychology. His counseling and research interests include behavioral interventions, spirituality as a coping mechanism, and early influences on psychopathology.

Virjeana A. Chambers, B.A., received her Bachelor's degree in Social Sciences with a minor in Psychology. She is currently a student in Portland State University's Graduate School of Education, pursuing a Master's degree in Counselor Education with an emphasis on both community and rehabilitation tracks.

Daren E. Gilbert, M.A.T., is a school counselor at Sandy High School in Sandy, Oregon, where she previously taught English for 14 years. She is working toward a Master's degree specializing in School Counseling from Portland State University. She completed her Master of Arts in Teaching at Lewis and Clark College. Her professional interests include issues related to eating disorders, adolescent pregnancy, and teen pregnancy.

Melinda Haley, B.S., is an Oregon Laurels Scholar and member of Chi Sigma Iota, an international counseling academic and professional honor society. She is currently pursing dual Master's degrees in Community and Couples, Marriage and Family Counseling and plans to pursue a Ph.D. in either Counselor Education or Counseling Psychology. Her areas of interest and planned specializations are couples, marriage, and family counseling, issues pertaining to the single parent, and psychiatric disorders. Ms. Haley is also interested in building a writing career in nonfiction and fiction. In addition to her scholarly work, she is also working on two novels; one is historical fiction *(Yanqui)* and the other deals with contemporary racial issues *(American Holocaust)*.

Susan E. Halverson completed her Ph.D. in Counselor Education at the College of William and Mary in 1999. After teaching first graders for five years, she helped establish the elementary school counseling program in the Virginia Beach Public School System. Working as an elementary counselor for ten years, one of her goals was to train peer helpers and peer conflict mediators at Point O' View Elementary School. During this time, she also achieved her license as a Professional Counselor (LPC). While completing her doctorate at William and Mary, she was director of New Horizons Family Counseling Center and added her Marriage and Family License (LMFT). Part of Susan's internship included counseling families on site at an elementary school in Williamsburg. Dr. Halverson is currently an assistant professor at Portland State University.

Debra Holmes, B.A.E., has her Bachelor of Arts in Secondary Education from Pacific Lutheran University in Tacoma, Washington. She is currently teaching seventh-grade language arts and social studies in Tigard, Oregon, and pursuing a Master of Arts degree in the School Counseling Specialization of the Counselor Education program at Portland State University.

Beth Hunter, B.A., is a second-year student in the Counselor Education program at Portland State University. Her particular area of interest is the brief solution-focused emphasis of employee assistance programs. Beth's professional background includes experience in human resources, financial planning, and employee benefit consultation.

Kristin A. Kahler, B.A., is currently pursuing a Master of Science degree in the School Counseling specialization of the Counselor Education program at Portland State University. She became interested in a career in counseling while co-facilitating domestic violence support groups at a shelter for women and children. Her interests include self-esteem enhancement, domestic violence, peer mediation, and communication skills.

Susan A. Kelsey, B.A., is currently a graduate student in the Counselor Education program at Portland State University. She is a member of Chi Sigma Iota, an international counseling academic and professional honor society. Susan also received an AAS degree, with highest honors, in Chemical Dependence counseling. She has owned and operated three successful businesses with her husband.

Barbara A. Klym, currently a graduate assistant in the career center at Portland State University, plans to work as a career counselor in a university setting.

Lisa Langfuss, a student in the Counselor Education program at Portland State University, works as a counselor to parenting and pregnant adolescents. She currently serves as a consultant to an inpatient psychiatric facility for youth diagnosed with multiple psychological disorders and facilitates groups for victims of domestic violence. Ms. Langfuss has served on the Psi Chi Steering Committee for the Annual WPA Convention (1999) and as a student coordinator of the 1998 IACCP Silver Jubilee Conference. Her interests include working with youth and their families with a primary emphasis on the psychosocial impact of behavioral and emotional disorders on the family system.

Martha L. Larsen, B.S., is a graduate student in the School Counseling specialization of the Counselor Education program at Portland State University, where she is a chapter member of the Chi Sigma Iota Honor Society. She is employed as a counselor at an alternative high school in the Portland area. She has experience training peer mediators at the middle and elementary school levels. She has worked as a substitute teacher in elementary schools and has been a volunteer in schools in many capacities for more than a decade. Ms. Larsen received her B.S. in Forest Resources from the University of Washington, which led her to her first career as a Forester with the U.S. Forest Service. She plans to find ways to integrate her background in natural resources with the theory and practice of counseling young people, as she believes in the importance of a deep spiritual connection to the natural world.

Rachel Lilienthal-Stair, B.S., currently is a teacher in the Cascade School District. She is enrolled in the Counselor Education program at Portland State University. She has worked with students in various school settings including an alternative school for third and fourth graders, self-contained programs for students with emotional problems, and Special Education programs in the middle school setting. Rachel Stair obtained her Bachelor of Science in Human Development with a specialization in Special Education from Wheelock College, Boston. She is a member of the American Counseling Association and the American School Counselor Association.

Jeff Morris, M.S.T., serves high school students in his role as guidance counselor at Wahtonka High School in The Dalles, Oregon. He is especially concerned with the unmet needs of teens, particularly those who struggle for success in traditional class settings. He thoroughly enjoys his wife and four sons, and hopes his students find the same familial support.

Kelly Peterson, B.A., obtained her Bachelor of Arts degree in Psychology at Portland State University. She is currently in the Master's program in Counselor

Education, also at Portland State University. Kelly's choice of focus on behaviorally challenged children and their families is an outgrowth of her experience as an educator for early childhood education. She uses her experience and education to advocate in her community on the importance of quality child-centered programs.

Sharon Smith, B.S., is a graduate student in the Counselor Education program at Portland State University. While working toward her Master's degree, Sharon is employed by a pediatric oncology clinic at a local area hospital. She received her B.S. in Psychology from Western Oregon University in 1997.

Marci J. Warnecke, B.A., is currently employed at Jesuit High School in Portland, Oregon, while completing the school counseling specialization of Portland State University's Counselor Education program. She is a member of the American Counseling Association and the Oregon Educational Association. Marci has worked with students at all levels in academic settings, in a residential treatment center, as well as on the athletic field as a coach. She plans to incorporate knowledge gained from these varied experiences and her counseling coursework into her role as a secondary level school counselor.

CONTENTS

PART 1

GROUP WORK WITH CHILDREN

In addressing group process as applied to young children, the authors in Part One explore a variety of subjects that are basic to counseling, yet profoundly important to such a vulnerable group of clients. For example, Chapter 1, "Using the Arts in a Bereavement Group for Children," recognizes that children are at a developmental and cultural disadvantage when faced with grief and loss. The use of creative arts allows children to grieve in nonthreatening ways and allows them to draw on the support of their peers, understand the nature of their loss, express feelings, and memorialize the person who died.

Chapter 2, "Life-Threatening Illness in School-Age Children: A Transition Group," addresses how a traumatic diagnosis can affect communication between children and their families. "Even when treatment is going successfully, the lives of the patient and family members are influenced by the illness and its treatment and side effects." Therefore, some goals for group members are to meet others who share the same illness, explore fears and anxieties in a safe environment, learn to deal with change within group members and their families, and have the opportunity to ask questions and receive honest answers pertaining to their illness.

Chapter 3, "Trust and Support: Children of Alcoholics Build Their Own Identities," aims to address the feelings of isolation, frustration, and powerlessness while, at the same time, addressing issues that will help children learn about the disease of alcoholism and identify resources to cope with its effects. Foundational to this particular group are the recognition that children are their own best resource and can recover regardless of their parent's behavior and that education is the most powerful weapon in the fight against the effects of this disease.

Chapter 4, "Friendship Groups: Make a Friend and Be a Friend," focuses on increasing children's understanding of themselves and empathy for others. As a developmental group within a school setting, it should be structured (yet flexible) and age appropriate. The goals for this group include learning respect for self and others, learning life and social skills, identifying feelings, and increasing self-knowledge and self-esteem.

Chapter 5, "Kids Helping Kids: A Group Training for Peer Helpers and Beyond," recognizes the moral and cognitive developmental growth that results from peer help. Various skills developed through the peer-helping relationship can aid individuals to function more appropriately in society. This group is structured to help members demonstrate strength-building skills, listening skills, open-question skills, clarifying skills, problem-solving skills, and journaling and reflection skills.

CHAPTER 1

USING THE ARTS IN A BEREAVEMENT GROUP FOR CHILDREN

Lisa M. Carbone

PURPOSE

"You've got to feel it to heal it" is a simple way to phrase an essential component of successful counseling. In the case of children who have experienced the death of an important person in their lives, this is equally true. To resolve grief, it must be expressed. Yet, children are often unable to express their feelings because of their immature cognitive and language abilities. In addition, the prohibition against showing the pain of loss is strong in our Western culture and many children are reared in families that follow this cultural taboo. When death touches the life of such a family, the child is at a developmental and cultural disadvantage for being able to express the feelings that are generated by the experience. In addition, according to Erickson, children ages 6–12 are undergoing the challenges of industry versus inferiority. They are so active with this developmental task that they tend to hide any emotional turmoil they may be experiencing (Schaefer, Johnson, & Wherry, 1982).

Smith (1991) lists three necessary tasks for resolving grief: "understanding the person is no longer there, feeling the feelings, and reinvesting in life" (p. 171). The purpose of a bereavement group for children is to assist them to fully experience and express the feelings they have about the death of an important person in their lives. It is hoped that by participating in such a group, children will be able to overcome the developmental and cultural barriers they face, claim the rightful and complete expression of their feelings, and from there move into a place of healing.

CONCEPTUAL FRAMEWORK

Given that it is imperative for children to process their feelings of grief, it is important to understand some of the unique ways they understand and respond to death. A child's reality upon experiencing a death is multifaceted. This variety begins with the type of loss experienced. It is not only a death in the family that impacts a child's life. The death of other known, important people also affects a child (Seibert, Drolet, & Fetro, 1993). In addition to the relationship the child had with the deceased, the child's support system and the psychological health of the child also influence the grieving process (The Dougy Center, 1999).

Certainly, children experience the same full range of emotions that adults experience when someone dies. However, their process of thinking about and understanding those feelings is quite different. Their age and cognitive abilities limit what they can communicate and comprehend about deep emotional issues. Play, sound, sight, touch, and the here-and-now are more potent and accessible than the words in their heads (Kissel, 1990). So it is through their behavior, affect, and play that information is gained about how children are resolving their grief.

Much has been written about how children understand the concept of death. Age divisions vary somewhat from one author to another, but most are in agreement about the overall comprehension abilities of children at different ages or stages of childhood. Not surprisingly, Jean Piaget's designations of childhood into preoperational, concrete operations, and formal operations are referred to in much of the literature.

At the preoperational level, death is experientially and emotionally equivalent to separation. Children may erroneously believe, through magical thinking, that they caused the person to die. Death is an abstract concept, and children at this age also believe it is reversible (Pritchard & Epting, 1991–1992). By the time children reach the concrete operations stage, they have a more complete and mature understanding of death. However, they are still troubled somewhat by feeling responsible for the death or feeling that other loved ones may soon die as well. Finally, within the formal operations stage, children have a complete "death concept" and understand the four commonly described components: death is irreversible, inevitable, universal, and attributable to the cessation of bodily functions (Singer, 1993).

The literature is clear about the beneficial effects of group counseling for children as well as adults. Groups are often organized around things children have in common and the counselor facilitates exploring and understanding how they feel about what's happening (Moore, 1983). Healing is gained by being directly involved in a discussion or activity, although children can also find release by observing others do things that feel too frightening at first. Then, they may find the courage to slowly move from only watching to actually participating (Ginott, 1968). Within a group setting, relationships develop that provide support and acceptance (Slavson & Schiffer, 1975), and the children have a chance to share things they have in common while showing empathy and offering to help each other (Moore, 1983). Children who have experienced a death especially need this safe place of understanding and support since their peers "on the outside" often do not know how to be helpful. One of the wonderful by-products of a group counseling experience is that simply by being there, whether directly involved or quietly watching, children learn and heal. Even when children cannot or will not express their feelings verbally, those emotions are seen symbolically and verbally (Segal, 1984).

One specific group counseling approach for grieving children becoming more prevalent is the use of creative arts as the focus of the group's activities. Zambelli, Clark, Barile, and de Jong (1988) are clear in their support of this approach, having seen from their own experience how it gives children nonthreatening permission to grieve. Consequently, the children's ability to understand and express their feelings grows. This occurs when children are given symbolic ways to express their feelings. "A creative arts approach enables bereaved children to transcend the intellectual and emotional limitations associated with understanding and conveying feelings about death" (Zambelli et al., 1988, p. 44). This combination of art, music, and movement is different from other kinds of counseling, because it uses these nonverbal techniques as therapeutic strategies. Children can access thoughts and feelings they may be unaware of or afraid to reveal directly, and, therefore, they become involved in their own process in a way that is accessible to them (Zambelli et al., 1988).

The process of a creative arts counseling group for bereaved children allows them to approach feelings in a safe and supportive atmosphere and learn how to manage those feelings. Therein lies the healing (Segal, 1984). "Grief is not a specific emotion like depression or anger but rather a constellation of feelings that can be expressed by many modes and symbols" (Gordon & Klaas, 1979, p. 62). Therefore, a creative arts approach is uniquely suited to helping children face and resolve their grief.

GROUP GOALS

As much as possible within the 8 weeks, the children will:

1. Access the support and acceptance of the other children in the group.
2. Reach an understanding that the person who died is no longer present and will not return.
3. Access, feel, and express the feelings unique to their grief experiences.
4. Find ways to memorialize the person who died.

PRE-GROUP SCREENING AND ORIENTATION

The 1-hour sessions described in the following section are intended for a group of no more than seven children, ages 6–12. A review of the literature shows that most authors recommend children be within a year or two in age and grouped by gender in the elementary school years (Ginott, 1968; Schaefer et al., 1982; Slavson & Schiffer, 1975). However, depending on the population available, it may not be possible to follow this best practice. Children with preexisting, major psychiatric concerns are not suitable for this kind of group until sufficient individual counseling has been undertaken. Screening should focus on selecting children who had good prior functioning, who are experiencing problematic grief reactions, and who need and/or want support. There is no limit on the type of death experienced (illness, accident, suicide, and so on) nor on the time elapsed from the death event. Finally, having parental support is essential. This will help ensure that a child attends all sessions.

In terms of orientation, conduct an intake interview with the family, on the phone or face-to-face, at which time all customary informed consent and confidentiality information can be discussed. Also, collect the Pre-Group Information Form that had been mailed to the parents before the appointment. This collects information on the child's behavior, attitudes, affect, and school performance since the death. At this time, also provide information to the child about the purpose and basic format of the group, and the concept of confidentiality. It is recommended that this information be drafted in a child-friendly style so it can be reviewed by the family at home prior to the first session. Give information to the parent(s) regarding the general work of the group which can be supported and continued in the home. Finally, a timely postcard sent directly to the child would be a warm and welcoming reminder about the upcoming experience.

OUTLINE FOR EIGHT GROUP SESSIONS

Session 1

Purpose. Access the support and acceptance of the children in the group.

Theme. "I am not alone."

Activities. Introductions Game, Group Rules, and Group Format

In this first session, the emphasis is to introduce the children to each other, review why they are gathered together, and teach them how the time will be spent.

The Introductions Game is the author's modification of the old Concentration game. In advance of this first session, prepare pairs of cards with matching symbols for school, family, friends, happy times, sad times, angry times, and fun times. To play, the cards are shuffled and laid face down on the floor in the center of the circle. In turn, the children say their names, reveal two cards (trying to make a match) and share some life details relevant to those categories shown. If the cards do not match, they are turned face down and the next child takes a turn. The object is to remember where the matching cards are. In the process, the children talk about themselves and get to know each other.

The group rules activity is similar to what the children have probably done in their school classrooms before. First, solicit from the children their understanding of why they are there. Perceptions may vary, so it is important for the counselor to gently correct misinformation as it arises. This is a place where the children will come together once a week to explore the things they have in common because someone close to them has died. Then ask what rules or guidelines the children believe are important to follow. They may offer ideas like "pay attention" and "one person speaks at a time." These can be written and drawn on a poster by the counselor as they are listed and left in place for reference during the duration of the group. Be sure to guide them to include the concept of confidentiality, as it is unlikely they will bring it up.

After all pertinent rules have been covered, describe the format the group will follow from one week to the next.

1. *Check-in.* Some form of check-in will be used. One example is to have the children describe an aspect of their week such as how school went or how happy they felt.
2. *Activity.* After the check-in time, the group will move into a creative arts activity centered on art, music, movement, or stories.
3. *Sharing Circle.* When the activity is over, the children will reconvene in a circle to debrief the activity by sharing as much of their experience as they are comfortable with.
4. *Checkout.* End the session, taking a brief moment with each child.

After explaining the format, it would be useful to briefly practice the entire process, starting with check-in. Depending on the time remaining, the arts activity could be a free drawing time. Then, a brief checkout should be conducted.

Process. Expect that during this first session the uncertainty and anxiety of the children will be quite high. Be attuned to various manifestations of those feelings and maintain a calm, organized, and accepting atmosphere.

During the Introductions Game, it is important to use the children's names frequently to give them a sense of being welcomed and enable the others to start learning names. Highlight any authentic similarities that come forward from the details shared during the game. This will start to create links between the children and reinforce that they have things in common besides the death of someone important to them. In turn, this will lead to a sense of safety and acceptance from which deeper sharing can later emerge.

Once the focus shifts to talking about the group rules and format, take the opportunity to make clear why the children are there. They will have the opportunity to understand their feelings about death and get help with the things that confuse them. Reiterate this idea every week. For the check-in procedure, as stated earlier, ask the children how they would like to have everyone share from week to week. They could agree to let each child choose something different for the group each week such as name of school, favorite movie, and a detail about the deceased. Doing so will increase the children's sense of belonging and belief that this is their special place and time. Within reason, gently encourage the choices to be related to the grief process. However, flexibility is the hallmark of a successful encounter with children.

Many children are uncomfortable showing their artwork to others, feeling shy or embarrassed or unworthy. Make it clear that participating in the sharing circle is always optional.

For the checkout, a simple statement from each child about something they learned or responded to in that session will suffice. Skillful group management will be necessary with a loquacious child or spontaneous conversations that begin.

Two final notes about process that will pertain each week are, first, it is imperative to be alert to the amount of time activities are taking. Gauge the time remaining and adjust the plan accordingly. Always give the children a 5-minute warning when they are about to make a transition from one activity to another. This is especially important when reconvening the group after an individually focused activity such as drawing. Second, each week, ideally with the children's involvement, review the number of sessions remaining. Avoid adding to the children's feelings of loss and abandonment by not preparing them for the eventual ending of the group.

Session 2

Purpose. Access the support and acceptance of the children in the group.

Theme. "I am not alone and other people understand how I feel."

Activities. Check-in, Review Group Rules, Yes/No/Sometimes Game, Sharing Circle, Checkout.

After doing the check-in, review the group rules listed on the poster from last week. Once that is complete, give each child a set of three differently colored cards marked "yes," "no," or "sometimes." Explain that they will be playing a game where different statements are made, and everyone tells their response by showing the appropriate card. After each statement, anyone who wants to comment on that topic may do so briefly. Start with safe statements phrased in the first person, such as "I like ice cream," "I like to play outside," or "I like to eat bugs for breakfast!" As the level of the group's relaxation and willingness to talk rises, move into more sensitive statements like "I felt sad when my important person died," "My friends don't know how to help me feel better," "I don't like my family to know I'm upset," or "I feel like it's my fault that my important person died."

Once the game is concluded, allow the children to draw a picture of one of the statements that meant something to them. While they are drawing, circulate around the room, checking in with each child. This should not be done as praise or a quality judgment but simply by reflecting on what the child is drawing. For example, saying "I see you're putting lots of green on that part of the page" is sufficient to let the child know she or he has been seen and accepted. During the sharing circle, the children may choose to share their pictures or talk about their experience of the Yes/No/Sometimes Game.

Process. Since the check-in process is still new to the children, a more directive role must be taken than will be necessary later on. If the children have chosen to take turns picking the category, keep track of the turn taking and make sure everyone is included.

During the Yes/No/Sometimes Game, use good attending skills to make sure each child feels seen and heard even if a verbal explanation is never offered by that particular child. Good eye contact, summarizing the responses given, and linking common answers will help with the recognition and also serve to strengthen the bonds forming between the children. An additional part of the process can be to ask a quiet child if she or he would like to speak or to ask a highly verbal child to choose another child to comment on the topic. It is hoped that by this second session the children will have begun to realize this is a safe place in which to explore feelings and experiences their peers outside the group cannot understand (Le Vieux, 1999).

In directing the children to draw about one of the topics that was meaningful to them, it is helpful to review the various statements made and summarize the stories told as a way to remind them about what was shared. Art is a way to symbolically express fears and other feelings such as anxiety or stress (Moody & Moody, 1991), and so it is helpful if the children feel the counselor's supportive, but not intrusive, presence as they work. Move about the room and take time with each child. Reflect the content of the drawing and offer observations about the underlying feelings if that seems appropriate. Slavson and Schiffer (1975) assert that offering a deeper level of understanding teaches children about their feelings and helps them learn about themselves and how to manage their feelings and circumstances.

Session 3

Purpose. Understand that the person who died is no longer present and will not return.

Theme. "We have trouble believing people are really gone when they die."

Activities. Check-in, Musical Emotions, Sharing Circle, Checkout.

Start the Musical Emotions activity by talking about the concept of change, of before and after. Use examples such as the transition from summer vacation to school resuming, or having a cold and then being healthy. Describe how ideas can be expressed in different ways; one method is with sound and/or music. Allow each child to choose a simple instrument from an assortment, such as tambourines, hand bells, small drums, claves, and xylophones. Demonstrate how different sounds can be made to show the "before" of an example (summer sunshine = light, airy) and the "after" (sudden rain storm = heavier, discordant). Have the children practice the example and then give them other scenarios. Begin with more neutral examples and then move into ones specific to their loss situations, such as "I liked to play with my important person. Now I can't do that anymore because that person died" or "I always shared my candy with my important person. Now I eat it all myself because that person died." They can create the sounds as a group, individually, or in pairs. It may feel safer to them to do it all together and then allow individuals to volunteer to share their "musical emotions" creation. In the sharing circle, have the children describe the experience they had in the activity. Begin to generalize their comments to the notion that music is one way to manage our emotions, any time we need to.

Process. The challenge in the Musical Emotions activity will be to handle the amount of noise generated. To many adults' ears, children and noisemakers go together like oil and water. Establishing some ground rules like "all instruments on the floor until I finish the sentence, then begin" and a signal for stopping the sounds would keep the activity more organized. A way to expand the activity and allow the children to feel ownership is to solicit their ideas. It is especially important to focus on those ideas related to the death of their important person. Be sure to rephrase a child's suggestion, if necessary, so it's applicable to more children in the group.

Another thing to remember is not to be too concerned if responses to the death-specific examples are lackluster. These children are still learning how to identify and express the feelings they have about their loss and may be unable to share much. Another attempt at getting the children to personalize the experience of emotions and music or sound can be made during the sharing circle. According to Schaefer et al. (1982), children can be helped to achieve insight through discussion with a group.

Session 4

Purpose. Understand that the person who died is no longer present and will not return.

Theme. "We have trouble believing people are really gone when they die."

Activities. Check-in, Calendar, Sharing Circle, Checkout.

Since children are very much oriented to the here-and-now, they may not have thought ahead to the fact that their important person will not be present at their next birthday or other special event. The Calendar activity is an attempt to expand this time orientation a bit. It speaks to the child's need to understand that the person who died will not be returning and able to participate in important life events like before. Have the children brainstorm a list of situations or events that the deceased will not be present for. Place this list in a prominent place so they can refer to it as they draw. Ask the children to divide their paper in half vertically, letting one side be a depiction of the event with the important person present and the other side showing what it will be like without them there. Encourage the use of paint or pastels, as these are more fluid media and tap into deeper emotions

(Geldard & Geldard, 1997). As described previously, make contact with each child while drawing or painting to reflect on and recognize the work being done. There should be plenty of time for the children to share their drawings with the group in the sharing circle.

Process. Compared to the music activity of the previous week, the Calendar experience will be much more sedate. However, the children may experience troubling feelings or be resistant to contemplating the fact of their important person's absence at special times. Wolfelt (1998) describes that anniversaries, holidays, and birthdays are especially painful times. Approach this activity as a rehearsal for the feelings each child may experience as those significant dates come along. Acknowledging this truth in the course of the activity may be difficult for some, if not all, of the children. As always, encourage as much participation as possible, yet allow an alternative if necessary.

The primary concern in this session will be to reflect the work each child is doing and then managing the sharing circle. No one should be forced to share, but all should be asked. Pointing out similarities in the children's stories of loss and change should be easy to do with this activity, as it is likely they have common birthday and holiday expectations. As with all sharing and discussions after the activities, take every opportunity to validate feelings, normalize experiences, highlight commonalities, and show faith in the children's ability to heal and grow.

Session 5

Purpose. Access, feel, and express feelings unique to each child's grief experience.

Theme. "We have lots of different feelings when someone important to us dies."

Activities. Check-in, Move to the Music, Sharing Circle, Checkout.

Thus far in the group, the approach to expressing feelings has been weighted on the cognitive side. The activity for this session is much more kinesthetic. Choose in advance a variety of musical selections that evoke different feelings when listened to. With the children seated on the floor, play a selection and model how the body wants to move a certain way in response. Invite the children to join in, still seated. Stop the music and ask what kind of feeling it elicited for them. Now, hand out sheets of paper divided into four equal, numbered parts. Explain that after the next four selections, they are to draw a quick picture that matches how they felt as they moved to the music. It could be a scene or an arrangement of colors and shapes. Play the next selection with the children still seated, let it continue and have them stand (still moving in whatever way feels appropriate), then encourage them to move around the room. Stop the music and have the children return to their places to do the quick response drawing. Repeat three more times with different styles of music. During the sharing circle, children may choose to share verbally or with their pictures what they experienced during the activity. It is important during this round of sharing to normalize the variety of feelings children experience in response to a death (depression, anger, withdrawal, sadness, confusion, and so on).

Process. Move to the Music requires a fair amount of trust and risk taking to get up and move with others watching. If there is some reluctance, suggest the children close their eyes or only move as much as they are comfortable, such as staying seated or standing in place. Throughout, offer reflective statements; for example, "You're feeling the music in your body" or "You know how you need to move" or "You can move in any way that feels comfortable to you." While doing the activity or talking about it afterward, there may be some feedback from the children that it was silly or stupid. Accept this as a valid response and gently probe for any connection possible between the music and the feelings in their bodies. Do not be distressed if the discussion stays at a surface level. Movement alone is a useful way to access what the child feels (Segal, 1984) and, therefore, is therapeutic even if the child has no words for it later.

Session 6

Purpose. Access, feel, and express feelings unique to each child's grief experience.

Theme. "We have lots of feelings when someone important to us dies."

Activities. Check-in, Clay Creations, Sharing Circle, Checkout.

This activity requires sufficient clay and a clear table top with plenty of space for each child. In addition, have a selection of soothing, instrumental music ready to play. The instructions are simple. Each child is given a quantity of clay and asked to quietly listen to the music without talking to anyone. While listening, they are to think of the important person who died and then to create whatever they would like. As has been the process all along, each child will be given the chance to share what was made and talk about it during the sharing circle.

Process. Depending on each child's level of trust and risk taking at this point in the group, a fair amount of redirecting may be needed during Clay Creations. Conversations may spring up as the children get busy with their hands. Discourage this gently and ask the children to just be with themselves right now. If a child is especially resistant to participating as directed, remove the aspect of it being related to the important person who died. Let the child make whatever she or he wants. Chances are, having heard the initial directions, the end product will be related in some way after all!

In fact, the odds are low of having a child be completely against the activity. Many children enjoy getting messy and clay serves that purpose well. As an art medium, it helps the children feel powerful through physical expression and encourages the release of emotions. Clay has an open-ended, expansive quality and facilitates interactive, adventurous, introspective, and private behaviors (Geldard & Geldard, 1997). For these reasons, this activity is likely to be enjoyable to the children and successful from a therapeutic standpoint.

As the children work, slowly and thoughtfully move around the room. Spend time with each child making reflective comments on what they are creating.

During the sharing circle, invite each child to share but do not insist upon it. Whatever level of communication is offered should be accepted. A mere show and tell ("I made a horse") is as valuable as a longer, more fluent explanation ("I made a horse because my grandma who died had horses and I used to get to ride horses when I would visit her and I always loved doing that with her"). The healing happens as much in the activity itself as it does in the sharing.

Session 7

Purpose. Find ways to memorialize the person who died.

Theme. "We will always love and remember the people who have died."

Activities. Check-in, Discuss Termination, Memory Collage, Sharing Circle, Checkout.

Although the children have known from the beginning that the group would only last 8 weeks, it is important to remind them they have tonight, next week, and then it ends. Plan for plenty of time to discuss what it means to end the group, and allow any expression of feelings and asking of questions.

For the Memory Collage, have on hand a large quantity of magazines, a pair of scissors and glue stick or glue bottle for each child, and paper of various sizes and colors. To set the stage, brainstorm a list of ways that people know and remember things. Guide them to delineate sights, sounds, tastes, textures, smells, places, actions, objects, and feelings. Post this list where they can see it as they work. Now that they have the idea of how memories are captured, ask the children to each make a collage of memories they have about their important person who died. These may be happy or sad memories, or concrete or abstract reminders.

Process. Be prepared for the level of trust and type of behavior to change during this session. Discussing termination may trigger the issues of pain and loss that brought the children to the group in the first place. For this reason and so they can continue to connect with each other, allow quiet talking while they work on their

Memory Collages. As they leaf through the magazines, they will see interesting or unusual pictures. It is natural to exclaim aloud and want to show them to someone else. Be tolerant of the conversation, yet always guide the children toward the end goal.

Hopefully, any anxiety the children are feeling about the group ending will not prevent them from being able to share their collages. It is unlikely that the entire group will be so affected, but accept this if it does happen. However, by selecting magazine pictures representative of their feelings and memories of the deceased, a bridge is created from the symbolic to the actual. This allows the child to make an easier transition than by simply talking from their experience and can facilitate getting closer to emotional material that previously was too scary to reveal (Segal, 1984).

Session 8

Purpose. Find ways to memorialize the person who died.

Theme. "We will always love and remember people who have died."

Activities. Check-in, *Cemetery Quilt*, Sharing Circle, Closing Checkout.

The book *Cemetery Quilt* by Kent and Alice Ross is a beautifully written and illustrated story of a young girl's experience of her grandfather's death. It describes her feelings, questions, fears, memories, and growing acceptance. Read the book aloud, taking plenty of time to look at the illustrations and allow the story to sink in. Depending on personal preference or the spontaneous responses of the children, discussion may occur during the story, afterward, or both. Focus on those areas already emphasized during the group: accepting support from others, understanding the deceased person's absence, expressing the feelings of grief, and remembering the relationship with the deceased.

Alter the checkout process this last time. Remind the children of the kinds of activities they did and the benefits they gained. Use a sentence-completion exercise as a means of having each child check-out. Some examples are "Before I started this group, I felt _____ and now I feel _____," "From being in this group, I learned _____," or "Something I will always remember about this group is _____." Select three or four statements and have them on a poster for the children to refer to. They may choose one or more of the sentences to complete. Finally, it would be appropriate to give each child a small remembrance token as a tangible symbol of their work and growth in the group. A polished stone or other small, natural object serves this purpose nicely.

Process. Everyone is likely to experience a range of feelings during this last session. Using a book as the arts focus is a contained, more cognitive approach that will help the children gain mastery and improve communication skills in a way that is familiar and stable (Geldard & Geldard, 1997).

It is important to care for the children by not beginning an emotional process that cannot be finished. Their experiences with books in the classroom have probably been more cognitive than emotional—thus, the choice to use a familiar, somewhat limited approach for the last session.

Of course, other books may be just as appropriate. The *Cemetery Quilt* is only one suggestion. Moody and Moody (1991) have found the following books to be useful in helping to normalize and explain feelings of grief and loss to children: T. DePaola, *Nana Upstairs and Nana Downstairs.* Putnam, 1973; M. W. Brown, *The Dead Bird.* Addison-Wesley, 1965; D. Cazet, *Christmas Moon.* Bradbury Press Inc., 1984; B. Eggert, *Marianne's Grandmother.* Dutton, 1987; J. Fassler, *My Grandpa Died Today.* Human Sciences, 1971; C. Zolotow, *My Grandson Lew.* Harper, 1974; and C. Carrick, *The Accident.* Clarion Books, 1976 (p. 598).

Preface the giving of the remembrance token with a statement about the importance of objects as holders of memory. A few of the children may have included pictures of objects in their memory collages and these can be referred to. Have more than enough objects and let the children choose the one they want. As a closing statement, tell the children about future availability for more help if the children and/or families feel they need it. Giving each child a business card in conjunction with this offer is a strategy used by Le Vieux (1999).

STRATEGIES TO EVALUATE THE GROUP

Certainly, there will be an intuitive sense of the progress of each child by the conclusion of the group. However, a more formalized assessment is always useful. A revised version of the Pre-Group Information Form (Post-Group Evaluation Form) can be utilized to informally assess the outcomes of the group (see Appendix A). Give a clean copy to the adult(s) at the last session, along with a self-addressed, stamped envelope, and ask that it be returned within a few weeks. Be prepared to make follow-up phone calls in order to get them back.

REFERRAL PROCEDURES FOR FOLLOW-UP

A cover letter can be attached to the post-group evaluation giving information on further treatment options. If individual child or family counseling is available, that information should be included. At least three other qualified individuals should also be listed. Parent(s) would surely also appreciate the offer of a telephone consultation to discuss whether further treatment is needed for the child or the entire family. Lastly, if attending the group again would be a helpful intervention for a particular child, that can be offered as well.

PRE-GROUP INFORMATION FORM

Child's name _____ Birthdate _____ Age _____

Adult name (please print) _____

Address_____ Phone Number_____

School name _____Grade _____

Children experience their grief in a variety of ways, just as adults do. It will help me help your child if I have an understanding of how she or he has been doing lately. Please fill out the information below as fully as possible.

Who died in the child's life? _____

Relationship to the child _____

When did the death occur? _____

Did the child attend the wake, funeral home, funeral, graveside service, or other rituals? _____

_____

_____

_____

How was the death and later events explained to the child? _____

_____

_____

_____

PLEASE CIRCLE ANY THAT APPLY AND EXPLAIN BELOW.

Fighting . . . more angry than before . . . clinging to adults . . . fearful . . . excessive crying . . . change in energy level . . . change in appetite . . . change in sleep habits . . . change in friends . . . bedwetting . . . no apparent reaction to the death . . . refuses to discuss it . . . wants to discuss it all the time . . .not following ordinary rules . . . change in school performance . . . depression . . . other concerns. . .

_____

_____

_____

_____

_____

_____

_____

_____

POST-GROUP EVALUATION FORM

Child's name_____Birthdate _____Age _____

Adult name (please print) _____

Address_____ Phone Number _____

School name _____ Grade _____

Children heal from their grief in a variety of ways, just as adults do. It will help me improve my future work to hear how your child has changed since doing the group. Please fill out the information below as fully as possible.

PLEASE CIRCLE ANY THAT APPLY AND EXPLAIN BELOW.

Fighting . . . more angry than before . . . clinging to adults . . . fearful . . . excessive crying . . . change in energy level . . . change in appetite . . . .change in sleep habits . . . change in friends . . . bedwetting . . . no apparent reaction to the death . . . refuses to discuss it . . . wants to discuss it all the time . . .not following ordinary rules . . . change in school performance . . . depression . . . other concerns . . .

_____

_____

_____

_____

_____

Please remember I am available for brief telephone conversations about finding more counseling. Take care.

Jane Doe
Generic Counselor
(xxx) xxx-xxxx

REFERENCES

The Dougy Center (1999). *Facilitator training manual.* Portland, OR: Author.

Geldard, K., & Geldard, D. (1997). *Counseling children: A practical introduction.* London: Sage Publications.

Ginott, H. G. (1968). Group therapy with children. In G. M. Gazda (Ed.), *Basic approaches to group psychotherapy and group counseling* (pp. 176–194). Springfield, IL: Charles C. Thomas.

Gordon, A. K., & Klaas, D. (1979). *They need to know: How to teach children about death.* Englewood Cliffs, NJ: Prentice-Hall.

Kissel, S. (1990). *Play therapy: A strategic approach.* Springfield, IL: Charles C. Thomas.

Le Vieux, J. (1999). Group play therapy with grieving children. In D. S. Sweeney & L. E. Homeyer (Eds.), *The handbook of group play therapy* (pp. 375–390). San Francisco: Jossey-Bass.

Moody, R. A., & Moody, C. P. (1991). A family perspective: Helping children acknowledge and express grief following the death of a parent. *Death Studies, 15,* 587–602.

Moore, H. B. (1983). Person-centered approaches. In H. T. Prout & D. T. Brown (Eds.), *Counseling and psychotherapy with children and adolescents: Theory and practice for school and clinic settings* (pp. 223–286). Tampa, FL: Mariner.

Pritchard, S., & Epting, F. (1991–1992). Children and death: New horizons in theory and measurement. *Omega, 24*(4), 271–288.

Ross, K., & Ross, A. (1995). *Cemetery Quilt.* Boston: Houghton-Mifflin.

Schaefer, C. E., Johnson, L., & Wherry, J. N. (1982). *Group therapies for children and youth.* San Francisco: Jossey-Bass.

Segal, R. M. (1984). Helping children express grief through symbolic communication. *Social Casework: The Journal of Contemporary Social Work, 65,* 590-599.

Seibert, D., Drolet, J. C., & Fetro, J. V. (1993). *Are you sad too? Helping children deal with loss and death.* Santa Cruz, CA: ETR Associates.

Singer, D.G. (1993). *Playing for their lives: Helping troubled children through play therapy.* New York: The Free Press.

Slavson, S. R., & Schiffer, M. (1975). *Group psychotherapies for children: A textbook.* New York: International Universities Press.

Smith, I. (1991). Preschool children "play" out their grief. *Death Studies, 15,* 169-176.

Wolfelt, A. D. (1998). *Healing the grieving heart: 100 practical ideas for families, friends, & caregivers.* Fort Collins, CO: Companion Press.

Zambelli, G. C., Clark, E. J., Barile, L., & de Jong, A. F. (1988). An interdisciplinary approach to clinical intervention for childhood bereavement. *Death Studies, 12,* 41–50.

CHAPTER 2

LIFE-THREATENING ILLNESS IN SCHOOL-AGE CHILDREN: A TRANSITION GROUP

Sharon Smith

PURPOSE

One of the most unsettling events a person can face is the diagnosis of a life-threatening illness. This event is even more unsettling if the diagnosis is for that of a child. In our society, the death of a child is one of the most disturbing, shocking, and unacceptable events that can occur. It is a death out of season. More so than the death of an adult, who has at least to some extent "lived life," the death of a child is against the natural order of things, disrupting our sense of purpose and of future promise (Judd, 1989).

Studies of children with leukemia age 6–10 reveal that, despite efforts by parents and medical personnel to conceal the truth, the children somehow sense the seriousness of the illness. Perhaps the loneliest of all are those children who are aware of their diagnosis but recognize that their parents do not wish them to know. As a result, there is little meaningful communication; there is no one with whom the child can openly express his or her feelings of sadness, fear, or anxiety. A child's realistic fears and concerns, as well as unrealistic fears and fantasies that are not addressed openly are more likely to lead to a loss of hope and optimism critical to survival (Leukemia Society of America, 1998).

Establishing a group for those children who are diagnosed with a life-threatening illness can allow for the opportunity to share and hear the sadness, fear, and anxiety of other children who understand and share the child's concerns. The educational component of the group would allow children to ask questions to uncover any myths they may have about their illness. An additional purpose of a transition group would be to create a supportive and safe environment in which children can explore their own feelings related to their diagnosis. Because of the importance of family support in a life-threatening diagnosis, some group sessions may include the opportunity for all family members to be present. For the purpose of consistency within this publication, focus will be on school-age children diagnosed with leukemia and other related cancers. However, sessions can easily be adapted to work with any life-threatening illness.

CONCEPTUAL FRAMEWORK

Treatment of a life-threatening illness, such as leukemia, can create changes in a child's appearance. For example, surgery can be disfiguring, chemotherapy can cause hair loss, radiation can cause fatigue, and changes in appetite can create weight loss. Due to the shock parents face upon the diagnosis of their child, knowing how to inform the child of his or her illness and its side effects can be difficult. Due to the child's level of development, the amount of information told to the child will vary.

As reported by the Leukemia Society of America (1998), studies of children under age 5 show that fear of separation, fear of abandonment, and fear of loneliness are most important to the seriously ill child. These children seek comfort from their primary caregivers, and they see parents as magical beings that can make illness and discomforts go away. From the ages of 6 to 10, children have fears relating to physical injury and bodily harm. The fear of abandonment is overshadowed by a fear of bodily harm. Because children in this age group often feel powerful in causing illness, they may view their illness as punishment for their thoughts and actions. Children over age 10 show a fear of illness and death. In the preadolescent and adolescent, this fear takes precedence over all other fears. Open communication with this age group is vital in allowing the individual to express and accept the illness.

However, regardless of age, it is important to be honest with children about trips to the hospital and procedures that may hurt. Allowing them to make simple, safe decisions about their care will add to their self-confidence and feelings of safety. It is very important to keep the lines of communication open with children. Although parents do not want to burden their children with their own feelings of anger, fear, or sadness, children are often very aware of how their parents feel and will often hide their own feelings to protect their parents (National Cancer Institute, 1994). Children who sense that their parents do not want to acknowledge the illness may try to protect them by not discussing their own feelings and fears. This feeling isolates the child from an important source of support and may only increase concerns, due to the child imagining the situation to be far worse than it actually is.

Like adults, children with life-threatening illnesses feel uncertain, anxious, and afraid at times. However, unlike many adults, children often cannot talk about their fears. Instead, they may express their feelings by being unpleasant, boisterous, or bossy, or by being quieter than usual. Play is a way for a child to express and reduce fears and anxieties. Drawing pictures and playing with puppets, dolls, and even medical supplies are ways children may show that they do not understand what is happening or that they need more reassurance and love. Nightmares, changes in eating habits, or behavioral difficulties are also seen in children who have problems expressing their feelings. Changes in school performance may also become apparent, as does the reoccurrence of behaviors that are otherwise outgrown such as bed-wetting and thumb sucking (National Cancer Institute, 1994).

The diagnosis of a life-threatening illness affects everyone in the family. For the patient, the restriction of certain activities and the inability to attend school may be among the two largest changes. Reduction in energy levels often make attending a full day of school impossible. For this reason, many hospitals have special hospital-based school programs that children can attend while receiving treatment. In addition, many families from rural areas must receive services from a treatment center many miles from home. This may require part of the family to take up temporary residence away from home. Even when treatment is going successfully, the lives of the patient and family members are influenced by the illness and its treatment and side effects. Schedules are rearranged to accommodate hospitalizations or clinic visits, family members may be separated in order to access treatment, and siblings may feel neglected. The finances of the family may create additional pressure as hospital bills accumulate. The changes within the family will not go unnoticed by the child, who may develop feelings of guilt for "causing" the changes. In order to prevent these feelings from occurring in the patient, it is important that life continues as normal as possible under the circumstances. To see that this happens, the sick child should be treated as normal as possible, the needs and feelings of the patient's siblings should be attended to, and sources of support for the family as well as the patient should be sought to help deal with the illness.

GROUP GOALS

The following goals for a school-age (6–10 years) life-threatening illness transition group could be incorporated to help guide the sessions:

1. For members to experience a safe, supportive, and educational environment to explore their fears and anxieties surrounding their illness.
2. To provide members with the opportunity to meet others who share their illness.
3. To provide play and personal growth for members facing a life-threatening illness.
4. To help members deal with personal changes that may accompany their illness.
5. To help members cope with changes that may be occurring within their family.
6. To provide members the opportunity to ask questions and receive honest answers pertaining to their illness.

PRE-GROUP SCREENING AND ORIENTATION

As with any counseling group, pre-group screening is critical to the success of the group. Leaders must screen prospective members of a group to select individuals whose needs and goals are congruent with the group goals, who will not be detrimental to the group, and whose well-being will not be jeopardized by the group experience (Capuzzi & Gross, 1998). Some individuals should simply not become members of groups. They include those who are so threatened by the prospect that they cannot be expected to function in a group and could be damaged by it, those who are too disorganized and potentially disruptive, and those who are so caught up in the personal crisis that they are unlikely to gain from a group or to function effectively within it (Whitaker, 1985). Before group screening can begin, the size of the group and its composition must be considered. The size of the group should be kept to a minimum in order to keep the length of each session short. The composition has to do with the homogeneity and heterogeneity of the group, more specifically the age, sex, and other human characteristics that the leader feels necessary to promote the effectiveness of the group. Next, a method for pre-screening the members must be decided upon.

In terms of a group for children diagnosed with a life-threatening illness, groups could be conducted as either single-sex or coed. When combining participants of varying ages, the developmental level of each child should be considered. In respect to this publication, sessions are directed to those children between the ages of 6 and 10. A key feature in group organization for this age group is the child's level of acceptance of his or her illness. Conducting individual interviews with each prospective member and asking age appropriate questions will provide good insight into their level of acceptance. Doctors, nurses, and parents are also valuable resources. Group membership may not be helpful if the child is in a state of shock but may be very useful once the child begins to emerge from it. According to Whitaker (1985), during the period in which shock predominates the individuals, they do not have access to their full range of defenses and coping devices. Individuals are likely to fall back on such defenses as denial and distancing themselves from the event. When in the shock stage, the individual is not yet in the position to confront the implications of the illness, and membership in a group where others are sharing and supporting one another may prove to be a disservice to the child. During the pre-screening interviews, careful attention should be paid to recognize those individuals who are in this shock stage, as acceptance time will vary for each individual. One-to-one counseling may be most effective for this population.

For those patients emerging from the initial period of shock, group counseling can be very beneficial. Exploring feelings associated with the illness and beginning to anticipate the future is facilitated by sharing and comparing with persons in a like situation. A group experience can facilitate a reduction in an individual's sense of isolation and allow for expression of anxiety and fears. Group counseling can be of great use in this working-through stage. For this reason alone, funneling out those individuals who have not yet emerged from the shock stage is vital to the experience of the group. Having members who have not yet accepted their illness will inhibit those who have from working through their feelings, thus interfering with the benefits of group membership.

For those children whose seriousness of their illness is kept secret by their parents, group membership would obviously not be beneficial. Careful interviewing and consent from the parents would lead to an understanding of the child's level of knowledge. Other factors that should be kept in mind during the pre-screening interview are the child's attention span and ability to concentrate on the issue as well as their desire to be in a counseling group with other similar children. Asking questions that directly relate to the child's feelings, fears, and anxieties can provide insight into where the individual is at in coping with the illness. With children diagnosed with a life-threatening illness, duration and timing of the group counseling sessions are critical. Duration of the sessions should be short (six to eight sessions) as health can change at any time, and short in length due to the short attention span of this age group. Essentially all children in the group should be at the same energy level, whether this means conducting an outpatient group for those who are feeling healthier, or an inpatient group for those children whose illness may be at a more critical point. Regardless of which type of group is conducted, working with this population may mean adjusting to a loss at any time. A method to help the group cope with any unfortunate member loss should be established prior to its need.

OUTLINE FOR EIGHT GROUP SESSIONS

All sessions should take place in a quiet area that is familiar to the children; for example, a quiet room in the hospital or clinic in which the child receives treatment. The room should be as free from distraction as possible so that the children can receive an optimal group experience. Prior to the start of each new session, any thoughts or feelings stemming from previous sessions should be discussed. All sample sessions are approximated at 45 minutes.

Session 1

Purpose. The purpose of the first session is primarily to introduce members to one another and to allow the children to form a basic understanding of what the group will be like. For many, this will be their first experience in a group setting and anxiety is likely to be present. It is essential that the ground rules be established at this initial meeting, as children at this age need to know structure and expectations.

Theme. The theme of the initial meeting can be thought of in terms of an orientation. Each member arrives uncertain of what to expect, and the idea behind the first meeting is to begin having the members feel comfortable with one another and with the facilitator. For some of the children, being away from their families for the group time may be difficult, so establishing a safe, fun, and accepting environment is critical to their enjoyment and to the success of the group.

Activity. Upon entering the room, hand group members a label on which they are to write their name and to decorate as they choose. Colored pens, crayons, stencils, and stickers should be provided for the children to use. Allow approximately 5–10 minutes for this activity. Be sure to create a name tag as well. Once name tags are made, they should be placed on the shirt where visible to all group members. Have members sit in a circle and as a fun way of introducing one another, play a name game. One variation of the name game is to have each member think of an adjective that begins with the same letter of their name (for example, Talkative Tina) and a gesture representative of the adjective. Beginning on one side of the facilitator, go around the circle, with each member stating their creative name and doing the gesture that they chose. After going around the circle once, start again with the first child. After the first child's turn, continue to the second, but before the second child can go, he or she must first state the name and do the action of the first child. Continue around the circle in this manner. Before the third child can go, he or she must state the name and do the action of the first and second child. This is a fun and exciting way for children to learn new names.

After the warm-up introduction activity, it is important the group rules be established. Explain to the children that you have met with them each individually, but now that everyone is together as a group some rules, just like in school, need to be made. Have a large sheet of paper available that can be brought and hung on the wall for each session. Allow the group to aid in the rule-making process if their cognitive level is significant enough. Some basic rules for this age group could include: (1) do not speak while others are speaking, (2) keep hands and feet to yourself, (3) be considerate of others at all times, and (4) be on time and attend all sessions unless absence is prearranged by the facilitator. Other rules can easily be applied and most children will enjoy being able to help think of them. It is important that the rules are brought to each and every session and gone over immediately following check-in. Once the rules have been decided and agreed upon, speak briefly as to what will happen during the group sessions. Inform the members that they will meet together for a total of eight 45-minute sessions. Let the children know that group will be a time for them to play with each other, but it will also be a time to explore their feelings and to ask questions about their illness. Allow the children to ask any questions they may have about the group process. Before dismissing the session for the day, play the name game again and ask the members to bring a favorite photograph of themselves (either alone or with someone else) to the next session. It may be helpful to design a letter to parents asking for their assistance in helping their child select a photo that can be used at the next session.

Process. The first session is designed primarily to begin building a safe environment for future sessions. By playing the name game, children are introduced to one another and to the facilitator in a safe and fun way. By having each child repeat the names of other children in the group, the unfamiliarity of the group members will start to deteriorate, leading to a more relaxed, comfortable environment. By allowing the children to help set the rules for the group, they gain a feeling of ownership and control of the group. Control is an important feeling for them, considering they are in a world of doctors, nurses, hospitals, and medications where they have very little control. Providing the children with an explanation of the ideas intended for the group and providing them with opportunities to ask questions adds to the comfort level of the group members by reducing any anxiety they may be feeling. The first session is kept very safe and general to allow the children the chance to feel comfortable with other group members and the coordinator before being encouraged to self-disclose.

The facilitator plays an important part in all sessions but especially during the initial meeting of the group members. An appropriate level of control needs to be established to keep the group focused, however, the session needs to remain relaxed and fun so that the children are excited to return to future sessions. Too much structure may take away from the therapeutic aspects of the group. Not only does the facilitator want to encourage the children to get to know one another, but the facilitator must also become familiar with each child and vice versa. It is important that each child feels comfortable and supported by the facilitator. By creating a fun, safe environment where the children have some control over what is done, the feeling of comfort should come naturally for this age group.

Session 2

Purpose. To provide the children, through play interaction, the opportunity to explore their feelings surrounding their illness.

Theme. Play is an excellent way for children to express their feelings. With this population, providing a room full of dolls, stuffed animals, and medical supplies will allow the children to play the role of the doctor rather than the patient. Fears in relation to treatment may surface as well as the children's feelings towards their treatment staff.

Activities. At check-in, give each member a small notebook to use as a journal for the duration of the counseling sessions. The journal will be theirs to take home to write or draw pictures in between sessions if they feel the need. This allows for continuity between group sessions. To personalize their journal, have each member place the photo they brought from home on the front of the notebook. Provide glue or other necessary items for this. As a check-in, go around the circle and have each member state their name for review and briefly describe the photo that they brought. Have each child explain the significance of the photo and why they selected it as their favorite. After each child has a chance to share, review the rules that were agreed upon at the last meeting. Allow the children to discuss any more rules that they may have thought of. Be sure that the rules are clearly written where each child can view them.

After completion of the check-in and rule review, bring out a bag consisting of various medical supplies that are used in the treatment of the illness. Provide a fair amount of supplies so that all the children can participate in the activity. Provide white doctor coats for the children to wear during their play. Have a doll or stuffed animal for each child so that he or she can play doctor to the object. There are some wonderful dolls made especially for this type of activity that can be purchased if funds are available. Allow the children to use the medical equipment for its intended use. Observe how the children play, especially in terms of how they prepare the patient for the procedure and how they reassure the child. This provides great insight into the child's fears and concerns. Most children will really enjoy this activity. It is very important, however, that as many related materials as possible to the children's treatment are provided, in order to allow for a full range of exploration by the children. It may be helpful to record what is observed on each child so that the information can be discussed during future sessions. Allow ample time for this activity. As a checkout, have the children share what they liked and/or disliked about the activity. If a certain behavior was observed in several children, this could be brought up as a checkout by the facilitator, and the children could discuss their feelings relative to the behavior.

Process. Generally speaking, most children will enjoy the chance to play the role of the doctor using the materials provided. However, the facilitator must be prepared with ideas of what to do if one or more of the children choose not to participate in the activity. Engaging in play with the child may encourage him or her to participate, or perhaps having the child share a doll with another child where one member plays the doctor while another plays the nurse may add to the excitement of the activity for the child. Through pre-screening interviews, the facilitator may gain an idea of how each child would react to this type of activity. A group of older children may prefer to do role-playing in front of other group members rather than have an individual doll. Here again, the team approach to treatment, with one member playing the doctor and the other the nurse, could be explored.

The facilitator has an important role in this session to closely observe the interactions of each child with his or her doll. How each child treats the "patient" may directly relate to how he or she feels when having treatment. This activity can also be modified to provide for more group interactions. For example, one doll can be

used for every two children, thus encouraging the children to cooperate with one another for the benefit of the patient. A general list of observations could be provided to treatment doctors and parents to advise them of the potential fear and concerns of their children during the treatment process.

Session 3

Purpose. The main purpose of session 3 is to encourage children to explore and share their feelings, including the fears surrounding their illness.

Theme. "Changes, feelings, and fears."

Activities. Ask all members of the group to open their notebooks to the first page and draw a picture of something they enjoy doing using the materials provided. This can be something they enjoyed doing before the limitations of the diagnosis or something they enjoy doing now. Allow appropriate time for the art and then ask that each child share his or her picture with the group. Arranging chairs in a circle provides for an excellent sharing opportunity. Encourage members to speak about their pictures as they show them to the group. Allow the group to ask questions to the speaker regarding his or her picture if they desire. Once check-in is complete, again review the rules for the session.

As a lead in, ask members to share personal changes they have noticed since their diagnosis, for example, loss of hair or energy. If a chalkboard is available, a list could be generated on the board of the changes the children mention. After an adequate list has been established, ask the group how it feels about the changes or what fears the changes create. Encourage the children to give very thoughtful answers. If the discussion falls short, ask questions surrounding how the children deal with the changes they are experiencing, for example, purchasing wigs to deal with hair loss. This may help others in the group learn how to deal with similar issues. Some probing may be necessary to get the children talking, but after a few examples are provided for them, they should be able to add to the discussion. If desired by the facilitator, an age-appropriate self-esteem discussion could also be implemented into this session. When it is time for checkout, explain to the members that next week a physician and nurse will be available to answer any questions they have surrounding their illness. Brainstorm some appropriate questions the children can ask during the next session. Have children write any additional questions they think of in their journal to bring with them to the next session.

Process. More direction and control on the part of the facilitator may be necessary during this session than of the last two as self-disclosure is introduced. How comfortable the children have begun to feel in the group will guide how easily they self-disclose. For this reason, establishing a comfortable and safe group during the first two sessions is especially important. Children are not going to tell you how they feel if they fear ridicule or punishment for what they have to say. This is why establishment of group rules and an understanding of the purpose of the group are critical. Once the children feel they can speak without fear, most will enjoy the opportunity to talk about themselves. Pay careful attention that each child has an opportunity to share. This may mean limiting the amount of time that each child is able to share. Encourage children to speak, but for those who are still uncomfortable with the idea, they may wish to listen and determine for themselves when they feel the environment is safe enough to share.

Session 4 (Allow for family members to be present)

Purpose. To allow children to ask questions about their illness and have honest professional answers given in terms they will understand.

Theme. Having knowledge about a subject, such as an illness, can often put any unnecessary fears and concerns to rest. Children diagnosed with life-threatening illnesses are often not given the opportunity to ask questions. Instead, they are left with lingering questions and uncertainties that lead to increased anxiety. This anxiety can be reduced if they are able to obtain an age-appropriate understanding of what the illness is.

Activity. This session will be more of a psychoeducational session and in order to provide adequate time for questions, no check-in will be conducted. However, a review of the group rules may be helpful. Have children sit in the front of the room, with parents (if attending) seated behind them. Invite a physician and nurse familiar to the children to the session. Have them begin with a brief overview of the illness, but reserve most of the time for questions and answers. The physician and nurse may wish to bring materials with them to help with their explanations to the children. Have an outline created (based on fears that were uncovered during the last two sessions) in case the children are reluctant to ask questions. Questions should be as general as possible so they relate to all members of the group.

Process. Be sure that the medical staff you invite are aware that their audience will be children ages 6–10. Some medical personnel have a hard time formulating medical answers in a way that children of this age will understand. It may be helpful to share the questions that the group thought of during the last session with the medical professionals to give them an idea of the type of questions to expect. The facilitator will need to help redirect the members to ask questions relative to their illness if things seem to get a little off track. It may be left up to the members of the group if they wish their parents to be present at this session. However, it is impor-

tant that if parents do attend that they know the session is an opportunity for their children, not them, to ask questions. The main reason for having the parents present is so they can gain an understanding of the concerns and questions that their children have. Often, parents are unaware that their children have concerns as well. Because of this session, it is important during the pre-screening process that the family isn't wishing to keep true knowledge of the illness away from the child. If that is the desire of the family, the child should not be put in the group.

Session 5

Purpose. To explore feelings surrounding the changes happening in the family since the diagnosis.

Theme. Many new stresses occur in the family upon learning of the diagnosis of a life-threatening illness. These changes do not go unnoticed by the sick child and often the child may internalize feelings of guilt. The family must learn to adapt to these changes without too much interference of daily functioning.

Activity. As a check-in, have each member think of something that makes them feel good and something that makes them feel bad. Go around the circle and have members share with the other group members. Upon completion of check-in and review of the group rules, introduce the topic to the group. Suggest that they share examples of positive changes that they have experienced in their families as a result of the diagnosis; for example, one positive change may be that their mother or father is home more often. Give every member an opportunity to share. After adequate time has passed, introduce the idea of negative changes, such as more arguing at home between parents or siblings. Ask for members to share negative changes that they see at home and how these negative things make them feel. Allow for children to comment on each other's thoughts. As a wrap up, speak with the members about the feeling of guilt and how they should not feel guilty because of the changes that are happening at home. Explain to the children that change, whether good or bad, is a naturally occurring process. It is also a good idea at this point to begin preparing members for termination of the group. Notifying group members that they are now more than half way through the sessions and only three sessions remain helps prepare them for the upcoming change. Allow time to answer any questions the members may have pertaining to termination of the group.

Process. The facilitator takes an active roll in directing this session. A significant amount of material is covered and time must be monitored to allow the session to be as beneficial as possible. It is also the facilitator who does the wrap up of this session. The wrap up is very important as it is during this time when the topic of guilt will be addressed. It is important that the children leave the session realizing that they are not to blame for the changes that they see happening.

Session 6 (All family members invited, including siblings)

Purpose. To provide families the chance to talk about the illness openly and create ideas for family activities.

Theme. Family activities often get put on hold when the diagnosis of a life-threatening illness is made. Family support at this time is more important than ever. Many changes occur within the family once a diagnosis is made, but it is essential to continue life as normal as possible.

Activities. Invite families to join the group for the day (you may wish to increase the length of this session). As a check-in, have the members of the group introduce the family members that are joining them (name tags may be useful during this session as well). After check-in, have the families create a poster that reflects several aspects of the family together. The poster can contain, for example, artwork, words, and magazine clippings. Have the families include activities that the family enjoys doing together. Have large butcher paper and other art materials available. Have each family come up with one activity that they would like to do together that they haven't had the chance to lately (this could be anything such as reading a book together or going out to dinner). Once everyone has completed his or her activity, have the children share with the group their posters and the activity the family would like to do together. Mention that you would like the families to try and do whichever activity they decided upon before the last session.

Process. This session provides an excellent opportunity for family quality time. Not only does it allow for families to share some thoughts with each other, but also with other families dealing with a similar problem. Through inviting several families to join the session, family support networks may be established indirectly. You may even wish to pass around a phone number list to provide the families the opportunity to stay in contact with one another. When dealing with a life-threatening illness, one can never have enough support networks. During this session, continue to provide the members the opportunity to do most of the talking. You may wish to clarify this with the families beforehand.

Session 7

Purpose. To have members reflect on previous accomplishment as well as acknowledge future hopes and dreams.

Theme. "Achievement, hopes, and dreams."

Activity. As a check-in, have the members speak of an achievement that they are proud of. This achievement could be as simple as learning to tie their shoes or ride a bike. Use the discussion of achievements to lead into a discussion about hopes and dreams. After you feel the children have a sense of what hopes and dreams are, have them draw a picture of a hope or dream that they have on a sheet of 8.5 × 11-inch paper. This can be an individual hope or a family-centered hope, a short-term dream or a long-term dream. Set few guidelines for this activity, allowing the children to be as creative as they wish. Once everyone has had a chance to complete a picture, have members of the group share their picture and briefly, as a group, discuss the hope or dream. Before members leave, remind them that next week will be the last session, so they can prepare emotionally for the change.

Process. Even for those children whose futures may be questionable, having dreams and goals are important. Staying optimistic about even the near future can be therapeutic. This session includes much self-disclosure, thus, direction will be required of the facilitator. Again, a complete understanding of the rules is necessary to ensure the safety and comfort of each and every group member.

Session 8

Purpose. To evaluate the group and to bring closure to any left over material from previous sessions.

Theme. "Effective termination of the group."

Activity. First, have the children mention whether or not their family was able to do the chosen family activity that they decided upon two sessions ago. Whether the activity took place or not, have the children express how this made them feel. Remind the children that this is the last scheduled group meeting and that this session will be used to continue with any unfinished business from previous sessions. If no unfinished business exists, allow the children to lead the discussion. It can be safely assumed that at least one child of this age will have something significant that they would enjoy sharing with the group. Allow the children to direct the discussion for the final session as much as possible. Toward the end of the session, ask each child to complete the evaluation form that you created. Be sure to tell the children that this is not a test and that there are no right or wrong answers. It is also appropriate to allow the children to share addresses and phone numbers with one another so they may remain in contact after the group ends.

Process. When dealing with children of this age group, allowing them as much control as possible will add to their feeling of self-worth. That is the idea behind this final session. A majority of the previous sessions have been facilitator directed, primarily due to the age group of the members. As a facilitator, however, you will still need to assert control to be sure that the group rules are followed during this final session. As a closure, provide the children with a referral sheet in case further therapy is desired.

STRATEGIES TO EVALUATE THE GROUP

A way to evaluate the effectiveness of this type of group would be to create a survey for each member to complete during the last session. For children of this age group, the survey should be very simple, short, and easy to complete. The statements on the survey should relate directly to the pre-group goals. The statements should be worded simply and for ease of the younger age group members and be in true/false or smile/frown face format.

The following are some example true/false statements that could be used for evaluation purposes:

1. I felt safe to share my feelings with other group members.
2. I enjoyed hearing about other group members feelings.
3. I learned new things about my illness because of this group.
4. Other people have feelings just like mine.
5. I met new friends during group.
6. Activities that we did in group were fun and helpful to me.
7. I feel all alone with my illness.
8. The changes that are happening in my family are my fault.
9. I am okay with the changes that are happening to me.

Other statements may be developed related to additional group goals. Provide a section on the evaluation form for members to add any additional comments.

REFERRAL PROCEDURES FOR FOLLOW-UP

As with any group, referral procedures must be developed upon termination of the group. A list should be generated of individual, group, and family therapists within your area that work with children and their families dealing with life-threatening illnesses. Be sure that the therapists that you are including are reputable and familiar with this type of population. Some children and families may not need additional services, but for those who do, providing a list of options for them will prevent them from having to do the research. You may also wish to make yourself available for any additional individual or family services depending on your level of expertise.

REFERENCES

Capuzzi, D., & Gross, D. (1998). *Introduction to group counseling*. Denver, CO: Love Publishing.

Judd, D. (1989). *Give sorrow words*. London: Free Association Books.

Leukemia Society of America. (1998). *Emotional aspects of childhood leukemia* (Brochure). New York: Author.

National Cancer Institute. (1994). *Talking with your child about cancer* (Brochure). Bethesda, MD: Author.

Whitaker, D. (1985). *Using groups to help people*. London: Routledge & Kegan Paul.

CHAPTER 3

TRUST AND SUPPORT: CHILDREN OF ALCOHOLICS BUILD THEIR OWN IDENTITIES

Kristin A. Kahler

PURPOSE

The purpose of this support group for ages 8–11 is to create an atmosphere of safety and trust where children of alcoholics can share their feelings and learn information about the disease of alcoholism. The intent here is to impart information to assist in combating feelings of isolation, frustration, and powerlessness. Children of alcoholics can begin to use each other as resources as they rebuild their self-worth and learn positive methods of coping with a disease that has affected their families' systems. The focus of these sessions centers on surviving with an alcoholic parent/guardian.

CONCEPTUAL FRAMEWORK

The following sessions were designed with three main facts in mind. The first is that children are their own best resource. The second is that the children of alcoholics can recover regardless of the addicted parent's behavior. The third fact is that education is the most powerful weapon against alcoholism (Robinson & Rhoden, 1998). Essentially, these sessions are psychoeducational by nature but also hope to provide the support that will bolster the child's self-confidence and survival skills.

Children in middle childhood (ages 6–12 years) begin to evaluate their self-worth through social comparisons (Sigelman, 1999). At approximately age 8, the child's evaluations of him- or herself are likely to become increasingly realistic. Although the child's image

of him- or herself is more factual, he or she is simultaneously garnering information about the "ideal" self. Children of this age group run the risk of believing that they are inadequate and are not what they think they "should" be (Seligman, 1999). Children of this age group who reported higher self-esteem more than likely had parents who were warm, communicated approval, consistently nurtured, and were democratic in their parenting practices. From this information, it is possible to see how a group counseling effort can be effective for children of alcoholics between the ages of 8 and 11.

When children of alcoholics were asked to verbalize their feelings when their parents were drinking, they listed: worried, angry, frightened, sad, and neglected (Laybourn, Brown, & Hill, 1996). Research, compiled by Robinson and Rhoden (1998), suggests that children of alcoholics often suffer from low self-esteem, anxiety, shame, suppressed anger, feeling out of control, poor coping skills, depression, and fear. Children as young as age 5 were able to identify direct negative consequences they experienced as a result of parental drunken behavior. Of the consequences mentioned, emotional withdrawal, experiencing physical or verbal violence, and unpredictability were among the most distressing (Laybourn et al., 1996). Another significant consequence included the parentification of the child. Children of alcoholics need a safe place to build their self-worth, learn to trust, build their own personal values and goals, learn constructive ways of dealing with problems, and develop effective peer relationships (Ackerman, 1983). Most importantly, children of alcoholics need emotional and physical support to combat their feelings of power-lessness (Ackerman, 1983).

The following sessions were designed for children ages 8–11. The sessions should last anywhere from 1 hour to 1 hour and 15 minutes. Since children of this age group will have difficulty talking for the entire length of a session, activities were developed to meet their developmental and emotional needs.

GROUP GOALS

The main goals for the group include, but are not limited to, the following concepts:

1. For members to realize that they are not alone and that it is healthy for them to be able to talk about the parents'/guardians' drinking.
2. For members to identify and express the different ways they can take care of themselves.
3. To realize that as the children of alcoholics they are not the cause of, cannot cure, and will not be able to control the disease of alcoholism.
4. To assist members in identifying and using support systems outside of their families.
5. For members to learn positive and constructive methods of getting attention, building self-worth, and developing personal values and goals.

PRE-GROUP SCREENING AND ORIENTATION

Screening for a children of alcoholics counseling group is a sensitive issue at best. In addition to the usual pre-group screening process, including weeding out potentially harmful members and providing prospective members with information about the goals of this particular group, the facilitator must also receive parental/guardian permission. Due to the denial present in both the children and the adults involved, many children of addicts will not voluntarily come forward nor will their parents/guardians willingly place them in counseling groups with this type of focus. In addition to the denial factor, most children feel protective of the "family secret" and may not talk even if they really want to reveal their issues. Ackerman (1983) adapted a list of questions in order to identify and assess children of alcoholics:

- Have you ever worried about your parent's/guardian's drinking?
- Have you ever felt responsible for the drinking?
- Are you ever ashamed of the way your parent/guardian behaves while he or she is drinking?
- Have you ever felt hatred toward your parent/guardian when he or she drinks and later felt guilty for having this feeling?

- Have you ever kept track of how much your parent/guardian drinks?
- Have you ever tried to keep your parent/guardian happy so that the adult would not drink as much?
- Have you ever felt like you have had to keep the drinking, and the way you felt about it, a secret?
- Have you ever thought that if your parent/guardian really loved you that the adult would not drink?
- Do you want to start feeling better?

Since trust is a crucial issue for the majority of children of alcoholics, confidentiality should be discussed at length. The children must understand that although they can say anything in the safety of the group, they must not talk about what another member says or does outside the group. The members should also be clear on the point that the facilitator is mandated to report acts of abuse committed against them—and that this could have a direct impact on the family structure. The facilitator should give examples that demonstrate how a child can be removed from the parents'/guardians' household. It is through the use of clear examples that the facilitator can be certain that the members understand the consequences their words may have on their family lives. The group members must understand that certain pieces of information about abuse, neglect, suicide, and homicide cannot be kept secret by the facilitator. Since the group can only be effective if the members feel safe, the members will have to agree to certain guidelines that ground their behavior. These guidelines include respect, tolerance, acceptance, support, confidentiality, and open-mindedness. Members should also be made aware that although they will be in a group with other children of alcoholics, everyone will still have different experiences, and all of these perspectives are valuable.

OUTLINE FOR EIGHT GROUP SESSIONS

Session 1

Purpose. The purpose of the first session is for group members to meet other members and develop a sense of trust with people that share common life experiences. Members will also become familiar with and understand the ground rules.

Theme. The theme for the first session is one of acceptance and understanding. Members are most likely going to feel a certain amount of anxiety about sharing this type of information about their home lives. It is important to reassure members that none of this information will be used against them and that no one will be discussing them behind their backs.

Activities. Every member should have a partner. The pairs are given about 5 minutes to share the following information: name, one thing they know to be true about alcoholism, and one fear they have about being in this group. (Members should feel free to write it down if they are afraid of forgetting when it is their turn to speak.) The members will share the information about their partners. The facilitator should go first and share the same information about him- or herself with the members. As the information about alcoholism is revealed, validate all points of view and model trust to other members. After the members disclose their fears, address the fears directly and make certain that fears about confidentiality, acceptance, and whether or not anyone will believe them will all be addressed in the ground rules.

As facilitator, thank the members for sharing and for coming to the group. Begin discussing the ground rules. Examples of appropriate ground rules are:

- I will not talk about anything that anyone else says in here outside of group.
- I will not talk about the people who come to group with others who are not members.
- I will not talk while another member is talking.
- I am mindful and accepting of the fact that everyone has had different experiences and that no one experience is more correct than another.
- I will wait my turn to share. If I am uncomfortable, I do not have to share.
- I will try to trust my group members and be aware that they are trying to trust me as well.
- Every feeling I have is okay. I am right to have these feelings.
- It is okay for me to talk about my family and my feelings here in the group.

Elementary-age children are very good at coming up with rules, so ask their opinions about the rules they want for their group. Write down their rules and add the key points of confidentiality, respect, and acceptance if they do not hit on those. Explain the importance of each rule, and ask the members to explain theirs.

Once the group has agreed on the rules, pull out a giant sheet of paper and ask the members to trace each other onto the butcher paper. (One person is the outline for the head, another is the shoulders, another the torso, and so on). Then ask the members to write down the rule that holds the most meaning for them on any part of the body. The group will then be asked to name their "bodyguard." In effect, the outline is the group bodyguard that will keep the members safe while they are in the group meetings. Since the bodyguard is composed of all the members' bodies, and the rules they felt were important, all of the group members are responsible for keeping themselves and each other safe. Ask the members to explain the rules they chose and their significance.

In closing, ask the group if they feel any less awkward than when they first arrived for group and if anyone has something they want to bring up during the next group.

The materials needed for the first group include a long sheet of butcher paper (at least 6 feet long), colorful markers, pencils, and blank paper.

Process. The only way the first session is going to go smoothly is if the members feel that they can trust the facilitator and each other. The facilitator must model trust, acceptance, and respect for all members. Children are incredibly perceptive and will notice a lack of genuineness or false praise. It is important to remember that children of alcoholics have tremendous survival skills but that most of them have been denied trust, feeling, and honesty.

Asking the members to introduce a partner, rather than oneself, takes some of the pressure off the members to feel obligated to disclose information that they may later regret. Often members may feel shy when asked to share information about themselves, so introducing a partner is a little easier to swallow on the first session.

Having a group "bodyguard" allows the member to feel a tangible ownership of the rules. Often, rules are thrust on children without their consent, so it is important that they understand that this is their group. These rules were made by them, for them, from their own bodies. This "bodyguard" is also something that the facilitator can bring to each session as a reminder to the group members of their commitment to each other. The "bodyguard" is also a tangible way of saying that each member deserves to feel safe and protected from their fears.

As facilitator, be organized and have all of the materials ready before members begin to arrive. The facilitator should be willing to interrupt inappropriate talking or harmful interactions. The facilitator should also be aware of the responsibility of being a role model. Every member should leave feeling respected, safe, and valued. Children of alcoholics have incredible survival skills and should be praised for their abilities whenever possible. Often, they do not realize just what they have accomplished.

Session 2

Purpose. The purpose of the second session is for members to reclaim some power and control over their safety. The members will think of safe places they can go to when they do not feel safe with the inebriated parent/guardian. As the group progresses, members will come to see that they do have control over some situations and that they can rely on themselves.

Theme. The theme for the second session is twofold. In addition to imparting safety information, this session hopes to demonstrate that the members can have confidence in their abilities to solve problems. They can begin to feel a sense of pride about themselves, while taking an active stance in keeping themselves safe in dangerous situations. The sharing of artwork at the end of the session also demonstrates how the members can use each other as resources for information and support.

Activities. The first activity will be a brief introduction followed by a check-in. For the check-in, ask members to state one thing that they did, or thought of, in the last week that they took some personal pride in. Explain that the act or thought need not be heroic, but rather simple—since it happens that the smallest thing individuals do for themselves or others is sometimes the most meaningful. For example, a member might say that he or she was proud of the fact that the class homework assignment was completed. Another example could be that the child was proud that he or she decided to take the dog out for a walk just to have some time away from the house. The facilitator can model these statements, and "break the ice" by going first.

After the introductions and check-in, it may be helpful to reiterate the ground rules. Since trust and safety are significant issues to children of alcoholics, it is important to stress confidentiality, respect, and acceptance. (Bring in the "bodyguard" from the first session as a reminder to the members.)

At this point, explain that the focus for the session is on safety. Ask members to brainstorm about places where they have gone, do go, or can go where they feel safe during a violent/upsetting situation. (The facilitator may want to write these down to show to members who have trouble getting started on the artwork later.) It should be clear to the members that these must be realistic safety options. As different ideas come up, be ready to explain certain facts about alcoholism. For example, you may want to add that alcoholism is a disease where everybody gets hurt, not just the addict, and that is why it is important to have a safe place. It may also be appropriate to share that members are never alone in the situations they are facing—that both members of this group and other people in their lives (e.g., neighbors, teachers, and friends' parents) are resources that can be accessed.

Once several options are listed, ask members to draw the options that they think they will use most often. Explain that the artwork need not look exactly like the real life place but that it simply needs to represent this place. Honesty, creativity, and taking part in this project should be valued above all else. It may be necessary to remind members that nothing will be graded or judged and that this is an exercise to help them think of different ways to keep themselves safe.

Once members have completed their artwork, they should be brought together as a group and asked to share their work. Praise should be handed out liberally to all members—including those who do not wish to share. You can also encourage members to praise each other by asking each member to name one thing he or she liked about another member's artwork. Keep in mind that, more than anything else, this was an exercise in building member confidence. In closing, members should be asked if there is anything they wish to add to a discussion on safety.

The materials needed for session 2 include several sheets of 11 × 17 paper, pencils, ink markers, crayons, pastels, scissors, ribbon, glue, multicolored construction paper, foil, and glitter.

Process. This session can only work if the facilitator is mindful of how challenging it will be for this group to open up and share. Feel free to acknowledge these difficulties and the frustration members may feel when confronted with divulging the "family secret." Members should feel a sense of trust with each other and with the facilitator. Appropriate personal disclosure could help the group move forward in this process. Remember that the facilitator is a role model. Be careful to allow each member the same opportunities to share. Always model encouragement and genuine praise.

Session 3

Purpose. The purpose of the third session is to continue with the safety planning that began in the second session. It is through this process of sharing information and feelings that facts about the nature of alcoholism can continue to be shared and confronted.

Theme. As in the second session, this session hopes to impart information while increasing the members' confidence in themselves and their problem-solving abilities. In addition, this session should assist members in realizing that they are not alone in their struggle against the disease of alcoholism.

Activities. This session begins with members introducing themselves and briefly explaining what kind of moods they feel they are in. Ask if anyone has any thoughts or questions about what happened in the previous session. Also ask members if they would like to bring up a special topic for discussion with the group.

Once every member has had a chance to speak, address the theme of safety by asking what the members know about keeping safe when someone is drunk. If this leads to some sharing of stories, that is fine; however, remain mindful of the fact that the issue here is safety. Keep stories focused so that the members do not begin to frighten one another, or "compete" for attention. It is important to point out a member's survival skills since they may not be aware that they have done anything out of the ordinary. This is also a good way of demonstrating that children of alcoholics are not powerless but can make a better life for themselves regardless of their parents/guardians actions.

If members are not sharing, it may be time to try using the sock puppets. There should be two puppets, and a list of situations to act out. Situations may include:

- What do I do when I know my mom/dad is too drunk to drive me home?
- What do I do when my mom/dad is so drunk that she or he locks me out of the house at night?
- What do I do when my drunken mom/dad kept me up all night and I was too tired to get my homework done?
- What do I do when my mom/dad forgets to pick me up at school because of the drinking?
- What do I do when there is no money left to buy food and I am hungry?
- Whom do I call when my mom/dad has the DTs and will not stop shaking?

Ask members to add situations of their own and to act out solutions to these questions. They can work together as a group or break off in pairs. Encourage members to have a special place to write down the answers to some of these situations. This special place could also include emergency telephone numbers and names of people who are safe to contact. (A small notebook or several sheets of folder paper stapled together can be the special place that kids use to record important information.)

After members have found some solutions to the situations, ask the members about how they felt during the exercise. Remind members that all feelings are valid and important. For a closing, ask members to share something positive that they noticed about themselves during the problem-solving exercise.

The materials needed for the third session include eight sock puppets and copies of the prepared list of situations.

Process. The facilitator should be willing to take more of a backseat role as the members warm up to one another. Although the facilitator should be talking less, it is still important to be modeling the respectful, accepting behavior that the group agreed upon. Also be prepared to jump in and correct any false impressions that arise during disclosure. For example, if a member shares that she felt it was all her fault that her mother started drinking again, the facilitator, while taking care not to invalidate the member's feelings about the situation, should be ready to correct that false impression. You can explain that guilt, anger, and hatred are often common feelings that children of alcoholics share. Also be prepared to draw out certain members who may be reluctant in sharing. This may mean attempting to curb other members who are talking more often.

If there is any storytelling, it is important to be aware that some types of storytelling could send some members into flashbacks where they might be reliving a hor-rible event where they felt powerless. The point of these sessions is not to torment the members with bad memories, but to emphasize the strength it took for them to get here and that they have the resilience it takes to survive an alcoholic parent/guardian.

Session 4

Purpose. The purpose of the fourth session is to learn how to confront drunkenness directly. This helps members share concrete information about the disease, and helps them see how alcohol has affected their lives. The main goal is to impart information about alcohol while addressing the fact that children of alcoholics are at risk of becoming addicts themselves.

Theme. "What is life like for me when my parent/guardian is drunk? How would my life be different if my parent/guardian never drank again?"

Activities. This group begins with a check-in. The members are asked to briefly describe how their week has gone and if they have any questions from the last session. The members are also asked if they have any special concerns that they would like to discuss with the group.

In this session, ask members the theme questions. The group should discuss them thoroughly before beginning the exercise. (If the discussion is going along well, the exercise should be discarded.) The members also are given the choice of continuing the discussion or beginning the collage with the same theme. This is a good time to share information about alcoholism. For example, alcoholism is a disease that the addict literally has no control over, therefore, it is natural that everyone in the addict's life feels a loss of control and power. It is also natural to feel anger and hatred toward the addict.

If members decide to work on the theme collage, it should be a group effort. A giant piece of butcher paper is divided into two equal sections, one for each theme question. Give the members a generous amount of time to go through various magazines to cut out pictures, words, and letters. They need to communicate with one another to get this project completed. Model this interaction by asking questions about the collage; although encouragement and not necessarily active participation in the collage is important.

Once the project has been completed, ask the members to explain which contributions were theirs and what significance they hold. The sharing of stories should be encouraged. In closing, openly acknowledge the courage it takes for the members to share and talk about their family lives. Give out praise liberally.

The materials needed for the fourth session include a giant sheet of butcher paper (5 feet long and 3 feet wide), at least 20 magazines, scissors, glue, colorful markers, crayons, pencils, ribbon, (metallic) origami paper, and glitter.

Process. Continue to model the appropriate behaviors but remain vigilant for those who shy away from participating. It is the facilitator's obligation to ensure that all members get equal airtime. Although the members should be doing most of the talking by now, be mindful of how painful it is for the children of alcoholics to share this kind of information. It is significant that they have overcome some of their defense mechanisms enough to be present in a group counseling session. This kind of bravery should be openly rewarded with praise.

Session 5

Purpose. The purpose of the fifth session is to assist the members in resolving interpersonal conflicts. In supporting the members when they learn alternative methods of relating with peers, the group serves two purposes: it teaches the members positive and constructive techniques of getting attention, and it opens new avenues of outside support. In addition to combating the isolation children of alcoholics often face, the members can recognize that they do have control over certain aspects of their lives.

Theme. "I can resolve interpersonal conflicts in constructive and positive ways." Hopefully, as the members trust one another, they can begin to trust themselves and develop confidence in their decisions and actions.

Activities. The group begins with a check-in. Ask members to describe one thing that they took pride in over the past week. Be ready to compare these to the last responses that occurred during this same exercise. In addition to noticing when the members are displaying more self-confidence, liberal praise should be laced throughout the check-in. Acknowledge how difficult it has been for the members to continue meeting week after week and that the group members should congratulate themselves on doing so well. Also ask the members if there is anything special they would like to discuss with the group.

After the check-in is complete, introduce several scenarios of peer and adult conflicts. Also ask members to add any scenarios. Add the members' scenarios to the list. Examples of some scenarios include:

- What do I do when a kid in my class starts telling everyone about the time my mom/dad came to school drunk?
- What do I do when my teacher starts in on me because I could not get my homework done the night before because I was nursing my mom/dad through another hangover?
- What do I tell people who ask me questions about my family life?
- What do I do when I am really angry with another kid on the playground?

- What do I say when other kids offer me a drink, or some pot?
- What do I do if a friend is over at my house and asks to try some of my parents'/guardians' alcohol?

(Make it clear that the resolutions to these scenarios should take several minutes each to explain.) Then introduce the sock puppets. The group members can split off into pairs to discuss and plan their role-plays. Offer suggestions to the pairs but take a backseat during this stage to allow the members opportunities to use both themselves and each other as valuable resources.

Reconvene the group and ask members to demonstrate their solutions using the sock puppets. Encourage all members to offer constructive comments and to say at least one thing that they liked about the role-plays. Encourage any discussion that stems from any of the role-plays. The point here is for the members to find alternative solutions and also to begin to rely on themselves.

In closing, suggest that the members try at least one solution that they saw role-played during the session in their lives outside of the group. Ask each member in the group to name one situation to try out during the coming week.

The materials needed for the fifth session include eight sock puppets, pencils, and the list of scenarios (one copy for each pair).

Process. If the facilitator has succeeded in the previous sessions, the group should be trusting one another and feeling more confident about sharing with each other. The facilitator now can ease out of the "teacher" mode and allow the group members to help and heal each other. As usual, you are responsible for modeling appropriate behavior and can offer suggestions. This being said, refrain from interfering as this can undermine the confidence group members are attempting to build. As the members share their experiences and resolutions, model empathic listening.

Session 6

Purpose. The purpose of the sixth session is to continue to increase the members' self-awareness and self-confidence. Since the group has offered alternative methods of resolving conflict, the members need to feel the self-confidence it takes to act on those new concepts.

Theme. "I am the hero of my own story."

Activities. This session begins with a check-in about any alternative methods of behaving that any member has tried since the last meeting. Other members can check-in with a brief statement about how they are feeling. Make certain that all of the members feel comfortable about bringing up special issues that they would like support or information about during this check-in period.

After the check-in, introduce the meeting's focus as being the hero of one's own story. Ask group members to think of an incident (involving their drunken parent/guardian) where they believe their behavior helped themselves or someone else. Attempts to rewrite history should be gently interrupted and refocused. The point here is to demonstrate that children of alcoholics already have excellent survival skills and that they can and should trust themselves. Offer some suggestions of what being a hero means in reality (i.e., not "leaping tall buildings in a single bound").

Ask members to draw a picture of how they behaved as heroes. Once the artwork has been completed, ask members to share their stories and their drawings with the group. Encourage all sharing and only interrupt self-effacing and derogatory comments. (If some members are experiencing great difficulty coming up with appropriate stories where they played a hero, then offer support but express confidence in the member to remember an incident on one's own.)

In closing, encourage members to write down two things during the week to come that they really like about themselves. The members should know that they will be asked to share these in the next session.

Process. As in the fifth session, the facilitator takes a backseat. The facilitator's role is really one of emotional support and practical advice at this stage of the group counseling. The facilitator is still actively focusing the flow of the discussion to avoid having members inflict psychological harm on themselves or each other. Be aware of the more quiet members of the group and ask them if they need anything from the group in terms of emotional support, information, or time to discuss a current issue.

Session 7

Purpose. The purpose of the seventh session is to continue the building of the members' self-esteem. The group members should realize that they are their own best resource. As the members move forward in the group process, they gain confidence in their abilities to problem solve and reach viable, safe options.

Theme. "I am . . . someone wonderful and valuable who deserves to feel healthy and safe."

Activities. This session begins with a check-in about the two things that the members really liked about themselves. If a member becomes stuck, ask other members to help their peer. Open the discussion to any concerns that group members may have from the last session. It is important to mention to the members that this is the second-to-last meeting and to listen to concerns or thoughts about the impending termination.

Once the check-in is finished, begin the "I am" poetry exercise. Have a hat full of index cards, all of which have a different adjective written on them. Pass the hat

around the group circle several times. Each member gets five different adjectives before the hat can stop doing rounds. Each member should also have a blank piece of folder paper and a pencil. When the cards are all given out, each member can begin the poem. Each line of the poem begins with "I am." The members should complete their poems with their adjectives. Suggestions for adjectives include, but are not limited to, insightful, caring, talented, brilliant, curious, precious, capable, reliable, intelligent, strong, lovable, valuable, resourceful, trustworthy, phenomenal, and sensitive.

Once the poems are complete, ask the members to share their poems with the group. After everyone has shared, and the group has had an opportunity to discuss what it felt like to do this exercise, ask the members to share the different ways that the disease of alcoholism has affected their opinions of themselves. After the members have shared, you should take great pains to make certain that all the members are aware of how much they have grown from the beginning of the group process. Impress on the members that although alcoholism is a disease that has affected their lives, they are in control of their own behavior and have the power to survive an alcoholic parent.

In closing, do a second check-in with the group members to make sure that no one is leaving the group session with negative feelings toward themselves. In addition, extra time should be left at the end of group to broach the subject of group termination. Ask the members if they have any thoughts about only having one more meeting together. There should be enough time left to discuss closure.

The materials needed for the seventh session include index cards with adjectives printed on them, pencils, a hat, and folder paper.

Process. The group dynamics should be operating on roughly the same level as they have for the past two or three sessions with one exception. Although the group members should be trusting and confiding in one another, they may also be feeling uneasy due to the imminent termination of the group. They should also be demonstrating increasing levels of self-confidence and self-reliance.

The facilitator's role becomes increasingly visible and important as the group faces the concept of termination. Be aware of the significance of this for the members. For the last meeting, be ready with a wealth of pamphlets and information about alcoholism and the support systems available for the members to take with them.

Session 8

Purpose. The purpose of the final group session is to validate all of the growth that the members have experienced. Give all members an opportunity to talk about how they feel about the termination of the group.

Theme. "Growth and new beginnings for the children of alcoholics."

Activities. The last session begins with a check-in about how everyone feels about leaving the group. Ask members to name a positive thing they can do for themselves after group has ended. (For example, a member might go for a bike ride to clear his or her thoughts.) It is the facilitator's responsibility to ask the members how they plan to continue keeping themselves safe after the group has ended.

If there is time, introduce the name exercise. Ask members to draw what they think their names mean. (For example, a member named "Mila" drew musical notes coming from her mother's heart because she believed that her name meant that she was her mother's song.) After each member has finished drawing, the group member should be asked to share the drawing and the meaning behind the art. Ask each member to say something positive about what the other member has just shared.

In closing, encourage members to share what they feel they have gained from this group process. Thank the group members and commend them on their courage and strength. At this time, ask the members to complete a brief evaluation questionnaire in order to determine the efficacy of the group.

The materials needed for the last session include the questionnaire, blank paper, multicolored construction paper, crayons, colorful markers, pencils, scissors, ribbon, glue, and glitter.

Process. The affirmation that members receive from their peers is the most powerful part of this last group. The facilitator should participate in this exercise and validate the positive feedback that members receive. Since the facilitator is the group's role model, it is significant that the members feel some confirmation of these new positive statements from the facilitator. Ask the members what they plan to do after the group is over. The main focus is to help the children walk away from the group with a wealth of information about alternative support systems and a healthy self-confidence that will allow them to rely on their own survival skills.

STRATEGIES TO EVALUATE THE GROUP

As facilitator, have the group members answer a brief questionnaire at the end of the final session in order to determine whether the group has met its initial goals. The questionnaire should not be excessively long because elementary-age children will most likely not wish to sit and fill out an extensive worksheet—it may feel too much like schoolwork for them. The following is an example of such a questionnaire:

- Did you feel safe while sharing your experiences with the group?
  Yes, because _____ No, because _____
- What is the most valuable thing you feel you learned from the group?
- Would you recommend a group like this one to a friend or peer who was facing similar issues with alcoholism?
  Yes   No
- If you begin to feel overwhelmed in the future, would you consider joining another support group for children of alcoholics?
  Yes   No
- Has your opinion about yourself changed during the group? If yes, how? _____

REFERRAL PROCEDURES FOR FOLLOW-UP

In addition to handing out pamphlets of information about the disease itself and support alternatives for the members, be aware of members who may need references to individual counseling or another group. Also, leave information regarding AA, Al-Anon, NA, crisis telephone numbers, domestic violence, and so on, with the group members. If the members do not feel safe walking around with these pamphlets, then they should be encouraged to record pertinent telephone numbers and addresses in their special notebooks.

REFERENCES

Ackerman, R. J. (1983). *Children of alcoholics: A guidebook for educators, therapists, and parents.* Holmes Beach, FL: Learning Publications.

Laybourn, A., Brown, J., & Hill, M. (1996). *Hurting on the inside: Children's experiences of parental alcohol misuse.* Brookfield, VT: Avebury.

Robinson, B. E., & Rhoden, J. L. (1998). *Working with children of alcoholics: The practitioner's handbook.* Thousand Oaks, CA: Sage Publications.

Sigelman, C. K. (1999). *Life-span human development.* Pacific Grove, CA: Brooks/Cole.

CHAPTER 4

FRIENDSHIP GROUPS: MAKE A FRIEND AND BE A FRIEND

Lori Butler

PURPOSE

Friendship groups are designed to provide a safe environment where children can openly discuss their thoughts and feelings while learning about the thoughts and feelings of their peers. The purpose of this type of group is to increase children's understanding of themselves and others, and to help them be more accepting of the similarities and differences between themselves and others. Through participation in the group process, children develop a stronger sense of empathy as they become more aware of how their actions can affect others. Many also experience a boost in self-esteem due to a sense of acceptance, belonging, and a forum to express themselves in the type of nonjudgmental environment that a group can provide.

Friendship groups are typically used in school settings, and the group's focus can be modified to address the needs of a particular school population. In most cases, students participating in groups are referred by teachers and parents, although many school counselors announce their groups in the classrooms and put sign-up sheets around the school in an effort to ensure accessibility to groups for all students.

Participation in a Friendship Group can have positive long-term effects on a child. Helping children to be aware of feelings and empathy, tolerance, and ways of being a good friend provides them with social skills that can increase positive peer relations in the elementary school. These skills remain with the children as they mature and become productive members of society.

CONCEPTUAL FRAMEWORK

Counseling groups are an integral part of the guidance programs at most schools. They are seen as an effective way to reach many children when a counselor's typical caseload would make individual contact with as many children impossible. While there are many types of groups used in schools today, developmental guidance groups play a large role in school guidance curriculums (Paisley & Hubbard, 1994). While developmental group counseling can have preventative goals, in general, it is growth-oriented in nature and is intended for children who "do not require extensive personality change and whose concerns center on the developmental tasks of childhood" (Orton, 1996, p. 193).

A Friendship Group would be designed primarily for children in an elementary school setting and would be considered a developmental group. Under the umbrella of "Friendship Group" many issues can be addressed, including how to make and be a friend, communication and cooperation skills, and exploring the concepts of feelings and empathy. Self-esteem and self-concept, which tend to have an influence on healthy relationships, can also be addressed in a Friendship Group.

While developmental groups focus on issues children face naturally as they grow and develop, the term "Developmental Guidance Group" also implies guidance themes and activities that are appropriate to a group's developmental level (Duncan & Gumaer, 1980). When structuring a group and planning group sessions, it is important to keep in mind the developmental stage of the group members. Things such as attention span, level of cognitive development, and writing abilities must be considered when working with elementary school children because abilities vary so widely among the grades, and even within the grades. Group sessions should have a planned hands-on activity component with related discussion and sharing time rather than relying on discussion and sharing for the entire session. Children learn better and are more engaged when they are actively involved.

Research shows that groups with children tend to be more successful when a structured rather than free-flowing format is used (Gibson, Mitchell, & Basile, 1993). A structured (though flexible) group environment provides children with a sense of security and safety, giving them some guidance and direction combined with freedom to explore and express themselves in a nonthreatening atmosphere.

GROUP GOALS

The goals and focus of Friendship Groups can vary according to the needs of differing school populations. The Friendship Group presented on the following pages has four main goals:

1. Students will learn to respect themselves and others, increasing their awareness of how their actions affect other people.
2. Students will learn such basic life and social skills as effective communication, problem solving, and conflict management.
3. Students will learn to identify their feelings and develop a greater sense of empathy for the feelings of others.
4. Students will experience an increase in self-knowledge and self-esteem, which will positively influence their relationships with others.

In the setting of a supportive, nonjudgmental environment, it is hoped that students will feel safe in freely exploring issues relating to themselves and their peers. The combination of self-concept, friendship, and empathy awareness activities presented in the group format on the following pages is designed to address this goal.

PRE-GROUP SCREENING AND ORIENTATION

Individual pre-group screening and orientation interviews are a vital component of setting up any group (Brigman & Early, 1991). A counselor needs to make an effort to combine group members who will be compatible with one another, taking care not to include a member who might be detrimental to the group process. At the elementary school level, developmental compatibil-

ity is also an important consideration. Screening can also identify students with issues requiring a deeper level of counseling than a group can provide. Students who are in an abusive home situation, or who have recently experienced trauma or the loss of a loved one, would probably be better served through individual counseling.

A pre-group screening and orientation session provides an opportunity to discuss group expectations and issues such as attendance and confidentiality. An interview session might include the following:

- General description of the group and brief discussion on why student has been asked, or has volunteered, to participate.
- Discussion of what the student might hope to gain from group participation; any goals the student might want to accomplish.
- Group leader expectations (e.g., attendance, participation, and confidentiality).
- Depending on the school district policy, a letter may be sent home to the parents informing them of their child's participation in the group, or a consent form may be needed. In such case, the counselor can explain procedures for these during the interview.

Some important considerations for setting up a group include:

- Similar developmental stages of students.
- Group size. Six to eight students is ideal at the elementary school level. With a larger group, a counselor may encounter the need to take on a disciplinary role, which would defeat the feeling of openness and rapport-building so important to the group process (Orton, 1996). A larger group also means that each student has less time to speak.
- The counselor should decide whether the group will be homo- or heterogeneous. In the case of a heterogeneous group, an effort should be made to balance the sexes.
- The duration of the group (usually 6 to 8 weeks) should be predetermined and the sessions should be planned to give structure and momentum to the group.
- It can be helpful to include peers who have successfully dealt with issues the group might explore, or who can serve as positive role models (Gibson, Mitchell, & Basile, 1993).

OUTLINE FOR EIGHT GROUP SESSIONS

The following group, "Make a Friend/Be a Friend," has been developed for use with upper elementary (grades 4–6) students. Each of the eight sessions will be roughly 30–40 minutes long. With some modifications of content and length, this group could be appropriate for use with younger elementary students as well.

Session 1

Purpose. The purpose of session 1 is to introduce group members to each other and to begin the process of rapport-building between members themselves, as well as members and the group facilitator. During the first session it is important to discuss and agree upon ground rules for group sessions. This introductory session may be a bit longer than the others.

Theme. "Getting to know one another as a group." Establish procedures and, as there is usually some nervousness around the first session, strive to make students feel at ease. Students learn a little bit about the other members through introductory activities and experience sharing a little bit about themselves with the group for the first time.

Activities. Session 1 begins with introductions. Going around the circle, students say their names and tell the group something unique about themselves. This can be anything, ranging from simply "I have a cat," to something more revelatory.

After students (and the facilitator) have introduced themselves, the topic of ground rules can be introduced. Clarify that these are rules made by and for the group, in order to make the group a safe place for all to share. Students can brainstorm ideas, with the facilitator recording them. The group as a whole can then narrow down the choices to four or five. Sample ground rules might include:

- Respect others and ourselves.
- Confidentiality.
- Don't use names when bringing up examples.
- Everyone has the right to pass.

After the ground rules are agreed upon, group members can discuss any goals they would like for the group. Write these goals down for use during the last session as part of a group evaluation discussion.

The second part of this group session involves an exercise in cooperation (Orton, 1996). Students can volunteer their ideas of what cooperation means. Then break the students up into smaller groups of two or three and instruct each group to work together to build a tower. Provide construction paper to each group, and place scissors, tape, and glue in the middle for groups to share, encouraging further interaction among the group. The small groups are given 15 minutes to plan and construct their towers.

At the end of the allotted time, students get back into the group circle and discuss how it felt to work cooperatively on the towers. Did they feel supported by their partners? Did they experience frustration with themselves or others during the process? What are some of the benefits of working cooperatively?

In closing this session, students name one thing they have learned from the group experience that day.

Process. Much has taken place on this first group session. Students came into the group with varying degrees of nervousness that they have confronted by introducing and sharing something about themselves. By working together to decide on ground rules and goals, the students contributed to the group and made the group partially their own. Through this process, and the cooperative tower-building activity, students hopefully have established a degree of comfort and rapport with the group leader and fellow members.

The presence and leadership of the facilitator in this first session is fundamental in promoting a positive, supportive environment and establishing boundary and safety rules. The facilitator provides structure and direction while letting students have control over many aspects of the group. This allows for students to develop confidence in the importance of their roles as group members.

Session 2

Purpose. The purpose of this session is to have students be able to define and recognize their feelings and to talk about situations where various feelings might occur. They explore their own feelings, as well as see how others in the group have felt in similar or different circumstances. Children often feel that they alone have felt or experienced something. This session will help the group be aware of how others may feel at different times, and of others who have had similar feelings as themselves, creating a closer bond among group members.

Theme. This session's theme revolves around emotions and feelings; being able to express one's own feelings, and understanding that others might have shared similar feelings.

Activity. Before the group gets underway today, it would be a good idea to go over the ground rules together and make sure there are no questions from last week.

Students begin this session with a review of each other's names. The first person in the circle says her or his name. The second person in the circle says her or his name and the name of the first person. The group continues thus, with the third student saying her or his name and the names of the first and second students until everyone has had a turn, with the facilitator going last.

Next, go around the circle having each member of the group complete the following sentence: "Today I feel ____ ." Then show the students eight (number can vary depending on how many are in the group) slips of paper, each with a different feeling word (e.g., happy, sad, angry, frustrated, proud) written on it. The group as a whole can discuss the meanings of the various words. Then place all of the words into a hat. The hat is passed around and each student draws a paper out of it. Then, going around the circle, students tell about a time when they experienced the particular feeling they pulled out of the hat. The hat can go around the circle two or three times, depending on time constraints.

In closing, students can share times when they have felt like someone else in the group, with the purpose of bringing about the idea of similarities among group members.

Process. As in the first session, the positive presence of the facilitator is vital to the group's feelings of security and comfort. As the students do not know each other very well yet, the warmth and guidance of the facilitator will play a major role in drawing them out and making them feel safe enough to talk about their feelings. Take care during this initial stage of the group to make the distinction between encouraging a reticent student to talk and putting that student on the spot.

Provide structure by being prepared, bringing in materials for the group activity, and making sure that all students have a turn to speak if they want. By maintaining the format of going around the circle rather than having students randomly volunteer to speak, quieter students will feel that they have an equal opportunity to share. Some students who wish to share might be hesitant to do so if they think they will be the only ones speaking up.

Session 3

Purpose. The purpose of session 3 is for students to become aware of and discuss some similarities and differences between themselves and others within their group. This activity is meant to spark in students the idea that even though they might think someone is completely different from them, they probably have more in common with them than they realize.

Theme. "We are different, we are the same."

Activity. As an opening activity, group members in turn say their names and make a physical gesture (i.e., "Shari," snap fingers; "Jason," flap arms). The entire group then repeats the student's name, copying the gesture.

Give students paper and a pencil and instruct them to write 12 characteristics that they feel are representative of them (i.e., likes/dislikes, pets they have, eye color). Those who finish early can draw a decorative border around their paper. Then invite students to read their lists to the group. After all students have shared their lists, ask if anyone noticed people having similar characteristics.

Next, have group members stand in a circle and tell them they will be doing an activity to see what things different members of the group have in common. Say "Step into the circle if you ___ ," finishing the sentence with any topic (e.g., "Step into the circle if you like

pizza"). Those students who like pizza step into the circle, while those who do not remain in the original circle. The topics can start out general, getting more personal as the game progresses (e.g., "Step into the circle if your parents are divorced; if no one is home when you get there after school; if you sometimes feel lonely"). When suggesting a more personal topic, ask the students in the circle to say a word describing how they felt. After several turns, have students choose the topics for a couple of rounds.

When everyone is seated again, have the group talk about how it felt to share in the circle, and then close the session by having the children name one thing they have in common with another group member.

Process. Again, the group facilitator leads the actions of the group and is vital in providing safety for group members by reminding them of their right to pass during the "Step into the circle" game. By setting up a format where students can reveal things about themselves without necessarily having to speak, the facilitator provides an opportunity for students to confront things about themselves while realizing that others often share similar issues. Having students identify how they felt around certain topics continues the process of being aware of one's feelings brought up in session 2.

Session 4

Purpose. This session is designed to get students talking about the qualities they value in a friend, things good friends do and do not do, as well as explore ways in which they can be a better friend. Tying ways of being a good friend in with feelings in a discussion during the activity can help promote a feeling of empathy for others. Hearing their fellow group members' views on what makes a good friend can help students become more aware of the behaviors one can adopt in order to make friends.

Theme. "Being a good friend."

Activity. This session begins by going around the circle, with students introducing the person to their right and telling the group something about that student that was learned during last week's session (e.g., "This is Amy, and she likes to read").

Next, hand out paper and crayons and ask students to draw a picture of their best friends. It can be a real or imaginary friend. After they have finished drawing, on the other side of the paper students can list how or where they met their friends, how long they have known them, and something they really like about them. Students can then take turns sharing their pictures with the group.

After all students have shared their pictures, write on the board the categories "Things a good friend does" and "Things a good friend does not do." Students can brainstorm several ideas to put under each category.

This can be followed up with group members sharing a situation where they or a friend behaved as a good friend does, as well as a situation where they or a friend did something good friends do not do.

The session can close with students naming something they learned about being a better friend during the session.

Process. This session is more discussion-oriented than the previous sessions. The group facilitator takes a less prominent role in this session by initiating the activities but then letting the group guide its own process. As children can be very spontaneous, the primary task of the facilitator in a discussion-based group with children would be to ensure that the more vocal kids do not monopolize group time and to reiterate the need for equal sharing time for all members. The facilitator may also need to enforce the group rule of not using names when bringing up examples.

Session 5

Purpose. Why do children act different ways? What are the reasons behind their various behaviors? What do they really want when they misbehave in class, push someone around on the playground, or betray their best friend's secret?

The purpose of session 5 is to have students discuss different behaviors they or their peers engage in, and look at possible reasons for misbehavior.

Theme. This session's theme revolves around figuring out what motivations can lie behind different behaviors.

Activity. This session begins with a thumbs-up, thumbs-down game. Ask the following questions, telling the students to put their thumbs up if they:

- Like it when their teacher tells them they have done good work.
- Feel good when they are included in a game with friends.
- Get frustrated and give up when they feel they don't understand their schoolwork.
- Sometimes act out in class.
- Have ever wanted someone's attention but weren't sure how to get it.
- Sometimes try to act quiet in class so the teacher won't call on them.
- Have ever acted like a bully on the playground.
- Have ever treated a friend badly and felt sorry afterward.

Then explain that behavior, and misbehavior, often has a purpose. Tell the group they are going to listen to some stories about children, and their task is to figure out reasons for the different behavior exhibited by the children in the stories.

Story 1.   Sarah is always very quiet. At recess time, she sits by herself at the far end of the playground. The other kids leave her alone now because she never wants to play, and whenever the teacher calls on her in class, she only bows her head and turns red. During free time in class, she doesn't use any of the things from the activity center. She just sits at her desk and draws horses.

Questions: How do you think Sarah feels about herself? Do you think she feels very smart in class? Do you ever feel like Sarah? What can you tell yourself if you do feel like that? How could we help Sarah feel better about herself?

Story 2.   Ellen and Alix were best friends, until Emma, the new girl, came to the school. Now Ellen ignores Alix and only wants to be with Emma. At recess they go off together to play hopscotch or play with the neat toys Emma always brings in her backpack. One day Emma was very upset to find her new Shelley doll missing from her backpack. It was later found in Alix's book bag with the braids pulled out and crayon marks all over its face.

Questions: How do you think Alix felt when Ellen began to ignore her and spend all her time with Emma? Why would she take Emma's doll and ruin it? Has one of your good friends ever started to ignore you and hang around with someone else this way? How did you feel? What else could Alix have done?

Story 3.   Tommy is always acting silly in class. He tries to make other people laugh when the teacher is talking. He calls out the wrong answer on purpose and talks without raising his hand. His teacher asks him to use behavior more appropriate for the classroom, and sometimes the teacher puts him in the thinking chair, where he clowns around even more.

Questions: Why does Tommy act like this? Does he really want to be in trouble? Can you think of more positive ways Tommy can get the attention of his classmates and teacher?

As a closing activity, group members can share something they learned about why people act different ways.

Process. These stories present a short form of bibliotherapy, where situations are presented in narrative form. Children often find something in stories that they can relate to their own lives. By living these situations vicariously through the stories of other children, they can gain insight into their own situations or behaviors. The discussion questions at the end of each story can promote feelings of empathy as group members look at behaviors through the eyes of the person acting out and see a situation from that person's point of view.

Session 6

Purpose. The activities in session 6 are designed for group members to become more aware of how we are all affected by the words, negative or positive, of those around us. They will also become more aware of how words they use can be hurtful to others and sometimes have a lasting effect on others' self-esteem.

Theme. "Positive and negative words: Sticks and stones can break my bones, and words can sometimes hurt me." This session ties in the exploration of feelings from previous sessions and takes a look at the motives behind peoples' words.

Activity. Begin this session by having group members around the circle complete the following sentence: "Something I like about myself is ___ ."Ask the group if anyone has said anything to make one of them feel really good that day. If so, what words did they use, what were the circumstances, and how did they respond? Next, ask if anyone has said anything to make one of them feel bad that day, and if so, ask the same questions as above. Point out how our words can have a strong effect on other people, even if we did not mean them very seriously. Then bring up the terms "plus" words and "minus" words, explaining that plus words add to our good feelings about ourselves (our self-esteem) while minus words often take something away from our self-esteem. On a dry erase board or chart paper, write the headings "Plus Words" and "Minus Words." Group members can brainstorm words and phrases that would fall under each category. Some examples of "plus" words or statements might be: "Bobby draws nice pictures." "Maya is my friend." "John is nice to people." Examples of "minus" words or statements could be: "Katie is ugly." "Jack is stupid." "Kristin says dumb things."

Bring out a picture of a boy or girl's face (a picture from a magazine or a hand-drawn picture would work well). Students are "introduced" to the child in the picture. Then say that they will go around the circle and each say a negative statement to the child in the picture. As each group member says something negative, write that statement under the "Minus" heading if it is not there already and crumple a section of the paper, until all members have spoken. At this point, the paper is a crumpled ball. Ask the children how they think the child in the picture is feeling right now. Then have the group members go around the circle again, this time each saying something kind to the picture. As each person says something positive, write the statement under the "Plus" heading and uncrumple a section of the paper, until the picture is opened up again. Ask the group members what they notice about the picture (the wrinkles in the paper will always be there).

The session can close by going around the circle, having the children turn to the person on their right and telling that person a plus statement. These statements will be more effective if they name something specifically about each child rather than being general statements (i.e., "Mary has a nice singing voice" rather than "I like Mary").

Process. The combination of sharing personal experiences and the visual activity of the crumpled picture allows children to explore the concept of the effects of positive and negative statements in both a cognitive and affective way.

Although the facilitator plays a prominent role in guiding the session today, the students were at liberty to share personal situations or not. The facilitator encourages but does not require students to share plus or minus statements they have received, and at no point is anyone put on the spot. Since the group has been together for several sessions now, it is possible that many of the students will feel that the safety of the group environment provides an opportunity to share their experiences.

Session 7

Purpose. The purpose of session 7 is for group members to continue learning about each other, using what they have learned about themselves and their fellow group members in a collage-building activity.

Theme. "What makes us who we are?"

Activity. The group begins this session standing in a circle in front of their chairs. Hold a ball and tell students they are going to play "Favorites." The game is played by one person selecting a topic relating to favorites (i.e., favorite food, favorite color, favorite animal, and so on). The ball is then thrown randomly around the circle, with the recipient naming a favorite item and then tossing the ball to someone else, saying that person's name as the ball is thrown. The last person in the group to get the ball gets to choose the new topic. This game moves quickly and there is time for everyone to have a couple of turns at naming a topic.

Today group members create collages as a celebration of themselves. Bring in magazines, paper, scissors, and glue. Using the magazines, as well as written words and pictures they care to draw representing something about themselves, the students each put together a collage. As part of this exercise, they are encouraged to share pictures with each other if they find something that reminds them of another group member.

The activity closes by going around the group, with each member telling something he or she appreciates about one of the other members of the group.

Process. Apart from the opening activity, the facilitator plays a background role in the group process today. Students continue to learn and explore things about themselves and the other group members through the favorites activity and the collage building. By sharing pictures with other members, the children demonstrate a knowledge and thoughtfulness about each other brought about by the group's interactions thus far.

Session 8

Purpose. As the last session, this will serve to provide a sense of closure for the group. Evaluation of the group goals and the group experience will take place, and the group activity for today is designed to terminate the group on a positive note.

Theme. This session's theme revolves around evaluation and closure.

Activity. The group begins today by having everyone complete the following sentence: "Something I like about myself is _____."

Hand out pieces of tag board. It can be square, or cut into the shape of a person, a heart, or something else. Students write their names on them and pass them around the circle. As the papers come around, students write something they appreciate about the other members of their group.

When the affirmation papers are completed, it is time to begin the closing activities for the group. Bring out a list of four or five goals that the group members decided on during the first session. The group as a whole can evaluate whether the group has successfully met its goals, and if any were not met, possible reasons for this. The group also evaluates what worked well and what didn't during the sessions. As a final activity, the group members identify one way they feel their participation in the group has changed them.

Finally, all group members fill out an anonymous evaluation form about their group experience. A sample evaluation form follows.

Process. Just as there were feelings of nervousness and anticipation during the first session, students may experience feelings of loss and separation as the group comes to a close. It would be a good idea to address this and discuss with the group members that it is normal to have these feelings. By ending the group with affirming and positive statements, the intent is to leave the group members with an uplifted feeling and heightened self-esteem. As many group members may continue to process feelings of loss after the group ends, make it clear to the students that you are available to them at any time for them to come and talk with.

STRATEGIES TO EVALUATE THE GROUP

In a school group of this type, evaluation procedures need not be elaborate. The facilitator needs to know such things as what worked well with the students, activities the students found most and least helpful in the group experience, and what students feel they have gained from the group. An evaluative discussion during the last session, as well as a group evaluation form to be filled out anonymously at the end of the last session, provide two viable methods for group evaluation that will be helpful in organizing future groups.

Sample Group Evaluation Form

Please answer the following questions regarding your group experience. Your responses are anonymous and will be considered by __(facilitator's name)__ in designing future groups.

1. On the first session I felt _____.
2. On the last session I felt _____.
3. Some things I learned from this group are _____.
4. The most helpful part of this group for me was
   _____.
5. Something I will use in the future from this group is
   _____.
6. Something I would change about the group would be
   _____.
7. My favorite activity was _____.
8. I would recommend this group to my friends
   YES   NO

REFERRAL PROCEDURES FOR FOLLOW-UP

A school group is special in that the facilitator is generally the school counselor and is therefore available to the students even after the group sessions end. On the last session, the counselor can tell students they are always welcome to come back and talk for any reason, that a counselor is their friend and is there to help and support them in any way.

The groups serve to acquaint students with the counselor and develop trust so that if students have a problem, they might be more likely to seek the counselor's help or advice. Equally, the group sessions might bring to the attention of the counselor something that a student might need additional work on. If it is found that a student has a problem that can benefit in any way from help through an outside agency, the counselor needs to make appropriate referrals. If there is a family problem, the counselor can also act as a resource for the family and aid them in getting the assistance they need.

REFERENCES

Brigman, G., & Early, B. (1991). *Group counseling for school counselors: A practical guide*. Portland, ME: J. Weston Walch.

Duncan, J. A., & Gumaer, J. (1980). Developmental groups for children: An overview. In J. A. Duncan & J. Gumaer (Eds.), *Developmental groups for children* (pp. 3–35). Springfield, IL: Bannerstone House.

Gibson, R. L., Mitchell, M. H., & Basile, S. K. (1993). *Counseling in the elementary school: A comprehensive approach*. Needham Heights, MA: Allyn and Bacon.

Orton, G. L. (1996). *Strategies for counseling children and their parents*. Forest Grove, CA: Brooks/Cole.

Paisley, P. O., & Hubbard, G. T. (1994). *Developmental school counseling programs: From theory to practice*. Alexandria, VA: American Counseling Association.

CHAPTER 5

KIDS HELPING KIDS: A GROUP TRAINING FOR PEER HELPERS AND BEYOND

Susan E. Halverson, Ph.D.

PURPOSE

Students helping other students produces a wonderful dynamic in which both parties are enriched by the interchange. The purpose of this group training is to present a series of activities that can help educators match students with opportunities to experience and grow in their increasingly complex social skills and interests. Peer helping is an activity that benefits the helper and the person receiving assistance. Students who are peer helpers experience moral and cognitive developmental growth. Students paired with, and helped by, a peer helper get assistance with math, reading, writing, social needs, and communication skills. Teachers get extra assistance for students who need more help and also are able to provide meaningful activities for other advanced students who finish their work ahead of time and need challenges.

Sprinthall and Thies-Sprinthall (1983) identified five essential elements to promote development in educational programs. They named this developmental model of education the Deliberate Psychological Education (DPE) model, and it is the basis for many cognitive developmental interventions. The students engage in:

1. A significant new role-taking experience as a helper in a real-world context such as counseling or peer helping.
2. Careful and continuous guided reflection where the individual is given the opportunity to reflect on new experiences and receives guidance verbally or through written instructor responses to journals.
3. A balance between experience and reflection.
4. Continuous program that allows enough time for significant cognitive structural growth to occur.
5. Adequate support and challenge where the learner is supported by the instructor and at the same time challenged with experiences that cause disequilibrium when trying new behaviors, ideas, and ways of approaching problems.

This group training extends beyond the 8-week training sessions. It includes monthly follow-up group meetings and responsive journaling with the leader during the time that the students are in helping roles. Techniques successfully employed for promoting growth include reflective and responsive journaling. This provides students with the opportunity to think about and personalize the ideas presented, receive encouragement for thoughtfulness and insight, and yet be challenged to think beyond the boundaries of their conscious knowing. It also helps counselors keep closer supervision on what is happening in their peer-helping activities. A system must be set up to facilitate careful matching of students with those in need of a peer helper.

CONCEPTUAL FRAMEWORK

Cognitive developmental theories describe human thought processes and how these thought processes influence human behavior. The fundamental premise of the cognitive developmental stage model is that an individual's cognitive structural development is orderly, sequential, and invariant, moving in the direction of greater complexity, differentiation, and higher order integration (Blocher, 1980). Piaget defines four stages of cognitive development for children and adolescents: sensorimotor stage (birth to 2 years), preoperational or intuitive stage (2–7 years), concrete operational (7–12), and formal operational (12 and older). Students in fifth through seventh grade are on the edge of transforming concrete operational thinking to formal operational thinking. This means students can begin to: (1) think about themselves in a nonabsolutist way, (2) conceive of self and future in terms of probability trends and possibilities, and (3) change their hypotheses as new information is brought to light (Sprinthall, 1978). According to the cognitive developmental perspective, people at higher levels of development tend to take a wider view of things, have more empathy, and are able to deal with dichotomous situations more effectively (Foster & McAdams, 1998; Rest, 1994; Sprinthall, 1994; Sprinthall & Thies-Sprinthall, 1983). These skills help an individual function more appropriately in society. As upper elementary/middle school students begin the journey of self-exploration, schools need to assist them in ways that match their increasingly sophisticated social skills and interests.

Kohlberg (1977) reviewed many studies on childhood predictors of adult performance. He found little evidence that academic achievement in school is an accurate predictor of adult success. Rather, Kohlberg discovered that psychological development predicted life success, as measured by occupational achievement, expert ratings of life adjustment, and absence of crime, mental illness, and unemployment.

Research conducted with high school students trained as peer helpers showed that high school students made significant progress in their developmental growth when the five conditions for growth were in place. However, student helpers who did not receive guided reflective support but only engaged in a helping role did not evidence the same growth (Sprinthall, Hall, & Gerler, 1992).

GROUP GOALS

Students who participate in this group are trained in helping skills. By the end of the training they should be able to demonstrate:

1. Strength building skills
2. Listening skills
3. Open-questioning skills
4. Summarizing and clarifying skills
5. Problem-solving skills
6. Journaling and reflection skills

PRE-GROUP SCREENING AND ORIENTATION

This group training is only one part of a peer-helper program. Cooperation between the administration, faculty, and staff will be necessary for this program to work. Identification of students who are good candidates for the role of peer helper is one of the important steps in the success of a helping program. Deciding on candidates in need of help is also vital. It will be crucial to find teachers who are agreeable for student peer helpers to leave the classroom in order to perform peer helping functions. These teachers must also be able to identify and support troubled students who are in need of peer helper services.

There are a number of ways to identify students as candidates for helpers. Teachers may nominate them or they may be self-referred, with teacher approval. They do not have to be straight A students to be helpers. They do need to have a desire to help and a willingness to participate. An information session may be conducted to inform students what helper requirements are. It is also important for students to have parental permission and support.

Group sessions will last 45–60 minutes and contain no more than six or eight members. It is important to have even numbers due to the amount of pairing used for practice in the group sessions. After the eight-session training, peer helpers will engage in helping another student, and this necessitates continued supervision and reflection. Therefore, it is imperative that monthly group sessions continue during the time peer helpers are helping. Journaling, which will begin during the eight sessions, will continue as well. Having a drop off and pick up location for journals allows the helpers to keep in touch with the leader. This is necessary for several reasons: (1) It allows the leader to spot and help students with difficulties that arise in the helping process and (2) it provides continuous reflection and dialogue between student and leader that facilitates growth.

Training student helpers in small groups is much wiser than trying to train larger groups. With an eight-session format, new groups may continuously be trained until you have enough for the helping need. There are advantages to this step-wise approach. When the new group is done and begins helping, they also join the monthly group. Here they come in contact with helpers who have already been working for at least 8 weeks. These more experienced helpers will provide valuable information and support for the new helpers. Thus the spiral nature of helping will continue to provide benefits to all.

OUTLINE FOR EIGHT GROUP SESSIONS

Session 1

Purpose. Develop group cohesiveness and promote individual comfort.

Theme. *"We are helpers."*

Activities. Introductions, Group Rules, and Mission: Possible Game.

Introduction. During the introductions, discuss the concept that a person's name is a very important part of one's identity. First have students introduce themselves to the group and have all the other students go around the circle and say "Hi, Dave" or "What's up, Sue?" greeting students as they choose but always using their names. Handshakes or high fives could also happen as long as they say the name.

Group Rules. The Group Rules activity begins with a discussion of what kind of group experience the students want this to be and how they can bring it about. Some rules may be different than classroom rules while others remain the same. Write a list of the rules on a chart to be displayed during group. The idea and practice of confidentiality should be introduced and discussed.

Mission: Possible is a game used to introduce and define the role group members will assume and the subsequent helping activities in which they will engage. The game begins by putting pieces of paper in envelopes; one envelope is given to each student. Each envelope contains several messages that students take turns reading to the rest of the class. If it is a task that they as helpers choose to accept, put it up on a poster. If it is not a task they can reasonably be expected to do, then put it in another envelope that the leader runs through the shredder (or find some other way for the message to destruct). The following are examples. *Acceptable:* Your mission if you choose to accept it would be to "Be a friend to a student who needs a friend" or "Help another student better understand math." *Unacceptable:* Your mission if you choose to accept it would be to "Make all your friends like the student you are helping" or "Make sure the student you are helping gets all As on his or her report card." When the positive roles are listed on a poster board, review them and allow them to ask any further questions.

Process. The first session is essential to the future of the group and their continued work together. The threads connecting them to each other and the mission of the group will be laid out here. *Introductions* is a way for students to get to know each other's names. Names are a powerful part of who a person is and calling someone by name is affirming to most people. In their roles as helpers, remembering that information will be the first of many lessons they will learn in the group. They also get to know each other better through the game.

Rules decided upon by the group are easier to reinforce than those imposed by others. Self-choice also gives members a chance to discuss and make choices about moral questions. If they are more comfortable with raising their hands to talk, that is their choice. If

they can wait for one another to finish and then talk, that is all right too. If things aren't going well, the leader can revisit the list and adjust it to fit actual current needs. The leader's job is to facilitate the participants' development of their own productive group.

Confidentiality is hard to promise. A good discussion about what it is and why it is a good idea will at least increase the chance of it happening. Talking about prior good and bad experiences with confidentiality can add to the reason and motivation concerning talk outside of the group.

Mission: Possible game defines the scope of students' expectations for their role as helpers. The leader can create these assignments to fit the tasks that the helpers are being asked to do. It is important that they understand the boundaries of their role and see the limitations of what they are expected to accomplish in their tasks. They should not force their own ideas, talk too much, be bossy, look down on the student, or give advice. These are some of the things that cause problems between helpers and helpees. Students are not counselors, teachers, or parents to those they help. They are helpers, a role that is noble, good, and valuable. The mission of the leader is to help the young people see how valued their contribution is, while keeping them from exercising too much power over others in ways that are not helpful to themselves or others.

Session 2

Purpose. Build resilience in student helpers by identifying their strengths.

Theme. "Strength building."

Activities. Group Juggling, Trait Talk, NWDT.

Group Juggling. Students stand in a circle. One student starts the throwing pattern with a small soft object (beanbags, stuffed animals, tennis balls). Students always throw to the same person and always receive from another same person. Once the pattern is complete and has included everyone, practice with just one object going around a few times. Then gradually begin adding more and more objects until they have five or six going at once. The trick to keeping many objects in the air at once is that the individual receivers only look at the person throwing *to* them, then quickly look away to carefully throw to their receiver, and then look back to watch their thrower.

Trait Talk. Participants begin by talking about someone they know of that is an admired helper. It may be Mother Teresa, Abraham Lincoln, Mahatma Ghandi, Martin Luther King, Jr., Ceasar Chavez, or someone closer to home in the local community. List descriptive traits such as compassionate, generous, and kind. Next, build a *strength tower* with the words on blocks, bricks, or pictures of blocks or bricks. Then, move to what their reasons are for wanting to be a helper and elicit strengths they posses. Finally, participants should draw a wall of bricks labeled with their own strengths in their journals.

Name It, Watch It, Do It, Teeq It.   Introduce the Name it, Watch it, Do it, Teeq it (NWDT) process for the group, as they will be using it in each subsequent session. Tell them that they will always know what skill they are working on because it will always be named. Then they will always be able to watch someone do the skill. They will always have a chance to practice it themselves, and they must always critique (teeq) their efforts, which leads to mastery of the skills.

Process.   The Group Juggling activity warms children up and starts the session out with fun. It also reconnects them with each other and prepares them for what comes next.

Helping peer helpers identify admirable traits in others helps them find the words to define their own strengths. Coming from a place of strength will help them be a better helper. Encourage them to look for the strengths in the students they will be helping, reminding them of how it feels to hear their strengths talked about.

Journaling is a crucial part of this training and learning process. Begin teaching the students to use their journal in the group, and gradually expand its use to record their thoughts and reflections between groups. When they, as helpers, are working with their students, use of the journal will be very important for the leader to keep in touch with them. The peer helpers will drop their journals off once a week or so in a prearranged location and the leader will read and write a response. Then the student will pick it up again. It is especially important to have a way of communication in case helpers are having any difficulties with their student. If difficulties arise, the leader will know if and when it is necessary to call students in for consultation or intervention. Responsive journaling also helps the leader shape the student's experience, reinforcing, questioning, and challenging as needed. Sprinthall, Hall, and Gerler's (1992) research with peer-helping groups indicated that growth in moral development occurred when students maintained a helping role over an extended period of time *and* had adequate chance for reflection, both by journaling and group support. Volunteering as a helper alone did not produce significant growth.

An advance organizer called NWDT should be posted for every session. The skill they are learning that day is named, then students know they will watch a demonstration of the skill, either by the leader or by seeing other peers doing it. The named skill for this session is *Strength Building.* At some time during the session, students have a chance to do and practice the skill themselves. Finally, they critique (teeq) their own and others' performances of the skill. The posted organizer helps them all remember not to miss any steps. Students also

post the daily NWDT in their journals. Journals are required and must be brought to each group session.

Critiquing (teeqing) certainly needs to be explained, and it is truly the most difficult part of the process. It is the process of students looking at what they are doing and figuring out how to improve it. It does not mean criticizing themselves or others. The leader must make this distinction. An example might be, "When I was listening to you, I was kind of nervous, and I think I was looking out the window. Did you notice that? Next time I will be conscious of looking at you." or "When I asked you what to do about my teacher, you told me I should just go and talk it over with her. You forgot to take me through the stepping stones of problem solving. Could we try that again?" Some other examples of questions students can ask of themselves and others in this process are:

- What went well?
- What were the problems?
- What was it like to be a peer helper?
- What was the best part?
- How could I do it differently next time?
- How do you think Jessica felt when . . . ? Why?

Session 3

Purpose.   Learn listening skills.

Theme.   "Listening or hearing?"

Activities.   Group Picture, AB Sharing, NWDT.

Group Picture.   Divide students into groups of three or four. The group gets a sheet of paper and one marker for each student. Instruct them to draw a picture without talking. Give them about 5 minutes. After they are done, ask them to tell about their pictures. Find out what was difficult about the task and how they worked it out. Discuss reading each other's eyes and bodies to make some decisions. Then give them another paper and again have them draw a picture. This time they can talk. Give them another 5 minutes and then talk about how it was different. Was it better or worse? What did they have to do to accomplish the task?

AB Sharing.   One student is *A*, the other *B*. They will be partners to practice and watch each other using their listening skills. Partner *A* will talk about any topic you choose for 30 seconds. Partner *B* will sit with his or her hands on knees and listen. *B* won't nod, move, smile, or do anything except look at Partner *A*. Then the process is reversed with *B* talking and *A* listening but not responding. At the conclusion, discuss how it felt to talk when the listener did not respond. Also, ask how it felt to listen and not be able to move or respond. Ask, "What did you learn about listening?" Now have them take turns talking to their partner about anything they would like. This time they can respond naturally. Instead of 30 seconds, give them 3 minutes each. Now ask them what they noticed about this talking. What was better? How did they feel? Give students 5 minutes to write in their journal on what they learned about themselves as listeners.

NWDT. "Listening" should be written on your chart at the beginning of the session so it is *Named* as the skill of the day. The *Watching* and *Doing* should be checked off as they are doing AB Sharing. The *Teeqing* is giving them a few minutes to do their journal writing: teeqing their listening skills and their experience with the AB sharing activity. Ask questions like "How did it feel when you were talking and Sara didn't seem to be listening?" "What did you do well when you were being a good listener?" "How do you know you were effective at listening?"

Process. The Group Picture activity addresses many issues in communication. The discussion should reveal that they had to read other student's body language when they couldn't use words. When they could use words, it was usually more difficult because they have to get everyone's opinions, reach consensus, negotiate, and make decisions. These other perceived needs make picture drawing more complex. This gives the leader a chance to list some of the processes needed for good communication. These hopefully include verbal and nonverbal listening skills, problem solving, questioning to find out what others want, and clarifying and summarizing in order to reach consensus.

The AB Sharing activity heightens their awareness of two ways to listen, verbal and nonverbal. It helps them understand what it feels like to not be affirmed when they are talking. The processing helps them transcend their experience and apply it to listening in the real world and how they will accomplish the helping tasks they are getting ready to undertake.

NWDT is a continual process during the session, tying it all together. *Naming* is "listening", *Watching* and *Doing* happens during sharing, and *Teeqing* is writing in the journal.

Session 4

Purpose. Learn about open questions.

Theme. "How do you help without giving the answer?"

Activities. Roundtable, Jeopardy, NWDT.

Roundtable. When students arrive and sit in the circle, inform them that they are going to be learning about using questions. Go around the circle and ask each student a closed question such as "Which team won the kick ball game?" or "What grade did you get on the poem you wrote, Michael?" Then ask students an open question such as "How did your test go yesterday, Lisa?" or "Could you tell us about your game this week, Joseph?" You can extend this by having them ask each other questions and then help them decide if the questions are open or closed. Further discussion about which questions pro-

mote the best conversation or make them feel better could round this out.

Jeopardy. In the traditional television show, contestants must reply with a question. Students in the group take turns being the contestants. They can choose categories and slap the table when they have the answer. The leader is the game show host. Students must answer in questions: two points for open questions and one for closed questions as judged by group consensus. The categories could be tailored to meet the needs of the group. Examples of categories and answers fitting the category:

Troubles Kids Have	It Helps How?	Teacher Woes	Cool Stuff About It
My boyfriend	Better grades	Missed classes	Feeling good
A failing grade	Friendly attention	Making up work	Helping helps
Friend fears	Someone to talk to	No place to go	The future
Teasing hurts	Helping steps	Great expectations	Strength building

Open-question examples:

Troubles Kids Have

My boyfriend: "How are things going with your boyfriend?"

A failing grade: "What do your grades look like right now?"

Friend fears: "How are things going with your friend?"

Teasing hurts: "Could you tell me a little about it?"

It Helps How?

Better grades: "How will it help you to have a student helper?"

Friendly attention: "What is the benefit of having a peer helper?"

Someone to talk to: "How can talking about your feelings help?"

Helping steps: "What are some things that helpers do to help?"

Teacher Woes

Missed classes: "What happens when you are helping?"

Making up work: "How do you find time to make up your own classwork?"

No place to go: "What do you do when you can't find a place to work with your student?"

Great expectations: "How does it feel when teachers expect your helping to make a difference for their students?"

Cool Stuff About It

Feeling good: "How are things going with your peer helping?"

Helping helps: "What is the best thing about being a helper?"

The future: "How does being a helper affect your future?"

Strength building: "What does strength building mean?"

These are examples, but leaders can determine their own categories and answers based on the experience of the peer helpers in their school. This makes it more meaningful to individual settings. Peer helpers already working could help design better examples from their experiences as one of the tasks of their monthly group meetings.

NWDT. The topic "Open Questions" should be listed on the chart at the beginning of class. Roundtable and Jeopardy both give students a chance to watch and practice using open questions. The Teeq will include discussion of how easy or hard it is to ask open questions and how they think they did. The homework should be to pay attention to the questions people in their school ask. Before they leave class, they should write in their journal words that facilitate open questioning and words that lead to closed questions. Encourage them to write some of the questions they discover during the week and bring them back to class.

Process. Prepare questions to ask the students before the session begins. Using open questions is really rather challenging. Some words lead more readily to closed questions like *Who, Where,* and *When,* which seem to ask for single answers. Questions requiring a "yes" or "no" are closed as well. *How* and *What* lead to more open questions. Sometimes *Why* will work but it may lead to defensiveness as well. Students will probably use a combination of closed and open questions when working as a helper. The open ones are harder and therefore require more practice.

Prepare the Jeopardy board using a chalkboard, white board, or poster. Write the categories on top and cover the answers with paper. The kinds of helping the students will be doing will dictate the answers you use. Students working as a PE helper, tutoring, or working with a handicapped student all have their own kind of issues. Giving the students a list of open questions for starters should facilitate the process.

The NWDT process is ongoing. *Naming* is "Questioning". *Watching* the leader ask closed and open questions informs students when *doing* it themselves during the game. *Teeqing* their own skill is valuable and a great transition to using it in their life outside of group. Do not be surprised if they do not write in their journals

outside of group. Having encouraged them to write, don't get upset with them for not doing it. Check to see if anyone did, and encourage that person by discussing what he or she noted. Comment on how much easier it is to remember to pay attention to the homework assignment if observations are written down and how much easier it is to remember what they did observe over the week's time if it is recorded.

Session 5

Purpose. Learn clarifying and summarizing skills.

Theme. "What's that you say?"

Activities. Homework Check-in, Mirror Mirror on the Wall, Parrot Talk, NWDT.

Mirror Mirror on the Wall. Check student's homework assignments on questioning first. Then, pair the students and have them face each other. One is the mirror and the other will look at the mirror and do things like stick out his or her tongue, wave a hand, or dance around. The mirror should reflect the movements. Change roles. Talk about how hard it was to anticipate the movements and how hard they had to concentrate to reflect what the other student was doing.

Parrot. If the pairings for the first activity worked well, let them keep the same partners. Ask for a volunteer to help with a role-play. The leader is the helper and the student can talk about anything. Model clarifying and summarizing responses. Ask students to do the same with their partner and then switch so they each have a chance. If there is enough time, ask a volunteer pair if they would share one of their role-plays with the group.

NWDT. Name "Summarizing" and "Clarifying" on the board. Note that they are able to *watch* and *do* it themselves. Have each pair *teeq* their partners, telling what they thought they did particularly well. Allow them to share their partner's strengths with the whole group, if the partner agrees.

Process. Mirror Mirror on the Wall is a fun way to demonstrate beginning clarifying and summarizing skills. It helps children pay attention and anticipate what the other children will do, which are the first steps to clarifying and summarizing.

Parrots who can talk often listen to a conversation and, not having a large vocabulary, repeat a few words they hear. The leader doesn't want the helpers to parrot back exactly what their students say. However, if students watch for the main words and ideas when their partner is speaking, and then summarize or ask for clarification, they will have learned a helpful skill. The leader will have to model teeqing his or her own role-play so that the students will be able to identify clarifying and summarizing skills. This will be vital when students teeq their own clarifying and summarizing skills. Some helpful teeqing questions include: "Did I repeat exactly what was said or could I explain using my own words?" "Did I really get what my partner was saying or was I off the mark when I summarized it?"

Continue to do NWDT at the end of every session. Sharing strengths is the best way to encourage students that critiquing does not have to be painful and can be really helpful. Make sure students get their partners' approval to share their strengths with the group. Model for them how to give constructive critiques. Example: "You seemed to really hear what I said, and then you summarized it well."

Session 6

Purpose. Teach problem solving skills.

Theme. "Steps to solving a problem."

Activities. Pretzel, Stepping Stones, NWDT.

Pretzel. Students stand close together in a circle, extending both hands to the center. Each hand should grab and hold a different student's hands; neither can be the hands of the students beside them. Students untangle themselves into a circle without ever letting go of anyone's hands.

Stepping Stones. Begin Stepping Stones by asking students what they know about solving problems. Then, brainstorm about how the students solve problems. Ask them how they like to be helped with their problems. Share that people usually just want someone to help them figure out what to do and tend not to want or take advice. Tell the students there are five steps that will aid them when someone asks for help making a decision. Following these steps is more helpful than giving advice. Make large circles out of poster board with the numbers 1 through 5 on them and put them on the floor. Get a student to stand on the first one, "What is the problem?" Sometimes it is easy to figure out and sometimes it takes using those open questions, summarizing, and clarifying skills they have just learned. Put down the second stone, "What have you tried?" It helps to know this so some possible solutions that didn't work can be eliminated right away. It also helps to find out what happened when they tried the solution and how long before they gave it up. The third stepping stone is "What else could you do?" When problem owners come up with other, new ideas, ask them what might happen if they choose this solution? Sometimes people with problems will have trouble thinking up anything new to try. Continue to help them think. Priming questions such as, "Have you thought of trying _____" or "What might happen if you _____" may help. Using statements like "Why don't you just _____" will usually not be helpful because it is like giving advice. The fourth stone asks, "What is your next step?" Encourage problem owners to choose one of the ideas they just came up with to solve the problem. The fifth stepping stone should be placed further away from the first four to indicate that this is done later. It asks, "How did it go?" This lets the problem bearer know that someone cares and is interested in the success of the chosen solution. If the solution didn't work it may be necessary to go through the steps again and choose another possible solution to the problem.

Next, the leader chooses a real-life problem observed in the school and conducts a role-play, going through the five steps. Finally, pair students and instruct them to practice solving another real problem with their partner.

NWDT. Problem Solving is posted as the skill of the week on the chart. Watching and doing are very important to this learning. Teeqing themselves at the end of this time by writing in their journals quietly can be very important. Ask them to write about how they have helped their family and friends with problems in the past and what might be hard for them in using the five-step process.

Process. Pretzel is a problem-solving task that is also physical and fun. It helps them prepare for the rigor of the rest of the session.

Brainstorm how students solve problems and how they liked to be helped with their problems as a way of examining their current practice of problem solving. It will help the leader evaluate how different their current practice is in comparison to the five-step process being presented. It might be helpful to give students a sheet of paper with the five stepping stones drawn and listed for them to refer to when practicing this skill.

The critiquing process is getting more complex as the skills become more complex. Remember: training students to teeq and journal is vital. As they reflect about what they are learning, these skills teach them to think about their thinking. This thinking about thinking is probably one of the most important parts of this whole process and is what helps them grow developmentally.

Session 7

Purpose. Find out whom they will be helping and puzzle out problems.

Theme. "Discovery."

Activities. Homework Check-in, Puzzler, Pairing and Sharing, NWDT.

Puzzler. Check to see who has written in journals and briefly discuss what they wrote, as well as how the process of journaling is helpful. Give each student one half of a puzzle picture. Have them find their match and work together to come up with a story about their picture. Each pair will then share their story with the group.

Pairing and Sharing.   Students are given the name of the person they will be helping. In groups of three, have them figure out what kind of fun they will have with their friend. Also think about what might be problematic for them, so they can plan ahead. Then have them share with the group some of those thoughts.

NWDT. "Discovery" is the *name* of this lesson. *Watching* and *doing* includes discovering who their peer-helping partners are and how they feel about being assigned to those students. Teeqing expands this discovery with the journaling of their thoughts about their peer assignment. Instruct them to reflect on their assignment and then write about their reflections in their journal before returning to group for the last session.

Process.   Picture puzzles are easy and fun. Find pictures in magazines, old recycled books, or make copies of covers of their favorite CDs, books, and so on. The pictures the leader chooses will influence the kind of stories the students create. Pictures of kids helping kids might be good examples. Cut the pictures in half in fun ways. Mix them up and hand them out randomly, or if the leader wanted certain pairs to work together, a little preplanning could effect that result. Random pieces could give them a chance to work with someone they may not have worked with before.

The story-creating session is linked with this activity in that thinking creatively about someone else's life can help children imagine their peer assignment. Students are always excited to find out who their assignment is. They also have lots of questions and need to air their thoughts about what it might be like to work with a mentally handicapped person, someone in Mrs. Jones' class, or whether they feel capable of helping a third-grade student with math. Giving students time to think and share their feelings will help them feel better prepared and supported in the role of peer helper. Sharing thoughts of fun and also worries with the whole group gives the leader a chance to allay some of their fears, help them think of what to do if they have a problem, and focus on strengths and the positive aspects of being a helper. Some of the difficulties students may encounter in their roles as peer helpers include: uncooperative students, teachers not having things for them to do when they arrive, not having a good place to work with their students, students telling them highly personal or dangerous things such as abuse, and other students teasing the student they are trying to help. The students can expand this list themselves as they begin their roles as helpers. Use this list judiciously so the helpers are not frightened away.

Teeqing for this session is accomplished by reflective writing in their journals between sessions. Ask them to write about how they are feeling about being a peer helper.

Session 8

Purpose. Put all the skills together and practice.

Theme. "Putting it all together."

Activities. Check-in, All Together Role Plays, NWDT, Awards.

Check-in. Check-in with journals and continuing thoughts they may have had about their role as peer helpers.

All Together Role Plays. Review the list of skills students have learned: strength building, listening, questioning, clarifying and summarizing, and problem solving. Teams of two should take turns role-playing what to do when they first meet the student they will be helping. If time allows, other role-play situations could include a session of something they might expect when working with their peer assignment. They should be using the skills they learned in the previous sessions.

NWDT. "Putting it all together" is the *name* of the session. Practice provides both *watching* and *doing*. Checklists of the skills should be used in the teeqing for this session. After each student role-play, students *teeq* with their partner about which skills were used and which weren't needed and why. The leader should be overseeing the role-plays and the teeqs.

Awards. Conclude this session with a discussion of how to begin their assignments, when their regular monthly meeting will be, what to do if they have a problem, and how to pick up and drop off their journals during the month of helping on their own. Then award each student a certificate of promotion to peer helper, reflecting on what you see as the strengths of each student. Be honest and generous.

Process. If homework has been assigned, it is very important to begin each session with a review of that homework. Students will have had time to think about their role in relationship to their assignments and may have come up with questions that you need to hear and address. Then give them as much time to practice being a helper as possible. Coach them about what they should do, say, and ask in the first meeting with their student, reminding them how important it is to start with a good impression. Remember to take time to review the skills the helpers have learned. A checklist of the skills in their hands may prompt them. Some problems or scenarios will not require students to use all the skills. Discuss this possibility with them so they don't feel they have to use all the skills, and identify when using them might be inappropriate. Move around and oversee how they are doing. Help them with their teeqs, reminding them to be gentle in their teeqing of each other. You may be tempted to skip the critique part because it is often difficult and time is short, but don't do it. It is very important to the process. When students are on their own, they will have been trained to write teeqs in their journals. This is a very important activity for promoting growth. Taking on a helping role is very good for students, as critiquing their work magnifies the value.

STRATEGIES TO EVALUATE THE GROUP

Evaluation for evidence of successful mastery of the skills learned in this group is very important because these students will be working with a fellow student after the group concludes. It is therefore imperative that the leader know if each student possesses the skills necessary to be a helper. Leaders must also assess affective areas such as helpfulness, compassion, and kindness of the students. The leader may already have a good idea of the student's skills from close scrutiny of the Getting Acquainted activity practiced in the last session. If the leader has any concerns or wants to conduct a careful observation, he or she may individually practice a role-play activity with the student to further assess their skills. In either case, the leader should assess the students on the basis of their journal entries and also complete a checklist of the students' abilities. Students should be able to identify and demonstrate these skills:

- Listening skills
- Open-questioning skills
- Summarizing and clarifying skills
- Problem-solving skills

Students should be:

- Willing to be a helper
- Not looking for power over other students
- Demonstrate kindness and compassion in their writing, thinking, and practice
- Demonstrate an ability to assess their own behavior and skills

When the leader is satisfied that students have acquired the necessary skills, they will introduce the peer helpers to the students they will be helping.

REFERRAL PROCEDURES FOR FOLLOW-UP

Letters are sent home with each student at the end of the session. The letter informs parents that the student has completed training to become a student helper and lists the skills that the student has been working on. It also encourages parents to notice and reinforce the skills when they see their children using them. Limited information about the student assigned to their child also is included, such as first name, grade, and classroom. Parents are encouraged to call the leader with any concerns or questions. Dates and times for the monthly continuing meetings are included so parents understand that their child will receive continuing support, supervision, and opportunities for growth.

REFERENCES

Blocher, D. (1980). Developmental counseling revisited. *Counseling and Human Development, 13*(4), 1–7.

Foster, V. A., & McAdams, C. R., III (1998). Supervising the child care counselor: A cognitive developmental model. *Child & Youth Care Forum, 27(1)*, 5–19.

Kohlberg, L. (1977). Moral development, ego development, and psychoeducational practices. In D. Miller (Ed.), *Developmental theory.* St. Paul: Minnesota Department of Education.

Rest, J. (1994) Background: Theory and research. In J. R. Rest & D. Narvaez (Eds.), *Moral development in the helping professions*, (chap. l, pp. 1–26). Hillsdale, NJ: Lawrence Erlbaum Associates.

Sprinthall, N. A. (1978). A primer on development. In N. A. Sprinthall & R. L. Mosher (Eds.), *Value development as the aim of education* (pp. 1–15). New York: Character Research Press.

Sprinthall, N. A. (1994). Counseling and social role taking: Promoting moral and ego development. In J. R. Rest & D. Narvaez (Ed.), *Moral Development in the Professions: Psychology and Applied Ethics,* Hillsdale, NJ: Lawrence Erlbaum Associates.

Sprinthall, N. A., Hall, J. S., & Gerler, E. R., Jr. (1992). Peer counseling for middle school students experiencing family divorce: A deliberate psychological education model. *Elementary School Guidance and Counseling, 26,* 279–294.

Sprinthall, N. A., & Thies-Sprinthall, L. (1983). The teacher as an adult learner: A cognitive view. In G. Griffin (Ed.), *Staff development: Eighty-second yearbook of the National Society for the Study of Education* (pp. 13–35). Chicago: University of Chicago Press.

■ PART TWO

GROUP WORK WITH ADOLESCENTS

The purpose, concepts, and goals of working with teens are reflective of their developmental needs as shown in Part Two. In Chapter 6, "School Success Skills: A Group for At-Risk Students," it is noted that many students lack necessary skills that ensure school success. Preventive measures that help keep teens from giving up on school include teaching teens skills and goal setting. Group goals include: increasing members' feeling of connectedness, practicing goal setting and planning, practicing organizational strategies, and gaining increased self-esteem and efficacy in school.

Chapter 7, "Moving to a New School: A Transition Group for Young Adolescents," addresses students' feelings of isolation and lack of coping skills when adjusting to a new school environment. Grieving loss of attachments is an integral component of helping teens adjust. Some group goals are that members will see the universality of their situation, help each other deal with losses, help each other make new friends and become oriented to their new community, and learn how to provide a safe environment for sharing concerns.

Chapter 8, "Peer Networking to Build Resiliency among High School Youth: A Violence Prevention Group," addresses the problems that can occur when students feel tumultuous emotion and social detachment. This group aims to strengthen members' bonds with "positive, presocial family members, teachers, and friends" and to encourage development of healthy behaviors. The goals of the group are to create a positive social orientation among group members and allow opportunities to work with peers and teachers to build bonds within the school.

Chapter 9, "TAG, I'm It: A Counseling Group for Talented and Gifted Adolescents," illustrates how talented and gifted teens have unique issues in counseling that are often overlooked. Group work helps "essentially healthy children draw on their own strengths to better deal with life's challenges." Goals for such a group include exploring the meaning and value of individual giftedness, providing opportunities to have successes in building and sustaining relationships, and using gifts as a personal asset.

Chapter 10, "Effective Communication for Conflict Situations," is geared toward students who are faced with disciplinary action due to the manner in which they respond to conflict situations. The group methods include role modeling, role-playing, goal setting, and identifying consequences of behaviors. The group goals include: recognizing conflict as part of life, identifying conflict responses, and learning tools for communication.

Chapter 11, "Adolescents of Divorce: A School-Based Intervention," describes how peer support can help students come to terms with the facts and feelings of divorce when it affects their lives. "The built-in presence of counselor and peers within a school setting is a natural first-line of nurturance and continuity in a time of family upheaval." Some group goals are: identifying, expressing, and understanding feelings; clarifying divorce-related misconceptions; developing problem-solving skills; and learning to understand the feelings of others.

Chapter 12, "High School Students Rediscovering Academic Success," addresses the issues of students who are "stuck in unhealthy academic patterns and appear well on the way to becoming high school dropouts." When seen through Ellis's Rational Emotive Behavioral Theory, students' problems are seen as the consequence of irrational beliefs about themselves and their abilities. Goals for this group include: separating the worth of a person from performance and abilities, recognizing and correcting irrational thought patterns, and formulating a reasonable and workable plan for academic success.

Chapter 13, "The Safe Survivors Group: A Psychoeducational Counseling Group for Adolescent Survivors of Relationship Violence," "is designed to supplement individual counseling following an adolescent's break from an abusive dating relationship." The five-stage process of victim-to-survivor behavior is illustrated. Some goals for this group include provision of emotional support, identification of components for safety, redefinition of self as a survivor, and replacement of learned helplessness with empowerment.

CHAPTER 6

SCHOOL SUCCESS SKILLS: A GROUP FOR AT-RISK STUDENTS

Daren Gilbert
Portland State University

PURPOSE

Students today have difficulty in school for a variety of reasons. Some either do not care or do not see the value of doing well. Some lack fundamental academic or intellectual abilities. Others seem to have the desire to succeed but lack the know-how to apply the academic ability that they have. For whatever reason, some students seem unequipped with basic skills that are necessary to succeed in school, placing them at risk. At the high school level, students are presumed to already have these skills in place, and there is little space in an already crammed curriculum to try to address the deficits in a systematic way. Students are expected to learn these skills with little or no organized instruction (Genshaft & Kirwin, 1990). Feeling overwhelmed, they find giving up and dropping out attractive options.

The purpose of the school success skills group is to teach students skills they may be lacking. In addition, communication will be highlighted in order to enhance student and teacher interaction. Attitudes toward self and success will be investigated as part of a discovery of the connection between expectations and success.

CONCEPTUAL FRAMEWORK

The conceptual framework of this group is one of prevention. One of the highest correlates for dropping out is lack of academic success (Natriello, Pallas, McDill, & McPartland, 1990). Helping students develop these skills early in high school will reduce the likelihood of drop-

ping out by helping them feel more successful and more connected to the school.

Because of the clientele and goals of this group, Wubbolding's (1999) WDEP system based on Glasser's Reality Therapy, is a straightforward framework from which to proceed. Reality therapy asserts that people are responsible for their own behavior, behavior involves choices, and in most situations, people have a number of options to choose. Thus, the power to change a situation clearly lies within the individual. Wubbolding's WDEP system applies Reality Therapy. Using this system, the counselor helps clients explore their **W**ants, then **D**escribe their current situation and the direction of their lives. Self-**E**valuation is the third step, where clients examine the efficacy of their current choices. The final step consists of making **P**lans that will be more effective in attaining the clients' goals (Wubbolding, 1999). Explained in this clear language, the simplicity of Reality Therapy will be appealing to many teens.

Many at-risk students are unaware that their learning strategies are ineffective (McWhirter, McWhirter, McWhirter, & McWhirter, 1993). Students who see success as a function of native intelligence alone rather than a result of know-how and effort are likely to give up, thinking nothing can change the situation (Robertson, 1997). Using WDEP to help students to identify what they are doing well and building on those strengths will help bolster self-confidence and a feeling of efficacy. Students are initially asked to target their efforts in one or two classes in order to put into practice the skills they are working on. Progressing incrementally helps students realize the value of setting attainable goals and keep them from being once again overwhelmed by what they see as their own lack of intelligence.

GROUP GOALS

The goals for the School Success Skills group are as follows:

1. Group members increase their feelings of connectedness to other group members and, therefore, to school.
2. Group members practice goal setting and planning.
3. Group members practice organizational strategies.
4. Group members gain a sense of increased self-esteem and efficacy in the school setting.

PRE-GROUP SCREENING AND ORIENTATION

The group should consist of six to ten freshman and sophomore students. Initial referrals may come from counselors, teachers, parents, or the students themselves. Interested students must fill out a questionnaire asking about their attitudes toward school (see Figure 6–1). Students should attach a copy of their most recent report card to the questionnaire. Students should also read a handout briefly describing the group process and the expectations for group members. Students need to agree to commit to the goals of the group and to make an honest effort to attend and do their best. Students also need a signature giving parent/guardian consent for participation in the group.

SCHOOL SUCCESS SKILLS GROUP INTEREST QUESTIONNAIRE

Name _____   Gr   9   10

Phone _____

Address _____

Parent/Guardian name_____

Please answer each item honestly and completely. Make sure to explain your answer.

1. In general, my attitude toward school is _____

   because _____

   _____

2. I'm interested in this group because _____

   _____

3. These are things I hope to learn from this group: _____

   _____

4. Currently, I'm having these problems in school: _____

   _____

My son/daughter has my permission and support to participate in the school success skills group.

Parent/Guardian signature _____

If I am selected as a participant in the school success skills group, I will do my best to attend every session, abide by the rules agreed upon by the group, and participate fully in all group activities.

Student signature _____

Figure 6–1.   Sample success skills group questionnaire.

Applications are screened by the facilitator and selected on the basis of interest in the group as well as school performance. Selected participants are given a handout that explains more fully group rules which will be discussed at the first session.

OUTLINE FOR EIGHT GROUP SESSIONS

The group will meet for approximately 45–60 minutes during or after the regular school day. Eight sessions are outlined here and should occur in the sequence given. The group could encompass as many as 12 sessions. The additional meetings, to be added where appropriate, could expand on the information presented in these sessions or introduce topics like note taking, test-taking strategies, and test anxiety.

Session 1

This is the initial meeting of the group. Materials necessary include a poster with group rules written on it, felt markers, and index cards with adjectives written on them for each group member.

Purpose. The purpose of the first meeting is for group members to begin to get to know one another and to understand the group rules. In addition, students have a chance to begin to explore their feelings about school.

Theme. "Group formation". Members discover that being in a group is a different experience than being in a traditional classroom session. Ideally, this will begin to alleviate some anxiety for group members.

Activities. The first activity is an ice-breaker to make sure that all group members are acquainted. Group members introduce themselves and answer a nonthreatening question such as "What television show would you like to guest star on and why?" The facilitator should go first to model an appropriate response.

Next, group members read and discuss group rules written on a poster or develop their own set of rules for the group. Rules might be similar to the following:

- I will really listen and not talk when someone else is talking.
- I will do my best to participate in all group activities.
- I will not discuss any personal information brought up in group outside of group.
- I will respect my fellow group members and not judge them.

The discussion that stems from creating and clarifying group rules can help members develop a feeling of investment.

For the next activity give each group member a set of 25 small index cards, each with an adjective written on it ("strong," "awful," "relaxing," "boring"). Each person then sorts the adjectives into stacks based on whether they describe "Home," "School," or "Myself." The group can then discuss the exercise and investigate the themes that are revealed in the separate card stacks, particularly the "school" stack. As a closing, each group member shares one or two cards and explains why the cards fit in the particular stack. As homework, group members could keep these descriptors in mind during the week and pay attention to how their own expectations played into the description.

Process. Steps in the first group meeting are designed to assist with group formation. Creating the rules or making modifications and/or additions helps students feel a sense of investment and control in the group. Topics of discussion are interesting but nonthreatening in order to encourage participation. Each member should speak so that all feel a part of the group.

Session 2

This session should immediately follow session 1. Materials needed include a poster with the group guidelines (optional), butcher paper, felt markers, index cards, copy of *Little Red Riding Hood* (optional), notebook, and pencils.

Purpose. Session 2 continues the formation and bonding of the group. Students learn the basics of the WDEP theory and how to apply it. Group members identify problem areas for them at school. Goal setting will come as an outgrowth of this.

Theme. The theme for the second session (as well as several more) is "learning to take control of your actions." As group members begin to apply WDEP to their own school situations and understand that the change must come from within themselves, they can begin to set goals and develop strategies to meet these goals.

Activities. As a warm-up, group members go around the circle and review the rules of the group, each person discussing one. (The poster with the rules could be up on the wall for a reminder if desirable.) The facilitator then briefly reads or tells the story of Little Red Riding Hood, asking the group members to pay close attention to the wolf's behavior. Once the story is finished, have students brainstorm what the wolf's needs were. Write responses on butcher paper under the column heading "W." Under the "D" column, group members describe the wolf's current actions. The "E" column is for listing evaluations of the wolf's current actions, and the "P" column is for suggestions for new strategies for the wolf. Once group members have gone through this exercise, explain the overall concept of the WDEP system. The group can discuss other examples (a basketball player in a game, a child locked out of the house, and so on).

Once group members seem to have a handle on the basic theory, ask students to make their own chart in their notebook and try to fill out the W, D, and E columns in regards to themselves in a school situation. The facilitator can model this if it seems necessary. Group members can be reassured that working on the P column is one of the things that this group is about. Members can be given an opportunity to share if they are willing.

In closing, ask students to take the chart they have created, think about their current class schedule, and write down at least two goals on an index card for next week.

Process. The group should be in the process of continuing to bond and establish some trust. Some activities in this session required participation from everyone; others ask for volunteers. This gives group members an opportunity to share if they feel comfortable but doesn't force sharing. The facilitator needs to help alleviate the anxiety that the WDE chart may create in some members. Assure students that this is a step-by-step process and most real-life situations cannot be solved in one group session (regardless of what they have learned from sit-coms!)

Session 3

An additional session could be added between session 2 and Session 3. Materials needed include butcher paper, masking tape, felt markers, and index cards.

Purpose. The focus of this session is goal setting and goal achievement. Group members will have set many goals for themselves in many areas of their lives over the years. Few of them will have had much experience in strategically planning the successful achievement of those goals.

Theme. "Go for the Goal." Group members learn the basics of goal setting—creating goals that are realistic, attainable, and fairly immediate. Many at-risk students have few if any goals regarding school. Helping them create attainable goals for themselves will aid in developing self-efficacy.

Activities. As an opening activity, group members can go around the circle and tell what they wanted to be when they were first graders. They can also include any more recent career goals if they want to share them. This activity can open into a discussion of goals and how vague those childhood desires really were. Most first graders do not really understand what it takes to become a police officer, much less how to go about accomplishing the necessary steps.

Have group members brainstorm on butcher paper the qualities necessary for good goals. Guide them to the concepts of specificity, realistic focus, and proximity—setting fairly short-term or intermediate goals on the way to an ultimate goal. Have group members practice setting realistic goals in relation to school. (This could be done as a whole group, or individually, then sharing results.)

Group members then take out their homework for this group session—two or three goals for school. Volunteer group members can share goals that they have set for themselves. The group can help the volunteer evaluate the goal in terms of attainability, specificity, and realistic time frame. Pass out more index cards for students who want to revise their goals.

Once everyone has two or three goals they intend to strive for, they need to write each goal at the top of a piece of notebook paper. On the piece of paper, they need to try to break the goal down into smaller, more immediate steps. Group members can share with a partner. Then ask students to identify one step that they can work on during the week. This will be the homework for this week. Students can go around the circle and share their goal for the week as a closing activity. For homework, have students bring their backpacks or book bags to the next group meeting.

Process. The facilitator's role during the session is to help group members create goals that are realistic and reachable. However, students need to be discouraged from creating goals that are too easy and do not require any work on the students' part. Finding a balance may be difficult for some individuals. Some students may not feel comfortable sharing their overall goals, so be aware of the level of ease each group member is feeling.

Session 4

This session should occur somewhere near the middle of the group. Materials needed include three-ring binders, sets of dividers, tape, and large permanent felt marker (for writing names on notebooks).

Purpose. The purpose of session 4 is to help students begin to develop an organizational plan. Students will apply the WDEP system to organization and learn some new strategies to help them keep their school materials and assignments under control.

Theme. "Put it in the notebook!" Students create an organizational system for themselves based on a large three-ring notebook with dividers and their school planners attached.

Activities. As a warm-up, students go around the circle and briefly share any progress they have made on their academic goals. Then the facilitator introduces the topic of organization. Since organization is frequently a downfall of students who are not academically successful, many of the group members will probably groan and roll their eyes. Give an example of a hypothetical student who is "organizationally challenged," and have the group members help generate possible alternatives to help the student gain some control. Then ask for volunteers from the group to bring up their organizational difficulties at school and how they have tried to deal with the issue. Students may bring up issues such as losing assignments, misplacing books/pens/pencils, and not finishing work because they cannot find where they wrote the assignment down. The group can discuss their common difficulties.

The next activity requires that each student have a large three-ring binder and a set of dividers. Students write their names on the notebook, label the dividers for each academic class, and tuck a pen and pencil into the binder pocket. Next, the fun begins. Students clean out their backpacks or book bags and put all papers in the appropriate place. More micro-organizational details like arranging papers by date and putting graded and returned assignments at the back of the section can be discussed as they are working. Students should be urged to check other places where they put papers—inside textbooks, jacket or pants pockets, on dressers—and place those papers in the appropriate spot. Inevitably, students will find assignments that they thought were lost, or assignments that need to be finished. The facilitator needs to stress the importance of following up on what they found and trying to continue to use the notebook system during the coming week. Students can take the goal cards that they did for homework and tape them somewhere inside the notebook where they can refer to them frequently. (Depending on time available, group members could take a "field trip" to their lockers and clean them out, organizing books and papers there as well.)

As a closing activity, students could go around the circle and mention the advantages of the one-notebook system. For homework, students should attempt to use the notebook system during the week. They should bring their notebooks and their school planners with them to the next session.

Process. In this session, the facilitator needs to be aware that some of the topics discussed (organizational problems) are a bit more personal than others covered so far. Rather than forcing everyone to participate, be aware of group members' level of comfort and let group members who are not comfortable listen rather than be called on at first. The bag clean out is a situation where the facilitator can provide some hands-on assistance, especially for group members who seem overwhelmed with the concept of dealing with the mess they have created.

Session 5

This session should immediately follow session 4. Materials needed include school planners or assignment books for the school year, butcher paper, tape, felt pens, and a handout with an outline of a social studies project.

Purpose. To take the general organizational skills learned in the previous session and begin to apply them to time management. Students will also begin to evaluate how organizational skills will help them achieve the goals that they have set for themselves.

Theme. "Use your planner!" Group members bring the school planner with them in order to learn how to use it as an organizational tool. Overall goals for academic improvement will also be integrated as part of each session.

Activities. As a check-in, each group member can briefly discuss a success or a difficulty with the new organizational system and can rate their success with it on a 1–10 scale. This may generate some general discussion about having to adapt a system to make it work for the individual. This can lead to a discussion about adapting goals if they are unreachable or unreasonable.

The next activity can begin with everyone bringing out their planners or assignment books. It would be interesting to go around the circle and have students admit how much they have actually used the planner. Have students look at the weekly calendar section and brainstorm how they could put this section to use—writing down due dates, tests, speakers, games, dances, work schedules, and so on. This concept should be very familiar to most of the group members even if they don't follow through. Urge students to keep the planner in their binder.

The concept of planning ahead in the planner may be new to many students. Have students work in pairs. Give each student a handout of a hypothetical social studies project, a large sheet of butcher paper, and some felt pens. Have each pair create a schedule for completing the project on time. Once everyone is finished, have each pair share their plan and have the rest of the group provide feedback. Group members will begin to see the need to occasionally modify a schedule.

The final activity will tie the time-management exercise to the goals that the students have set for themselves. Students continue to work with the same partner and discuss possible schedules or intermediate steps necessary to accomplish their goals. Volunteer pairs can share with the larger group. For homework, ask students to try to incorporate the planner into their school routine during the week.

Process. As in session 4, the facilitator also wears a "teacher" hat for part of this session. Some group members may be resistant to trying organizational systems, claiming, "I've tried that already" or "It doesn't work for me." If this occurs, then the entire group needs to be brought into the discussion. With any luck, one of the group members will bring up the WDEP system and then the individual, with the group's help, can attempt to apply WDEP to his or her organizational resistance.

It is also important that the facilitator affirm and praise successful efforts to apply the new organizational strategies. At-risk students, even more than most adolescents, need positive reinforcement for making progress. Reassure students that a "one-step-at-a-time" outlook is vital in order to combat frustration and avoid falling back into old habits.

Session 6

This session should occur at least half way through the group. Materials needed include butcher paper, felt markers, masking tape, and notebook paper.

Purpose. The focus of this session is for group members to apply the WDEP system directly to their own academic experience. So far, they have applied Reality Therapy theory to specific aspects of their school life (e.g., organization); the focus of this session is for them to look at the big picture and try to identify their academic needs. Students will begin to see school success as their own responsibility.

Theme. "Take Responsibility." Group members begin to see the necessity of taking responsibility for their own education rather than making excuses or blaming and scapegoating.

Activities. As an opening exercise, group members can go around the circle and share a success they have had in school since the previous session. The next activity requires that each group member divide a piece of paper into two columns. In the left-hand column, they should make a list of each teacher they have had since kindergarten. Since it is likely that some group members have attended school together for a number of years, there may be some reminiscing during this process. Tell group members to write descriptions of the teachers whose names they have forgotten. In the right-hand column, have students write a few words about their attitude toward school and how they viewed themselves as a student at that time. Give students a few minutes to reflect on what they have discovered through this process. Have each group member share something that the activity revealed.

This discussion can lead into the application of WDEP to their academic lives. On another piece of paper, have students brainstorm their own current academic needs. (It may be necessary to model this on butcher paper first.) Then have students list what their current attempts to get those needs met are. Have students pair off and share what they have discovered. For homework, group members need to evaluate what they are currently doing and try to identify those strategies that are not working and those that are successful. The facilitator needs to introduce the idea of termination so that group members can begin to come to terms with the ending of the group. For a closing, students can go around the circle and share one strength they think they have academically.

Process. This session requires more introspection and higher level thinking than most of the previous sessions. Some students will still be stuck in the "blaming the teacher" mindset. It is up to the facilitator and the other group members to remind reluctant students to take responsibility for their own education. There may also be group members who are so failure-oriented that they will refuse to see any successes. Again, the facilitator and group members need to combat the pessimistic attitudes. This topic was deliberately left until the second half of the program so that even group members with a traditionally defeatist attitude could possibly begin to see options and opportunities.

Session 7

This is the next-to-last session. It must immediately precede session 8. Materials needed include notebooks with paper and pen.

Purpose. The purpose of this session is to help group members become aware of the need for clear communication with teachers and administrators. Many students will not ask for help because they either do not know how to ask or feel like their questions are "dumb." Rather than risking unsatisfactory communication, they do not ask questions and get more and more confused.

Theme. "How to talk to teachers and other human beings." In this session, group members need to remember that teachers and administrators are adults who want to be helpful. Students also need to learn to ask specific questions and to communicate their needs clearly in order to get those needs met and to avoid conflict.

Activities. As a check-in, group members can go around the circle and briefly explain a frustration they are having in one of their classes. This can lead to a discussion of how effective communication with the teacher may be a solution. In order to illustrate effective communication, the facilitator can ask for a volunteer from the group to join in a role-play. The facilitator takes the role of parent and the group member the role of son/daughter. A scenario about cleaning the kitchen or bedroom can be used to model ineffective communication. Once the exchange is finished, the participating group member can share his or her feelings about it. The other group members can then brainstorm what was ineffective about the communication. The facilitator can guide them to notice problems with specificity, clarity, expectations, and so on. Then, two group members can role-play the scene again, this time communicating clearly. The group then can discuss the results of ineffective communication and what outcomes it might have in the classroom (teacher/student frustration, wasted time, teacher thinking student was not paying attention, and so on).

Each student can volunteer one poor question and then one or two effective questions to ask a teacher in order to highlight the qualities of clear communication.

Group members need to refer to the goals they have in their notebooks. Then they can take a few minutes to write a paragraph discussing how effective communication can help them achieve those goals. Volunteers can share what they have written as a closing. For homework, have group members write about the progress they've made towards achieving their goals and bring these to the final group meeting. Each group member can also bring food to share with the group for the final celebration.

Process. This session needs to help group members focus on the quality of their communication. It is vital that the facilitator models effective communication for them and helps them identify unclear communication even within the group. This may engender some conflict, so the facilitator needs to anticipate it and be prepared to help the group process it.

Effective communication is a topic that could easily stretch to several sessions. Other areas that could be touched on include appropriate time and place to seek help from teachers and effective communication with parents.

Continue to stress the proximity of termination during this session so that group members can continue to process the idea of the ending of the group.

Session 8

This is the final session of the group. It must follow immediately after session 7. Materials needed include food, drink, plates, napkins, and cups.

Purpose. This session is designed to help provide closure to the group experience and help group members feel prepared to continue with the progress they have made because of the group. It is also designed as a celebration of all that has been accomplished.

Theme. "Moving on—a celebration." For the final session, group members need an opportunity to feel a sense of accomplishment for all they have learned during the group. Food is an addition to the group that will help with the celebration atmosphere. Group members will also need to express their thoughts and feelings about the termination of group meetings and what will happen next.

Activities. As a check-in, students go around the circle and share one important thing they feel that they have learned from the group. Then group members need to get out their homework. Students need to either read or share something from their writing about the progress made on their goals. The group can provide feedback and affirmation. Help the group segue into a discussion

of how they intend to continue applying what they have learned in the group.

Hand out the evaluation forms to the students. Each group member gets four—one to be filled out by the group participant, and the other three to be given to parents or teachers of the group member's choosing. (Have them put the evaluations in their notebooks!) All evaluations need to be returned directly to the facilitator within a week. This is a reasonable time for the facilitator to discuss other resources available to students who feel the need for continued help: the school counseling center, community resources, and so on.

As a closing exercise, each group member and the facilitator identifies a strength or says something positive about each other member of the group.

Process. The facilitator needs, in this final session, to help the group balance the celebration with a meaningful termination. Starting with a focus on achievement of goals will help the group members see how much has been accomplished by the group. This leads into a discussion of how they can continue the progress they have made and where to get help if they need it. This is an important step in terminating the group. The group evaluations also help group members feel a sense of closure. Having them select who will evaluate their progress (academic, organizational, and behavioral) gives them a sense of control and also requires them to take responsibility. The closing affirmation exercise helps students feel that they have a continuing base of support from the individuals involved even though they are not meeting as a group anymore.

STRATEGIES TO EVALUATE THE GROUP

There will be several opportunities for evaluation. Each group member will be asked to fill out an evaluation form dealing with group efficacy and facilitator effectiveness (see Figure 6–2).

The evaluation sheets that group members give to parents and/or teachers will have a similar format and will focus on the academic performance, organization, and behaviors of the group member (see Figure 6–3). Getting feedback from both the individual and others who deal with the student will help the facilitator see where the group's greatest impact was for each group member.

An additional informal evaluation tool would be to organize a group reunion meeting after the next report card or progress report came out. Group members could share their grades and comment on the progress they felt they had made. The facilitator could informally assess the impact of the group by comparing the current grade report with the previous one which was attached to the group application.

GROUP PARTICIPANT EVALUATION FORM

	High				Low
1. In this group, I learned things I can use in school.	5	4	3	2	1
2. I have more confidence in my ability to do well in school.	5	4	3	2	1
3. I have made changes in my school work habits.	5	4	3	2	1
4. What we learned in group matched what I expected.	5	4	3	2	1
5. The facilitator helped me learn about myself.	5	4	3	2	1

Finish these statements on your own paper.

1. The most important thing I learned from this group was (explain): _____
   _____
   _____

2. I was disappointed in: _____

Figure 6–2.   Sample group participant evaluation form.

OBSERVATION OF GROUP PARTICIPANT

Participant's name _____

	High				Low
1. I have seen an improvement in the participant's attitude toward school.	5	4	3	2	1
2. The participant seems more responsible about school work since attending group.	5	4	3	2	1
3. The participant has made an effort to ask for assistance with school work if needed.	5	4	3	2	1
4. The participant has turned in all work/assignments for the past several weeks.	5	4	3	2	1
5. The participant has met school deadlines.	5	4	3	2	1

Other comments/observations: _____
_____
_____

Figure 6–3.   Sample observation of group participant form.

REFERRAL PROCEDURES FOR FOLLOW-UP

Since this group is held in the context of a school environment and the facilitator is likely to be a school counselor, the first and foremost resource for group members beyond the group is the school counseling center. The facilitator needs to remind students to contact their counselors if they feel the need for more assistance with academic or behavioral issues. Some schools may have additional student resources—peer tutoring programs, study halls, and so on. These, as well as community resources, will form the resource base for group members once the group has terminated.

REFERENCES

Genshaft, J. L., & Kirwin, P. M. (1990). Improving the study skills of at-risk students. In L. J. Kruger (Ed.), *Promoting success with at-risk students: Emerging perspectives and practical approaches* (pp. 109–130). New York: The Haworth Press.

McWhirter, J. J., McWhirter, B. T., McWhirter, A. M., & McWhirter, E. H. (1993). *At-risk youth: A comprehensive response*. Pacific Grove, CA: Brooks/Cole Publishing Company.

Natriello, G., Pallas, A., McDill, E. L., & McPartland, J. M. (1990). Keeping students in school: Academic and affective strategies. In L. J. Kruger (Ed.), *Promoting success with at-risk students: Emerging perspectives and practical approaches* (pp. 179–196). New York: The Haworth Press.

Robertson, A. S. (1997). If an adolescent begins to fail in school, what can parents and teachers do? *ERIC Digest*. Available: wyswyg://bodyframe.5. http:// ehostvgw2.epnet.com/ \fulltext.asp.

Wubbolding, R. E. (1999). Reality therapy theory. In D. Capuzzi & D. Gross (Eds.), *Counseling and psychotherapy: Theories and interventions* (2nd ed.) (pp. 287–314). Upper Saddle River, NJ: Merrill/Prentice-Hall.

CHAPTER 7

MOVING TO A NEW SCHOOL:
A TRANSITION GROUP FOR YOUNG ADOLESCENTS

Debra Holmes

PURPOSE

For all adolescents, especially those with low self-esteem, transition is a difficult yet normal process. Students go from elementary to middle school and from middle to high school. They are also dealing with the changes that happen to their bodies in puberty and changes in relationships with peers and family. One transition that not all adolescents must go through but is quite common is changing schools. Adolescents would greatly benefit from a group involving other students going through the same process.

The purpose of the group is to first and foremost provide an environment in which students realize the universality of their situation. They will understand that they are not the only ones who have been faced with a move to a new community and school and who must not only orient themselves to, and make themselves comfortable in, their new situation but also must say good-bye to their previous communities and friends. They will see that being the "new kid" isn't something that they must face alone and that there are others who can help.

Another significant purpose of this type of group is to teach students how to transition to the new environment in a relatively smooth fashion. This includes both dealing with the loss of contact with familiar friends and surroundings and the acquisition of new friends and a familiarity with the new community.

Self-esteem declines for a considerable amount of time during adolescence, and this change accompanies major transitions (Bukatko & Daehler, 1995). Considering this, a third purpose of this group is to provide a safe environment where students feel they can express their feelings without fear of ridicule or rejection.

CONCEPTUAL FRAMEWORK

When students move to a new school, there is much that is exciting. There is a new city to explore, a new house to settle, new friends to make, and an opportunity for a fresh start. However, much is also lost, especially in the adolescent world. Adolescence is a time of strong friendships, but also a time of vulnerability.

Adolescents need companions. There are a vast number of transitions, explicit and subtle, that they must face in their middle and high school years. Companionship, the enjoyable experience of interacting socially, gives them a sense of belonging, acceptance, cohesion, and affirmation from just being together (Cotterell, 1996). Adolescents spend more time socializing with their peers than with any other people including teachers, parents, and other family members (Berk, 1991).

Without this companionship, teens may experience social loneliness. This comes from a lack of being affirmed by others and is often experienced following a disturbance, such as moving, in the social network. Anxiety is heightened, security and self-esteem are lowered, and to make matters worse, the social support system in place at the city or school of origin has been removed. This leaves them vulnerable to psychological distress and larger problems later in life (Cotterell, 1996) such as anxiety or depression.

Changes in adolescence, especially in the early part of it, can make even the most secure and healthy adolescent feel like an outsider and a person whose very worth ought to be questioned (Barr, 1997). Considering the strong attachments that teens have to their friends, moving away from their friends is one of the most difficult changes they may have to face in their lives. Many adolescents face feelings that strongly resemble the grief feelings that one faces when a loved one dies. Attachment theory explains how humans make strong emotional ties with others which provide psychological security. The theory also helps us understand the strong emotional response that happens when these ties become threatened or broken (Worden, 1991). There are many ways in which these ties can be broken to cause grief. Although the most common is death, it can happen through separation as well.

There are four widely accepted tasks of grief through which a grieving person moves. The first is accepting the reality of the loss. When the loss occurs, there is a tendency of the person grieving to deny its reality. It is the counselor's job in this stage to help the individual come to accept it and understand that it is irreversible. The second task is experiencing and working through the pain of grief. In this stage, it is necessary to acknowledge and process the pain to prevent its deep manifestation. The third stage, adjusting to the new environment, involves realizing what life will be like after the change, and the fourth stage, withdrawing from loss and reinvesting emotional energy, has to do with moving on with life and putting emotional energy into productive areas of life (Worden, 1991).

Some students, after moving to a new school, may grieve for a long time and may never effectively work through it. This would be especially true if they are never given the opportunity to work through it and the support necessary to the process. A transition such as a move to a new school may be seen by many adults as relatively unimportant, and students may be denied help. Unless they are given the help they need, even seemingly insignificant losses may compound, and profound stress may result. When children move to a new school, it is important that they be given the opportunity to effectively and thoughtfully say good-bye to the old school, and hello to the new one (Jarratt, 1994).

GROUP GOALS

The following goals will help the counselor guide the group sessions and keep the foci on the purposes of the group.

1. For members to realize the universality of their situation; many students have had to move to a new school, leave a community and friends, and learn how to fit into a new community and make new friends.
2. To help members deal with the loss of contact with friends and family members left behind.
3. To help members make new friends in the new school.
4. To help members become oriented with a new community.
5. To provide a safe and affirming environment where members do not feel threatened in any way by any other member of the group, where members may freely share their fears and feelings, and where members can feel supported by one another.

PRE-GROUP SCREENING AND ORIENTATION

As with any group in which the counselor hopes for good counseling to take place, good client selection must take place (Yalom, 1995). Yalom (1995) suggests that selection of group members is more a process of de-selection, that is, deciding which applicants simply will not work out in a group and going about accepting the rest. In this type of transition group for middle school students, it will be important first to screen out students who have conduct disorder or have traits of personality disorders. Deeply depressed or suicidal students would probably benefit more from individual counseling where they can get the attention they need.

Students who make ideal group members are those who are willing. They will come to group on their own accord and will have goals for themselves and the group that are congruent with the goals established by the counselor. The students will be productive and participatory and will not be a detriment.

Finding these ideal group members is possible by first identifying students new to the school. They are interviewed by the school counselor to determine their willingness to be productive and participatory and to determine if there are any traits that would make the student nonideal.

As part of the pre-group orientation, in the personal interviews, the counselor makes clear the goals and rules of the group to help the students determine whether or not they would like to participate. The goals and rules are given to the students in written form. Considering the potential members are minors, it is important for the counselor to not only provide this information to the students but also to the parents. Parental permission must be obtained before the student may participate in the group.

OUTLINE FOR EIGHT GROUP SESSIONS

Session 1

Purpose. The purpose of session 1 is for introduction and to begin to put group members at ease. Group members introduce themselves, and they begin to get comfortable with each other and the idea of being in a group. The goals of the group are reemphasized, and the ground rules, including confidentiality and its specific implications, are explained.

Theme. The theme for the first session is "orientation and introduction" but also "assurance." The adolescent students will most likely enter the group with apprehension about who else is in the group, whether or not they will be accepted, what will be discussed, and just how much they will be expected to share. In the first session in the orientation and introduction processes, the students should become more confident and relaxed.

Activities. The first activity is the introduction of group members. The counselor starts with a brief introduction of himself or herself, his or her role in the school, and experiences with students who have moved to the community and have been new to the school. Then choose a student to begin introductions. Once that student has finished, let the student choose another one in the group to share next. Ask students to share their names, what grade they are in, and from where they recently moved.

Engage the students in a discussion of ground rules. It will primarily be the students' responsibility to develop the ground rules, but be sure that the following rules are included and encourage their inclusion if the members do not include them.

1. It is OK to talk about what you said in the group, but keep other information shared in this room, including the identity of other group members, within the walls of this room. Group members will not talk about what other people in the group have said.
2. One person will talk at a time.
3. Come to every group meeting unless you are absent that day or have a test in the class you are missing.
4. Everyone has the right to "pass" or not participate in a discussion or activity.

Write the rules on a large piece of paper that can be displayed in the room. For adolescent students in a transition group, these ground rules lead to greater success in the group.

It is important to thoroughly discuss the confidentiality rule, as there will be students who will not feel comfortable sharing if they feel their privacy will not be respected. Stress its importance by discussing different scenarios with the members. For example: "Is it OK for you to go home and tell your parents that your neighbor is in the group with you?" or "Is it OK for you to

write to your best friend and tell him or her that you're in a group with other students who have recently moved to this school?" or "Is it OK for you to tell another student about someone in the group who is so sad because he or she missed the cousins who used to live next door?"

Adolescents have the potential to turn group counseling sessions into times to merely complain about the negative aspects of their new situations. To avoid this as much as possible, address this potential problem during the first session, engaging the members in a discussion of what these "gripe sessions" may look like, why they could be detrimental, and how to turn them back into productive counseling sessions. The responsibility to keep the sessions productive rests primarily with the members, and they should be encouraged to redirect sessions when they notice other members beginning to complain excessively.

After discussing these rules, members have the opportunity to voice any additions they may have to the rules. The additions can be discussed and added to the original rules. When the ground rules are finalized and all members are satisfied with them, it is important for the counselor to make sure all group members have bought in. To accomplish this, members state their name and their promise to follow the ground rules. For example, "I, Mary, commit to following these ground rules." The members should further express their commitment by signing their names to the paper on which the rules are written.

It then is important for the counselor to explain his or her role in the group so the students know what to expect. In this type of transition group, the most important role of the counselor is to facilitate and maintain a safe environment in which the members feel comfortable sharing. This includes making sure everyone gets to be heard, intervening when one member is being disruptive or disrespectful, and pointing out common themes within the group. Ask for feedback from group members. The feedback can come in the form of expectations of the counselor and questions about his or her role.

To close the session, have members share in the same manner as before, beginning with the counselor, and then selecting a member, and having members choose others to continue. The counselor asks the members how they feel about the group now that the first session is at an end and what they hope to get out of group in the eight weeks they have together.

Process. In the first session, things are still at a very safe level. The students are together in a group setting, but they have only shared relatively surface information about themselves, and so the anxiety level should still be low. The students are, at this point, rather passive, and the counselor is doing the majority of the work and is the primary leader. Although this will change throughout the duration of the group, the members will most likely feel more comfortable with the counselor being authoritative.

It is important throughout the 8 weeks for the counselor to set an example of how members should relate to one another, but it is especially important at the beginning when the members do not know each other. The counselor is the only one that all the members know, and ends up as the transitional object. It is through the counselor that the group is unified, and the members relate only to each other through the common relationship with the counselor (Yalom, 1995).

The counselor provides snacks for the sessions. At the first session, these snacks are consumed at the beginning of the session. Snacks and a little bit of social time helps the new group members feel more comfortable with each other and breaks the expected tension, especially the first week. After the first session, bring the snacks out at the end so it will not be a distraction. This routine serves as some incentive to early adolescents to attend each meeting.

Session 2

Purpose. The purpose of session 2 is to begin the process of working through the four major tasks of grief. This session's focus is on accepting the reality of the loss. The discussion and activities are centered around the fact that the members experienced what will most likely be a permanent move and coming to terms with its reality.

Theme. "Where did I come from?" Members share with each other from where they moved and what was difficult about it. They should focus on what was and what they left.

Activities. The group starts with a check-in question. The members share how they would rate the week on a scale of one to ten, one being awful and ten being wonderful. The counselor also participates in the check-in. After the check-in, review the ground rules and answer any questions pertaining to them.

The group members each answer the question "What was the most difficult thing about moving?" Each group member gets a chance to share, and members are reminded that they have the right to pass.

Then have group members remind the others from where it was they moved, and after doing so, stick a pin in that city on a map on the wall. Provide both a map of the state where the school is located and a map of the United States and the world, if needed. After pinning their city, the members tie a string from the previous city of residence to the current city of residence. A discussion of these places follows covering how far away they are, how difficult it will be to keep in touch with people still there, and different ways to keep in touch with those people.

To close, group members share something special about their hometown. The content of the sharing can range from activities in which they used to engage, special friends or family members they left behind, or a description of their previous residence.

Process. An important role of the counselor in this session is to be a base of reality. While continuing to put the goodwill of the members first, have the courage to confront students when they seem to be unrealistic about how easy or difficult it will be to maintain relationships with people at a distance.

The counselor also needs to be focused on ensuring equal participation from all members. Although adolescents often only say the minimum required to answer a question, there are also those who monopolize time, especially when the topic is important to them. Gently remind all members that while everyone's stories are important, it is also important that everyone has an opportunity to share.

Session 3

Purpose. The purpose of the third session of the group is to begin experiencing and working through the pain of moving away from what was familiar to a place that is unfamiliar. The activities allow members to feel sad about the move, remember that others are going through the same pain, and begin to work through the pain to be able to start adjusting, preventing a possible later emotional breakdown. This will continue into session 4.

Theme. "This is how I feel." In working through this task of mourning, students are given permission to feel sad or angry or whatever emotion they may have.

Activities. The members should first be reminded that this is a safe place to talk, but they also need to be careful about the things they say to other people so they do not sound mean or judgmental. Pose the question, "What makes you sad?" to the group, expecting the members to volunteer to speak instead of being asked. Remind members that it is OK to feel sad, and without telling others and expressing how they feel, they'll bottle it up, and it will all come out later. By that time what it was that originally made them sad may have been forgotten. If it hasn't already been addressed in the members' answers, encourage members to also discuss what makes them saddest about moving.

As this is likely to be an emotional session, after everyone has had a chance to share, thank everyone for sharing and encourage members to respond to what others have said. They may have been able to relate to someone else's story or have been touched in some way. If the students have a difficult time getting started, the counselor can begin. Then assign homework to the group. Group members can brainstorm a list of things that is exciting and fun about the process of moving and adjusting to a new place.

Process. During this session, the counselor will need to be sure that the environment remains safe from judgment and ridicule for members so they feel comfortable grieving in front of their peers. There will likely be an unwillingness for members to share at a deep level, but once they see others do so, it will be easier. Therefore, this session's success partly depends upon the willingness of the first few people to share and the depth of their discussion. If they feel safe and protected, the rest of the group will imitate the ones who share first.

Session 4

Purpose. The purpose of this session is much like that of the third. The members continue to experience and work through the grief caused by moving and leaving people they care about behind.

Theme. "This is how I feel."

Activities. Begin the session by having members share what they wrote about the exciting and fun aspects of moving and adjusting to a new place. Then define the word "vulnerable" and begin the group by having members discuss briefly how it felt to be vulnerable with each other last week. After this discussion, group members share who their best friends were in the town from which they moved. Some members may want to talk about other people such as extended family members they are close to. Encourage students to talk about what made those friends their best friends and what were some great qualities about those people.

When everyone has had an opportunity to share, explain the term "unfinished business" and how it relates to moving away from people they were close to. The group discusses how some people have to move away quickly and do not get to say good-bye, some people might have been too sad to say good-bye, and sometimes best friends do not always get along and they may have not had an opportunity to make up before one moves away.

Make available different types of stationery and pens as well as a mobile computer lab for word processing or e-mail, and encourage all group members to write a letter to the best friends they left behind. In the letter, the members should express how they felt about having to leave, how they plan to keep in touch, and attempt to resolve any unfinished business with which they may have left. They should also include at least one exciting or fun thing they have experienced about moving. The letters can be mailed or they can be kept, whichever the members feel comfortable with. The activity can take the remainder of the time and can be finished as homework.

Process. What makes this session work is the counselor modeling acceptance of emotion from all members and interfering if some group members are not accepting the emotions of others. This session also allows students to express in written correspondence to a best friend what they may not have felt comfortable sharing in front of the rest of the group.

Session 5

Purpose. The purpose of the fifth session, continuing with the four tasks of mourning, is to help students begin to effectively adjust to their new environment and to continue to adjust after the group has finished. They have the opportunity to learn about what is available to do in the school and the community to start feeling more familiar with the environment, and they should begin to feel a sense of ownership of their new community. They are presented with information needed to adjust and are equipped with the tools needed for further adjustment.

Theme. "So, what is this place?" As members have been given the opportunity to accept the move as irreversible reality and have experienced and started working through the pain associated with that, they are ready to begin to look at the present situation and learn how to live in it.

Activities. The session begins by asking the students if they have questions about how the school runs. Questions about available sports and activities, field trips, teachers, choosing classes, and so on will likely be asked. Be ready with basic information about these topics to answer questions and to bring them up if students show hesitation or are just not thinking of questions to ask. Encourage students to answer each others' questions before supplying the information.

The students then brainstorm activities of any kind that they have found to do in the city; for example, video arcades, ice cream shops, shopping malls, or batting cages. The counselor or one of the members writes the ideas on a piece of butcher paper on the wall. The members of the group are also given the opportunity to peruse books or brochures brought by the counselor about the city and things to do in it.

Near the end of the session, begin to tie community learning to their need to make the new city their new home. Assign members homework. The homework assignment is to go to one of the places mentioned with a family member or new friend and to report back to the group the next week.

Process. In this session, the tone is more lighthearted than the two preceding. The counselor is providing information but is also putting more responsibility on the group members to help each other adjust. The members

members do not really have to as they are all in the same school and see one another daily. Encourage group members to stay in contact, especially if close friendships have started within the group. Then model saying good-bye to each group member by saying one thing that will be missed about each student and encourage the others to do the same (Morganett, 1990). If it seems appropriate, a group hug can be a good way to say a final good-bye.

Before the students leave, remind them one last time that what they learned about friendships and saying good-bye is not confidential, but what they learned about the other people in the group is.

Process. The success of this last session rests with the impact that will be made by adolescent students going outside themselves and recognizing positive attributes of others. Knowing that several of their peers are finding positive things to say about them, group members are affirmed and accepted, and this self-confidence helps them as they leave the support of the group. The review of what has been discussed over the time also helps group members keep what they have learned fresh in their minds as they go out and practice.

STRATEGIES TO EVALUATE THE GROUP

At the beginning of the last session, distribute an evaluation form for group members to fill out. It will consist of Likert scales on which the students can reflect the amount of growth they personally experienced in areas related to the group goals. The students also respond to statements using scales regarding the leadership of the group. There are also some open-ended questions for the students to answer.

REFERRAL PROCEDURES FOR FOLLOW-UP

In any group, it is feasible that one or more of the group members may need more help than the group process can provide. In this case, the group counselor should have several names of counselors experienced in working with young adolescents to provide the extra counseling. The counselor should speak with the parents of the student(s), explain that more assistance is needed and why, and share the names and phone numbers of the counselors.

REFERENCES

Barr, D. (1997). Friendship and belonging. In R. L. Selman, C. L. Watts, & L. H. Schultz (Eds.), *Fostering friendships: Pair therapy for treatment and prevention* (p. 21). New York: Aldine de Gruyter.

Berk, L. E. (1991). *Child development.* Boston: Allyn and Bacon.

Bukatko, D., & Daehler, M. V. (1995). *Child development: A thematic approach.* Boston: Houghton Mifflin Company.

Cotterell, J. (1996). *Social networks and social influences in adolescence.* London: Routledge.

Jarratt, C. J. (1994). *Helping children cope with separation and loss.* Boston: The Harvard Common Press.

Morganett, R. S. (1990). *Skills for living: Group counseling activities for young adolescents.* Champaign, IL: Research Press.

Worden, J. W. (1991). *Grief counseling and grief therapy: A handbook for the mental health practitioner.* New York: Springer Publishing.

Yalom, I. D. (1995). *The theory and practice of group psychotherapy.* New York: Basic Books.

CHAPTER 8

PEER NETWORKING TO BUILD RESILIENCY AMONG HIGH SCHOOL YOUTH: A VIOLENCE PREVENTION GROUP

Cathleen Callaway

PURPOSE

Today more than ever before, young people are facing "emotional turmoil and psychological storm and stress" (Sigelman, 1999, p. 279). At the same time, in an era of increasing diversity and divisiveness, "many adolescents are drawing bold lines between people they consider to be like themselves and people they view as different" (Roberson, 1991, p. 2). As evidenced by recent violence in schools across our nation, this combination of tumultuous emotion and social detachment can prove deadly. Any efforts that a school district can make to promote healthy, prosocial growth is a step in the right direction. A violence prevention group designed to decrease school and community violence and intolerance, and strengthen bonds between peers through effective communication and conflict resolution, would contribute to healthier schools and communities.

This proposal is to form a group of select students who would work as a team to establish trust, unity, understanding, and respect for cultural sensitivity issues; improve intra- and interpersonal communication skills, as well as small group communication skills; and create a network where information learned would be taken back to the diverse populations represented. Utilizing the natural channels of communication already in place in the school community, this group would eventually work to identify various school and community problems and attempt to resolve them through student collaboration as well as the facilitation of trainings, presentations, and mediations. By creating an environ-

ment of support, where students feel comfortable sharing personal, social, and community concerns, the group would be designed to specifically increase personal protective factors and decrease school and individual risk factors, including alienation, rebelliousness, and problem behavior.

CONCEPTUAL FRAMEWORK

Research has shown that there are a number of risk factors that increase the chances of adolescents developing behavior problems, as well as protective factors that help safeguard young adults from harmful school involvement. Schools can prevent problem behavior by reducing risk factors and increasing protective factors, creating a child that is more resilient to conflict and problem behavior. "Risk and protective factor-focused prevention is based on a simple premise: to prevent a problem from happening, we need to identify the factors that increase the risk of that problem developing and then find ways to reduce the risks in ways that enhance protective or resiliency factors" (Developmental Research and Programs, 1996, p. 3). Prevention is about protecting our students by reducing the contributing factors that often lead students down the road to violence, teen pregnancy, substance abuse, crime, and other problem behaviors (Western Center for the Application of Prevention Technologies, 1995, p. 1).

One of the most effective ways to reduce children's risk is to strengthen their bond with positive, prosocial family members, teachers, or friends. Children who are attached to positive family members, friends, school, and community, and who are committed to achieving the goals valued by these groups, are less likely to do things that threaten that bond, such as doing drugs, dropping out of school, or committing violence (Developmental Research and Programs, 2000, pp. 10–11).

This means that in order for risk-focused prevention to work, students also have to make a commitment to adopting healthy behaviors. According to prevention researchers, there are three specific conditions or processes that foster attachment and student commitment. These include "opportunities for meaningful involvement, skills to be successful at that involvement, and recognition for successful involvement" (Developmental Research and Programs, 2000, p. 11). This group will attempt to integrate these strategies, building resiliency among group members with a comprehensive, developmental approach and using meaningful activities, skill development, and positive school recognition.

GROUP GOALS

Ideally, this group of high school students work with their peers under the guidance of a group leader (teacher specialist or school counselor) with the goal of becoming an extension of the school's teaching and administrative staff. This means that as these students develop as a team, they are given peer mediation responsibilities, as well as classroom instructional time in various disciplines throughout the building, in coordination with the school district's current prevention curriculum. Eventually, this team of students could train peers, elementary students, and staff members during building in-services, in the resiliency skills listed above, and with special focus on conflict resolution, effective communication, and cultural sensitivity.

Ultimately, the goal of this group of highly influential youth is to create a positive social orientation among group members, and to allow opportunities to work with their peers and teachers to build positive social and cultural bonds within the high school building. Concrete group goals include:

1. Become a leadership team that represents the social and cultural diversity of the school.
2. Establish trust and team unity, so that the team can work effectively together on projects and presentations.
3. Recognize and respect cultural sensitivity issues.
4. Learn and practice effective communication techniques.
5. Identify school issues and work together to resolve them through presentations and mediations.
6. Transfer what is learned in the group to the behavior of one's everyday life.

PRE-GROUP SCREENING AND ORIENTATION

With such multifaceted group goals, the effectiveness of this group rests heavily upon how effectively group members are selected. It is imperative that the members of this group represent as much as possible the diversity of the school, including the social cultures ("skaters," "computer nerds," or "jocks") as well as ethnic cultures found within the building. Males and females should be proportionally represented. Group members should be socially influential students within the school building but not necessarily the "most popular" students, or the students who would independently opt to register for a leadership class. To ensure that all student populations are equally represented within the group, specific students have to be recruited and invited to be a part of the group.

To target these students, an advisory committee should be formed, including a minimum of three certified teachers, one administrator, one classified staff member (preferably a hall monitor or security officer), and one parent or community member, who are all committed to the goals of the group and to the confidentiality of the group formation process. The group facilitator should be included as one of the members of this advisory team. Each of these individuals will provide diverse perspectives of different student populations, offering for the committee a wealth of information and feedback about all students to be considered for group involvement.

The unified advisory committee should approach the entire staff with the concept of the group, description of desired group candidates, and request a confidential list of recommendations from all staff members. Upon collecting and consolidating this list of student names, the advisory committee then needs to categorize those students and attempt to narrow the list to a diverse group of approximately 20 individuals representing the social and cultural diversity of the school. This will be the preliminary group that is invited to participate, 8–10 of which will eventually form the group.

Logistics of the group need to be decided before inviting students to participate, as some students may not be able to be involved simply due to schedule conflicts. Group meetings need to be held consistently, for at least 45 minutes per day, and at a time when all students may be able to participate without having to leave another class or an after-school commitment to do so (including sports, employment, family, and so on). This may vary between districts, but the optimal time to offer this opportunity to students would be to schedule the group as a class period during the regular school day, perhaps even offering it as an elective social studies or communication credit (an important consideration, as many students, both college-bound students and low-academic achievers alike, may not have room in their schedule for a "useless" credit, making a diversified group more difficult to establish).

This group should be ready to begin in the fall of the school year, so depending on the school's forecasting and registration schedules, course decisions should be made in early spring. For the sake of simplicity, the author of this proposal will create all sample materials as though this group would be offered in a high school as a class beginning fall term; however, this could be easily adapted to another format.

After critical logistical decisions have been made by the advisory committee and approved by the school district, the pre-group screening process can continue. The advisory committee should invite the final 20 nominees to a general informational meeting, being sure to have all potential members in the same room at the same time, in an attempt to observe student behaviors when among very diverse and probably unfamiliar populations. Group members will most likely be uncomfortable; however, the advisory committee should pay close attention to any behaviors that seem dogmatic, that might be too disruptive to the effective functioning of the team, or that might require pre-group individual counseling.

The first meeting of the group is critical, in that it sets the tone for the group in the future. The entire advisory committee should not only attend the meeting, but also lead part of it so that students see the importance of the group to the school as represented by all of the adults involved. The primary components of that first meeting (see sample agenda on p. 71) include welcoming students to the meeting, introducing advisory committee members, explaining to students how they were nominated (keeping individual nominations confidential), and how the final group will be selected based on the necessity for diversity and degree of leadership ability. Candidates also need to be informed of issues such as how the program developed, how it will be conducted in the future, and the goals already established for the group (see sample student goals sheet on p. 71). Procedures should be outlined delineating how students will notify the committee of their interest in participating in the group (see sample student response sheet on p. 71). Finally, the meeting should allow substantial time for students to ask questions of the committee.

The student response sheet should not be a requirement of that initial meeting, but have a later due date to allow students time to consider the program thoroughly and discuss it with their parents if they wish. Some school districts may also require a parent permission slip to allow students to participate, and this may be designed by the district and given to students at this meeting, as well.

Based on the positive responses returned to the committee, the advisory team can then make final decisions about group participants based on the gender and cultural needs of the group. If the group is going to be held during the regular school day for academic credit,

before making decisions about final group participants it works well for the advisory committee members to meet with individual guidance counselors about prospective group members to see if student schedules will allow for enrollment in the course. This step helps prevent having to make continual changes to the final group selection. Final group participants need to be notified of their selection and encouraged to meet with their guidance counselor to arrange any final schedule changes.

OUTLINE FOR EIGHT GROUP SESSIONS

The format of each session depends upon the logistical structure established by the individual school district. As stated previously, for the purposes of this proposal, the group is assumed to be operating as an academic class within the regular school day. While this group would be meeting all year long, eight sessions are detailed for the purposes of this proposal, with the understanding that several different class periods would be consumed with each session topic. Sessions 1 and 2 are at the beginning, sessions 3, 4, and 5 are near the middle, and sessions 6, 7, and 8 are consecutive sessions near the end of the group experience. Throughout the entire program, members are expected to keep a journal of their experiences in the group and in their everyday lives between sessions.

Session 1

Purpose. The purpose of session 1 is for group members to become more familiar with one another, to learn the nature of the group and requirements of the class, and to begin to see similarities in their human experiences. In the first session, ground rules need to be established, and confidentiality emphasized. Students need to begin to trust one another, and perhaps the most critical element of that trust factor in a diverse student population is the understanding that what is said in any group meeting does not leave the group.

Theme. After taking care of administrative tasks, like reviewing the course syllabus, establishing ground rules (see attached sample syllabus on p. 72), and answering course expectation questions of the group, the theme for the first session should be one of personal introduction. Group members should be asked to share low-risk, personal background information in an attempt to begin developing relationships and identifying commonalities among group members.

Activities. One activity that could be used for the first session with the group is to have each group member create a "road map" and share it with the group. This involves several materials: glue, scissors, colored felt pens/pencils/crayons, recycled magazines for cutting things apart, 9×13 or larger construction paper, and five or six (two or three fewer than the total number of group members) matchbox-sized toy cars.

Students should individually create a chronological lifeline in the form of a road, including significant events or activities in their life. This road may take wide turns or follow a straight and even path; it may be bumpy or smooth, take dips or climb hills depicting the events and activities occurring during that period. Pictures from magazines could be used to represent visual images of the different events or "sightings" that may occur along the road map.

When students have created their "road maps," it would be appropriate to review again the confidentiality of the group and the basic ground rules, and then have group members choose one of the variety of matchbox cars and explain why they think that car best represents their individual style or personality. From there, group members take turns sharing their individual maps, driving along their roads in their individual car.

Process. This first session allows group members to relax and work creatively on a fairly low-risk project. The goal is to get students to share a part of themselves, talk to one another, and begin to see similarities between human life experiences: divorce experiences, siblings, birth order, adoption, school activities, and more. Different individuals within the group will have picked the same matchbox car to represent their personality and style, providing another connection between group members.

As students share to their individual levels of comfort, the group begins to develop a sense of trust in the fact that what they say to the group will stay with the group. The leader needs to establish the group as a safe place to communicate honest ideas and emotions early in the group formation process. The leader should also operate the group as if he or she is a participant in the group, and not just the facilitator, and this precedence needs to be set in the very first session. For this reason it is important that the leader of the group also create a road map and share it with the group, demonstrating a willingness to take risks and be a part of the group, while also maintaining appropriate control and giving the group a sense of security by providing structure and direction. Throughout this process, a feeling of safety will begin to be established and the group formation process will begin.

Session 2

Purpose. Session 2 further establishes trust within the group and helps students to begin to see things from a variety of perspectives. As they begin to take greater risks with one another, they will become closer as a group and be better prepared to take larger risks with the group as a whole. Furthermore, this activity strengthens their awareness of the similarity of human experience, regardless of ethnic or social background.

Theme. Establishing greater trust and awareness is the theme of session 2. As students participate in this activity they will be forced to rely on a partner for success and will be forced to open themselves up to a degree of vulnerability.

Activities. Students are given the opportunity to experience a "trust walk" activity. This involves cloth blindfolds and reflection journals (provided by the student). Move the group outside to a safe area that is less familiar to most students. Pair up students in teams of two, giving each student his or her own blindfold, and instructions to decide initial "leader" and "follower" roles. Leaders will direct their followers on a casual walk, adding dimensions of difficulty (such as stairs and other obstacles, a faster pace, or walking backwards) as they feel comfortable and prepared as a team. Partners switch roles after 15–20 minutes, and then debrief as a larger group after everyone has had the experience of both roles.

Process. As the partners return to the larger group a variety of prompts could be used to process their experience: What aspects of the activity were difficult or uncomfortable? What aspects were easier or more comfortable? Which role was least challenging? Which role was most important? What aspects of this activity parallel team or group processes you have experienced in the past? If you were to participate in this activity again how would it be different a second time? Why? Student responses to this experience should be related to the process of group formation and effective communication skills by the group facilitator.

Session 3

Purpose. This third activity is designed to teach students strategies of effective communication. By the end of this session students should be able to express their feelings and opinions in an assertive, yet nonthreatening way.

Theme. The theme of this activity is to improve communication. Students should be able to identify ineffective communication strategies that they have used in the past, and learn ways to rephrase the same information in a way that can be more thoroughly and accurately received by the listener.

Activities. This activity requires prior training for the facilitator in active listening and effective verbal and nonverbal communication, including the use of "I" statements. Materials necessary for this activity are simply that students have with them their reflective journal. The opening activity for this session is to ask students to share with the group any situation they remember when they were misinterpreted or when they felt like they were not heard at all. They can also share a time when they were having a disagreement with someone and felt like everything they said only escalated the problem.

This discussion and sharing could lead to the natural conclusion that knowing a more effective communication strategy could be a powerful tool in any relationship.

The second step is to give students information about effective verbal and nonverbal communication strategies, allowing time for discussion and facilitator demonstration of techniques. Students may ask questions for clarification, or ask the facilitator to apply the concepts to sample scenarios.

Next have each student pair up with another member of the group. Have each pair work together to write down an example of a disagreement that would be likely to happen at school (such as locker partner disagreements, disputes between social groups or athletic teams, or young relationship conflicts). When scenarios are finished have group members trade these stories with another dyad in the class. Each partnership will then individually role-play in front of the group an effective resolution to the conflict described.

Closure to this activity involves a discussion of how important effective communication can be in relationships. Homework for group members is to practice "I" statements and come back to the next group with an example of an attempt to use "I" statements effectively outside of class.

Process. The key to this session is facilitator knowledge of effective communication strategies and having the ability to relate them to real-world examples that students will understand. Students must also feel safe and comfortable in the group in order to risk practicing their communication skills in front of the group. The facilitator needs to guide students gently as they learn to incorporate new skills into their repertoire of knowledge. These skills should be integrated into all future sessions and used by students in every group interaction. In addition, at this point in the group process, the group should be nearing the group involvement stage of development, so group feedback should be encouraged.

Session 4

Purpose. Once students have mastered the skills of effective communication, they can then begin to focus energy into learning the skill of empathy. The purpose of this activity is to give students practice in effective communication and to allow them the opportunity to see situations from a variety of perspectives.

Theme. The theme for session 4 is that we all are capable of thinking from someone else's perspective. Students should be able to feel and begin to understand experiences described by a partner in the group, as well as others outside of the group.

Activities. This activity requires several supplies including construction paper, scissors, and writing utensils. Each group member should be paired with another member of the group and directed to trace the shape of their partner's foot onto a piece of the construction paper. When this is finished, ask members to think of a time in their life when they felt wrongly accused. Partner "A" will then explain his or her situation to partner "B" while partner "B" actively listens, asks for any clarification, and writes from the first person perspective about partner "A's" experience on partner "A's" foot shape. The roles are reversed, time is given for partner "B" to share, and then the group joins again into the larger unit. In the big group, individuals share the incident of false accusation that they heard from their partner, except that they should say it as if it had happened recently. The closure activity could be to ask the group what similarities in human experience they discovered as they each went around the group and shared, or as they told someone else's story. As homework, group members should attempt to demonstrate empathy and active listening skills outside of class, bringing their experiences to the group for discussion.

Process. As group members are paired together, it is important to make sure pairings are diverse in every session. Group members need the experience of working with everyone in their team individually and as a group. In this session, it also seems important that all group members are told up front of the fact that their experiences will be shared with the whole group at the end of the session so that group members are not uncomfortable or embarrassed. Because the foot shapes do not have names on them, arranging them along the wall in the group classroom could be a reminder of valuable lessons learned from members.

Session 5

Purpose. The purpose of this group session is to learn to apply the skill of empathy to various cultural and social perspectives. This session builds upon the knowledge developed in previous sessions.

Theme. The theme of this session is learning to understand different perspectives through literature. Students can gain valuable insight into their own lives and the experiences of others through stories and discussion.

Activities. This session can begin with a quick reminder of personal stories that were shared in the previous session by revisiting the foot shapes that are arranged on the wall. Students could share one story that they heard that they could really relate to personally.

Next ask students to read and react to various stories that describe unique human experiences and perspectives. Students could visit multicultural literature anthologies and each find a story to share with the group, or the facilitator could provide the literature for review. Facilitators may consider stories such as: "Little Things Are Big," by Jesus Colon; "I was Embarrassed for

My Race," by Janet Flips; or "Silence," by Maxine Hong Kingston. Closure could be to discuss how the messages presented in the literature could apply to school experiences, noticing specific examples in the school or community and bringing them to the group for discussion.

Process. Depending on the stories selected, multicultural literature lends itself to discussions of prejudice, false perceptions, stereotypes, and social change. Literature helps individuals see unique perspectives of issues that one would never have imagined prior to the reading. Work to help the group members uncover messages and discuss their relevance.

Session 6

Purpose. Session 6 builds upon skills developed in previous sessions and trains group members to become resources to students and staff within the building. Providing group members with the opportunity to become critical extensions of staff and administration makes group participants feel a growing sense of importance and builds resiliency among youth. The diversity of this group makes it an ideal resource to benefit all students and staff members.

Theme. The theme of this session is "peer mediation training."

Activities. There are a multitude of activities involved in any peer mediation program. One approach to this task is for the school district to plan a two-day retreat for the initial training of group members, with evening follow-up sessions planned for further rehearsal opportunities. Once group members have been trained, they also need to promote the program to students and staff. Everyone in the building needs to know that the opportunity for mediation exists, and where and how to refer students for mediation. The staff in particular needs to believe that peer mediators have the skills necessary to carry out successful mediations. All of these tasks can be completed in a variety of ways depending on the style and structure of the school district: classroom presentations, assembly presentations, staff in-service trainings, and more.

Process. This session is really the proof of the group's cohesiveness and ability to work together. The facilitator must be willing to allow group members the freedom to demonstrate their skills and focus his or her energies on coordinating the appropriate training and informational meetings. At this stage in the group formation process the group has power and energy, empowering group members to work as a unified team.

Session 7

Purpose. As this group becomes increasingly skilled, it is time for members to begin to teach others about cultural

awareness and communication. This session should occur as a culminating experience designed to reinforce and challenge group abilities.

Theme. The theme of this session is "public presentations."

Activities. To begin this session, ask the group where they see the greatest need for cultural education or training relative to increasing communication strategies. The group brainstorms different ways that they could reach out to fellow classmates and share bits and pieces of what they have learned. This challenges the group to not only consider who they would like to teach, but when, where, and how they would want to work with that population. They begin to evaluate their own learning and learning styles, their roles within the group, and apply that meta-cognition to the task at hand. Students should design, prepare for, and implement lessons to staff and students.

Process. The facilitator needs to allow group members the freedom to make group decisions and reinforce group progress. The facilitator also needs to recognize that not all group presentations will necessarily prove to be positive experiences; regardless of perceived success or failure, he or she will have to make sure that every session is debriefed as a group after every presentation, especially before another presentation begins.

Session 8

Purpose. Session 8 is the evaluation and termination of the group. This session is designed to bring closure to the group experience, arrange for any follow-up session that group members may require, and celebrate growth and change.

Theme. The theme of this session is "How have we impacted the group and others, and where do we go from here?"

Activities. Activities for the last session of the group require materials such as colorful paper and art supplies, glue, scissors, and tape, as well as the journals that they have been keeping throughout the sessions. The first activity is to ask students to separate themselves around the room and, using their journal as a reminder of the group's experience, create a "thank you" card for the group as a whole, representing what the individual group members have given to the group as a "gift" of themselves, and what personal/individual growth and change has resulted from the group involvement. Students are encouraged to write and draw pictures or symbols.

When all cards are complete the group members can then share their "thank you" card with the group, perhaps even sharing entries from their personal journals that demonstrate the process of change. The group could also brainstorm other avenues that members could take in their futures to maintain their growth and positive leadership abilities. A group follow-up session could be discussed to look at what efforts members have continued to make in their personal lives after termination of the group.

Finally, the group should celebrate their efforts to be a leadership team within their school. This may involve special treats or even an alternative meeting site, such as a local restaurant, and perhaps the distribution of individual certificates of achievement.

Process. Be prepared to assist students in their efforts to separate from the group by providing a safe environment for expressing emotion, as well as continued support in their violence prevention efforts. In this last session, the group is embracing an evaluative position. Gather feedback about the facilitation strategies used in this group for improving future groups. Student expression of positive growth and change is important. Students need to be engaged in a discussion about the impact that the group has had on the school and community as a result of their personal group membership, growth, and change.

STRATEGIES TO EVALUATE THE GROUP

As described in session 8, group members have an opportunity to discuss their personal growth and change, as well as their perceptions of the impact the group has had on the school and community. Students could also be asked to write post-group reflective papers, reacting to the group experience and evaluating its impact on them individually. Questions that students could reflect upon in their writing might include: How would you describe this group experience to someone outside of the group? To whom would you recommend this group and why? How have you changed since becoming involved in the group? How long will this group impact you? Did this group have any negative effects on you? How did the leader impact the group? Explain your feelings of safety and comfort in the group? What facilitator activities fostered or blocked these feelings? How have you used what you have learned in this group outside of the group setting? How did involvement in this group empower you or others to solve conflict differently?

REFERRAL PROCEDURES FOR FOLLOW-UP

In the school setting counselors are available for group members to seek out throughout the school year. This group, however, would be terminating near the end of the school year. Therefore, group participants should also be encouraged to serve as resources for one another, and summer phone numbers could be distributed among members. Local community resources could be made available to students as needed, and a follow-up session (as described in session 8) could be planned for later in the summer. Students transitioning out of high school could be referred to counseling and peer mediation programs at the collegiate or community level. Ideally, students will have developed healthy prosocial relationships, fostering resiliency among youth.

Sample First Meeting Agenda

AGENDA

1. Welcome
2. Introduction of Advisory Committee
3. Nomination and Selection Process
4. Explanation of Program Development and Goals
5. Explanation of Response Sheet—Due _____
6. Questions

Sample First Meeting Goals and Response Sheet

PROGRAM GOALS

1. To be a leadership team that represents the social and cultural diversity of our school.
2. To trust each other and build team unity so that we work effectively together.
3. To be thoroughly trained to recognize and respect cultural sensitivity issues.
4. To learn and practice effective communication techniques.
5. To identify school issues and work to resolve them through presentations/ mediations.
6. To make a personal commitment to practice these skills in our everyday lives.

Nominated Student's Name _____

_____ Yes! I am interested in participating in the leadership program and would like the committee to consider me for a position on this team.

_____ No, I am not interested in participating in this program.

SAMPLE COURSE SYLLABUS

COURSE TITLE

Course Description

Student leaders representing (as much as possible) the social and cultural diversity of our school and community are individually invited by an advisory team of administrators, teachers, and community members to participate in a program designed to address social and cultural sensitivity issues currently impacting our school and community. Team building, effective communication, developing cultural awareness and sensitivity, problem solving, anger management, group presentation strategies, conflict mediation, and other leadership skills will be introduced and utilized.

Course Goals

1. To be a leadership team that represents the social and cultural diversity of our school.
2. To trust each other and build team unity so that we work effectively together.
3. To be thoroughly trained to recognize and respect cultural sensitivity issues.
4. To learn and practice effective communication techniques.
5. To identify school issues and work to resolve them through presentations/mediations.
6. To make a personal commitment to practice these skills in our everyday lives.

Academic and Behavioral Expectations

Due to the unique nature of this group, it is extremely important for all members of the team to participate fully in all activities. Therefore, it is mandatory that students be present and on time every day in class. In addition, some training workshops may require students to occasionally miss other academic classes. While work that is missed will have to be made up by the student, our class time will always be given following a field trip to allow students time to meet with their other teachers and complete make-up assignments.

Ground rules:

1. One person talks at a time.
2. Everyone will have a chance to talk.
3. Everyone has the right to "pass" with explanation in any activity.
4. No put-downs are allowed.
5. We will respect the opinions of others.
6. Confidentiality is critical!! Everything addressed in class stays in class.
7. Other: _____

All other school rules also apply.

Grading System

All assignments and assessments will be worth a specified number of points. Points a student earns will be recorded in the gradebook. At the end of the semester, each student's points earned will be totaled. That total will be divided by the number of points possible to determine the student's percentage for the semester. The percentage scale is: 90–100 = A; 80–89 = B; 70–79 = C; 60–69 = D; 0–59 = F. Students are required to maintain an A or B average during the first semester if they are to remain in the class second semester.

REFERENCES

Developmental Research and Programs. (1996). *Communities that care. Prevention strategies: A research guide to what works.* Seattle, WA: Author.

Developmental Research and Programs. (2000). *Building healthy communities through prevention science: The research foundation.* Available (online): http://www.drp.org/Research.html.

Roberson, H. (1991). *The shadow of hate.* Montgomery, AL: Teaching Tolerance.

Sigelman, C. K. (1999). *Life-span human development* (3rd ed.). Pacific Grove, CA: Brooks/Cole.

Vernon, A. (1997). Special approaches to counseling. In D. Capuzzi & D. Gross (Eds.), *Introduction to the counseling profession* (2nd ed.) (pp. 257–285). Boston: Allyn & Bacon.

Western Center for the Application of Prevention Technologies. (1995). *Developing healthy communities: A risk and protective factor approach to preventing alcohol and other drug abuse.* Reno, NV: Author.

CHAPTER 9

TAG, I'M IT: A COUNSELING GROUP FOR TALENTED AND GIFTED ADOLESCENTS

Martha L. Larsen

PURPOSE

Educational systems often fail to meet the needs of talented and gifted (TAG) students. While the mandates to deal with gifted children are in place, the means often are not. Educators do not feel they have the resources and typically lack the understanding of what it takes to meet these students' needs. Even worse, they often also do not have the motivation. Even the counseling needs of gifted children seem to pale in comparison to the needs of other students who have problems that are more visible. The result is that gifted and talented students may well be the single most neglected group in terms of educational programming (Davis & Rimm, 1998).

From the point of view of the gifted and talented student, the toll for neglect is high. Most are bored senseless. Many find school impossible to tolerate. Feigned illness or disruptive behavior often seem to them like reasonable courses of action. Many feel weird, that they do not fit in, and feel the need to hide their talents from peers. Statistics show that as many as half of gifted children do not perform up to their abilities in school (National Commission on Excellence in Education, 1983). Twenty-five percent give up on school entirely (McDonald, 1990). Society loses their potential benefits, the students lose opportunities to rise to their potential, and classrooms are disrupted.

Talented and gifted students are not usually seen as prime candidates for mainstream counseling in our schools because of the strong emphasis on traditional "problem" students as a priority for counselor time (VanTassel-Baska, 1991). High expectations from themselves, from their parents, from their teachers, and from society create a very large burden for these students who are also struggling with the normal developmental pressures faced by all adolescents. Some talented and gifted students become lost completely when they do not receive help with their most acute problems.

"Preventive counseling is particularly effective in small groups, which can serve as support systems for gifted students" (Swassing, 1985, p. 72), especially those who do not have specialized services available to them in their schools. Many of these young people could greatly benefit from the personal growth, support, and new understanding about themselves that can come from connecting with their peers in a group counseling setting. Such a group can assist gifted teens who are struggling with adolescent issues. Although many of these issues are common to all adolescents, dealing concurrently with giftedness creates an additional dimension of complexity. Issues that are particularly important to gifted adolescents include:

- Accepting themselves and their giftedness
- Fitting in with peers
- Struggling through adolescence
- Coping with school and teachers who do not understand giftedness
- Exploring career choices
- Dealing with failure—preventing suicide
- Developing a philosophy of life

The purpose of this counseling group for talented and gifted students is to provide a safe and supportive context where members can work together with intellectual peers to explore and examine ideas, attitudes, feelings, and behaviors associated with their personal development and progress in school. It focuses on their affective needs, thereby helping them gain a greater awareness, understanding, and acceptance of themselves and others.

CONCEPTUAL FRAMEWORK

The intended outcome for this group endeavor is to provide support and empowerment for talented and gifted students at the developmental stage of adolescence. It follows a preventive model of counseling aimed at reducing the risks to this unique group of young people and reducing the potential loss to society of the contributions they might ultimately make (Bireley & Genshaft, 1991). Students in this group benefit from the basic affective experiences of group processes, from learning practical skills for surviving adolescence, and from thinking about deeper questions of identity.

The developmental group counseling approach used with this group draws from the theoretical underpinnings of both existential theory and reality theory. Elements of the existential quest contribute to talented and gifted students' search for answers to life's deeper questions and development of their own philosophy of life. Reality theory contributes the principles of responsibility, focus on evaluating present and planning future behavior, commitment, taking action, and paying attention to results.

Developmental groups for young people are distinguished from other forms of group counseling by their orientation to help essentially healthy children draw on their own strengths to better deal with life's challenges. "Developmental group counseling is growth-oriented but has a preventive and remedial function as well" (Orton, 1997, p. 194). Developmental groups focus on discovering inner strengths and using the group to increase their understanding and acceptance of values and goals or to change attitudes and behaviors. Developmental group theory provides an opportunity to reframe problems experienced by talented and gifted adolescents into challenges worthy of their attention.

Kegan (1980) recognizes that one of the imperatives of meeting adolescent's developmental needs is to guide them in making meaning of their lives and experiences. The world of gifted adolescents is large, including not only their family, school, and peers, but also the larger world. Gifted adolescents thrive on opportunities to sharpen their critical thinking skills. By facing existential questions, they have an opportunity to deploy their own very significant intellectual resources to understanding their situations and finding good reasons to act on their own behalf.

Frank (1999) notes that existentialism provides a contextual approach for group counseling that emphasizes choice, responsibility, and growth. In discussing applications of existential theory, May (1981) recognizes that problems, rather than being something to solve and dispense with, provide the basis for human creativity and supply the energy for change. Bugental (1987) characterizes the goals of existential therapy as aiding the client to experience more potency in his or her life and to recognize personal choice where formerly only compulsion existed. The developmental group approach framed by the existential quest for meaning is particularly well-suited for gifted adolescents because of their capacity for critical thinking, an emerging self-knowledge, and desire to explore the deeper questions of life.

Reality therapy offers constructs for group counseling that also fit the special needs of gifted students, many of whom are chronic underachievers. The central theme of reality theory is that people's problems arise from denying reality. The key to improvement is taking responsibility for, and control of, your own life and facing the consequences of your actions. This notion is applicable to the needs of gifted adolescents. The group counseling experience provides opportunities for adolescents to re-create their self-image by replacing patterns of ineffective behaviors with purposeful behaviors guided by intent.

Gifted students have a thirst for cultivating higher level thinking skills. The group activities are designed to teach and strengthen critical thinking skills, creative thinking, and metacognition. Socrates, who believed that true knowledge existed within everyone and needed only to be brought to consciousness, used a method of asking probing questions to force students to think deeply about the meaning in their lives. The group activities make use of this Socratic method to achieve the desired outcomes. Continued participation in group sessions is ensured when the activities are stimulating, valuable, and enjoyable for the students.

GROUP GOALS

The following goals will be the focus of this group experience:

1. To provide opportunities for gifted adolescents to explore the meaning and value of their giftedness among academic peers.
2. To provide opportunities for gifted students to engage in self-discovery and learn to accept themselves and their giftedness.
3. To provide opportunities for gifted students to have successes in building and sustaining personal relationships.
4. To aid adolescents in deploying their own giftedness as a personal asset.

PRE-GROUP SCREENING AND ORIENTATION

The group leader, the school staff, and the prospective member all play significant roles in pre-group screening. The purpose of screening is threefold: (1) to identify those whose goals are congruent with the group goals; (2) to identify those who could be harmed by or who, for some other reason, are not yet ready for group counseling; and (3) to identify those who could have an adverse affect on the group. The first step involves the school staff in assessing which students are eligible for participation and identifying those who would benefit the most. School records disclose which students have been identified as talented and gifted, and staff may also be aware of gifted and talented students who have not been formally designated.

The group leader next conducts an individual interview to assess each student's needs and readiness for participation in a group. During the interview, the counselor introduces the group concept to the student, explains the purpose of the group, listens to the student's responses, and assesses whether or not the student would make a good group member. At the same time, the counselor hears what the student expects from the group if he or she were to join. It is at this point that both the counselor and prospective member form independent conclusions about the goodness of fit between group and student. Gazda (1982) identifies a variety of desirable traits for inclusion in the counseling group. Those that are particularly applicable to this group include:

- A desire for growth
- A desire to empathize and form relationships with others
- A willingness to articulate goals for change
- The potential to be open and a willingness to give others considerate feedback
- A commitment and ability to attend regularly
- A willingness to take risks in dealing with problems and try new behaviors

Who needs to be screened out? Adolescents who need individual counseling before they are ready for group counseling need to be screened out. Examples include those who are suffering from an unresolved traumatic event or adolescents who are in crisis for any of a variety of reasons. Those with severe behavior problems who may be disruptive to the group process also need to be screened out.

The group is homogeneous from the standpoint that all students are gifted and talented adolescents. The group needs to have enough diversity to provide the opportunity for group members to learn ways of relating to and helping people different from themselves. The group would benefit from the inclusion of students from diverse ethnic and cultural backgrounds. The group consists primarily of students who express an interest in participating, but may also include some other students identified by the school staff who would benefit from this particular developmental experience. The group is a closed group, consisting of the same students throughout the duration of the group.

Following selection of the group membership, the facilitator conducts a pre-group orientation session where the purpose and main goals of the group are explained. Confidentiality and the critical role it plays in establishing safety within the group is discussed. It is also important to include a discussion of informed consent and ensure its understanding by all group members. Members have an opportunity to ask questions and share concerns. The expectation is shared that group members willingly and reliably participate and arrive at group sessions on time. The process of decision making by group consensus is explained. Members are asked to come to the first session prepared to identify personal goals related to the overall group purpose.

OUTLINE FOR EIGHT GROUP SESSIONS

Session 1

Purpose. The purpose of session 1 is for group members to get acquainted with each other and learn about the group. Group members may be apprehensive about the experience and unsure of how they will be perceived by other members. It is important in this first session that participants experience an environment in which they feel safe and accepted in the group.

Theme. The theme of the first session is "introduction."

Activity. The first activity serves as an icebreaker and provides an opportunity to begin the process of inclusion. The activity is designed to be stimulating for gifted adolescents because it includes elements of many learning styles. Begin the activity by assigning partners, including the facilitator. Three partners may be in a group if the number of members is uneven. The group stands and each person grasps hold of the group basketball with both hands, thus forming a tight circle. It does not matter where partners stand in relation to each other. Without letting go of the basketball, the group then navigates an assigned course around the school. While navigating the course, partners try to find out two things about each other that they will share with the group when it reconvenes. Upon return to the meeting site, members take turns stating their name, the name of their partner, and two things they were able to learn about their partner during the trip around the course. The facilitator begins the sharing to model the behavior desired.

Next, review the purpose of the group, fully exploring the topic of confidentiality and the vital role it plays in creating a sense of safety within the group. The group brainstorms and reaches agreement on a set of rules that guide how the group functions. The ground rules include ideas such as the right to pass (and that it is best if you explain to the group why you are choosing to pass), the need to respect each other, the need for acceptance of others' ideas, and the need to be on time.

Members identify one goal to work on inside the group and one goal for their own work outside the group. Keep the goals in a folder and bring them to each group session. Goals are reviewed weekly during check-in. In the course of the discussion, members of the group share their major concerns and the new behaviors they want to learn.

At the end of the discussion, summarize the progress of the group. Make a special effort to reinforce behaviors that help the group to be effective by recognizing such behaviors with positive comments. Introduce the closing activity to help members prepare for leaving the safety of the group and explain that the same activity will be used at the end of each session. The closing activity is 1 minute of silent reflective thought about experiences in the group and how the learning can be applied outside the group.

Process. Members learn to trust themselves and others and that the group is a safe place to disclose. They benefit from the experience of being together because it provides intellectual stimulation and opportunities to form friendships with intellectual peers. They learn that trust, acceptance, and mutual respect are necessary elements of group work. The role of the facilitator is to create a safe environment and to help members develop relationships with one another and with the facilitator. The facilitator models the behaviors of being understanding and accepting.

Session 2

Purpose. The purpose of the second session is to explore the meaning of giftedness. Due to their social isolation, uniqueness, feelings of not being normal, and self-analytic ability, many gifted youth experience severe identity problems regarding who they are and what they wish to become (Davis & Rimm, 1998). Bringing them together gives these young people a chance to express their feelings of isolation and loneliness in order to help them develop skills for functioning better with others.

Theme. The theme of this session is "self-awareness." It is important that gifted adolescents learn to accept themselves for who they are, not for what they do.

Activities. The group begins with a check-in activity that provides an opportunity to review the names of group members. To begin the activity, members are asked to take turns around the circle stating their name and then answering the question: If you described yourself in terms of a type of weather, what kind of weather would

you be and why? Invite participants to review or revise their goals if they desire.

Then initiate a life map exercise by passing out large pieces of paper and colored markers or crayons. Ask members to take 15 minutes to draw a map of their life—where they have been, where they are, and where they might be going. Encourage members to use their creativity in how they draw their path and how they illustrate points of significance. Points of significance can be people, places, events, experiences, feelings, or ideas. When the maps are completed, members form a discussion circle and share their work with the rest of the group. The discussion can be deepened by posing the question: What does it mean to be gifted? Related questions for the discussion can include: What do teachers and other students in school think it means to be gifted? What do your parents think it means? How is being gifted an advantage for you? How is it a disadvantage? What do gifted and nongifted individuals have to learn from each other?

Begin the discussion to model the desired behavior and to include the facilitator in the group. Members continue the discussion around the circle. Discussion of the nature and function of giftedness helps the group identify conditions that may impede the healthy development of the members. The session closes with 1 minute of silent reflection.

Process. Group members feel the support of the group and experience that they are not alone. They begin to feel more comfortable sharing information about themselves with the group. As the leader clarifies and summarizes statements of the group members, they learn to attribute meaning to their experience and begin to integrate what they are learning into their own experience. The role of the facilitator is to assist the group in developing its own leadership and social processes. The facilitator models the behaviors of being open and congruent.

Session 3

Purpose. The purpose of this session is to increase self-knowledge through emphasis on self-acceptance. Gifted adolescents find themselves torn between a need to conform to be accepted into a peer group and a need to develop their individuality and uniqueness. They often feel forced to deny the qualities and needs that define their giftedness. "Only when gifted students receive help in clarifying their true values and developing their sense of self-worth can they acknowledge their differences as positive and harness their abilities to the fullest extent" (Kaufman, Castellanos, & Rotatori, 1986, p. 239).

Theme. The theme of the session is "self-acceptance." This session helps members learn to capitalize on their personal strengths and shift their locus of control from extrinsic to intrinsic.

Activities. The session opens with members reading and reporting progress on their personal goals. After all have discussed their progress, pass out 3 × 5 inch cards. Instruct members to write three words that they would use to describe themselves and drop the card into a hopper. The hopper is passed around the group so that each member can draw someone else's card. Members take turns reading the cards aloud and guessing who the author might be. The guesser speaks directly to the person who is being guessed and says "I think this is you *(name)* because _____ ." The facilitator seeks out opportunities to elicit what it is about the person being guessed leads the guesser to his or her conclusion. The point of the exercise is to promote feedback and not to necessarily guess the right person.

Continue the discussion with questions about who we are in terms of our own and other people's perceptions and expectations: Are you weird if other people think you are weird? How can you deal with people who put you off or put you down because you are not like everybody else? How can you feel good about yourself in the face of ridicule from the people you want to be with? The session provides opportunities for members to learn to respect themselves and trust their abilities. The session closes with a minute of silent reflection.

Process. Group members learn to accept themselves and their feelings within the context of trust and support in the group. They begin to face and resolve personal problems. Members benefit from feedback and confrontation in the group as well as from reinforcement by peers and the facilitator. Discovering that other members within the group have similar problems helps members feel they belong and are understood. Having others discuss common problems openly and watching them learn new ways to behave motivates other group members to discuss their problems, too. Members are empowered by the realization that they can alter their perceptions of the world. They also learn that accepting themselves is an important way to cope with pressure from other people.

The leader encourages frank communication between members and helps them test their power as they define their identity within the group. The facilitator assists group members in exploration of ideas that will help them meet their goals. The facilitator helps them deal with overly high expectations of others by encouraging them to move from extrinsic motivation to intrinsic motivation.

Session 4

Purpose. The purpose of this session is to continue to provide opportunities for group members to explore who they are, but this time specifically in a social context. Psychosocial difficulties occur for gifted adolescents because many gifted students believe that nongifted peers and teachers hold negative views of them. They are often unsure of how to balance the developmentally appropriate need for conforming and peer acceptance with the realities of their differences. They are keen observers of others' behavior, but tend to be poor interpreters of the behavior they observe. They need experience interpreting nonverbal behavior to facilitate a greater understanding of themselves and others (Frey, 1991).

Theme. The theme of this session is "building successful relationships."

Activities. The opening activity is to have each member draw lines on a piece of paper dividing it into four equal quadrants. Members are given 10 minutes to fill each quadrant with a positive statement of appreciation: one to self, one to a best friend, a family member, and a classmate. They then take turns sharing their positive statements with the group. Members may be eager to get started and move directly to discussion, rather than do goal review at this session. The question of the day is: How can I be part of the group and still be myself? It may be helpful to initiate a discussion that focuses on a variety of social skills such as:

- Listening to others
- Asking questions to let others know you are interested in them
- Reaching out to others and initiating conversation
- Accepting others for who they are
- Finding other people who accept you for who you are

It is important that the discussion includes issues of peer pressure and conformity to ensure understanding that students do not need to deny their giftedness to have friends. The session closes with a minute of silent reflection.

Process. Group members engage in considerate and meaningful discussions that prepare them for the behavior changes that occur as a result of the group counseling experience. The group experience helps members explore how they appear to others. Members recognize they have choices about selecting their peer group. Strategies important to the development of social skills are also principal strategies for changing self-perceptions and enhancing self-esteem. Members are encouraged to express feelings and explore new behaviors. The leader stays closely tuned to the process and content in the group to make decisions about when it is appropriate to explore hidden thoughts, attitudes, and feelings that are not expressed verbally.

Session 5

Purpose. The purpose of this session is to explore the concept of risk taking. Gifted adolescents often tend to avoid taking risks. They typically weigh the advantages and disadvantages of activities and choose only those in which they believe they will succeed.

Theme. The theme of this session is the importance of "taking risks."

Activities. Open the group by observing that half the sessions are complete and half remain. The session opens with each member reporting progress on their goals for the group. Choose a bibliotherapy project activity, wherein the group reads a story together. A suggested source of applicable stories is *Gifted Kids Have Feelings Too: And Other Not So Fictitious Stories for and about Teenagers* (Rimm, 1990). The story provides the basis for discussion, stimulating questions such as: What can you control in your life? What does it mean to take risks? Is it OK to take risks? When is it a good idea and when is it not such a good idea? What would happen if you never took a risk? When can risk taking be important in helping you get what you want? The session closes with a minute of silent reflection.

Process. Group members thrive on support and encouragement from the facilitator and peers. They also derive a feeling of empowerment from recognition of their own real accomplishments. Members help each other examine how they deal with situations. Individuals begin accepting responsibility for their own growth. They develop a new set of standards and values that they use to test their sense of identity against the realities of the group (MacLennan & Felsenfeld, 1968).

The role of the facilitator is to draw out leadership behavior from group members and become more involved as a helper as members take over the leadership function. The leader models and affirms positive changes in members and cooperation in the group. It is very useful for the facilitator to encourage the group members to engage each other by looking at and speaking directly to one another (Yalom, 1985).

Session 6

Purpose. Gifted students often experience considerable stress as a result of high expectations. They are typically unprepared and poorly equipped to respond when they fail to meet their own expectations or the expectations of others. The purpose of this session is to provide a framework for healthy choices that will help students set realistic expectations and learn to cope with failure, thus strengthening personal assets that are important elements in the prevention of suicide.

Theme. This session focuses on "perfectionism and suicide prevention."

Activities. The members review progress on their goals as an opener. The activity begins by asking the members to express their experience of the past week as a type of

music or a type of art. The group then explores the topic of the day with questions related to perfectionism such as: "If I am so smart, why can I not do everything right?" What is failure? Did you know that Beethoven had a music teacher who described him as "hopeless" or that Thomas Edison's teacher said he was addled? Did you know that Bill Cosby was in a class for gifted students but dropped out of high school? Did you know that a person can be gifted in one academic area and be learning-disabled in another? Does perfection exist?

Howard Gardner (1985) proposed that intelligence exists in different forms. The leader may choose to teach Gardner's Theory of Multiple Intelligences, highlighting that there are different kinds of intelligence: linguistic, logical-mathematical, visual-spatial, musical-rhythmic, bodily-kinesthetic, interpersonal, intrapersonal, and naturalist, to emphasize the idea that a person may easily learn in some areas but have difficulty learning in others. "The beauty of Gardner's theory lies in the fact that you do not have to be #1 in everything in order to be considered gifted. You can have abilities in certain areas and still be a regular person" (Delisle & Galbraith, 1987, p. 12). Emphasize the importance of maintaining a positive self-concept, setting realistic goals, and accepting failure as an important part of the success. Encourage students to examine their self-talk and irrational beliefs regarding perfectionism. The discussion includes strategies for stress management, with particular reference to its usefulness in prevention of suicide, such as compartmentalizing, calming, active ignoring, humor, and methods of asking for help and support if circumstances seem dire. Prior to the session closing with a minute of silent reflection, ask members to reflect on all the different strategies and strengths they have built so far that would be useful for reducing stress and the risk of suicide from becoming a possibility in their own lives.

Process. Members have a chance to reflect on where they are in the group and how they are progressing with their personal goals. The development of more realistic self-expectations results in a more positive self-concept and desirable personal growth. They are building confidence in themselves and learning to function more collaboratively as a group. The facilitator helps the group members discuss painful issues and helps them decide how they can change maladaptive behaviors. The facilitator also reinforces positive change in members and emphasizes effective group dynamics.

Session 7

Purpose. The purpose of this session is to provide group members with an opportunity to think about and discuss how they can apply what they have been learning in the group to the world outside the group. Gifted students who have multipotentiality are often either immobilized by too many choices or unduly influenced by others to make choices prematurely (Kaufman et al., 1986). This session focuses on the application of acquired self-knowledge to career choice and development of a philosophy of life.

Theme. The theme of the session is "creating possibilities for the future."

Activities. The group begins with a reminder that the time for the group is nearing the end. Members are given an opportunity to express their concerns and feelings about closure. Ask members to reflect on their goals and progress in preparation for discussion at the next session. When the group is ready, move on to the topic of the day by asking questions including: What are your values? What matters to you in the world? How can you make a difference? How do you choose a career? Where can you go for good information? Do you need a mentor? The session closes with a minute of silent reflection.

Process. Members experience growth as they evaluate their own and others' thoughts and plans for the future. The discussion helps them clarify their own thinking and remember the importance of remaining true to themselves in their decisions. They accept responsibility for their own growth and commit themselves to action. The facilitator helps members identify and work on the remaining issues. The facilitator also leads members toward action by helping them identify resources and people whose assistance would help them enhance their ability to achieve their goals.

Session 8

Purpose. This last session helps the group collectively understand what has transpired during its existence—with emphasis on applying the changes in the outside world—and provides an opportunity for members to evaluate their experience in the group.

Theme. The theme of this session is "closure."

Activities. The group begins by forming a circle and holding hands. Instruct the group to work together to keep a balloon in the air. They may use all parts of their bodies until the balloon hits the ground. Each time the balloon hits the ground, the group loses the ability to use part of the body, starting with the head, then arms, and so on until they are just left with the feet. After the activity, focus the discussion on evaluation of goals. Members discuss answers to questions like: What have you learned? What do you still want to learn? Where will you go to get information? The discussion assesses how members feel the group functioned and how well it met its goals. Time is provided for members to share their feelings about how they met their individual goals for inside and outside the group. Members openly acknowledge the sense of loss they are experiencing as the group comes to a close and share appreciation of each other with other members. Members are asked to complete a written evaluation. The session closes with a minute of silent reflection.

Process. Students grow from an opportunity to evaluate and affirm the changes that have occurred in themselves, in each other, and within the group. Members affirm to the group what they have learned or experienced and how they will apply that outside the group. They experience the feeling of empowerment that comes with the knowledge and training to reliably get better outcomes in a world that does not understand them. The facilitator helps members evaluate individual and group progress, creates an opportunity for expressing emotions associated with ending the group, and helps members celebrate their success.

STRATEGIES TO EVALUATE THE GROUP

The evaluation takes a two-pronged approach, first where the group evaluates itself and its processes and second where members personally evaluate themselves and how useful the group was for them. The group evaluation is done in a group setting and serves to honor group processes while firmly cementing the notion of individual responsibilities for group outcomes. The individual evaluation is taken from a more personal viewpoint and asks individuals to reflect on their own progress and rate the group's efficacy.

The individual evaluation is conducted by means of a written questionnaire administered at the last session and three months later. It rates these following statements on a five point scale: 0—Strongly disagree; 1—Disagree; 2—Undecided; 3—Agree; and 4—Strongly agree.

_____ I enjoyed being a member of this group.
_____ I have made progress toward my written personal goals.
_____ My feelings of self-acceptance have improved as the result of group sessions.
_____ I have experienced personal growth.
_____ The counselor was an effective facilitator for group sessions.
_____ The group topics focused on issues that are important in my life.
_____ I feel more comfortable in social situations with other students.
_____ I can use my own special abilities to make a positive difference in my life and in the world.

REFERRAL PROCEDURES FOR FOLLOW-UP

The last remaining piece of business for the counselor in group termination is to ensure that each member has reached closure in the group experience. For students who are compelled to continue work on their issues, several options exist. Students can be referred to a counselor in school or private practice, directed to another group, or encouraged to find a mentor.

REFERENCES

Bireley, M., & Genshaft, J. (Eds.). (1991). *Understanding the gifted adolescent.* New York: Teachers College Press.

Bugental, J. (1987). *The art of the psychotherapist.* New York: W. W. Norton.

Davis, G. A., & Rimm, S. B. (1998). *Education of the gifted and talented* (4th ed.). Boston: Allyn & Bacon.

Delisle, J. R., & Galbraith, J. (1987). *The gifted kids survival guide II.* Minneapolis, MN: Free Spirit.

Frank, M. L. (1999). Existential theory. In D. Capuzzi & D. Gross (Eds.), *Counseling and psychotherapy: Theories and interventions* (2nd ed., pp. 151–178). Upper Saddle River, NJ: Merrill/Prentice-Hall.

Frey, D. E. (1991). Psychosocial needs of the gifted adolescent. In M. Bireley & J. Genshaft (Eds.), Understanding the gifted adolescent (pp. 35–49). New York: Teachers College Press.

Gardner, H. (1985). *The frames of mind: Theory of multiple intelligences.* New York: Basic Books.

Gazda, G. M. (Ed.). (1982). *Basic approaches to group psychotherapy and group counseling.* Springfield, IL: Charles C. Thomas.

Kaufman, F. A., Castellanos, F. X., & Rotatori, A. F. (1986). Counseling the gifted child. In A. F. Rotatori, P. J. Gerber, F. W. Litton, & R. A. Fox, (Eds.), *Counseling exceptional students* (pp. 232–251). New York: Human Sciences Press.

Kegan, R. (1980). *The evolving self.* Cambridge, MA: Harvard University Press.

MacLennan, B. W., & Felsenfeld, N. (1968). *Group counseling and psychotherapy with adolescents.* New York: Columbia University Press.

May, R. (1981). *Freedom and destiny.* New York: W. W. Norton.

McDonald, B. (1990). *Oregon handbook for parents of talented & gifted children.* Salem, OR: Division of Special Student Services, Special Education Section, Oregon Dept. of Education.

National Commission on Excellence in Education. (1983). *A nation at risk: The imperative for educational reform.* Washingtion, DC: U.S. Government Printing Office.

Orton, G. L. (1997). *Strategies for counseling children and their parents* (4th Ed.). Pacific Grove, CA: Brooks/Cole.

Rimm, S. B. (1990). *Gifted kids have feelings too: and other not so ficticious stories for and about teenagers.* Watertown, WI: Apple.

Swassing, R. H. (Ed.). (1985). *Teaching gifted children and adolescents.* Columbus, OH: Charles E. Merrill.

VanTassel-Baska, J. (1991). Teachers as counselors for gifted students. In R. Milgram (Ed.), *Counseling gifted and talented children: A guide for teachers, counselors, and parents* (pp. 37–52). Norwood, NJ: Ablex.

Yalom, I. (1985). *The theory and practice of group psychotherapy.* (3rd ed.). New York: Basic Books.

CHAPTER 10

EFFECTIVE COMMUNICATION FOR CONFLICT SITUATIONS

Marci Warnecke

PURPOSE

This group is designed for students in grades 6 through 10 (ages 11–16) and is geared for use in a school setting. It is assumed that sessions will be set up to occur weekly and last for approximately 1 hour. This is a psychoeducational group intended to address the needs of adolescents who are frequently faced with disciplinary action due to the manner in which they respond to conflict situations.

The purpose of this group is to create a safe environment in which students can become aware of their current conflict responses and the origins of these responses, learn new and/or alternative tools for dealing with conflict, practice these new techniques in a controlled environment, and begin to experiment with and practice these new response skills in their everyday lives.

CONCEPTUAL FRAMEWORK

The basis of this group relies most heavily upon Albert Bandura's Social-Learning Theory, which combines aspects of behaviorism and cognitivism (Domjan, 1998). His theory rests on the assumption that much important learning results from observing and imitating models. However, unlike strictly behavioral models, Bandura's theory recognizes the importance of our ability to think, to symbolize, to figure out cause-and-effect relationships, and to anticipate the outcomes of behavior (Domjan, 1998). This group relies upon Social-Learning Theory in that it assumes individuals have a variety of different anger response styles that they have learned from par-

ents, siblings, friends, caretakers, and other influential people in their lives. Students who respond to conflict situations with either physical or verbal aggression are often relying on the responses they have seen modeled over the years and do not possess a knowledge of alternative skills or tools. The cognitive abilities recognized by Bandura support our belief that people can change and can be guided to see that their behaviors are often ineffective and learning new behaviors may be beneficial. This group will, in part, educate students on various response options and give them opportunities to practice these new responses in a controlled environment.

The framework supporting the principles of this group also relies on the ideas of several other psychological theories. Feminist Theory emphasizes the goal of empowerment—gaining awareness of the guiding influences in one's life, and learning and practicing skills that allow one to gain control over these influences while respecting others' boundaries (Capuzzi & Gross, 1999). As previously stated, empowering students in this manner is an important objective of this group. Often people blame others for their troubles: When asked why she was suspended, a student might immediately respond, "That girl said things about me behind my back, so I had to show her she couldn't talk about me like that. I had to beat her up!" The empowerment principle places the responsibility for responses and behavior in the hands of each individual. Similarly, in the early days of Reality Therapy, Glasser believed personal responsibility for behavior must be emphasized, rather than allowing blame to be placed on the past or outside forces (Capuzzi & Gross, 1999). Through the methods of this group, students will learn that while they may not be able to control the actions of others, they can control and are responsible for their own behaviors.

The group methods also utilize the techniques of several different theories. The role-playing ideas proposed by Cognitive-Behavioral theorists are used throughout the group process as the primary method of acquiring new responses to conflict. Role-playing is an extremely valuable tool, as it generally involves hearing about a new behavior, seeing it demonstrated, and then having multiple opportunities to practice the new skill in a controlled setting before attempting it in a real-world situation (Gurman & Messer, 1995). Also, goal-setting and scaling techniques from Brief Solution-Focused Therapies are used throughout the group. These are useful in helping individuals to both look/plan ahead and evaluate progress and current feelings in the moment (Gurman & Messer, 1995). It is not necessary to completely understand these principles, as their procedures are described within the description of group sessions.

GROUP GOALS

The following goals guide the purpose, process, and activities of each session:

1. To help members recognize conflict as a normal occurrence/part of life.
2. To help members visualize conflict as a cycle with many alternatives at each phase.
3. To help members identify their conflict responses and the origins of these responses.
4. To encourage members to take personal responsibility for their behaviors.
5. To provide members with a "tool box" of techniques for communicating effectively and dealing with conflicts.
6. To provide members with opportunities to practice the various tools in a safe and controlled environment.
7. To provide support for members as they begin to try their newly acquired skills in daily life.

PRE-GROUP SCREENING AND ORIENTATION

As with any group, the facilitator should attempt to select individuals whose needs and goals are expected to be addressed by the group, and whose participation will not be detrimental to the individual or to the group as a whole (Capuzzi & Gross, 1998). As is consistent with the nature and setting of this group, members will likely be selected from students who are referred to the school counselors by a disciplinary team or other school personnel due to frequent angry outbursts in class, or violent verbal or physical reactions to conflict situations. It is suggested that potential members be met with individually and told about the goals of the group, generally what can be expected during sessions, and briefly informed about confidentiality. The students must be willing to explore alternative conflict responses and agree to be respectful of the other group members. As students will be expected to keep a journal and track their behavior between sessions, potential members should be informed of these expectations and agree to participate fully. The purpose, goals, and expectations of the group should be written out and verbally explained to each potential member, and members should sign a statement indicating they understand and will adhere to the expectations set forth.

Parents of potential members should be contacted and informed of the same information that was presented to the student, and they should be sent an information letter and permission form to be signed before the student is formally invited to join the group.

In addition, it is suggested that facilitators not include students with extreme behavior issues or antisocial tendencies as these students are likely to not only require more intense counseling but may be detrimental to the experience of other group members.

OUTLINE FOR EIGHT GROUP SESSIONS

Session 1

Purpose. The purpose of session 1 is for group members to introduce themselves to the group and begin to become comfortable with one another. In addition, the first session is an appropriate time to implement ground rules for the group. Finally, the concepts of mood scaling, goal setting, and anger cues should be introduced.

Theme. The theme of this session is introduction and beginning to understand how the group will be run. The members begin to develop relationships with one another, learn what the role of the facilitator is, and begin to find their voice and personal role in the group.

Activities. The first activity is an energizer or ice-breaker, which will serve to get members involved in attaining a cooperative goal with other members. It may also help to ease any tension students may be feeling as they enter this new environment in a positive, healthy way. While many ice-breaker activities exist, the following example is suggested: Ask that students use only positive encouragement/suggestions—no put-downs. Each student chooses a partner, and each pair receives a fully inflated balloon. A "finish line" is designated 30–50 feet away (distance determined by available space). Each pair must place the balloon between them (between shoulders, elbows, hips, or legs) and walk together from the start line to the finish line without dropping or popping the balloon. When each pair has successfully crossed the line, one pair joins a second pair. Now in groups of four with a balloon between each two people (three balloons/group), students attempt to again make it from start to finish without dropping or popping any of the balloons. If there are eight group members, the two foursomes now join with a balloon between each two people and complete the task again. Follow this activity with a brief discussion involving questions such as: What was most difficult about this game? What techniques did you discover to make the task easier? Was the task easier with more people, or with only two? What other things did you observe while playing the game?

The discussion of the first activity may lead naturally into a discussion of ground rules. If not, this would be an appropriate time to discuss ground rules and confidentiality issues. Explain what confidentiality means and its implications in the school setting. Examples of potential confidentiality challenges and appropriate resolutions may be extremely helpful for students. Invite students' questions regarding confidentiality. With a fairly mature and/or insightful group, the counselor may then ask for suggestions for group rules that will keep the group a safe and comfortable environment. The list brainstormed by the group may be summarized so that the final list has approximately five items. With a less mature/insightful group, it may be helpful to provide an initial list of ground rules that are then read and discussed. Then ask for additional suggestions from group members to be agreed upon by the group. The initial list may include the following rules: only positive or encouraging statements, ask for permission to give feedback before giving it, listen openly and quietly while others speak, and members may choose to pass during any activity.

Although a check-in period would usually fall at the beginning of a session, it is the third activity in this first session. The group members each introduce themselves and describe how they are feeling at the time on a scale of 0 to 10 (10 being the best a person could possibly feel, 0 being the absolute worst). The students should also be encouraged to give an explanation of the reported rating. Additionally, students may be asked to tell what they are hoping to gain from this group experience.

Following the check-in time, introduce the concept of personal goal setting. Stress that goals should be challenging, yet attainable; should include a long-term goal with several short-term goals that lead up to the long-term goal; and goals should be stated positively rather than negatively ("I will _____ " not "I will not _____"). Give students a few minutes to come up with a long-term behavioral goal regarding what the student would like to gain from the group. The long-term goal should be written on the second page of the Conflict Journal (spiral notebook). This will be the only goal established at this point but goal setting will be discussed further at future meetings.

As mentioned previously, students are asked to keep a daily conflict journal, in which they record each time they are faced with a conflict situation, what

words/actions triggered the conflict, any accompanying physical anger signs (face heating up, sweaty palms, locked jaw, and so on), how they responded to the situation, and a description of the results of the confrontation. Students should be encouraged to write the items to be included in each entry at the front of the notebook for future reference. Let students know they should bring the journal to each group session, as they will be invited to reflect on the contents and share with the group when they feel comfortable doing so. Students should not write their names in their journals, in order to protect their confidentiality should the journal fall into someone else's hands. A code name or word could be used if journals need to be identified.

Finally, a checkout time should conclude the group. Members may be asked to describe how they feel about being involved in this group and also may be encouraged to share any other observations, hopes, or concerns they may have regarding the group.

Process. The role of the facilitator is extremely important throughout all sessions, but especially during this opening meeting. The facilitator takes on the role of a teacher, encourager, and role model. Due to the strong basis of this group on the importance of modeling, the facilitator is encouraged to participate in activities and demonstrate appropriate ways of communicating with others. In addition, as this is a group of students with explosive tempers but without the tools to effectively deal with strong emotions, it becomes extremely important to put emphasis on ground rules that provide safety and a nonjudgmental climate of tolerance and respect. Behavior contracts may be used if a lack of adherance to ground rules is expected to be a problem. In addition, any in-group conflict situations may be used as teaching tools. The facilitator may ask the members to agree upon a group cue (raising hands, and so on) that signals that conflict is occurring before it gets out of hand. When the cue is given, group members involved in the conflict should agree to stop, and the facilitator may help them to resolve the conflict in an appropriate manner.

The opening ice-breaker activity is intended to assuage initial fears and tension of the members through physical activity. However, this activity is the members' first impression of the group and must be a positive experience. Therefore, although ground rules are not discussed until later in the group, the facilitator is encouraged to require that only positive statements (no put-downs) be used during the activity. Some students may benefit from examples of possible positive statements. The discussion following the ice-breaker facilitates the flow from physical activity to talking and reflection among group members.

It is imperative that the facilitator fully explain confidentiality given the school setting. Students should be told that while they are free to acknowledge their own participation in group, they may not talk about what others have said or identify other group members to friends, family, and so on. In addition, members should be made aware that even simple comments such as, "Hey, Kristin! See you in group!" are a breach of confidentiality if non-group individuals are within ear shot.

The Conflict Journal is introduced during this first session. In addition to the instructions given previously, students should have one-page sections set aside in their notebooks for goals and tools, and the rest for entries. Students may be asked to draw a large tool box on the first page of their journals with a section labeled "contents." As the sessions progress, each new communication tool gained will be written in this section.

Session 2

Purpose. The purpose of this second session is to guide students in beginning to identify their personal conflict responses and the origins of these behaviors.

Theme. The theme can best be thought of as one of becoming aware. Students are beginning the process of empowerment by identifying their common behaviors.

Activities. Session 2 begins with a brief review of the ground rules and a check-in period involving scaling and explanation, and an invitation to share observations from the Conflict Journals.

The second activity involves completion of the Discover Your Style! worksheet found in Appendix A by each member. This questionnaire is then discussed, including a description of each anger style and its implications for behavior.

Students then design an Anger Map, in which influential people in a member's life (parents/guardians, siblings, friends, and so on) are represented by circles drawn surrounding a "self circle." Within each circle the student describes how each of the people on the Anger Map reacts when feeling angry. Students should be invited to share their Anger Maps with the group and describe any similarities they observe between their own personal anger behaviors and those of the other people on their Anger Map.

The session should be wrapped up with a checkout, during which students may be given time to reflect on their conflict style and its origin and influences. In addition, based on what was learned during the session, students should be asked to make a note regarding the conflict style used each time anger is recorded in the Conflict Journal during the following week.

Process. The ability of group members to feel safe is extremely important in this session, making the review of ground rules absolutely necessary. The facilitator may also frequently find that students are not ready to begin divulging information and sharing personal experiences at this early stage. To help the flow of the group, the fa-

cilitator should participate in all activities and be willing to "get the ball rolling" if need be.

Prior to the conflict style activity, the facilitator should let students know that conflict is a part of everyday life—something everybody experiences, but our responses can be very different from those of other people and result in different consequences. This idea normalizes conflict and may decrease a certain sense of resistance and/or defensiveness. Following scoring of the questionnaire, the facilitator should let students discuss the possible positive and negative consequences of each style. The facilitator should guide students in discovering that attempts to talk calmly and get all the necessary facts is the most effective way to resolve conflict.

Before the Anger Map activity, the leader may explain that we usually learn some of our anger behaviors from other people in our lives. As the idea of learning one's behaviors from models is introduced, it is important that the facilitator begin to emphasize that once individuals are aware of the influences in their lives they become responsible for choosing which of these behaviors they will continue to use in their lives, and therefore become responsible for their own behaviors. While students will likely enjoy the feeling of empowerment, they may also be resistant to claiming full responsibility for their actions. It is not necessary to repeatedly make a strong point of this concept, but the facilitator should consistently work phrases emphasizing choice and ownership of behavior into discussions. These students have patterns of blaming others, and altering these attributions takes time.

In addition, by reviewing the entries in the Conflict Journals, students are held accountable for tracking and reflecting on their conflict responses.

Session 3

Purpose. The purpose of this session is to continue the awareness process while introducing members to a predictable cycle of conflict. Members also begin to identify many possible conflict responses and resulting consequences. Finally, students begin the process of acquiring tools to deal with stressful situations.

Theme. As mentioned, the theme of session 3 is one of continued awareness combined with the acquisition of skills.

Activities. Once again a check-in period begins the session. The check-in should consist of each member scaling their present mood with a brief explanation, and being given the opportunity to share observations from the Conflict Journal.

The conflict styles from last week should be briefly reviewed. Students should be asked to recall the characteristics of each style and be encouraged to give examples—preferably personal. For each style have members list the pros and cons of the style and the associated behavior.

Then ask students to construct an Anger Awareness Cycle, with only headings of each stage written at this point (see Appendix B). Give brief descriptions or examples of each stage as noted in the example. Following these descriptions, ask students to recall a situation from the past week in which they felt angry. On their Anger Awareness Cycle pages, members are given time to apply their particular situation to the cycle, listing specific characteristics of the anger situation under each phase. For example, under the "Early Warning Signs" phase, a student might write, "face got hot, jaw got tight, hands were sweaty, brow furrowed." Next, ask for volunteers from the group to share their situation by writing responses on a chalkboard or dry erase board. This is not a time for judgment or evaluation of the individual's responses.

Following the Anger Awareness Cycle activity, ask students to brainstorm as many different possible anger responses as they can think of (e.g., hit the person, walk away). There is no evaluation of responses at this point. These responses should be written on the left-hand side of a chalkboard or dry erase board, with room for two more columns. Once students have come up with a list of anger responses, they should be asked to think of pros and cons (possible consequences) for responding in each of the given ways (these make up the other two columns). Discuss which responses seem to have the most positive and least negative consequences.

After evaluation of the anger responses, introduce a breathing relaxation technique. Have each student visualize a situation in which they can feel themselves beginning to get angry. Encourage them to think about what they are feeling that lets them know they are starting to get angry (early warning signs). Then, ask members to close their eyes and take a slow breath in through the nose, feeling the chest and stomach rise with the breath. Students should hold the breath for one to two seconds, and then slowly release it through their mouths. Ask them to take four more breaths in a similar manner.

Ask students to make a note of the breathing technique in their Conflict Journals ("Tool Box Contents" section). Students should be asked to use the breathing exercise the next time they feel themselves beginning to feel their early warning signs. Let them know they will be given time in the next group to share how this technique worked for them.

Finish with a checkout period in which students scale once again, and are given a chance to reflect on what they have learned.

Process. As students share personal situations and responses during this session, it is very important that the facilitator help to maintain a safe and nonjudgmental climate. Members should never be asked "What did John do wrong?" or other such personally critical questions. Instead, members may be asked to brainstorm as many positive and negative consequences as possible that

would be likely to occur for a particular response style. This method objectively evaluates each response and recognizes that even responses that are ineffective overall do serve a positive purpose or function of some sort for the individual—if they did not, they would not be used repeatedly. Students are likely to begin to realize, however, that verbal and physical fighting have many more negative than positive results. The students may need to be guided to this discovery by the facilitator through open-ended questions.

The relaxation technique at the end of the session should be introduced as a method of relaxing oneself when one first feels the early warning signs identified during the session. Members may be told that sometimes taking a few seconds to relax and collect one's thoughts is calming enough to help the individual avoid reacting too quickly or aggressively to a conflict situation.

Session 4

Purpose. The purpose of session 4 is to help students become aware of the expanse of explanations for the precursors of any conflict situation, and the value of exploring these explanations before reacting to assumptions. In addition, the members are introduced to additional communication tools with an opportunity to practice within the safety of the group setting.

Theme. The theme is one of continued awareness, combined with the acquisition and practice of new skills.

Activities. This session's check-in includes scaling and an opportunity to share how the breathing technique worked for the individuals. Ask students to reflect on whether or not the technique was a good one for them and if they would use it again.

Next, beginning with one of the situations from the Discover Your Style! questionnaire used previously, ask members to answer the following questions either verbally or on notebook paper: What is the problem? What are possible explanations for the situation? (List at least three.) What are the alternatives for responding? (List as many as possible.) What are the consequences of each alternative? This activity may be done a second time using a situation suggested by a member. Discussion and sharing of ideas should occur after each situational evaluation. Students should be guided to recognize that for each situation, multiple explanations may make perfect sense, and until all the facts are gathered it is difficult to thoroughly assess the situation.

The students may then be introduced to "active listening" as a technique for gathering the necessary facts in a situation. Active listening skills include paying attention to both verbal and nonverbal communication (body language), clarifying and asking questions to get a clear picture and showing interest ("You mentioned your brother—is he older or younger than you?"), rephrasing and reflecting statements back to the speaker, and checking on the feelings of the speaker ("It sounds like you felt pretty frustrated when your brother wouldn't turn his music down"). Then, in partners, students practice these skills. This practice can be done in a number of ways. For example, students may be instructed to select one item their partner has with him or her and ask the partner about that object ("Could you please tell me about that pencil?"). An easier format may be to give the group a topic so each pair is discussing the same topic as other groups ("If you had a perfect day, what would you be doing?" "Tell about your favorite activity"). Each partner should be given an opportunity to be both the speaker and the listener, and each individual session should last around 5 minutes. This practice should be done multiple times with different topics, each followed by a brief discussion reflecting what students like about active listening, what was most difficult, and possibly sharing with the group one interesting piece of information learned about the partner through use of the technique.

Following this practice activity, ask students to brainstorm ways in which these active listening techniques could be helpful in a conflict situation and to contemplate when in the anger flow would be the most helpful point at which to use active listening.

Students should then write "active listening" in the Tools section of their Conflict Journals, accompanied by a goal to utilize the skills in their next conflict situations. Under "active listening" have students write "muscle relaxation," and guide them through progressive muscle relaxation: Students begin by lying on the floor spread out (for groups with more vulnerable members, sitting in chairs may feel safer). Members are guided quietly through systematically tensing and relaxing each group of muscles, beginning with the face and moving downward, ending with the feet. Each tensing phase lasts approximately 5 seconds, followed by 5–8 seconds of relaxing the particular muscle group. This activity may be accompanied by relaxing music (no lyrics).

The session ends with a checkout, including reflection on the techniques learned, scaling, and sharing of any additional goals students would like to work on for the following week.

Process. Often individuals make assumptions regarding others' feelings and/or reasons for action. It is important for the facilitator to help students to recognize that assumptions do not always create a true picture. By having students brainstorm many possible explanations for various situations, they are encouraged to consider multiple possibilities. The value of being in a group will be clearly seen in this activity, as each member is likely to see the given situations very differently, and peer interaction allows members to see differences in interpretation. As always, the facilitator must encourage respect for each member's contributions.

The active listening practice is a crucial bridge between becoming aware of the differing thoughts and feelings of others and actually learning to communicate with others in a way that allows members to rely on facts rather than assumptions. In addition, students should be guided to recognize that while active listening is most helpful at the very beginning phases of the conflict cycle, they can be used effectively at any point.

Session 5

Purpose. The purpose of this session is to begin to make connections between the principles learned and to put them into practice.

Theme. The theme here is effective communication through practice. As members begin to utilize their new skills in a variety of role-play situations, they will become more comfortable with the idea of using these tools in life outside the group.

Activities. The check-in period for session 5 includes brief scaling and an opportunity to share situations in which students used active listening. Students should also be encouraged to share difficulties they may have had with their goals and/or with using the active listening skills learned. Students should be asked if they would be open to receiving any feedback from other group members regarding the difficulties they encountered. If so, group members should be instructed to give only suggestions or positive feedback, rather than criticisms of the student's difficulties.

The check-in will likely open the door for the next activity, in which a student volunteers her or his situation for role-play. The student presents the trigger situation only at this point, and two members act it out. The group is then asked to identify the possible feelings of the people involved in the conflict and possible alternate explanations or misunderstandings that could have led up to this conflict. The group may even find it helpful to ask the role-players how they felt as they acted out the situation. Next, the group should be asked to brainstorm a list of possible responses to the situation, and time is taken to role-play each one. The possible consequences of each response are listed and discussed. This process may be repeated with multiple situations as time allows, but adequate discussion time should be allowed following each role-play. Give as many students as possible an opportunity to participate in the actual role-playing roles.

Then ask students to choose one of the techniques role-played to put into practice in their next conflict. They should be asked to write down how each conflict was ended or resolved, whether or not the techniques practiced were actually used in the students' particular situations.

Another relaxation technique may be introduced at this time, followed by a checkout (including scaling), and reflection on the session's activities.

Process. The most important part of session 5 is providing members with as many opportunities to practice their new skills as possible within the safety of the group setting. The facilitator should note that students may encounter frustration at first as they get used to using different communication styles than they are used to. The facilitator should remind students they have been using the same techniques for the majority of their lives and it will take some time and practice to become accustomed to using new methods. The climate must remain positive, geared toward practice, learning, and focused on the small successes. In addition, the facilitator should ask for student suggestions for situations to role-play as often as possible. Using student ideas ensures that the encounters and subsequent practice are applicable to the members' lives.

Session 6

Purpose. The purpose of session 6 is to teach another concept in effective communication after increasing personal awareness yet again, followed by additional practice time.

Theme. The themes, then, are awareness, skill acquisition, and practice.

Activities. Check-in for session 6 is very similar to that for previous sessions. Students do scaling and briefly discuss their goals for the previous week, including any successes and/or difficulties encountered. Students may be given an opportunity to bring up for discussion any situations they encountered but were unsure as to how to resolve.

    Members are then presented with an Assertiveness Questionnaire (see Appendix C), which they are given a few minutes to complete. Then, guide the students in scoring the questionnaire, followed by definitions of both assertion and aggression given by the facilitator. These definitions should be discussed in general, in comparison and contrast to each other, and as they apply to various conflict situations (see definitions in the process section). Address the concept of "I statements" ("When I hear, 'you're stupid,' I feel hurt and embarrassed," rather than "You make me feel . . .").

    Follow this discussion by role-playing situations suggested by students (format similar to session 5) in which assertiveness principles and "I statements" are practiced. Following one or two role-plays in front of the group, students may break off into groups of two or three and be given situations to role-play using the principles learned. After each practice situation, allow time for reflection and discussion. "I statements" and "Assertiveness" should be added to the "Tool Box."

    Goals for this session should revolve around "I statements" and using assertiveness, and should be written in the "Goals" portions of the Conflict Journal.

    Checkout is similar to previous sessions.

Process. Up to this session, many concepts of assertiveness have been presented and practiced without being given a name. Students should be told that many students say they fight to make sure others "don't mess with" them or walk all over them. Being assertive rather than aggressive allows individuals to feel that they have made a point without the severe consequences that often accompany aggression. Assertion involves standing up for one's own rights without stepping on the rights of others. The basis of assertion is that everyone is entitled to consideration and respect, including oneself (Goldstein & Rosenbaum, 1982). Students should be guided to see that aggression involves hurting others, and being passive often is hurtful to oneself. Assertiveness is identified at this point in the group as a preferred communication technique because now students have had experiences to support its effectiveness and also a framework in which to fit this direct information. Students should be asked to reflect upon the various techniques they have learned and practiced over the past few weeks and comment on which are assertive behaviors.

Session 7

Purpose. The purpose of this session is to reflect on any changes and/or successes seen in the past few weeks, in addition to a brief reflection on what has been learned thus far and an assessment of goals.

Theme. The theme here is one of beginning to wrap things up.

Activities. Check-in for session 7 is similar to that of previous group meetings. Ask members to spend a few minutes (approximately 15–20 minutes) reading through their Conflict Journals and reflecting on any differences between their anger responses in the first few weeks and their responses in the last couple of weeks. The students should be instructed to summarize these observations in a couple of paragraphs. This writing period may be carried out in an open fashion for some groups, but it may be more appropriate in most situations to guide their written reflections with specific questions such as: What was your most common conflict response during the first three weeks? What was your most common conflict response during the last few sessions? What techniques that we've learned have you found most helpful? Have you been surprised by any social encounters you've had in the past few weeks? What has been your greatest social success in the past 6 weeks? Students may then be given an opportunity to share their reflections with the group.

    Ask students if there is anything else they feel they would like/have liked to gain from the group. Attempt to meet any easily met needs, and help students brainstorm ways in which they can meet their other needs and accomplish these other goals.

    Checkout may be similar to previous sessions.

Process. The basic group process for this session is described within the description of this week's activities.

Session 8

Purpose. The purpose of this final session is to tie up any loose ends, review and reflect on the principles presented, and bring closure to the group.

Themes. The theme is one of summing up what has been learned and appreciating the successes that have occurred over the past couple of months.

Activities. Check-in is similar to previous sessions, but encourage students to express how they are feeling about this being the final session.

Now that students have had an additional week to reflect on their Conflict Journals and their progress, allow time for discussion of any further observations.

Briefly review each of the principles, ideas, and tools covered in the past 7 weeks, with time for discussion or clarification if needed.

Suggest that the group meet in 3 months and again in 6 months to evaluate further progress, any issues or difficulties which may have arisen, and for continued support from group members.

If a peer mediation/conflict mediation program is in place at the school, suggest that students apply to participate in the program, and remind students that even if they do not choose to become an official mediator, they still have learned many tools that are helpful in conflict situations and they can even help their friends and families to acquire these skills.

Checkout for this session may involve any reflection on the group in general. In addition, group members may be encouraged to express any appreciation they feel toward other group members.

Process. It is important that the facilitator allow adequate time for discussion of closure feelings, during both the check-in and checkout periods. Since students in a school setting will continue to see each other on a regular basis, departure may not be a significant issue. However, members may have other fears. For example, students may be concerned that they will not be able to remember and continue to practice their new skills without the weekly reiteration of the group sessions. Students should be reminded they have all the tools they need both inside them and in their notebooks if they need a reminder. Students should also be given a chance to express encouragement to each other, as peers are very influential during adolescence and because peer encouragement is not as expected as that from the facilitator.

Additional process points are mentioned in the description of activities.

STRATEGIES TO EVALUATE THE GROUP

The facilitator may use the evaluation form in Appendix D to assess the benefits obtained by group members in accordance with the original group goals.

REFERRAL PROCEDURES FOR FOLLOW-UP

This group is designed to meet the needs of a population of frequently disciplined students in a school setting. The activities and process are intended to help members increase awareness of personal conflict responses, develop new tools for dealing with conflict, and give students an opportunity to gradually become comfortable using their new skills. It should be noted that because every school is set up differently and all group members will have different needs and personalities, the facilitator is not expected to follow the activities and process precisely. The facilitator should remain flexible and be willing to adjust the group to meet the needs of the students involved. In addition, many related videos and books are available and may be added to any session if deemed appropriate by the facilitator, as long as they coincide with the goals of the group.

Finally, the facilitator may notice that some members have remaining needs that are significant and should be addressed beyond the scope of the group. As most school counselors do not do an extensive amount of personal counseling, the counselor should discuss options for referral with the student and parents. These referral options may include a list of local counselors and psychologists or community agencies that address the student's specific issues.

REFERENCES

Capuzzi, D., & Gross, D. R. (1998). *Introduction to group counseling.* Denver: Love Publishing.

Capuzzi, D., & Gross, D. R. (1999). *Counseling and psychotherapy: Theories and interventions.* Upper Saddle River, NJ: Merrill/Prentice-Hall.

Domjan, M. (1998). *The principles of learning and behavior.* Albany: Brooks/Cole.

Goldstein, A. P., & Rosenbaum, A. (1982). *Aggress-Less: How to turn anger and aggression into positive action.* Englewood Cliffs, NJ: Prentice-Hall.

Gurman, A. S., & Messer, S. B. (1995). *Essential psychotherapies: Theory and practice.* New York: The Guilford Press.

Lefrancois, G. R. (1996). *The Lifespan.* Albany: Wadsworth.

DISCOVER YOUR STYLE!

Picture yourself in each of the following situations. Select the response that best matches how you would react.

1. Your older brother is playing football with some neighborhood kids. When one of the boys asks if you'd like to join them, your brother tells them you don't play very well. You:
   a. yell at your brother, calling him a big jerk.
   b. go inside and kick the toy your little sister is playing with as you pass.
   c. go up to your room and look for something else to do.
   d. pull your brother away from the group for a minute and let him know that what he said hurt your feelings.

2. During the drama presentation you acted in you forgot a couple of lines and had to be prompted by the drama teacher. After the play some kids tease you about the incident. Among them is one of your close friends. You:
   a. push your friend down and scream at your friend.
   b. make fun of another actor who forgot even more lines than you did.
   c. brush past them, tell your parents you're ready to leave, and decide not to mention your anger to your friend the next day.
   d. wait until you have time alone with your friend and tell your friend how embarrassed and hurt you felt by what he said.

3. Your friend shows up at the prom with the exact same dress as you. She was with you when you picked it out and knew how excited you were about finding the "perfect dress." You:
   a. blow up at your friend and dump your punch down the front of her dress.
   b. glare at your date and step on his toes when he tells you how wonderful you look.
   c. try to hide how upset you are and try to forget that you two look like twins.
   d. send the guys to get punch and tell your friend you're embarrassed and ask why she bought the same dress.

4. You ask your friend to come to the opening of the new cool pizza place. He says he has to help his dad with yard work. You decide to take your brother instead, but when you get to the restaurant, you see your friend there with another kid from school. You:
   a. march up to your friend, call him a liar, and tell him your friendship is over.
   b. throw your brother's plate onto the table with such force you knock over his drink.
   c. decide not to say anything to your friend and go ahead and order your pizza like nothing happened.
   d. call your friend later that evening to ask for an explanation.

Count the number of times you selected each letter and write that number below.

a's _____ Act out your anger   c's _____ All bottled up!

b's _____ Take it out on others   d's _____ Attempt to resolve conflict

APPENDIX B

ANGER AWARENESS CYCLE

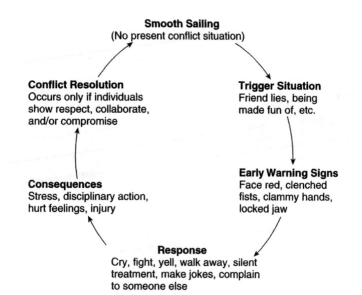

Smooth Sailing
(No present conflict situation)

Conflict Resolution
Occurs only if individuals
show respect, collaborate,
and/or compromise

Trigger Situation
Friend lies, being
made fun of, etc.

Consequences
Stress, disciplinary action,
hurt feelings, injury

Early Warning Signs
Face red, clenched
fists, clammy hands,
locked jaw

Response
Cry, fight, yell, walk away, silent
treatment, make jokes, complain
to someone else

APPENDIX C

ASSERTIVENESS QUESTIONNAIRE

Please circle your most likely response to each of the following situations.

1. You and a friend are seated at a restaurant waiting to have your order taken. Several people who came in after you have already been waited on, but you have not. You:
   a. remain quiet and assume they will eventually come take your order.
   b. angrily call out to the waiter that if you are not served immediately you will be speaking to his manager.
   c. calmly get the attention of one of the waiters and explain your situation.

2. A friend who doesn't have her license and doesn't like riding the bus asks you for a ride to school tomorrow morning. You were planning to get to school early tomorrow to set up some props for a presentation and talk to one of your teachers. The friend really wants a ride, but doesn't want to get up early and pressures you to leave at the regular time. You:
   a. explain you would be happy to give her a ride, but it's really important to you to take care of things tomorrow, and you will be planning to leave early. Then you suggest a couple of others who you don't think would mind giving her a ride.
   b. angrily yell that she doesn't care anything about your feelings or what's important to you and you don't need friends like that. Then you hang up.
   c. quietly agree to pick her up at the regular time, thinking angrily that you will probably get a failing grade on your presentation, because you won't be prepared.

3. Your basketball coach announces the starting line-up for tomorrow's game, and although you have been starting all season, this time your name is replaced by a teammate's. You:
   a. say nothing, but sit angrily on the bench, keeping track of the number of times the other player makes a mistake.
   b. pull your coach aside before the game and explain that you have been working hard in practice and thought you'd been playing well, and explain that you are confused as to why your starting position was taken away.
   c. jump up angrily and say, "What?!? Are you a moron? He can't play worth beans!"

(Remove this portion when giving questionnaire to students.)

Properly assertive responses:

1. c
2. a
3. b

APPENDIX D

GROUP EVALUATION

Please use the rating scale below to evaluate the following statements:

Strongly Agree	Agree	Undecided	Disagree	Strongly Disagree
4	3	2	1	0

1. The facilitator was knowledgeable and presented material clearly.

   _____

2. The facilitator modeled and encouraged positive interaction among group members.

   _____

3. Due to group activities, I discovered/became aware of my common responses to conflict.

   _____

4. I learned about new ways to communicate with others in conflict situations.

   _____

5. I was given adequate opportunity to practice new techniques (active listening, assertiveness, and so on) during group time.

   _____

6. I feel comfortable using the techniques taught in this group in my daily interactions.

   _____

7. I felt safe and comfortable sharing personal information and ideas with other group members.

   _____

8. I feel I have several tools for dealing with difficult conflict situations in my life.

   _____

Please feel free to comment on any of your responses above or any other matter concerning the group:

_____

_____

_____

_____

_____

CHAPTER 11

ADOLESCENTS OF DIVORCE: A SCHOOL-BASED INTERVENTION

Rachel Lilienthal-Stair

PURPOSE

Educators find that a growing proportion of their students come from divorced families (Scrivner-Blum, 1990). Divorce often brings about the severance of family relationships. Although the support of others cannot minimize the pain associated with these torn relationships, a network of supportive people can help to make the pain bearable. School counselors are a part of the students' daily environment and can serve as one component of the support system.

The purpose of this group is to provide a supportive, safe, and nonjudgmental environment in which adolescent students can express their feelings about the divorce. The group will also help members learn from others' experiences how to cope with problems arising from the separation/divorce of natural parents (Scrivner-Blum, 1990).

CONCEPTUAL FRAMEWORK

Each year, a new large group of adolescents joins the growing number of those whose parents have divorced. From the adolescents' viewpoint, the loss of the familiar everyday presence of the parent who has left the household is often a major event that initiates a cascade of consequences (Buchanan, Maccoby, & Dornbusch, 1996). Consequences that follow a divorce can contribute to the adolescent displaying at-risk behaviors. These consequences of divorce affect adolescents, family, and society.

Group approaches for adolescents of divorced families are powerful intervention strategies. Intervention in the schools is particularly likely to reach adolescents in need of help who are unlikely to receive help in other ways (Hodges, 1991). Without the group, adolescents may be hesitant or skeptical of resources available to them and not seek help in coping with their new family configuration. Research completed by Sprinthall, Hall, & Gerler (1994) has shown that such adolescents do not seek school counseling services because of the perception that school counselors are already too busy with other tasks. Once these obstacles are out of the way, and the adolescent is connected with a school counselor, the adolescent may begin to experience the benefits of being a member of a group and connected with a school counselor.

Several school-based interventions have been developed to help adolescents cope with the divorce of their parents. A supportive environment in which adolescents can learn more complex methods of processing their experiences will be most beneficial (Paisley & Hubbard, 1994). A research study completed by Richardson & Rosen (1999) found that adolescents of divorce who perceived themselves as having more overall support had lower scores on measures of post-divorce difficulties, anxiety, and worry, and higher scores on measures of openness about the divorce and positive resources. This research supports the effects of helping adolescents cope with their parents' divorce.

During a time of familial disruption, schools can play an essential part as a resource of nurturance and continuity. Parent, teacher, and peer support are components of the resources available to an adolescent at school. This support is one step in building a comprehensive intervention plan. In addition to these resources, skill building focused on emotional expression and coping is the second component. Finally, an intervention that is flexible and accommodates diversity in age, gender, ethnicity, and socioeconomic status is also significant (Richardson & Rosen, 1999). Including these three components will create a beneficial and comprehensive intervention plan.

Group interventions can be effective for a variety of reasons. An individual's need for belonging can be met in a small group in which members may share their thoughts. This process is instrumental in coping with a life change such as divorce. Divorce groups can also be an effective prevention-intervention strategy to support adolescents and maximize learning in the school environment.

Finally, school-based groups can be a powerful and potent method of meeting the needs of large numbers of students at risk from dysfunctional families (Costa & Stiltner, 1994). Structured groups can teach students how to cope with crisis, like divorce, through group discussions, role-plays, and the use of drawing and collages. School-based groups can provide the opportunity for positive personal growth in the wake of a divorce.

GROUP GOALS

These group goals are suggested as a framework to build upon. These goals may be accommodated to meet the needs of the students in the group.

1. To help members identify, express, and understand their feelings.
2. To promote understanding of divorce-related issues and clarify divorce-related misconceptions.
3. To develop and apply skills in regards to problem solving and communicating.
4. To emphasize self-worth and positive feelings toward themselves.
5. To listen to and understand the feelings of others in similar situations.

PRE-GROUP SCREENING AND ORIENTATION

Screening group members is a crucial task in preparation for the group. According to Fields & Smead (1998), 50 percent of a group's success can be accounted for by the appropriate selection of members. This task can be viewed as one with several steps in order to select members that would most benefit from the group experience.

The first step is identifying potential group members. This step can be accomplished by a referral to the counselor made by a parent, teacher, or administrator. If one of these people does refer a student, the counselor should follow-up by gathering additional information to help with the selection process. The additional information may include any academic or behavioral concerns

that could pertain to group placement. This information, in conjunction with the information gathered by an interview with the student, would assist the counselor in determining if the group is appropriate.

Referral is only one way a student may be connected with the group screening process. The counselor may identify potential members from daily interactions with the students. As a result of a comprehensive counseling program at the school, the counselor would be widely available for the students. Thus, the counselor would be aware of any students that are currently coping with a divorce and may need additional support from the group.

Once there is a group of students that the counselor believes would benefit from group, there are three guiding principles that Hodges (1991) identifies as part of the screening process. The first guiding principle is to select a few members that have relatively good coping skills. These members may prove to be helpful role models for the others in the group. Second, the counselor should assess the degree of problems a student has around the divorce, paying particular attention to comments made about depression and self-harm. Students that exhibit any immediate distress may be better served by participating in individual counseling sessions. By interviewing, the counselor is given the opportunity to screen for these areas.

During the interview process, the counselor should also explain to the student the purpose and goals of the group. In providing this information, the student will be able to make the educated decision if the group will be beneficial for him or her. If a student confirms that he or she is interested in participating, the counselor should obtain parental consent before the group begins. This practice can vary from each individual school district. Often, a letter is sent home to parents/guardians to inform them of the purpose of the group and ask for their consent.

Finally, the important outcome is that a group can function together and form a cohesive, supportive whole (Fields & Smead, 1998). The ideal group size ranges between 8 and 10 members. This number of group members works well with adolescents since it provides the opportunity for each member to share during the group sessions.

OUTLINE FOR EIGHT GROUP SESSIONS

Session 1

Purpose. The purpose of this session is to provide time for group members to become acquainted with one another.

Theme. "What do I represent?" Students provide their ideas on rules for the group. The introduction time provides students with the opportunity to share and understand what group will be like. Taking the time to get acquainted should help ease the anxiety that may be present from participating in the group.

Activities. Materials needed for this session: an assortment of pictures of people, flowers, scenes, animals, and objects cut out of magazines; glue; scissors; and small pieces of oak tag.

Once members are greeted by the leader, students take turns going around the circle they are seated in to say their name and their favorite cartoon character out loud. After everyone has had the chance to participate in the activity, ask students to select a picture out of the assortment that represents themselves. Once they select the picture (or pictures if they choose), they should glue them on the piece of oak tag. After each person is finished, there will be time for each member to share his or her picture. This time the leader begins and goes in the opposite direction from the opening activity.

After the members have shared their pictures, initiate a discussion to develop group rules. First ask if any group member has any ideas. As rules are suggested, write them down. Identifying behaviors that are acceptable for the group should be a part of the rules. Some examples of the group rules are the following:

- I will be a good listener. This means I will make eye contact and keep quiet while someone is speaking.
- I will show respect to other group members. This means I will respect opinions of group members even if I do not agree with them.
- I will keep what is said in group confidential. This means I will not tell anyone who is in my group or what anyone shares.
- I will use "I statements" in response or giving a member feedback.

The group's closing activity is to take turns going around the circle sharing what their favorite food is. Remind students when and where to meet for the next session before this session is completed.

Process. The leader is to set up an environment that is non-threatening and safe. The leader should set up the area in a way that promotes this atmosphere. The area should be in a private, quiet location with comfortable chairs set up in a circle. This should be taken care of before the session.

The leader also provides the group with structure by modeling appropriate sharing behaviors. Members are given the opportunity to get to know one another by engaging in these activities. Many students may know each other already, so these activities may give them a new dimension of a classmate.

By including the members in setting the rules, they become more a part of the group process. The members have contributed to making the rules rather than having the rules imposed upon them. This process can help to clarify the rules and get the members' commitment to them. By writing them down, they serve as a visual reminder for each future session.

Anxiety may be present during this first session. Group members may be feeling uncomfortable and unsure of what to expect from the group. Open and close the first session by using light-hearted and nonthreatening activities. By having the members state what their favorite cartoon character and food is provides them with something personal to share without disclosing a lot of information. Hopefully, by keeping this session relatively structured, it reduces the anxiety and uncertainty that the members may be feeling.

Each session is structured in the same format as session 1. There will be a check-in at the opening of the group, an activity focused on the theme of the session, and a closing activity. Each group member will be asked during the check-in time if he or she needs time to talk about any presenting issues. Flexibility in the session format will be necessary.

Session 2

Purpose. This session provides students with the opportunity to focus on skill building. Skill building includes the activities to help students express their feelings, and to increase their interpersonal relationship skills.

Theme. "Express yourself." Students are encouraged to identify, express, and share their feelings with the group. Students first practice these skills before applying them to themselves.

Activities. Materials needed for this session: pictures of an adolescent student displaying sad and happy emotions, paper, and pencils.

This session begins with a check-in activity. Members are asked to express how they feel on a scale of 1 to 10. (1 is having a bad day or feeling down and 10 is having a good day or feeling very good). After they rate themselves, they are given the opportunity to ask for "time" after the check-in.

After check-in, show a picture of an adolescent that is happy. Group members are to write down their answers to these questions in regards to the picture:

- What is the student feeling?
- How do you know the student feels this way?

Once members write down their responses to these questions, they take turns sharing their answers. Pay attention to the nonverbal cues for responses to the second question.

Next, select a picture of an adolescent that is angry and ask members to answer the same questions. After each group member is given time to share, ask the group the following questions:

- Why is it important to know how someone else feels?
- Have you ever had someone misunderstand how you were feeling? Were you able to tell him or her your true feelings?
- What could you do if you were not sure how someone else was feeling?

Each member should be given time to share his or her responses to these three questions. As members identify a strategy to clear up a misconception about feelings (whether their own feelings or someone else's), the leader should write these on a piece of paper for everyone to see.

As a closing activity, ask members to identify one strategy that they could use in their relationships with others.

Process. As the main activity begins, the leader should first answer the questions regarding the picture of the adolescent that looks happy. The leader should model for the members how to identify, using nonverbal cues, someone's emotions. By having the leader answer the questions first, the members are given an example of an appropriate response. This is important as the members begin to talk about their own feelings. The leader demonstrates a way to express.

The leader should also demonstrate a strategy on how to ask someone how he or she is feeling. Students may not have seen this modeled before. It could be a new experience for them to observe an adult that is expressing intense emotions without being destructive either physically or emotionally. Members should be encouraged to share their ideas. Members can learn from others that are especially verbal in expressing themselves.

Session 3

Purpose. The purpose of this session is to extend the emotional expression skill building from last session.

Theme. "My feelings about divorce." Students identify their feelings about divorce and express them using a list of "feeling words."

Activities. Materials needed-list of "feeling words" such as:

resentful	ashamed	discouraged
down	strengthless	bitter
special	depressed	depressed
thankful	nervous	relieved
excited	safe	courageous
concerned	brave	abandoned
frustrated	helpless	guilty
lonely	powerless	fearful
disappointed	afraid	unsafe
terrific	fine	joyful
betrayed	happy	protected
miserable	special	worried
anxious	left out	accepting

This session begins with a similar check-in from session 2. Members rate how they are feeling on a scale of 1 to 10. After everyone checks in, distribute the list of "feeling words" to each group member. Then ask mem-

bers to circle words on the list that describe how they feel about divorce. Members should be encouraged to share their feelings with the group.

The session closes with an appreciation activity. Members are given the chance to state who or what they appreciate today. They can acknowledge someone or something about the group or someone or something from their personal life.

Process. In this session, the leader is helping students begin to deal with their feelings about divorce. As the students reveal their feelings, the leader should keep in mind that this might not be a simple task for some. Members may need to vent their feelings. Venting their emotions may empower the member; however, the leader should be able to make the distinction between venting and continual griping. Focus on helping members problem solve to better meet their needs instead of allowing continual griping about the situation. This way, students also take control of the situation and thus start to gain empowerment.

Another skill the leader has a chance to build upon is empathy training. Having a group member state appreciation by paraphrasing something another member has said can be a catalyst. Paraphrasing is helpful training in building empathy. Members may find, in the closing activity, that they appreciate that group members' listen and can relate to what they are saying.

Session 4

Purpose. The purpose of this session is to explore reactions to positive/negative family changes and to clarify issues of concern in members' lives.

Theme. "Life lines." Members share their reactions and feelings to change in their family configurations. New family configurations may include stepparents, biological parents, and a parent's boyfriend or girlfriend.

Activities. Materials needed: long pieces of butcher paper and markers.

To begin the session, ask members to identify a color that they feel like today and explain why. After the check-in, ask members to draw a life line representing the major events in their lives—birth, where they lived, and things that happened to them in their lives up to the present time. The line can be straight, jagged, or curved. A reasonable amount of time should be given for each member to finish the life line so everyone can have enough time to share at the end.

For the closure activity, members identify areas of their own life line that they like or give feedback to other group members about their life line. The feedback should be positive—either something they identify with, have in common, or appreciate.

Process. Members are given the opportunity to share with the group how and when the divorce occurred in their life using the life line activity. Since this could be the first time the member has told his or her story to anyone, the leader should be aware of this situation. Confidentiality must be stressed again. Members should be encouraged by the leader to practice using active listening skills. Members should be encouraged to first listen to each person before responding using an "I statement" or sharing a life line. The leader should allow members to have their turn to share while controlling tangential responses from the members.

The leader should not be too worried about students that seldom talk as long as they are monitoring the process. Quiet members can learn from watching even if they do not feel comfortable speaking.

Session 5

Purpose. The purpose of this session is to promote understanding of divorce-related concepts and to clarify divorce-related misconceptions. This session also helps to enhance students' positive perceptions of themselves.

Theme. "Why did my parents get a divorce?" Members are given the chance to explore for themselves the reasons why their parents divorced.

Activities. Materials needed: large piece of butcher paper hung on the wall and markers.

This session will begin with members rating how they feel on a scale of 1 to 10. After the check-in, place a large piece of butcher paper on the wall. Members brainstorm ideas on why they think their parents divorced. If a student wants to list a reason that is already on the chart, make a tally mark next to the appropriate reason. By making this tally, the leader is showing the group that two or more students have the same reason.

After all students are given a chance to share their reasons, ask students to decide on two or three reasons that are most important to the group. Next, structure the role-playing of the problem situations.

The role-play should be kept simple and should only have 2–3 characters in each situation. Emphasize the point to be made in each situation and keep the role-play on that point. Students are assigned to parts in the role-play by selecting slips of paper with character names on them. Before the role-play begins, members discuss the individual characters' feelings, behaviors, and consequences. Group members not participating in the performing role-play should be observing.

After the role-play, each student is given time to focus on feelings, insight, and relate the role-play to personal experiences. For a closure activity, each member is asked to identify something or someone they appreciate from the role-play.

Process. The leader is opening the stage at this session for members to process why their parents divorced. Having members list their reasons helps the leader to

know if any members are blaming themselves for the divorce. This activity can also be a follow-up to the "feeling words" session—if members identified at that session that they were the reason for the divorce, see if they continue to feel that way.

Using role-plays is usually a tool to help students develop a better understanding of themselves and others as they relate to the situation. Processing after role-plays should focus on feelings or experiences in the different roles. Members should be encouraged to use "I statements" and describe their feelings. In the closing activity, members should be directed to share their appreciation rather than evaluate the role-play performance.

Session 6

Purpose. In this session the purpose is for members to share the important events in their lives. By sharing, members will begin to adjust to and accept their changing family situation.

Theme. "My family shield" (Brown, 1994). Members are encouraged to share their shield depicting their family. Members should also be encouraged to share the similarities and differences of their families.

Activities. Materials needed: blank pieces of paper, markers or colored pencils, example of family shield.

Members begin the session by rating how they are feeling on a scale of 1 to 10. After the check-in, ask members to draw the outline of a shield. (The leader should have a model of his or her own family shield completed ahead of time). Members should divide the shield into six parts. These parts do not have to be equal in size. The size can be left up to the member. Next, members can write statements of feelings or draw pictures about their family. If members need suggestions, they may put their responses to the following statements on their shield (Brown, 1994):

- Describe a happy time you spent with your family.
- Describe a sad time with your family.
- Describe a time you helped the family.
- Describe something your family does on the weekend.
- Draw three symbols or write three words that describe your family.

Once each member is finished drawing his or her shield, they can take turns sharing them. As a closing activity, ask members to pick out something in another group members' shield that they identify with or have in common.

Process. What makes this session work is that members are creating their own shield based on things that are important to them. By this session, members should be able to share their personal experiences and feelings since the environment is a safe one.

The leader is also disclosing more this session than in previous sessions by sharing their family shield. Thus, by doing so, it sets the stage for members to share their own experiences. Members are also encouraged to use "I statements" at the end of the session to express their appreciation for a fellow group member's shield.

Session 7

Purpose. The purpose of this session is to help members develop skills in problem solving and communication. Members also develop coping skills and ways to show empathy while expressing their own feelings.

Theme. "How do I cope with this?" Members learn to use the communication skill of empathic assertion. As a result of this skill, members feel more confident in coping with difficult family situations.

Activities. Materials needed: large piece of butcher paper and markers.

Members check in by rating how they feel on a scale of 1 to 10. After check-in, members list, on the butcher paper, as many problems of divorce that they can think of. Group members then select the two or three most important problems by group vote. Members first are given the choice for participating in a specific role-play. The goal is for each member to be involved in at least one role-play.

Members are given a situation that they will first practice in their small group. After they have come up with a coping strategy to deal with the problem, they will present their role-play. After each group performs, discussion should follow about alternative ways to cope with the problems that were not identified. As a closing activity, members are asked to select one coping strategy that they feel would be beneficial for them. Members should also be reminded that the next session is their last one and they should come prepared to share their appreciation for other group members.

Process. Members are encouraged by the leader to imagine how each character in the role-play feels and acts. By doing this, members are given the opportunity to develop strategies in dealing with the problems associated with divorce. Allowing the students to decide on the role-plays will increase the meaningfulness for them.

At this point of the group, members should be at the stage of applying the coping strategies and skills that they have learned from the group into practice in their daily lives. Identifying a coping strategy at the end of the session provides the members with a frame of reference for the rest of the week. Reminding members that the next session is their last prepares them for the culmination of the group experience. Informing the members to come prepared to share their appreciation reduces the feelings of being put on the spot, so to speak. This way, members have a period of time to think and reflect on the group process.

Session 8

Purpose. The purpose of this last session is to acknowledge the growth of each member and to talk about using the growth in the real world.

Theme. "Treasure chest." In this session, as a parting token of appreciation, each member takes part in filling a treasure chest for the other members. The items written down in the treasure chest should be a reflection of the growth process during the group sessions.

Activities. Materials needed: white sheets of paper with a treasure chest outline traced on it, markers, and colored pencils.

As the session begins, ask members to rate how they are feeling on a scale of 1 to 10. After the check-in, each member is given a copy of the treasure chest sheet. The leader starts with the member on his or her right-hand side. To begin, members pass their treasure chest to the member sitting next to them. They should draw a picture, write a few words, or write a symbol for how they see this member. Members are given the opportunity to explain what they are giving as the "treasure" and why. By the end of the session, each member should have a completed treasure chest. As a closing activity, members add to their own treasure chest a drawing, words, or symbol that is meaningful to them.

Process. Since this is the last session, this activity provides members an opportunity to do a perception check. Each item that is placed in their treasure chest serves not only as a reminder of the group, but as an affirmation of the member's contribution to the group. Adolescents at this stage of development often take peer comments to be very meaningful. By receiving a positive recognition from each member, it will contribute to their self-esteem and personal worth.

STRATEGIES TO EVALUATE THE GROUP

Give a survey to the group members at the end of the last session. This survey should be comprised of short-answer questions. These questions should be designed to measure the achievement of group goals and the procedures used to achieve the goals.

- What did you like about this group?
- What didn't you like about this group?
- What would you change if you were in charge of the group?
- Was there anything you really enjoyed or, on the other side, really disliked that we did in group?
- What did you learn by being in this group?
- Would you recommend this group to a friend that was going through a divorce? Why or why not?

REFERRAL PROCEDURES FOR FOLLOW-UP

As the group sessions culminate, members should be reminded of the resources available to them if they find they need support. One possible way to keep the connectedness and continuity of the group is by arranging a lunch time group once a month. This way, group members can stay connected and continue to be supportive of one another.

Another option for members is a referral to a peer-counseling group. Many schools have peer-counseling programs where students are connected to a peer (usually one that is a grade or two older). These peers can provide support to the student on a regular basis or as needed. Again, peer counseling can be a very effective and beneficial resource.

Finally, members that may need continued support could be referred to an outside agency. There are many resources in the community that can serve as an additional support for the student. Also, students should be reminded of additional support systems located within the school. The school counselor should follow-up with each group member individually after the last session. By doing so, the counselor will continue to be a part of the student's support network.

REFERENCES

Brown, N. W. (1994). *Group counseling for elementary and middle school children*. Westport: Praeger.

Buchanan, C., Maccoby, E., & Dornbusch, S. (1996). *Adolescents after divorce*. Cambridge: Harvard University Press.

Costa, L., & Stiltner, B. (1994). Why do the good things always end and the bad things go on forever: A family change counseling group. *The School Counselor, 41*, 300–304.

Fields, T. H., & Smead, R. (1998). Keys to leading successful school groups. In J. M. Allen (Ed.), *School counseling: New perspectives & practices* (pp. 55–58). Greensboro: ERIC/CASS Publications.

Hodges, W. F. (1991). *Interventions for children of divorce*. New York: John Wiley.

Paisley, P. O., & Hubbard, G. T. (Eds.) (1994). *Developmental school counseling programs: From theory to practice*. Alexandria, VA: American Counseling Association.

Richardson, C. D., & Rosen, L. A. (1999). School based interventions for children of divorce. *ASCA Professional School Counseling, 3*(1), 21–25.

Scrivner-Blum, D. J. (1990). *Group counseling for secondary schools*. Springfield, IL: Charles C. Thomas.

Sprinthall, N. A., Hall, J. S., & Gerler, E. R. (1994). Peer counseling for middle school students experiencing family divorce: A deliberate psychological educational model. In P. O. Paisley & G. T. Hubbard (Eds.), *Developmental school counseling programs: From theory to practice*. Alexandria, VA: American Counseling Association.

CHAPTER 12

HIGH SCHOOL STUDENTS REDISCOVERING ACADEMIC SUCCESS

Jeff Morris

PURPOSE

High school counselors across America face numerous challenges, and a variety of methods can be employed to meet these needs. Where appropriate, group-counseling sessions allow for efficient and effective personal growth. One often-overlooked need is the significantly large group of high school students who are not progressing in their coursework at a rate that ensures timely graduation. Many of these students themselves see their dire condition in time and make necessary corrections. However, many do not, and the counseling and cajoling done by teachers, counselors, parents, friends, and others do not turn all of them into graduates. These students, the subjects of this chapter's proposed group, seem to be stuck in unhealthy academic patterns and appear well on the way to becoming high school dropouts, or at best GED candidates.

The reasons for this lack of academic success are undoubtedly varied, and the group processes and member interactions will allow some exploration of the causes. However, the foci of the group are recognition of the academic situation, discovery of the value of education, and attempts to change failure into success.

The purpose of the group is to create a nonthreatening environment where students are free to share their fears and frustrations, but where they also are required to take ownership for their less-than-favorable situation. A key ingredient is the sharing of ideas; students sharing with each other ways of success, ways of coping with different teaching styles, and ways of handling emotions such as apathy and anger. Key also is naturally developed accountability among members, and the degree to which members are able to grasp the correlation between academic success and attainment of life goals. Ultimately, success must be measured largely by group members increasing behaviors and attitudes that really do result in increased accumulation of credit toward graduation.

CONCEPTUAL FRAMEWORK

Ellis's rational Emotive Behavior Theory aptly lends itself to work around academics, and it is this author's choice as the basic guiding conceptual framework for this group. Students lagging behind in high school coursework are quite normally capable of passing classes, but they are also very often victims of irrational patterns of thinking. Using the A-B-C-D-E therapeutic approach (Ellis, 1991), the group of unsuccessful students can be led to rational conclusions regarding their education. Applying this approach to our target group, we can broadly define pieces as follows:

A. The Activating Event actually is the lack of proper credit accumulation.
B. The Belief will vary from individual to individual, but will contain irrational elements regarding the reasons why one has failed to succeed academically.
C. The Consequences of A and B are feelings and behaviors counterproductive to academic success.

D. The Disputing attempts by the counselor will focus on efforts to correct thoughts and self-verbalizations for each individual in the group.

E. The Effects are the expected positive behavioral and emotional results: in this case, increased accumulation of credits toward high school graduation.

While any of Ellis's 11 irrational beliefs may be present (Ellis, 1962), 3 of them are frequently found in this population:

1. The idea that one must be thoroughly competent, adequate, and achieving to be of value. Many students do not complete and turn in work, or indeed even attempt it, because they fear they will be judged inadequate as humans for work they know is not perfect.

2. The idea that it is easier to avoid than to face certain life difficulties and self-responsibilities. Students frequently choose to avoid attendance and assignment responsibility, believing the resulting failure to be preferable to the unpleasantness of fulfilling these duties.

3. The idea that one's past history is an all-important determiner of present performance. Many unsuccessful high school students began this pattern in earlier years and believe it unchangeable.

GROUP GOALS

Goals for members of these groups can actually be individualized. However, the following general goals serve as guidelines for the "Rediscovering Academic Success" groups:

1. Establish a group environment characterized by safety. Members need to feel free, even inclined, to probe the true causes of their lack of academic success. Members of these groups are likely to have developed a plethora of irrational reasons for their academic plight, and a safe atmosphere may be necessary for them to lay aside falsehood and embrace reality and personal responsibility.

2. Separate the worth of a person from performance and abilities. This allows individuals to admit weaknesses, an exercise many either dance around ("Who needs to write a persuasive paragraph anyway?") or deny ("I can get an A in any class I want").

3. Lead individuals to see the errors in their thinking, and help them recognize how their irrational thought patterns result in poor academic performance. As the group progresses, this process will quite naturally be assumed by members, as well as the group facilitator. Some expected types of errant thinking include "No one in my family has ever graduated from high school," "I just can't do math," and "It doesn't matter if I complete high school." Also address student expectations, as unsuccessful students have "lowered

the bar," and have perhaps helped teachers to have lower than necessary expectations of them. Teachers may also need encouragement in this readjustment (make sure group members agree with this before communicating with teachers). Higher expectations on the part of the school, teachers, and students can play a powerful role in improved performance (Brookover et al., 1982).

4. Assist in correct thinking regarding member academic situation and potential. In response to the examples previously given, simple truths are that family patterns are changeable, study and tutors and persistence pay off, and career opportunities improve drastically when one graduates from high school.

5. Aid group members in formulating a reasonable and workable plan for academic success. This plan should be carefully crafted, allowing for the student's current situation. If a student is beginning an English class, and has always read and written well, goals of good grades may be very appropriate, whereas a goal written half way through a class for a student who has traditionally struggled in the subject requires a much lower expectation. Other student patterns need to be considered as well, including absences, tardiness, misbehavior, negative attitudes, and drug and alcohol use. The common objective of finding solutions to their difficulties provides a necessary adhesive for even a seemingly diverse group (LaFountain, Garner, & Eliason, 1996). Confrontation is a normal expectation in the group process during this phase, and it may well come from other members as well as the facilitator.

6. Accurately assess follow through on the individual plans. Once a plan has been implemented, weekly meetings focus around progress. Changes in the plan are not haphazard, but carefully thought out. Care is taken to ensure that lack of success is not blamed on the plan or others; responsibility lies with the student.

7. Change attitudes and behaviors related to academic success. The ultimate goal is that group members learn how to be successful academically, value that success, and prove able to continue being successful without group support.

PRE-GROUP SCREENING AND ORIENTATION

Counselors have easy access to the high school credit records. Indeed, it is generally their responsibility to keep these records and, therefore, they can readily see which students are approaching the point where graduation with one's class seems unlikely. Publicity about the group (how this is done should depend upon the counselor, the school environment, and other factors that should be obvious to the competent school counselor) is used to determine which students are genuinely interested in working to improve their academic situation.

Individual interviews can be used to gather valuable information that the counselor can use to group students as seems appropriate, considering such factors as desire and commitment to succeed academically, gender, year in school, and degree of credit deficiency.

OUTLINE FOR EIGHT GROUP SESSIONS

Session 1

Purpose. The first purpose of session 1 is for group members to begin relationships with each other. Since this group exists for a definite purpose of function—to bring about positive change in the academic endeavors of its members—the initial guiding from the counselor should bring this to focus. The second purpose of this session is for members to come to an understanding of how groups work, including the group rules. As these students have already proven themselves poor students, care should be taken to ensure they understand and agree to follow the rules, particularly those surrounding confidentiality.

Theme. The theme for session 1 is commitment. Having agreed in a private interview to take part in the group, members now need to commit before peers their determination to change in order to succeed academically. This commitment is encouraged by the rules of confidentiality and, perhaps, should be solidified by the signing of a contract.

Activities. The counselor begins by welcoming the students, and then gives an explanation of some general characteristics of groups. Included in this description would be a broad explanation of normal group stages. This would lead naturally to comments on the normal awkwardness of the first session, and the variance of comfort members might have regarding disclosure. Assurance is given that successive sessions become more and more enjoyable and less and less threatening.

Introductory activity can be tailored to the specific group. The school counselor may prefer to form groups that have specific common factors, such as age, gender, degree of academic deficiency, or serious histories of behavior problems. Some groups may well have members who know each other, while others may know little or nothing about the group members. The counselor can take all this into account as he or she determines how best to facilitate self-disclosure that allows the group to properly begin its process. For the first session a reachable goal is to have the members introduce themselves and explain why they are in the group and what they hope to get out of the group.

A special note is important here. Students who have not been academically successful will quite possibly prefer to focus on areas of common interest where they have seen success rather than on the purpose of the group. Counselors need to guard against the group spending its energy and time on off-the-topic issues such as drugs, dating, and even bragging about the very behaviors the group is designed to eliminate. The theme of commitment resurfaces here, as this group is only for those who seriously desire changing academic failure into academic success.

The counselor should briefly explain the necessity of the group rules, stressing the safety members need to feel before they are able to trust each other. A visual representation of the rules is helpful. If the room being used is commonly used for groups and has wall space available for the group, the rules may be posted for regular review. In addition to normal group counseling rules, there are two we strongly recommend be emphasized and enforced: (1) Use of appropriate language. Often in alternative learning situations language rules are not as strictly enforced: but this group has quite probably done themselves damage with the use of poor language, is currently in classroom situations where proper language use is advantageous, and are in need of a variety of exercises in discipline. (2) Use of proper respect for the counselor and each other. Be aware that some students have little in the way of family role models for showing proper respect toward others, and they may need some practical suggestions and modeling of appropriate respectful behavior.

A caution with working with this group; care should be taken regarding reading activities, such as asking each member to read one rule. This group may well have one or more members whose lack of reading skills has been hidden, and who are not yet trusting enough to publicly disclose this condition.

The first session can be closed by asking members to share something about the time together that they felt was positive. The counselor might suggest a few things, such as seeing that the group process was going to be better than expected, that it felt good to realize that others had similar struggles, or that they were beginning to feel some hope that they actually could start being successful in school.

An assignment of thought should be given, such as "For next week, think about ideas for change that you believe will help you be more successful in school. Come prepared to share these. Have them written down on paper. If you really believe in these ideas, did you begin to use them this week? Why or why not?"

Process. In describing how the group works, the counselor communicates that each member contributes throughout, so all are aware that abstaining from participation is not an option. Modeling appropriate disclosure (by role-playing as a member with academic deficiencies) can be done by the facilitator and can in fact be a powerful tool. An example of this technique would be for the facilitator to open this initial disclosure section as follows: "My name is John Doe, and I am in the group because I don't have enough credits to really be a junior. I really messed up my freshman year. I thought it was cool to be disrespectful to teachers, and I never did homework. Last year I skipped a lot of classes and got suspended a couple of times. Results? I've got about half the credits I should have. What do I expect to get out of this group? Help. I know I want to graduate, and maybe even go to college, but right now I need help to get headed in the right direction." This first session modeling shows students appropriate disclosure, length of talking time, and focus on the announced subjects.

Session 2

Purpose. In the second session, group members should continue to become acquainted with each other and should begin to feel a sense of group.

Theme. This session's theme is reality. In addition to the group-building activity, the major focus is on carefully and completely mapping out the current graduation situation of each member.

Activities. The opening activity can be a feelings check, where members share how they feel on that particular day. However, as this group focus is cognitive based, an appropriate follow-up can be about the reality that feelings cannot be what determines whether or not we act as successful students act; despite negative feelings, good students still attend class and do their schoolwork.

The day's second activity is a check on homework. Expect that several members would not have given it any thought, but do not allow this as acceptable. These students have committed themselves to constructive change, and change takes work; in this case, it requires doing homework. Have members share regarding their thoughts and actions about activities of change. Require those who did not do the homework to complete it by next week.

The final activity of the second session is for each member to individually figure out his or her graduation situation. The counselor aids in this process by providing a current transcript and a list of graduation requirements for each student. Model how the work can be done, either by using an overhead projector or whiteboard. Students then go to work, consulting with the counselor when necessary. Ten minutes before the session is to end students are given a file folder to place their work in, which they give to the facilitator.

Session 2 wrap-up is a check with members about how they felt the day went and, in particular, how the final activity helped them understand their situation. The counselor is careful to end the session with the next week's plan, which is to develop a strategy to reverse academic course and head for success.

Process. There is a hidden theme in this session, and it is hope. While the harsh realities of credit deficiency may be discouraging, students are never left without the hope of reversing course. Indeed, the group exists for this purpose. As each member comes to grips with his or her dismal situation, the facilitator includes the positive aspects (even in a cheerful manner) of recognizing the problem, committing to change, and gaining the help of this group that allows students to do what they have not done for quite some time—succeed at school! Pity parties, excuses, and acceptance of failure do not belong in the group. Positive steps, positive thinking, and positive attitudes are encouraged and praised. Be prepared to confront an attitude of blaming others or circumstances.

Session 3

Purpose. The purpose of session 3 is to give hope legs; to find the plan to address the current dismal situation. Proposed plans give hope, but also can cause doubts, such as, "Why should this plan work?" and "I've tried before and things did not get better—why should this be any different?" Each plan must identify those thinking errors that lead to failure, and correct the thinking with accurate appraisals fundamental to successful implementation of the plan.

Theme. An individual plan exists that each student can use to achieve success.

Activities. Begin the session by encouraging members to honestly share how they are feeling at this point. Be prepared for some discouragement. Remember, students are not in this group because they were doing well in the areas upon which you are focusing. Again, reframe reality in a positive light, reminding members of the success that lies before them.

Continue addressing the realities of deficient credit. Have each student draw up an academic plan for graduation. Allow that students would naturally prefer to graduate with their class, but that graduating a bit later is vastly more valuable than not graduating at all. Emphasize that the basic elements of all the plans are attendance, positive attitudes, and serious efforts on class work, homework, and tests.

With approximately 10 minutes left in the session, the counselor should again collect the work of the group. Final moments can be spent checking on each member's attitudes and emotions. The natural assignment for the week is to implement the fundamentals identified above, along with any particulars students feel fit individual classes. This assignment is serious work, to be undertaken by all. Next week's session will center around reports of this assignment being successfully implemented.

Process. By this time students should have either moved forward in their commitment toward success or excused themselves from the group. If at all possible, facilitators should not allow students to continue who will not stay committed. This does not preclude facilitators from working to get members to maintain commitment, but recognizes the reality that lack of commitment by this group spells failure. This stand communicates to members the absolute necessity of resolutely persisting until a task is completed.

The stark reality facing some students may be almost overwhelming. The counselor needs to prepare in advance, and to know which circumstances require special efforts, such as summer school, an extra year of school, or additional work at the local community college. Educational hope is always possible, and examples abound of those who completed educational goals in spite of difficult circumstances. The counselor needs to stay alert to spot the faulty thinking as it resurfaces, and assist the student in replacing it with rational thinking.

Session 4

Purpose. The purpose of session 4 is for members and the counselor to provide positive and helpful, but accurate, feedback as all discuss their week of implementing sound student behaviors. Attendance at this point is key, as results from one or two weeks of proper academic behaviors may be mixed. However, if serious efforts and attitudes were applied, each student will have positive stories to share.

Theme. This week's theme is "Proof! An individual plan exists that, if followed diligently, will lead to academic success."

Activities. By now, if the group members have remained sincere in their efforts to change, group sessions should take off with minimal direction from the counselor. However, success in class has also given more validation to the counselor, and his or her direction is more powerful than before. As members discuss their academic efforts, the counselor must be vigilant to spot the gloss overs—the tendencies to pretend all is going really well and victory is achieved. Amid the glow of success, the counselor must maintain distance by not allowing the warmth of positive results to diminish needed confrontation. Things are not fixed yet, and claiming they are is another example of faulty thinking that needs correction. This member-by-member critical evaluation lets success be praised, and still demands persistence and improvements. Moreover, the facilitator probes to find the hidden residue of old patterns and the lingering acceptance of mediocrity. These discoveries are once again cast in a positive light, as in "This is good—we've found something that needs work. Whew! We almost missed that, and it could really have got in the way of your success."

For session 4, allow at least 15 minutes at the end to respond to the question, "What are we missing?" Make sure each member responds.

Process. By this point the group dynamics should be very powerful. Depending on the individuals in the group, it is very possible that members are becoming very adept at spotting the thinking errors of others and, in so doing, are becoming better at seeing thinking errors they are making. The role of the counselor during some time periods may be reduced to ensuring that members frame things in ways that are positive, as well as truthful and factual. Also, the counselor must pay careful attention to all members, spotting any who are not seeing success but who are allowing the dynamics to pass them by, allowing others' enthusiasm and willingness to share to let them leave unspoken their frustrations and failures. The counselor cannot allow these individuals to pass on into the next week without the help of the group.

Session 5

Purpose. The purpose of Session 5 is to explore beneath the surface by searching for further-fouled thinking that hampers success. By now there should be considerable trust established, and members should be more comfortable with a deeper level of introspection. The counselor can suggest some possibilities not yet identified as blocks to progress, such as family expectations, lack of family academic success, poor reading abilities, struggles with mathematics, difficulties getting along with certain types of adults, work schedules, peer pressure, struggles with substance abuse, poor health, or unfavorable home conditions. Recognize that excuse making is counterproductive while still acknowledging that these types of circumstances may require special strategies.

Theme. This week's theme is refining the plan of academic success.

Activities. A quick check-in is done first. Clearly state that this is an inadequate evaluation of the week, but that the need to probe a bit deeper into our circumstances requires time. Then explain the idea of a more in-depth look at events in our lives that shape our thinking, give a list of examples of what might be beneath the surface, and perhaps open with some personal insight as a model to get things started. Ask volunteers to continue the sharing until all have taken part. Depending upon the time remaining, offer feedback to those who so desire. Sensitivity on the part of the counselor is required here, as some of what is revealed may be very personal and emotion laden. Reemphasis on group confidentiality should be included at some point in the session.

An absolute requirement is that this session not end without a refocus on academic success and without a reframing of negatives to positives. This reframing relates what has been learned to the individual plans for academic success, and students are again sent out with the task of continuing to improve as successful students.

Process. This session has tremendous possibilities, and the attention and available energy of the counselor are paramount. Hurts of serious magnitude may surface and anger may accompany these revisited wounds. The opportunity to confront, gently but firmly, the wrongs of the past that have so clearly led to errant thinking patterns is not to be lost! Once again, reframing the negative to a positive in light of the hope is crucial and must be done prior to group dismissal. The counselor must be ready to attend to individuals after this session.

Session 6

Purpose. The first purpose is to revisit the previous week's topic, and attend to any unfinished business. The second purpose is to honestly evaluate each student's plan as a continuing pattern that endures beyond the life of the group.

Theme. "New and continuing patterns for academic success."

Activities. Begin this week with a revisit of what was shared last week. Ask members for their personal reaction, and get permission before offering feedback. While permission is requested, the counselor should encourage that permission be given, instructing members to be constructive in their comments. By this time in the group, support for each other should be powerful, and the possibility is high that members will for the first time feel accepted by others who know of a particular weakness.

Check with members about their academic progress. Hopefully, by this time, patterns are emerging—patterns of regular attendance, homework remembered and completed, and passing grades on tests. Watch for decline in performance and commitment, and confront it aggressively.

Next, approach, perhaps for the first time, the reality of the group's end. At this juncture the point of doing so is to ensure that members realize the need for their academic success plan to be refined and working. For some it may be a wake-up call, a realization of reliance on something that will soon cease to exist. It may be a bit frightening, and a promise to explore this more fully at the next session can alleviate some fears.

Finally, let each member briefly share a success story from the week, and then send members out with the charge to make this week the best so far.

Process. The counselor must attend carefully to each member. It is very possible that probing has brought to mind terrible wrongs not even yet mentioned in the group discussions. The safety of these members is vital, as is follow-up work for them.

As the group begins to approach its end, members may well find themselves surprised by their reactions. Many may have felt indifferent toward the others at the beginning, but now feel attached and do not want the group to end. Reminding members of the purpose of the group fits the cognitive model adhered to throughout, and should help members with the group completion.

Session 7

Purpose. The purpose of session 7 is to reinforce successful patterns, to refine academic plans, and to prepare for academic success beyond the life of the group. The facilitator now must work a bit harder to focus on positives, as members see the end looming. One easy positive is the fact that the students will still be attending the same school, and can continue and enhance friendships that began in the group.

Theme. The same as session 6, "New and continuing patterns for academic success."

Activities. The major activity this week is an in-depth evaluation of what is working and what needs attention. Allow group members to help one another as each shares. Incorporate the new concept; namely, what concerns are there when taking into account the fact that the support group will dissolve in one week?

End with each member sharing a positive experience related to the group.

Process. The facilitator can allow the warmth of the group and the sorrow at its passing to exist, but must still require refocus on the task of succeeding academically. It is also important to look for the member(s) who is giving signs that he or she fears a return to old patterns of academic failure without the group support.

Session 8

Purpose. The purpose of session 8 is to examine the effects of the group, and to debunk any faulty thinking concerning the lack of power of the members to succeed without it.

Theme. You have all you need to succeed in school.

Activities. Open with members sharing something about a group member that they appreciate. If this goes well, as it probably will, consider having them make a second round, but only if this is a fairly quick process, as time for later discussion is desired.

Follow this with members sharing what they have learned about groups, what this group has come to mean to them, and the continued growth they expect because of belonging to the group.

Next, facilitate a discussion about the group, including what members will miss about it and what fears they face without its support, but focusing more on how they will survive and flourish without it, because of what they learned in it. Encourage open and frank group evaluation of the process and content, accepting criticism and suggestions for future groups. If this is done effectively, the counselor should note this input.

Finally, offer to facilitate a session in 1 month with the express purpose of checking on academic success.

Process. This final session can be melancholic or upbeat, and the counselor can determine which it will be. Refreshments, and even a bit of ceremony for a job well done, can help set the tone. Reminders of confidentiality are appropriate. Allow real warmth and affection.

STRATEGIES TO EVALUATE THE GROUP

During the portion of the final session that is devoted to group evaluation, members are asked to candidly speak about the effectiveness of the group. Written evaluations may also be used, asking students to respond to such questions as: How effective do you feel this group has been for you? Did participation in the group help you become a better student? If you were helped, what are the things that helped you most? Do you feel you think more clearly about your potential and how to reach it? What were some group highlights? What changes would you recommend for future groups?

In addition, the group's effectiveness can be assessed by its academic outcomes. Did members actually become successful students? This can be measured simply by looking at credits accumulated by these members over time.

REFERRAL PROCEDURES FOR FOLLOW-UP

As mentioned several times in the chapter, the counselor must be attentive to individual group members and their more serious needs. Should serious issues present, the referral process used by the school district must be employed. This will entail parental contact, and probably will require offering a list of suitable therapists in the area.

Many students will also need continuing support in order to maintain and cement new academic and cognitive patterns. The counselor can evaluate individual needs and recommend further support systems. The formation of ongoing groups that meet less frequently may be of significant help to students.

REFERENCES

Brookover, W., Beamer, W., Efthim, H., Hathaway, D., Lezotte, L., Miller, S., Passalacqua, J., & Tornatzky, L. (1982). *Creating effective schools.* Holmes Beach, FL: Learning Publications.

Ellis, A. (1962). *Reason and emotion in psychotherapy.* New York: Stewart.

Ellis, A. (1991). The philosophical basis of rational-emotive therapy (RET). *Psychotherapy in Private Practice, 8,* 97–106.

LaFountain, B., Garner, N., & Eliason, G. (1996). Solution focused counseling groups: A key for school counselors. *The School Counselor, 42,* 256–267.

CHAPTER 13

THE SAFE SURVIVORS GROUP: A PSYCHOEDUCATIONAL COUNSELING GROUP FOR FEMALE ADOLESCENT SURVIVORS OF RELATIONSHIP VIOLENCE

Lisa Langfuss

PURPOSE

As the very nature of childhood changes, evidence of relationship violence among children and adolescents is increasing. Young people are finding themselves caught in cycles of violence and emotional abuse before they are educated about the impact of an abusive relationship. Although education about relationship violence is increasing among many student and community populations, adolescents who have been in violent relationships need to learn how to empower themselves so as to stay out of violent and unsafe relationships in the future.

The Safe Survivors Group is designed to supplement individual counseling following an adolescent's break from an abusive dating relationship. Relationship violence requires emotional and physical isolation from a victim's support system so that the abuser may maintain control. The group process helps alleviate the sense of isolation felt by the adolescent victim during this time when peer acceptance and involvement is developmentally crucial.

Furthermore, this group aids in recovery from the abusive relationship and helps strengthen skills to identify and avoid abusive relationships in the future. The adolescents redefine themselves as Survivors. As such, they practice acting as Survivors, incorporating past trauma into current action for a more beneficial outcome (in this case, emotional, physical, and sexual safety). The participants engage in active exploration of what safety means to them while discovering how they are largely responsible for their own well-being. Furthermore, participants mourn the losses incurred as by-products of the

violent relationship while embracing newfound control over their own roles in future relationships.

This group helps young women break the cycle of violence by giving them the opportunity to gain skills to avoid future abusive relationships. These young adults will carry awareness of the destructive nature of abuse and will be able to identify unhealthy relational patterns as they emerge. The participants redefine themselves as able, worthy young women capable of making safe decisions in their emotional and physical interactions. Finally, group participants have a safe environment to work through the emotional damage of their previous relationship while building support in the knowledge that others are working through similar issues.

CONCEPTUAL FRAMEWORK

Mills (1985) designed a framework of positive coping techniques for the termination of relationship abuse. The underlying principle is that the victimization is a gradual process resulting from abusive behavior rather than from qualities within the victim. This is a key factor in working with survivors of abuse: The abusive behavior was a choice made by the abuser and the victim is not to blame. Mills describes five stages that occur within victims during the life of an abusive relationship. First, the victim *enters a violent relationship,* usually unwittingly. The victim has needs that she or he believes may be fulfilled by the new relationship. The second stage is *managing the violence.* This is when the victim develops coping strategies and attempts to attach meaning to the violence. At this point, victims may be engaging in thinking errors as they try to cope by believing themselves to have the ability to control the violence despite the fact that it is not their behavior to control. Self-blame is useful in this stage because it further allows the victim to avoid feelings of hopelessness and powerlessness by imagining responsibility for the abuse.

The third stage is experiencing *a loss of self.* This stage progresses from the increasing isolation and devaluation of the victim as a worthy individual. Victims may be very confused at this time as they continually question their perceptions. This stage is especially crucial to identify when working with adolescents who may have less self-knowledge and ego strength to successfully resolve the dilemmas faced within this conflict. The average adolescent has not yet developed a strong sense of self and may come to group with a sense of self derived entirely from what she has been told by the abuser. She may have difficulty realizing that she has a personality that exists separately from that described to her by others and that she is unique and that her characteristics and needs are definable and valuable.

Victims of abuse *evaluate the relationship* in the fourth stage of coping. Most savvy abusers will identify when the victim is experiencing this reevaluation and may choose this time as an invitation to make promises of a better relationship, increased safety, and increased love and affection. Victims in this stage attempt to make sense of contradictory internal and external messages and insights. Adolescents who maintain excessive self-doubt and low ego-strength are easily manipulated during this time by abusers who know what the adolescent most desires at this time: promises of safety and unconditional love.

Finally, *restructuring of the self* is the fifth stage when individuals learn to view themselves as survivors rather than victims. With adolescents this stage may be extremely challenging, as restructuring the self implies that the adolescent has a sense of self to reconstruct. Practitioners may instead choose to view this stage as structuring a survivor self, where the adolescents learn to view themselves as someone who was a victim but has made the choice not to be victimized anymore.

The redefinition of self as a survivor is of principle importance to this group practitioner. Members of this group will have been out of an abusive relationship for a period between 4 months to 1 year so they will have presumably passed through each of these phases and into the fifth. This group is designed to aid adolescents in that restructuring of the self as a survivor. Adolescents who experience abusive dating relationships tend to leave those relationships with low self-esteem; a low sense of self-worth; a distrust in others, society, and themselves; depression; anxiety; fear; an inability to handle anger; intense feelings of helplessness; and symp-

toms of Post-Traumatic Stress Disorder (PTSD) (Krupnick & Horowitz, 1980). With effective facilitation, the group experience can decrease the sense of loneliness and isolation and increase awareness of a social support system. Survivors may feel an increased sense of control and accuracy of self-perception as they engage in the group process. The group design requires members to be fairly active as they work through many of the negative results of their previous relationship in preparation for future relationships, both romantic and nonromantic in nature. Members are responsible for their own healing.

Researchers have determined that many victims remain in abusive relationships because of a rational cost-benefit analysis of the relationship itself (Frisch & MacKenzie, 1991). Victims may determine that it is more beneficial to remain in the relationship than to leave, oftentimes due to psychological and financial dependence on the abuser and fear of violent repercussion as one attempts to disengage from the abuse. However, this group will be working with adolescents who are still operating within a family-of-origin structure. This is an ideal time to help adolescents evaluate the costs of abusive relationships before actually reentering one where the individual's very lifestyle creates dependence. Realistic cost evaluation may help young adults make safer choices while building a relationship rather than waiting until the cost of leaving is higher than the cost of remaining. In keeping with the idea of a safe survival, this group is designed to teach adolescents to expect an emotionally and physically safe life where they make safe choices for themselves while recognizing that they cannot make choices for others.

GROUP GOALS

The goals for this group are as follows:

1. To provide a safe group environment where members gain emotional support from peers who have shared similar circumstances, thus decreasing feelings of isolation.
2. To define and identify emotional, sexual, and physical components of safety and to explore how and why one chooses to remain safe.
3. To redefine self as a survivor while discarding a "victim" identity.
4. To celebrate the emergence of a survivor while identifying and mourning the losses experienced as a victim.
5. To replace feelings of learned helplessness with empowerment and self-control.
6. To perform a cost-benefit analysis of safety versus potential victimization.
7. To define abuse as an issue of control and power, not anger.

PRE-GROUP SCREENING AND ORIENTATION

Safety within the group is of significant concern. It is imperative that group members be screened prior to acceptance in the group. Members should be completely out of their abusive relationship for a period of not less than 4 months and no more than 1 year. Four months should be sufficient time for most adolescents to regain some sense of safety if the abuser is not stalking or harassing them. Adolescents who are being harassed or stalked may not yet participate in the group for the safety of all members. Clients must also be evaluated for alcohol and substance use, PTSD, and major depression as well as personality disorders to determine whether individual counseling prior to group would be most useful. If the client has a recent history of suicide attempt or ideation, individual counseling must precede the group experience. The group will involve some grief work and may be harmful to the individual who is still psychologically unstable and engaging in deliberate self-harm. The 1-year limit is recommended so that the abusive relationship and factors therein are more fresh in the client's recent memory.

This group is designed to be most effective for clients who attend voluntarily. Furthermore, clients should have some knowledge base in basic issues of domestic violence (as may be taught in school guidance classes, community awareness courses, or widely available educational curriculum). It may be useful to provide a packet of reading to each participant 2 weeks before the group that contains basic informational handouts about the nature and warning signs of abuse, plus definitions of abuse and control. This group expands upon knowledge of some basic tenets of violent relationships such as signs of abuse, methods of abuse, and who is most susceptible to abuse. Victims of abuse may be extremely angry and be on the verge of aggressive release; therefore, it is imperative for the safety of the group that the facilitator screen for anger management issues and current emotional functioning. It is recommended that the screening interview be done in person and that the screener ask specific and extensive questions about anger management, aggressive tendencies, and patterns of emotional release.

Participants should also be screened for learning disabilities and educational development. Participants should have the ability to engage in some abstract thinking and must be able to read and write at a minimum ninth-grade level. An individual with difficulty remaining on task for longer than 15 minutes may be distracting to the group and would not be able to complete the tasks at hand. Distractibility and high anxiety may be the result of the abusive relationship itself in which case prior individual counseling would be most useful before the group experience to maximize effectiveness.

Prior to group, the facilitator should determine a location with minimal distraction and optimal safety features (e.g., locking doors and windows). Clients will be concerned (rightfully so) about safety first and foremost, so remember that protection from possible stalking and attack is key. Many local law enforcement agencies are willing to send an officer to walk clients into and out of relationship violence classes and seminars to increase feelings of protection. Be certain that all clients consent to this service, as an officer's presence may be a trigger for a client or may compromise confidentiality.

This group would be most effective with between six and eight members. Six members would be optimal so that participants are more able to fully engage in each activity and will have more time to contribute and process following each activity.

OUTLINE FOR EIGHT GROUP SESSIONS

Session 1

Purpose. The purpose of the first session is to introduce group members and create group rules as the foundation to a safe group environment. Session 1 is designed to facilitate safety so that interpersonal exchange and personal revelation may begin. Members express what they would like from the group experience while learning what can be gained from group. Finally, members learn how the safety journals will be used.

Theme. The central focus of session 1 is the creation of safety. The session is designed to encourage participants to realize that "We are each worthy of a safe environment and need to take responsibility to keep our environment feeling safe."

Activities. The materials needed include posterboard and marker, overhead projector, or chalkboard; notebooks for each member; pens; and a bowl or bag. The group begins with the facilitator introducing herself or himself to the group. Then the facilitator explains to the group the purpose of the upcoming introduction activity (to be aware of who is around us and why they are here). Next, members of the group go around in a circle and say their name, their birthday, and one word to describe the room where group is being held. The third expectation (to describe the room) gives the members permission to investigate their surroundings without fear of seeming odd or "weird" to their peers. Furthermore, the adolescents may uncover factors within the environment that need adjusting to facilitate feelings of safety. The circle then reverses and members are asked to describe why they have come to the group and what they would like to get from group. Since this will be difficult for the clients, the facilitator should model first. Explain that clients may choose to pass with or without giving a brief reason why. The choice to pass is as respected as the choice to participate.

Next, the members are invited to contribute to a list of group rules. The facilitator leads by introducing some key rules for safety: use listening skills (wait until someone is done speaking before talking, pay attention, respect what others are saying, agree to disagree), what is said in group stays in group and may never be discussed outside, and respect the safety and cohesion of the group at all times (e.g., let the group know if you can't attend, inform the group of potential physical danger or recent threats). Invite group members to add to this list in an open discussion. If members feel unsafe speaking yet, they may write their idea down and ask the facilitator to read it aloud (members are likely to respond directly to the member who originally wrote the note—intervene if the member appears overly distressed by this). Following the creation of the rules list, explain to the members that they will each receive their own copy next week at group and are expected to tell the group or the facilitator if any of the rules are violated.

Then explain to the group the purposes and goals of the group as defined earlier. The group is not created to relive their stories of abuse. It is to take the past and incorporate it into a more hopeful and healthy future. At this time, pass out blank notebooks to the members. Explain that these are safety notebooks. If a member feels the need to disclose a personal story or memories, they may be recorded in this book until it is time to share personal recollections. This will help keep members from monopolizing group time by excessive sharing yet allows an outlet for safe disclosure. If the members choose, they may ask the facilitator to read and comment on the writings in private and then, if permission is granted, in front of the group as deemed therapeutic.

Next, members create a mantra to be read together at the beginning and end of each group. Each member will be given 2 minutes to think of a line to the mantra. It may help to set the tone by providing a line such as, "I have come here to experience togetherness." Each member writes a line down on a piece of paper, then places the paper in the bowl. All pieces are chosen in random order to create the poem. The members pass the bowl around so that each person reads one line. The facilitator records the lines, then asks for a volunteer to read the finished product. The members then copy this down into their notebooks and practice the mantra together (be aware that some will be uncomfortable and may withdraw or giggle at this point).

Finally, ask members to write a number down on a scale of 1 to 10 describing how safe they felt at the start of group, how safe they now feel, how safe they have felt over the past week, and how safe they expect to feel this week. In future sessions, this will be called the personal assessment of safety scale. Invite the group to repeat the mantra once more, then congratulate the members on their group attendance.

Process. The facilitator sets the emotional tone for the group from the first moment. It is crucial that the facili-

tator be constantly aware of the respect levels within the group; in other words, that group members are being treated with value and not cut down or insulted for any contribution. Anxiety of the group experience will create enough energy so that the facilitator may need to demonstrate deep breathing and settling down techniques at times. The facilitator must demonstrate active, encouraging listening and must reinforce positive group member behavior. Lavish praise will put members off, as their low self-esteem may not allow them to believe the praise. Instead, calmly and sincerely thanking them for their contributions may be most effective.

Group members will probably be uncomfortable speaking to one another quite yet. In fact, many will probably have difficulty making eye contact or holding focus on the activity as many will be especially concerned with their surroundings as they assess for safety concerns. The facilitator may point this out to members and let them know that it may take awhile for group members to trust each other, as everyone has endured a lot of pain and violation. Affirm that this is acceptable and valid; after all, they are doing a good job at assessing their own personal safety in a way that works for them as individuals. Express excitement for the time when group members realize how much they are looking out for each other and express how much of a relief it will be to not have to hold that burden alone.

Session 2

Purpose. Members create working definitions of the term *safety* and discuss how to create a safe group experience. Members begin to consider how safety affects their lives and relationships.

Theme. The theme may be described as "How will I know I'm safe if I don't know what safety is? Today I define safety on my terms and starting today I expect safety above all, from all."

Activities. The materials needed include copies of the rules list, clock or timer, six posterboards, and markers. Group begins by group members reciting the group mantra. Following this, group members rate safety on a scale of 1 to 10 (as done in the previous group). The facilitator then tapes three posterboards to the wall. At the top of the first, write the word "emotional." The second should be titled "physical," and the third, "sexual." Group members then are encouraged to write definitions of safety as pertaining to each of these three components. Next, members are asked to come up with a list of words and phrases that answer the question, "How do I know I am physically/sexually/emotionally safe?" To enhance group cohesion, the facilitator tells the group they have 8 minutes for each list. The facilitator stands aside and acts as timekeeper after placing one marker in the center of the group. The members then have to choose a recorder or pass the marker around while the facilitator models positive listening skills. Encourage members to examine the list of emotional safety factors and compare them to the group environment so as to adjust the environment as needed to maximize safety. Lead members in discussion about how they feel after creating these lists. Do they feel empowered? Sad? Anxious? Finally, engage members in relating these feelings to feelings of safety within their everyday lives. Then inform members that next session's topic will be power and control. Invite members to participate in reciting the closing mantra together and congratulate them on finding the courage to come to group.

Process. The leader once again serves a key role in facilitating safety within the group. Emotional safety will be most compromised if one or several group members bully or overpower the more quiet or withdrawn members. It is at this point that the facilitator must quite actively intervene by modeling assertive intervention. For example, the leader may say, "Jenny, it sounds like you were just interrupted. I wonder if you would please tell me the rest of what you were saying because it may really benefit the group." The facilitator must also be aware that some members may sense an opportunity to dive into the sharing of personal anecdotes. These anecdotes should be kept to a minimum. Brief sharing as it relates to the topic is beneficial. In-depth sharing may be recorded in the notebook for sharing at a later time. It must be constantly reinforced that their stories and memories are important and worth listening to, but that this group is to learn how to rewrite the future by using lessons learned from the past. Sharing stories takes members out of the present and into the past. Instead, the facilitator may help rephrase anecdotal information so that the member can apply the information to future functioning. For example, a client says, "One time I felt unsafe when my boyfriend wouldn't let me out of the car." The facilitator may validate how scary that must have been, then rephrases by saying, "When you were a victim, (abuser's name) made the choice to hold you hostage to have control over you. As a survivor you will recognize unsafe situations and will be able to disengage from dangerous people before they choose to hurt you." The facilitator must emphasize that this was the abuser's choice and was not the member's fault. Continually emphasize that the abuser was very skilled at making the victim feel powerless, but that a survivor will have more skills and strength than a potential abuser because as a survivor she will know how to recognize and avoid danger.

Session 3

Purpose. The purpose is to impart knowledge that relationship violence is a control issue and is not caused by victim characteristics, substance use, or anger manage-

ment issues. Members define control and examine how perceived power and control affect daily functioning. Clients gain empowerment by examining where in their lives they have control and power that can be used for positive gain and healthy functioning. Members begin to define control in terms of emotional, physical, and sexual safety.

Theme. "Survivors are powerful. I am a survivor, therefore, I am very powerful. I am learning to have control over my safety and my choices and will have a future regardless of others' choices."

Activities. The materials needed include posterboard and pens. Members recite the opening mantra, then write safety scales in their notebooks (how safe I feel today emotionally, physically, sexually; how safe I felt this past week emotionally, physically, sexually). Members begin by playing "popcorn." Give members 1 minute to go around the circle as many times as they can as members say one word at a time that they think of when they hear the word "control."

Members then discuss and create definitions of power and control as prompted by the previous popcorn game. Members are asked to describe what a person looks like who has no control versus someone who has a healthy amount of control versus someone who exerts excessive control. Members are asked to discuss whether people who seek to exert control over others actually feel a lot of control over themselves. The facilitator then begins discussion about when members felt in control of their lives and when they felt out of control. Discuss the relationship between safety and control, relating incidents of abuse to an abuser's ploy for control.

Group members are then asked to spend 10 minutes as a group writing a letter to a young girl explaining to her how she might be able to keep herself safe as she journeys through life. Focus on explaining to her what she has control over and what she doesn't have control over, and who to turn to if she is feeling unsafe. This may become an emotional and sad project for group members. Encourage them to share with the group what they need most right now: Is there anything the group can do for them? Is there anyone else who has ever felt this way? Emphasize the importance of realizing that others too have felt alone, scared, and sad and affirm the loss of innocence and trust that results from violent relationships. Before closing, encourage group members to share one method they will use this week to deal with sadness or anger. Recite the group mantra.

Process. The facilitator will have to be quite active in this group to keep the momentum going. As members become sad, allow the sadness to permeate the group. Allow and encourage silence so that group members can fully absorb the resulting emotions. Members will be more relaxed and comfortable than before, so it may be necessary to review group rules and reinforce acceptance and positive listening. Most importantly, evaluate group members at the end of group for excessive anger or depression. Address concerns to the group in general. If the client appears to not personalize the concern or appears disengaged, speak with the client directly following group to assess the client's safety through the course of the week.

Session 4

Purpose. This group is designed to redefine self as a survivor rather than a victim and to identify the qualities that help turn a victim into a survivor.

Theme. "I will survive and will use my newfound power to keep me safe. I have power and control over my choices and will make choices that keep me safe."

Activities. The materials needed include two posterboards, markers, flowerpots, potting soil, plant seeds, water, and cups or spoons to use as shovels. Group begins by reciting the mantra and writing down a personal safety scale assessment (as in the previous session). The group then discusses the definition of "victim" versus "survivor." This should be recorded by the facilitator on posterboards placed in the center of the group. Lead members into discussion about how each person in the room is a survivor. Members may volunteer to complete the sentence, "I know I am a survivor because _____."
Group members now pair off into couples. Explain that, using no words, one member will sculpt the other to look like a victim by arranging the partner's body to tell a story, much as a sculptor would. Members must first gain permission to touch the other member. Discuss the sculpts with group members. Why were the members sculpted that way? Do any members feel as if they are seeing themselves in one of the sculpts? How does it feel to be in that position? Next, the same sculptors reposition the partners to look like survivors. How is the body language different? What happened as you became a survivor instead of a victim? Which feels more comfortable to you? Members then switch positions and sculpt the partner, followed by a repeat of the earlier discussion so that all members physically experience a survivor's posture.

Following these sculpts, members write a memorial for the victim that they were when involved in the abuse. Explain that you cannot expel a part of yourself or your experiences, but you can grieve for what was lost during the relationship. Next, pass out flowerpots and paper cups to each member. A bag of dirt and seeds are placed in the center of the circle. Members plant seeds into their flowerpots as a way of symbolically burying the "victim." However, the seed, representing the victim, is not dead. Instead, it is now going to be nurtured to create new life and beauty. Survivors will care for and nurture their seed as symbolic of the victim

within themselves. We do not expect to see the seed again looking like a seed (a "victim"); instead, we will see the seed in a transformed state as it plants roots and blossoms (a "survivor" who will have strong days and weaker days but has evolved from the seed it once was). Continue to help group members make analogies between the seeds and the nurturing process and the transformation from victim to survivor. Group closes with the mantra and congratulations on planting "new roots."

Process. The facilitator is especially sensitive during this session to grief and loss issues and should address members with sympathy and support rather than pity. It is essential that the leader model appropriate support and then encourage members to ask for support when needed by demonstrating "safe" ways to ask for peer support. The facilitator may find a discussion on typical responses to grief and loss beneficial to group members at this time as members process their losses.

Session 5

Purpose. This session is designed to help members connect issues of self-esteem and self-worth with safety issues. Members engage in cost-benefit analysis of the psychological price paid when involved with an abuser.

Theme. "I am worth too much to allow someone else to tear me down. I am strong and will make the choice to be with people who value my strength."

Activities. The materials needed include 40–50 paper "bricks" (rectangular sheets of brown or red construction paper shaped to look like a brick), markers, "control caps" (strips of white construction paper), and scotch tape. Group begins with the mantra and a safety scale assessment (as in previous sessions). The group leader checks in with members about their flowers and the grief experience. Discussion may follow as needed. Next, pass out paper bricks to each member and place markers in the center of the circle. Instruct members to write words or phrases on the brick describing what is special about them or what makes them worthy of safety and love. Members may answer the question, "Why am I important?" Once members write the words, they tape the bricks to the wall in the shape of a house. Members should continue this until all the bricks are used (approximately 40–50 bricks are recommended). Next, pass out the control caps (paper strips to be placed around the forehead like a headband). Before putting the bands on, members should write a statement on the front that reminds them of something an abuser would say as he or she seeks to gain power over another's psychological self. Members then put the bands on and are instructed to make a statement that is meant to decrease another person's strength. As the statements are made, the members tear one brick down (as the statement would tear at the psyche). Once each member has made the statement twice, note what has happened to the once-sturdy house of bricks. Members are invited to discuss how it felt to create weakness in a once-strong structure and are then invited to take the caps off and rip them into shreds. Members may then rebuild the house as survivors and may add additional bricks. Members are encouraged to share the personal meaning of this experience. Group ends with recitation of the mantra.

Process. The facilitator must use special care in this session to ensure that members are not experiencing flashbacks or extreme anxiety as a result of the role-playing. If anxiety and energy feels intense, the facilitator may lead members in brief "cooling off" moments of taking a deep breath and refocusing. It is imperative that the facilitator helps members remain in the present while making connections with the past. Remember, the focus of group is to use past experiences for present and future skill-building.

Session 6

Purpose. The purpose is to build esteem and redefine self as a strong, capable human.

Theme. "I am worth protecting. My emotional self is valuable, my body is valuable, and I am worthy as I am."

Activities. The materials needed include "Survivor of the Year" awards. Group begins with a recitation of the mantra and a brief check-in with each member. Members are asked to record their safety scales. Then, members are asked to leave notebooks open and record on a scale of 1 to 10 how much self-esteem they feel they have at that moment. Then, record how much they have had over the past week and over the past month. Ask members to determine how much esteem they had before their most recent abusive relationship, at the start of the relationship, as the relationship progressed, and then as the relationship ended. Then invite members to share and discuss these results with special focus on how the esteem levels affected safety and choices within the relationship.

Members then pair off with partners to interview one another for a pretend TV report on the "Survivor of the Year." Members ask questions such as "What have you accomplished this month? How did you keep yourself safe today? Who are your role models?" The task is to find out how the survivor became a survivor and how he or she will continue to be one. Members have 10 minutes for each interview and are requested to take careful notes and ask clarifying questions. Each member then presents the other member to the group as a reporter would and awards the partner with a "Survivor of the Year" award. Discussion follows and group ends with recitation of the mantra and congratulations on being the "Survivors of the Year."

Process. At this point, the facilitator continues to reinforce supportive peer behavior and points out signs of peer acceptance and approval. The facilitator should also encourage peer involvement by giving less-involved members of the group tasks that connect them with other peers (such as passing out materials or pairing off partners).

Session 7

Purpose. The purpose of this group is to continue a cost-benefit analysis of controlling and abusive relationships.

Theme. "I will recognize unhealthy control because I have too much to lose if I let myself get involved in verbal, physical, or sexual relationship abuse."

Activities. The materials needed include strips of newsprint or butcher paper at least 7 ft. long by 2.5 ft. wide, markers, and red triangles (from construction paper) approximately 4 in. long. Group begins with the mantra, safety scale assessment, and brief verbal check-in. Members are all given a 7-ft. long piece of butcher paper and are instructed to trace each other's outlines onto the paper (draw self if uncomfortable otherwise). On the figure, draw symbols to represent different positive aspects of your personhood (e.g., draw a heart, a brain, a smile to represent happiness, and so on). Around the body, write the names of five people who support you or care about you, then two places you like to hang out or visit. Next, the facilitator passes out red triangles (about 4–5 in. long) to group members. Members then label triangles with "red flags" of abuse (such as "isolation from family" or "not allowed to go to movies"). Members then take the red flags and determine where on the body (or on surrounding words) the flag should be placed based on what functioning that behavior interferes with. Activity ends when bodies are covered in red flags. Discussion follows: Has the abuser left any part of functioning unaffected? How much of the real person underneath the flags do we actually see? Can the person under all those flags breathe? Members can then remove red flags by making positive self-statements or by role-modeling how one might respond when that red flag issue appears. Group concludes with mantra and congratulations on being survivors.

Process. The facilitator must once again be certain to keep members focused on the present. Members must be continually reminded that they did not choose to be abused and that the abuse was not their fault. Now, though, they do have the skills and knowledge to avoid future relationship abuse as they invariably encounter others who decide to use abusive tactics.

Session 8

Purpose. The purpose is to solidify the redefinition of self as a survivor and to celebrate the acquisition of new skills, new emotional support, and solidarity with a larger population of adolescents who have shared similar abusive experiences.

Theme. "I am now a survivor and will remain a survivor for as long as I live. My survival is worth celebrating. I am worth celebrating."

Activities. The materials needed include paper and decorative items, glue, markers, birthday cake, and juice or beverages. This group begins with a recitation of the mantra and a safety scale assessment. Next, invite members to design a birth announcement for their own rebirth as a survivor. The facilitator may have an example ready including a statement such as "This is _____. She is a survivor and will be for the remainder of her life. Today we welcome her to the world. She is looking forward to a life of love and happiness. She continues to build skills and support and will handle every situation with safety and esteem. Welcome!" The members should decorate their invitations, then share each with the group. Members should then share cake and soft drinks and sing Happy Birthday to each other. Discussion centers on the ending of group and resultant feelings. Members then sign the covers or pages within each other's journals to commemorate the support and learning that took place together. Group closes with the mantra.

Process. Group members may feel anxious and sad over the ending of the group and may fear loss of support and isolation. Remind members that they now possess the ability to strengthen and support their self-esteem and safety skills. The facilitator may help group members explore options for further support-building by helping them identify community resources and informational networks that will continue to facilitate the survival experience. Members in this session should be encouraged to offer one another sincere comments of praise and admiration as each member has accomplished an extraordinary task of creating a safe, skilled survivor.

The group may choose to meet for "tune-up" sessions following the close of the formal group. It may be useful to meet to discuss progress of support-building outside of the group setting, continuing informally the process of identifying social and familial supports and engaging those supports in strength-building. A follow-up group may be formed with a more formal agenda that may include themes such as "Now what? Finding friends and partners who value my continuing survival" and "Actively finding red flags for violence and what to do with them."

STRATEGIES TO EVALUATE THE GROUP

The group facilitator is encouraged to hold a post-group session with each group member individually. At this ses-sion, the facilitator may work with the client to chart a safety graph. This graph is a visual representation of the client's self-assessments of safety as recorded each week in the client's notebook. The facilitator may discuss fluctuations with the client and may compile this information from all clients to determine group increases and decreases in safety assessment. Furthermore, the facilitator should design a concrete questionnaire to be sent home with the group participants along with a pre-addressed, stamped envelope. The questions would consist of a Likert scale format where clients determine whether group goals were met, whether personal goals were met, and whether the facilitator helped or hindered progress.

REFERRAL PROCEDURES FOR FOLLOW-UP

During the last session, referral procedures for follow-up should be discussed. The facilitator should let group members know whether he or she will be conducting any additional groups and allow members to continue if they so choose. If the facilitator believes any group member needs to continue, that member should be taken aside confidentially and have this option discussed. If the facilitator is not going to conduct more groups in the near future, he or she should provide three recommendations for other groups that are appropriate. It should be noted that if the adolescent is a minor, then his or her parent(s) or guardian(s) should be provided the same information. In addition, all group members should be invited to contact the facilitator of this group in the future if needed for further follow-up or referrals.

CONCLUSION

Children and adolescents today exist in a society more violent and unsafe than in recent decades. As children are more frequently left to fend for themselves, many seek to find control in situations where they feel they have little or none. Children seek power for a number of reasons, yet safety and predictability are two main reasons that teenagers seek control over others in their environment.

One potentially disastrous outcome of a child's search for control is that the child may attempt to assert control over others in the form of physical, emotional, and sexual aggression. The child may learn this vicariously through familial patterns of interaction and perceived societal expectations (such as that evident in the media and entertainment industries), or it may be reinforced in assertion of control as he or she receives positive consequences for such acts. A child who aggresses against others in power or control struggles may receive internal reinforcement such as comfort or predictability or increased feelings of power and control where previously lacking. Thus begins a new life cycle of the search for power and control, the building blocks of relationship violence and physical aggression toward others.

Physical abuse is the most common source of injury among women, and domestic violence was deemed by the United States Surgeon General to be the nation's number one health problem (Murphy-Milano, 1996). In addition to the loss of health and safety, victims often lose a sense of hopefulness about the future and one's own abilities. This learned helplessness leads many abused persons into lives of continued victimization. Adolescents who do not interrupt the expectations of abuse will most likely end up in another abusive relationship and are less likely to succeed in other areas of life functioning such as education and employment (Strube, 1988). Chronic feelings of powerlessness may also surface as abusive behaviors toward other individuals such as the victim's children, thus expanding the cycle of abuse. Victims of violence are simply less likely to avoid abuse in the future as abuse becomes an expectation. Survivors are created as we help free victims permanently from this suffocating cycle.

REFERENCES

Frisch, M. B., & MacKenzie, C. J. (1991). A comparison of formerly and chronically battered women on cognitive and situational dimensions. *Psychotherapy, 28,* 339-344.

Krupnick, J. L., & Horowitz, M. J. (1980). Victims of violence: Psychological responses, treatment implications. *Evaluation and Change (Special Issue),* 42–46.

Mills, T. (1985). The assault on the self: Stages in coping with battered husbands. *Qualitative Sociology, 8,* 103–123.

Murphy-Milano, S. (1996). *Defending our lives.* New York: Anchor Books.

Strube, M. J. (1988). The decision to leave an abusive relationship: Empirical evidence and theoretical issues. *Psychological Bulletin, 104,* 236–248.

 **PART 3**

GROUP WORK WITH ADULTS

In Part Three, group work with adults takes on many forms for addressing the wide variety of concerns that face adults today. Chapter 14, "Planning Your Career Adventure: A Group for Career Planners," shows how group work can help members clarify their skills, interests, and goals. A variety of theoretical approaches help to achieve identified goals for these groups. These include clarifying interests, skills, and goals; using career center resources; normalizing the anxiety of indecision; and developing information and network resources.

Chapter 15, "Grieving Our Losses," illustrates how a group for those who have suffered a loss through death, illness, or transition can provide emotional support, a source for information on grieving, and a place to gain the tools necessary for coping in the real world. Goals for these groups include creating a safe environment for expression of feelings and supporting others to accept their loss.

Chapter 16, "Simplify Your Life," identifies how such a group can provide support, information, and an ongoing exploration in "voluntary simplification and becoming a force for change in society." Various routes to simplicity are illustrated that lead toward some common goals for group members such as exploring options for change, becoming more committed to personal values, and taking steps toward a cleaner, safer, more sustainable environment.

Chapter 17, "The Transition Into Parenthood: A Group for Expecting Couples," describes how "to get couples talking about things they may not have considered and to contemplate their fundamental parenting assumptions." Some goals toward this end are generating positive perceptions about parental aptitude, developing more accurate expectations of parenthood, recognizing parental attitude as a choice, and developing a parental mission statement.

Chapter 18, "Using the Wheel of Self-Discovery: A Career Transition Tool," addresses career redesign or new career choices for currently employed women. Such a group can help address anxieties about change, offer peer support, and provide a cost-effective way to obtain professional guidance. The goals of the group include identifying interests, abilities, and values; selecting career fields, researching and evaluating career options; and establishing an ongoing, online support group.

Chapter 19, "Returning Women Students: A Transition Group," describes a group experience for providing a forum for women to share resources, information, and emotional support within a university setting. By addressing certain psychosocial and cognitive issues, members learn to see themselves as successful in their new environment. Some goals of the group include replacing old coping mechanisms with more relevant ones, defining a sense of self during transition, and identifying resources for member success.

Chapter 20, "Codependence Recovery for Adults Abused as Children," depicts such a group as "especially effective at eliciting symptomatic behavior, thus bringing the client's problems into the counseling session." Addressing members' relationship with themselves and others helps achieve this objective. Some goals are learning about codependence, confronting core symptoms, and developing a sense of identity.

Chapter 21, "A Positive Approach to Disciplining Your School-Aged Child," discusses the skills parents need to create a positive environment for their school-aged child. Group goals are directed by using the six components of positive discipline. Goals include dealing with guilt over parenting/disciplining choices, recognizing the history behind parental discipline choices, and learning a variety of discipline choices and skills to achieve goals.

Chapter 22, "Transitioning Into Single Parenthood," identifies this group as one where members' intense feelings can be normalized and feelings of isolation can be minimized. Recognizing that psychological adjustment is greater when members are involved in social networks, the group goals include identifying feelings of grief and loss, analyzing adaptive and non-adaptive coping mechanisms, and sharing resources and information.

Chapter 23, "Systematic Desensitization for Specified Phobias," has as its purpose "to alleviate or lessen the intense anxiety response to a feared stimulus." Deep muscle relaxation is used to counteract anxiety reactions. The goals for these groups are learning that fear is a natural and healthy response to threatening stimuli, understanding that stressors are not aberrant, and learning relaxation techniques to aid in overcoming fear.

CHAPTER 14

PLANNING YOUR CAREER ADVENTURE: A GROUP FOR CAREER PLANNERS

Barbara Klym

PURPOSE

The purpose of this group is to help adults who are undecided about career direction begin to clarify their skills, interests, and goals, and benefit from the support, information, and networking possibilities of a group, as well as the expertise of a career counselor as the group's facilitator. The group would be offered as a service of a university career center and made available to students and alumni of that university.

CONCEPTUAL FRAMEWORK

The conceptual framework for this group is the current understanding of the career decision-making process and the usefulness of groups in that process.

Depending on theoretical orientation, career indecision may be seen as (1) a problem of matching one's interests, needs, or skills with the appropriate occupation; (2) problems of development or vocational immaturity; (3) problems in the decision-making process; or (4) problems with barriers posed by the social environment (Vance, 1997).

Emerging theories emphasize the importance of other factors in decision making, including cognitive information processing, social-cognitive processes, individual values, and the social environment as a shaper of self-concept. Another emerging discourse calls for theoretical unification (Zunker, 1998).

Zunker (1998) states, "The major difference among the theories is the nature of the individual factors in-

volved in the career decision-making process, but all the theories have common implications for career guidance." He notes those common implications as:

1. Career development takes place in stages, is influenced by sociocultural factors, and is lifelong.
2. Career development tasks involve transitions requiring individuals to cope with life stages, and helping individuals with these transitions is key.
3. Career maturity is acquired through successful accomplishment of tasks within developmental stages, and points of reference from this continuum provide relevant information.
4. Each person brings a unique cultural and historical self to the career development process.
5. Self-concept—which is not static, but a process—affects career decisions.
6. Stability of career choice depends on the strength and stability of personal characteristics: finding congruence between work environments and those characteristics is a key objective of career development.
7. Individual characteristics can be assessed through standardized assessment instruments. Use of these assessment tools may not dominate career counseling but are a viable option.
8. Identifying learned beliefs and generalizations is a key ingredient in counseling strategies.
9. Introducing occupational information and training in its use is a relevant goal for all educational institutions.
10. Career development involves a lifelong series of choices, for which effective decision-making skills

are necessary. Understanding individual decision-making processes enables counselors to be of better assistance during the decision-making process.

11. The concept of human freedom is implied in all career development theories and, as such, implies that all counselors should provide avenues of freedom from both the external and internal barriers in clients' lives.

12. The importance of cognitive development and its relationship to self-concept is an important focus in challenging clients' self-limiting beliefs about their options.

Miars (1998) notes several advantages to group delivery of career guidance services, including the enhancement of career counseling outcomes, support of group members, the efficient use of time and cost effectiveness, the enhancement of feedback, the personalizing of information, and the enhancement of enjoyment and variety from group members. Traditionally, group counseling has involved less formal structure, more affect, and greater utilization of the resources of group members. However, attempts at group counseling with a career focus in higher education often combine the structure of information delivery and planned activities with the relative nonstructure of group interaction, discussion, feedback, and sharing. Research supports this combination as improving outcomes (by increasing the number of exploratory activities completed by students) over individual counseling, pure group guidance, or pure group counseling (Herr & Cramer, 1992).

GROUP GOALS

Group goals include:

1. Providing activities that aid members in clarifying and articulating interests, skills, and goals.

2. Instructing members in the use of career center resources, the Internet, and the broader community to optimize access to current world-of-work information.

3. Normalizing members' anxiety regarding indecision through the support of the group.

4. Facilitating group discussion of the variety of approaches to anxiety and decision making among members.

5. Facilitating information and network resource sharing among members.

PRE-GROUP SCREENING AND ORIENTATION

As with any group, screening for significant problems in social functioning is primary. Members would be screened for social and life functioning within the normal range, with any chronic psychiatric conditions being stable and well-managed, as would be expected for attendance at any post-secondary educational institution. A fairly broad range of life experience and reasons for career indecision would be acceptable in members. The group is intended to be equally useful for alumni, returning students, and first-time students early in their academic careers. This set of categories would represent a fairly homogenous group if each person has the desire to "start from scratch," with a fresh look at identity, preferred skills, and life goals.

The physical setting would be a career center conference room with a flip cart or chalkboard and comfortable seating for five to ten people around a conference table. This would allow for a circular seating arrangement with a work surface for each person to complete written activities. Members will frequently pair-off to discuss written work, followed by discussions in the larger group. Each session is 90 minutes.

The screening interview would include the following components. First, informing prospective members of:

- the general group goal of providing exercises and information to help with career decisions as well as the support of one another through the group process
- rules regarding confidentiality, participation, completion of the whole process, arriving on time, and respectful listening

Second, assessing prospective members for:

- a match between individual needs and group purpose
- appropriate social functioning
- no apparent psychiatric instability

(Students better served by a one-time appointment for the purpose of specific industry information would be directed to that resource.)

OUTLINE FOR EIGHT GROUP SESSIONS

Session 1

Purpose. The purpose of the first session is to orient members to the group and allow them opportunities to get acquainted as well as to begin assessment and self-awareness processes.

Theme. A theme could be: "What will this journey be like?"

Activities. The first session starts with introductions, an overview of planned activities for the duration of the group, and a discussion of group rules, followed by administration of an assessment tool. The last 10 minutes will be spent in discussion of the homework assignment: "My Five Stories" to be completed for the following week (see Appendix A).

Introductions should be straightforward, starting with the request that members tell the group their name and answer the question, "What will you never do again, no matter how much you need a job?" Estimated time for this activity is 15 minutes.

The next activity is a discussion of the group rules and includes respectful listening, confidentiality, completion of the whole process, as much participation as possible while still taking care of oneself, and starting and ending on time. Ask the group for any suggestions to add to the list. Estimated time for this activity is 10 minutes.

The overview describes the format of the group: for example, "In the first few weeks we will be doing several activities, including some homework, which should be fun and valuable in clarifying career and life goals. We will also have ample opportunity to discuss homework and get to know each other better, in pairs and as a group. As the weeks pass, we will be able to spend more of our time functioning as a support group, but right now, we need to get the 'aha' process rolling (as in, 'Aha, I used to love doing X' or 'Aha, I really do not like X at all.')" Estimated time for this overview is 5 minutes.

The next activity is administration of the MBTI/SII which takes roughly 45 minutes. Five minutes are allowed for passing out test materials. (The test would be mailed to the scoring service with expected return within 1–2 weeks.) The final 10 minutes will be spent discussing the Five Stories exercise.

Process. The structure of this session provides enough information about group format and expectations to allow members to relax and participate. The introduction allows members to begin to open up to each other with the option of a low-risk self-disclosure and allows members to begin a clarification process for themselves. The assessment is completed in this session for two reasons: (1) the results may take up to 2 weeks to come back, and (2) this activity might disrupt the group process in later sessions.

Session 2

Purpose. The purpose of the activities planned for session 2 is to return and discuss assessment results to group members, as well as to encourage members to begin forming relationships with one another through telling their five stories.

Theme. A theme might be: "Where have I already been?"

Activities. The second session is spent discussing test results and the homework assignment, with the first third of the time allocated to interpretation of the MBTI/SII, and the remaining time on the Five Stories. A few minutes is used at the end to assign the My Forty-Year Plan exercise (see Appendix A).

In handing back tests results, it is important to say something like: "What the list of job titles means is that other people whose preferences and interests are similar to yours have had these jobs for at least three years and said they liked their work. These are suggestions based on statistics, not your only option. Also, if you were hoping to see a particular job title on the list and it is not, do not worry about it. It does not mean you would not be good at it, or would not like it. You may love some job based on something other than your interests, or that job may not be on the list. The job database for these tests has only a few hundred of the possible 15 or 20 thousand job titles in the world at this time." This discussion should take about 30 minutes.

For discussion of the Five Stories exercise, members should have listed and ranked the five most satisfying accomplishments in their lives so far. The facilitator asks that someone volunteer to tell their #1 story, which the facilitator should analyze by asking such questions as, "What was the main accomplishment for you? What did you enjoy most? What did you do best? What led up to you getting involved? What was your relationship to others? What was the subject matter?" Ask the member to share another story and work through the same questions. The group and facilitator then look for common features in the two stories. This should take about 15 minutes.

The group then pairs off and takes about 20 minutes each telling as many of the five stories as they have time for, interviewing each other about them, and identifying similarities. This should take about 40 minutes.

The last 5 minutes are spent assigning the My Forty-Year Plan exercise for the following week.

Process. In the first session the only "group time" members have is the short introduction and sharing in the first 15 minutes, so the second session would really be the start of group formation. The process of talking in pairs about their most satisfying accomplishments should be a largely positive experience, allowing members to get to know each other better using self-affirming disclosures, which should provide a supportive atmosphere.

Letting the group know that this exercise will be discussed as a larger group activity next time should reduce anxiety in low-risk taking members for immediate wrap-up. The last few minutes are used to assign the Forty-Year Plan exercise.

Session 3

Purpose. The purpose of this session is to have members share their long-range plans with one another and be supported in their goals.

Theme. A theme could be: "What are the qualities of my dream destination?"

Activities. The first 30 minutes of group is a wrap-up of the Five Stories exercise; allowing members to share anything they would like with the larger group—about their five stories or the process of thinking, writing, or talking about them with a partner. Any difficulty identifying themes could be addressed at this time as well.

Questions that should be asked of the group include: "How was it for you to talk about something you feel proud of? How did you feel about dissecting *that* information for clues about the real you, instead of your fears and worries? Is there anyone who's proudest accomplishments are several years old? Do you want to change that?" Ask members to give the notes they took on their partner's five stories to their partner, as the group will be using them in the future.

Following that, the Forty-Year Plan is discussed. Having completed it as a homework assignment, members now pair-off with someone other than their prior partner to talk about their fantasy of life 5, 10, 30, and 40 years into the future. They have 50 minutes, which can be structured however they prefer—perhaps taking turns discussing each time segment, or taking turns going through the whole exercise.

Instruct members to get details about how their partner will get from the 5-year goal to the 10-year goal, and so on. They also have the option of going further into the future with goals if they like. The last 5 minutes are used to give the Perfect Moment assignment (see Appendix A).

Process. Spending 30 minutes wrapping up the prior session is intended to facilitate continuity between sessions and clear up any unfinished business.

The process of talking with a partner and having dreams and goals supported and clarified should support member comfort and group cohesion. Members become better acquainted and feedback is structured to be positive. Members should be instructed that "reality checks" (such as, "You cannot do that, that is impossible") are not permitted, but questions that help clarify action steps, such as, "How will you do that?" are encouraged.

Session 4

Purpose. The purpose of the activities in session 4 is to complete the self-assessment activities and begin integration of the information gathered.

Theme. A theme could be: "Which real places match the qualities of my dream destination?"

Activities. The first 15 minutes are spent wrapping up discussion of the Forty-Year Plan, followed by discussion of the Perfect Moment, the assignment given for this session. This is a more detailed vision emerging from the Forty-Year Plan. Pairs have 20 minutes to discuss their ideal scene, then the group begins to integrate the information gathered through the activities. The remaining hour is spent in this discussion.

Summarizing is done using the flip chart or chalkboard to grid the results of the MBTI/SII, themes of the Five Stories, goals of the Forty-Year Plan, and salient details from the Perfect Moment. The group and facilitator then brainstorm possible matches of job titles for each member. Estimated time for each member is 20 minutes, so three members will complete this process during this session.

Process. Again, allowing wrap-up of the prior week's discussion paves the way for integration and forward movement. Pairs again discuss the exercise and then rejoin the larger group. At this point, everyone will have interacted with the majority of the larger group in a twosome, and members will have hopefully had three positive, fun, supportive conversations, so group cohesion would presumably be quite high.

The larger group should be a very positive place for all members, then, with brainstorming being lively and enjoyable for everyone.

Session 5

Purpose. There are two purposes of the activities planned for this session: (1) to continue the integration of self-assessment activities, hopefully finishing the process of plotting assessment results and discussing each member's activities, and (2) to orient members to the use of career center resources, allowing them to conduct independent research for world-of-work information.

Theme. A theme for this session could be: "Which real places…continued."

Activities. The first hour of this session is spent gridding results and brainstorming for the remaining group members. As in the last session, summarizing is done using the flip chart or chalkboard to grid the results of the MBTI/SII, themes of the Five Stories, goals of the Forty-Year Plan, and salient details from the Perfect Moment. The group and facilitator then brainstorm possible matches of job titles for each member. The last half hour is spent orienting the group to career center tools and the use of the Internet for career research. This prepares members to explore five of the job titles generated in the brainstorming session.

Process. At this point the group should be quite well-functioning, since all activities have been supportive and positive. The transition from a primarily educational group to a counseling/support group is expected to be smooth since the group has been interacting for a few weeks.

Session 6

Purpose. The purpose of the activities planned for this session is to check in with members to discuss any issues or concerns, followed by introducing informational interviewing to the group. Informational interviewing is emphasized here because members presumably have gotten a clear idea of how to conduct more general research from prior activities.

It is now appropriate to introduce informational interviewing as a tool allowing more focused research within targeted fields/organizations. Many people express anxiety about this activity, so it is important to allow time for full exploration of the rationale and protocol of informational interviewing. Through brainstorming, members also directly experience the potentially painless process of developing and utilizing one's network in a job search.

Theme. "How will I get there?"

Activities. The first 20 minutes of session 6 are spent introducing the idea of informational interviewing to the group. The remaining 70 minutes are spent in group session discussing members' concerns and progress with research, and brainstorming as a large group identifying potential organizations within fields and contacts within targeted organizations.

This discussion could be easily facilitated by focusing on one member at a time, with members volunteering ideas or potential contacts, which could then be mapped on a flip chart, showing relationships within possible courses of action. Each member would then have his or her own map to take home. Members are given an opportunity in the last few minutes of the session to request the needed contact information. The understanding is that in the intervening week, the member with the contact will obtain permission from that person to be contacted, and will bring the needed information the following week.

Process. The group process should continue as it has, with members relating directly to one another as much as possible, and experiencing one another as supportive. They should hopefully be well into stage three by this time, disclosing about specific concerns that the group can help normalize and support. The leader can then provide individual career counseling or other interventions that would potentially benefit the whole group. The networking activity should be fun and supportive, contributing a great deal to group cohesion. Of course, the possibility exists that not everyone will end up with good contacts, but there should be no shortage of ideas. It is important for the counselor to state that even if the group cannot provide a contact directly in line with the target organization or job title, any connection is one degree closer. Members need to be prepared to talk to several people, and for the process to take some time.

Session 7

Purpose. The purpose of the activities planned for this session is to begin to get members ready to work inde-

pendently, and to continue to increase their network beyond the group.

Theme. A theme could be: "Last-minute travel tips."

Activities. The session starts by addressing any unfinished brainstorming activities from the prior week. In addition, the topic of "life after group" should be introduced, with the idea that members need to begin to consider how they stay on track with goals and continue to gather the information they need to be able to make career decisions and achieve those goals. Discussion focuses on responding to member concerns and issues regarding that or prior topics of discussion. The last few minutes are set aside to exchange contact information.

Process. The group process continues as it has with members enthusiastically supporting one another and sharing ideas, suggestions, concerns, and practical solutions with one another. It is also expected that they express feelings of sadness as they recognize that the group will only meet one more time. This session, then, serves as an open forum for members to share whatever they would like, with the understanding that full consideration will be given to group closure next week. It might be important for the facilitator to moderate discussion to allow equal time to individual issues and members.

Session 8

Purpose. The purpose of the activities planned for this session is to facilitate satisfying closure of the group for members.

Theme. The theme for this session could be: "Off we go!"

Activities. Closure for the final meeting includes tying up loose ends, appraising achievements, and allowing members to talk about what they will do next in their process. The facilitator could structure this session with comments such as: "We've looked at a lot of information about ourselves and the world of work and tried to understand it in terms of career direction. I appreciate the hard work you've put into the process, and hope it pays dividends for you and your future. In completing this process, you are aware that there is no final answer to career and lifestyle development. It is an ongoing process." (Miars, 1998).

In addition, members have the opportunity to address any concerns or feelings about ending and proceeding alone with goals. Estimated time required for group closure discussion is 1 hour.

Following that, 10 minutes should be used to provide information regarding additional community resources for members wishing to continue with group counseling, referrals for individual counseling for members wishing to work on other life issues, or appointments with the facilitator for career counseling sessions.

The final 20 minutes are reserved to allow group members to complete a 1-page evaluation and to connect individually if they would like to exchange contact information between members and the facilitator for follow-up.

Process. The group is now in the "termination phase" in this session. Predictably, member's responses to this ending range from anticipation and excitement regarding their newly acquired skills and self-understanding to sadness at the loss of this structured opportunity to be assisted and supported by others.

Since the themes of "travel" and "adventure" have imbued the activities of this group, the final meeting could be orchestrated as a "bon voyage" party if the group and facilitator wish.

STRATEGIES TO EVALUATE THE GROUP

Evaluation processes are included in the last session. They include group discussion of gains in confidence and self-awareness, members' plans for next steps, saying good-bye, and providing verbal and written feedback for the facilitator (see Appendix B).

REFERRAL PROCEDURES FOR FOLLOW-UP

These issues are discussed in the final session. Information is provided regarding community resources for continuing with group or individual counseling re-garding issues other than career planning, and individual appointments with the facilitator or other career professionals for career counseling.

Follow-up is addressed with the suggestion that anyone who wants to stay in contact with the group can exchange contact information with others at the same time they are exchanging it with the facilitator, who will contact them via e-mail to follow-up on progress.

REFERENCES

Herr, E., & Cramer, S. (1992). *Career guidance and counseling through the lifespan: Systematic approaches* (4th ed.). New York: Harper Collins.

Miars, R. (1998). Group counseling: Career and lifestyle issues. In D. Capuzzi & D. Gross (Eds.), *Introduction to group counseling* (2nd ed., pp. 231–250). Denver, CO: Love Publishing.

Vance, M. (1997). *Career indecision among academically talented college students.* Unpublished master's thesis, University of Maryland, College Park.

Zunker, V. (1998). *Career counseling: Applied concepts of life planning* (5th ed.). Pacific Grove, CA: Brooks/Cole.

APPENDIX A

ACTIVITIES

MY FIVE STORIES

List the five most satisfying accomplishments in your life so far. It may be easier to remember your stories if you finish the statement, "There was a time when I. . . ." Rank your stories 1–5, and write down in detail what you actually *did*. Partners: Ask each other the following questions and write down the answers for your partner.

- What was the main accomplishment for you?
- What about it did you enjoy most?
- What did you do best?
- What led up to your getting involved?
- What was your key motivator?
- What was the subject matter?
- What was your relationship to others?

MY FORTY-YEAR PLAN

What do you want your life to be like in 5, 10, 30, and 40 years? How do you imagine the details? Partners: Ask each other the following questions and write down the answers for your partner.

- How old are you?
- What is your life like right now?
- Who are your friends? What do they do for a living?
- What is your relationship with your family?
- Are you married? Single? Do you have children? What are their ages?
- Where are you living? What does it look like?
- What are your hobbies and interests?
- What do you do for exercise?
- How is your health?
- How do you take care of your spiritual needs?
- What kind of work are you doing?
- What else would you like to note about your life right now?

MY PERFECT MOMENT

Pick a day sometime in your future. What's going on? Partners: Ask each other the following questions and write down the answers.

- Describe a typical day.
- Who are your friends?
- If you're working, what is it like?
- What kind of people do you work with?
- What kind of work are they doing?
- What is the atmosphere? (Relaxed or frantic?)

APPENDIX B

MEMBER EVALUATION

Directions

Circle the number that indicates how strongly you agree with each of the following statements below:
1 = strongly disagree, 2 = somewhat disagree, 3 = agree, 4 = somewhat agree, 5 = strongly agree.

1. The presenter provided activities that aided me in clarifying and articulating my interests, skills, and goals.

    | 1 | 2 | 3 | 4 | 5 |

2. The instruction in the use of career center resources, the Internet, and the broader community was useful to me.

    | 1 | 2 | 3 | 4 | 5 |

3. The support and ideas of the group helped reduce my anxiety about my current career/job circumstances.

    | 1 | 2 | 3 | 4 | 5 |

4. The information on informational interviewing and network resource sharing among members was useful to me.

    | 1 | 2 | 3 | 4 | 5 |

5. Please use the space below and on the back of this form to give the presenter any additional feedback.

CHAPTER 15

GRIEVING OUR LOSSES

Ann Strachan Bethune

PURPOSE

The purpose of this group is to provide an opportunity for people who have suffered loss through death, illness, or transition to experience, explore, and process their feelings in a safe and supportive setting. It is also to provide information related to the grief process that will help group members to understand their process and to work toward release and renewal. Finally, it is hoped that group members will gain tools that will help them to better support their process after the group ends.

CONCEPTUAL FRAMEWORK

We live in a society where people are viewed as individuals—autonomous, independent, and free—and where we experience separation from others (Glick, Weiss, & Parkes, 1974). Discussion of death or loss is not generally welcomed. For a person who is grieving a loss, a group can provide support that is not available elsewhere (Price, Dinas, Dunn, & Winterowd, 1995). Yalom and Vinogradov (1988) point out that people who have recently lost a loved one through death are at risk themselves. In their view, grief and loss groups comprise an important preventative intervention, in terms of both the bereaved person's physical and mental health.

The terms *grief* and *bereavement* are often used interchangeably in describing groups that focus on dealing with loss. *Grief* refers to the actual process that occurs when one perceives oneself as experiencing a loss—a

person's thoughts, feelings, and reactions. *Bereavement* refers to the state of having experienced a loss. The term *mourning* is used in psychoanalytic theory to refer to the conscious and unconscious processes created by loss; in this context, it can be used interchangeably with *grief*. More commonly, it is used to denote the cultural aspects of the grieving process (Rando, 1984).

We experience loss throughout our lives. O'Conner (1984) states that the most difficult losses are those that bear close relationship to ourselves. Loss of our own life or a part of our body or ability to function is the most extreme. Also profound is the loss of important people in our life, whether through death, divorce, or some form of abandonment. Developmental change, such as finishing school, getting married, moving, having a child, or growing older, comprises another level. Finally, material possessions, financial security, dreams and expectations, along with environmental, political, and socioeconomic change are all areas that hold the potential for loss.

To a greater or lesser degree, one experiences grief following loss in any of the aforementioned areas. This occurrence of grief is considered to be normal. Avoiding, repressing, or denying grief can have serious consequences, in terms of a person's emotional and physical well-being. While each person's process is different, it is important that grief be *experienced*—not just intellectualized or observed. One must *feel* the pain of one's loss in order to get through it.

Worden (1982) has defined four tasks that must be completed in order for a person who has experienced loss through death to move successfully through the grieving process. They are: (1) accepting the reality of the loss, (2) experiencing the pain of grief, (3) adjusting to the fact that the deceased is missing, and (4) withdrawing emotional energy from the deceased and reinvesting it elsewhere. Feelings that are normally experienced as a part of the grieving process include sadness, anger, guilt, anxiety, helplessness, frustration, and depression. How they are expressed will be influenced by a person's culture, religious orientation, and gender (Vernon, 1998).

Worden's (1982) four tasks are applicable in situations involving loss of all kinds. A life change or symbolic death results in a grief process similar to that caused by physical death. In terms of their process, both loss and grief are universal (O'Conner, 1984).

GROUP GOALS

The goals for this group are as follows:

1. To create a safe environment for the open expression of feelings.
2. To support group members in accepting the reality of their loss and in experiencing their grief.
3. To provide information about the grief process.
4. To help group members gain a sense of normalcy about their feelings and experience.
5. To provide tools that will be helpful to group members in better supporting their process after the group ends.

PRE-GROUP SCREENING AND ORIENTATION

Establishing a procedure for pre-group screening is important to insuring the well-being and safety of the group as a whole, along with that of its individual members. Capuzzi & Gross (1998) point out the importance of selecting group members whose personal goals align with the goals of the group and who are ready for a group experience. Individuals who are at risk or who would put the group at risk should not be included.

It is recommended that prospective candidates for the group be interviewed on an individual basis. The interviewer should begin by explaining the importance of determining whether people are ready for group work and whether the issues that they hope to resolve are appropriate to the group that is being formed. The interviewee should then be asked to talk about their loss and what they hope to gain by participating in a group. As the interviewer listens, it will be important to note any signs of pathological grief—grief that is prolonged, exaggerated, or masked by somatic or behavioral symptoms—as well as for loss through death or divorce that is very recent. If depression seems to be present, the interviewer may want to assess the prospective group member for risk of suicide. A person experiencing any of the aforementioned

symptoms or circumstances may need more help than the group can provide. If so, they can be encouraged to seek individual counseling (Price et al., 1995; Worden, 1982).

Assuming that the interviewer and the interviewee feel comfortable in proceeding, information can be offered regarding group process and goals. The interviewer will want to emphasize that while information about grief and loss will be offered, the group is primarily process oriented. Examples of group process can be provided and the group goals reviewed. Discussion should then focus on the importance of the prospective group member: (1) defining personal boundaries within which they are willing to share, (2) being open to the *experience* of their grief, and (3) accepting and allowing others to express their feelings. During this segment, the interviewer should address any issues, attitudes, or values that could negatively affect the group process. Pronounced resistance to experiencing or sharing feelings, along with judgmental attitudes toward others who cry or who express anger, are possible examples. Again, it may be necessary to postpone the interviewee's involvement in a group setting, offering instead to refer him or her for individual counseling.

In completing the orientation, the interviewer should share that the group will meet for 2 hours once a week for 8 consecutive weeks. It will consist of 7 to 10 people, all of whom are dealing with some type of loss. The starting date and time, along with methods of payment, can also be reviewed.

Issues of confidentiality need to be explained and their importance emphasized. Finally, the interviewer should share the ground rules for the group, which are defined as follows:

1. Group members are expected to attend every session. Please call the group leader if for any reason you are unable to attend. More than two absences will be grounds for termination.
2. You may contact and/or ask to meet individually with the group leader at any time. However, it is possible that you will be asked to share the nature of the contact with the full group at the next session.
3. It is important to define what you want from the group and/or hope to accomplish in the coming 8 weeks before you attend the first session.
4. Honor the rules of confidentiality and do not discuss group members or process outside of the group.
5. Wear comfortable clothing and be on time (Capuzzi & Gross, 1998).

OUTLINE FOR EIGHT GROUP SESSIONS

Session 1

Purpose. The purpose of the first session is for group members to meet one another and to initiate the group process. It is also to review group goals, issues of confidentiality, and ground rules; in addition, material on the leader's role and expectations are introduced.

Theme. Members enter the session with some degree of uncertainty about who and what to expect. Beginning the work of establishing a sense of safety and support—"setting the tone"—while allowing people to become familiar with one another and with the group experience—"transforming the unknown into the known"—will be the theme.

Activities. The group leader opens with a simple exercise intended to help people connect with themselves, referred to as *center and ground.* Once seated in chairs in a circle, ask group members to place their feet flat on the floor, to lower or close their eyes, and to allow themselves a full minute of silence. They can be quietly coached to follow their breath and to feel both the chair and the floor solidly beneath them. When the minute is up, they should open their eyes and allow their focus to return to the circle.

The leader welcomes the members of the group and initiates a preliminary round of introductions: "Tell us your name and one thing that you like to do. I will begin—I am Ann and I like to walk in the woods with my dog!" Using a flip chart, the leader then reviews pre-written lists of the group goals, confidentiality issues, and the ground rules. At the end of each list, group members should be encouraged to ask questions or express concerns. Also ask members if they want to add anything to the list. If someone has a suggestion about which the group can reach consensus, his or her point can be added.

Again, using the flip chart, a pre-written list of leader responsibilities, roles, and expectations is presented, as follows:

1. It is the leader's responsibility to ensure a safe and supportive environment in order that group members can share their feelings and their experience openly.
2. The leader will intervene if a group member (a) interrupts or is disruptive while another group member is sharing, (b) expresses negative judgment or disapproval regarding the feelings, values, or beliefs of another group member, or (c) attempts to dominate or control the group.
3. The leader has the right to ask a member to leave the group if it seems necessary for the safety of the member or the group.
4. The leader expects group members to listen closely when others are sharing and to communicate with others from a place of caring and respect (Capuzzi & Gross, 1998).
5. The leader acts as timekeeper and may on occasion interrupt the group process in order to restore balance, complete an exercise, or arrive at closure.
6. The leader will confront group members who consistently intellectualize, tell stories, or offer advice as a means of avoiding their own feelings of grief (Price et al., 1995).

As with the previous material, the leader answers questions and concerns, adding any points around which the group can arrive at consensus.

With the groundwork laid, the leader asks that during the second hour every group member share (a) their name, (b) the nature of their loss, and (c) what they hope to gain and/or accomplish as a member of the group. Each member is given 3–5 minutes, depending on the number of people present, and is given a 1-minute warning when his or her time is about to end. Group members can use any leftover time for open processing.

During the last 10 minutes the leader explains that future groups will open with a short educational offering on grief and loss, followed by group processing. Ask members to bring a photograph or a symbol representing their loss to the next session. Also ask them to start a journal, an assignment that will be discussed in more detail at the next group meeting.

Process. This session is more highly structured and task oriented than future sessions due to the leader's decision to review materials relevant to the safety and process of the group. Grieving a loss can be a very emotional event, one that requires a strong group foundation. It is hoped that through discussion and review of group goals, confidentiality issues, ground rules, leader responsibilities, and roles and expectations, members will deepen their awareness and understanding of what is required to safeguard the group process. Inviting members to add goals, ground rules, or other agreements encourages their consideration of what is required, as well as their involvement in taking ownership and helping to define the group.

Group members are given an opportunity to begin sharing personal material in the second hour. This segment, while structured and time-limited, allows group members to identify themselves and to take their place in the group. Naming their loss out loud helps to bring home the reality of it. Sharing their goal with the larger group helps establish and make clear their intent.

This session requires preparation, organization, and an active role on the part of the group leader. Successfully guiding the group through a task-oriented process during the first hour and initiating a process of personal sharing in the second requires flexibility, skill, and adeptness. However, the leader's most important role is in establishing a sense of safety. In addition to the steps that have already been described, this requires that the leader maintain a certain level of control within the group at all times, enacting and modeling interventions as needed.

Session 2

Purpose. The purpose of sessions 2 and 3 is the same—to provide a safe and supportive environment wherein group members can share the story of their loss and are open to feedback from other group members if they choose. As each group member shares, he or she will be working toward accepting the full reality of the loss, as well as experiencing his or her grief.

Theme. "This is the story of my loss" is the theme of sessions 2 and 3. This may be the first time that group members have had the opportunity to share the full story of their loss, along with whatever they choose to share about their current situation. This experience helps them to get their bearings on where they are—and where they're not—related to the grief process. It will also provide an opportunity to listen and to empathize with others, deepening the trust within the group.

Activities. After welcoming members back to the group, the leader takes the first 10–12 minutes to talk about the importance of *experiencing* feelings that are a part of the grieving process. Common ways of avoiding feelings of grief should be discussed, along with possible consequences of short-circuiting the grief process altogether.

Group members are encouraged to keep a journal during the course of the group, writing daily or several times a week, as they prefer. Explain that a journal is a tool that can help them to deepen and to move their grief. It also acts as a history of where they have been and quite possibly yield insights and points of awareness that they would not otherwise have had.

After concluding discussion of the above, guide the group in observing a minute of silence (described in session 1). Then ask members to participate in a brief check-in, once more stating their name and how they are feeling about themselves and the group. Following that, they are asked if there are any leftover issues or unfinished business from the week before. Once all business is cleared, the group can move on to the main activity for this session.

Ask members to share the story of their loss with the group, using the photograph or object that they have brought with them to help them disclose. Remind members that they can share as much or as little as they care to—that the group will respect and support them in establishing and maintaining their boundaries. They can choose to take their turn in the current session or wait until the following week. Instruct group members to listen quietly while each member takes a turn. Upon finishing their story, presenters are asked if they would like questions and feedback from the group. If their response is affirmative, the leader can open the group process to members for that purpose.

At the end of the group, those who have not had an opportunity to share should be reminded to bring their photograph or object with them the following week.

Process. During this session, group members begin to get a better sense of who is in the group. Assuming that the leader is successful in establishing and maintaining a sense of safety, trust and cohesion will begin to build as members disclose. During periods of open processing, it is particularly important that the leader demonstrate an ability to protect the member who has completed sharing his or her story and who is receiving feedback.

During this session it is possible that group members will begin to express their feelings of relief and elation at having found a safe haven where they can experience and share their grief. Too often family members and friends have become impatient with the intensity and duration of their grief process and have withdrawn their support. Both Yalom & Vinogradov (1988) and Price et al. (1995) indicate that cohesiveness tends to form quickly in grief and loss groups due to a strong need to bond.

Session 3

Purpose. The purpose of this session is the same as that described in session 2—for group members to share the story of their loss and open themselves to possible feedback in a safe and supportive setting.

Theme. "This is the story of my loss" continues to serve as the theme in this session.

Activities. The group leader presents an overview of the feelings that members can expect to experience as a part of the grief process, as well as the myths that often block us in finding the courage to grieve (Tatelbaum, 1980).

During the group check-in, ask members to comment briefly on (1) how they are feeling generally, (2) how safe they feel in the group, and (3) how they felt as they drove home following the last session. From this segment, the group leader should get some idea of how the group is doing as a whole.

Otherwise, the leader guides the group through the same format as in session 2, with the remaining group members sharing the story of their loss.

Process. Since the group is still in the definitive stage, the leader needs to be sensitive to the insecurities that members are experiencing and model a supportive and caring approach (Capuzzi & Gross, 1998). The leader, as well as the group members, should be getting a sense of what they can expect from individuals in terms of roles and responsiveness. A sense of trust and cohesiveness continues to deepen.

As each member of the group shares his or her story, it will become clear that people can experience loss in many ways. Similarities in the grieving process over a broad spectrum of loss also become apparent.

Session 4

Purpose. The primary purpose of sessions 4–7 is to support group members in grieving their loss. Identifying and experiencing their feelings, exploring the issues that are related to their feelings and loss, and gaining a perspective on where they are and what lies ahead in completing the grief process—all are important to supporting that purpose. Also important are the insights and opportunities for new learning that come with observing and interacting with others who are also struggling with grief and loss.

Theme. The theme of session 4 is "Where am I?" and/or "Where do I go from here?" Having shared their story and listened to the stories of others, group members are now free to explore feelings and issues surrounding their loss. A major portion of group time is spent in open process. While the falling away of structure is a source of relief for some and a point of anxiety for others, *all* members are expected to be wrestling with identifying where they are and/or how they want to use group time in support of their process.

Activities. The group leader opens the session with a description of the four tasks of mourning, as defined by Worden (1982) (see Conceptual Framework). Using a flip chart, focus and expand on the tasks one at a time, using examples from the members' disclosures for purposes of illustration. Emphasis should be placed on the fact that it is necessary to complete each task in order to finish the grieving process.

Next, ask group members to observe a minute of silence, followed by a check-in, where they briefly state how they are and talk a little about their experience in keeping a journal (see session 2). Finally, ask members if there are any leftover issues from the week before. When the discussion has run its course, move to the next and final segment.

The leader announces that for the remainder of the session—approximately 1 hour, 15 minutes—the group process is open to members who wish to share and receive feedback. Members are encouraged to recall their goal or what they ultimately hope to gain from their group experience. With their goal in mind, they may become clear about ways in which the group can support them. They will, of course, need to risk asking the group for the help they need.

As processing begins the leader should pull back, blending into the circle. Attentive and supportive, the leader re-emerges when opportunities appear to model desired behaviors or when interventions are needed. Five minutes before the period ends, alert the group and

assist members in reaching some form of closure before the group disbands.

At the end of this session, the leader should give a homework assignment, to be shared with the group during session 7. Group members are asked to create something that expresses their grief and their sense of loss. Possibilities include drawing, painting, collage, clay, sculpture, poetry, prose, songwriting, sewing, needlework, collecting, and arranging things—whatever medium or process is comfortable and healing to them.

Process. By now the group has entered the personal involvement stage, a period when members are beginning to experience their identity within the group and when power struggles, testing, confrontations, resistance, and defensiveness tend to emerge. In addition to a focus on active listening, empathizing, modeling, and protecting, the leader may now need to reflect and help members clarify their feelings. Challenging members to explore feelings at a deeper level through questioning, interpreting, or providing feedback may also be useful. The leader's capability may be openly challenged by a group member during this stage; if that occurs, it is important that the challenge be acknowledged and discussed (Capuzzi & Gross, 1998; Price et al., 1995).

For this and remaining sessions an open process will occupy a large portion of the group time. Yalom & Vinogradov (1988) report that in their experience with bereavement groups, structured activities or exercises are not always well received; rather, group members tend to prefer an open forum. The writer tends to support this view but, when acting as a group leader, arrive prepared to provide a structured exercise should the group energy falter.

Session 5

Purpose. The purpose of this session is the same as that described in session 4—to support group members in grieving their loss.

Theme. As group members gain in their familiarity with an open process and have an opportunity to reflect on their direction and needs within the group, the theme becomes one of "identifying and experiencing feelings and issues related to the loss." Risk-taking in terms of sharing and inviting help from the group is closely linked to this theme.

Activities. During the first 20 minutes of the session, the leader talks about tools that can be used to facilitate and enrich the grief process. Keeping a journal, writing a letter to whomever or whatever has been lost, talking to an empty chair—each of these alternatives are discussed, along with any ideas offered by group members.

Following this, group members observe 1 minute of silence—breathing, grounding, centering—then, proceed with their check-in. For the latter, they are asked to state how they are feeling, what aspect of their grief they are most aware of, and how safe they feel in the group. Finally, they are asked if there is unfinished business from the previous week.

Before proceeding with the open process, remind members that the group is half over. The leader may want to speak to the fact that while it is not recommended that members push themselves, it is important for them to think about what they want to accomplish or risk within the group before it ends. A gentle reminder to remain within the boundaries that they have set might also be useful at this point.

Process. The "empty chair" technique previously mentioned could easily be incorporated during group processing. Borrowed from gestalt therapy, it is a powerful tool. It involves setting an empty chair in front of a group member and asking him or her to speak directly to "who or what" has been lost in the present tense. Worden (1982) used this technique as an alternative to allowing his clients to talk to him about the departed; he felt that they needed to address the person directly, expressing their feelings about the relationship and the loss. Jacobsen, Kindlen, & Shoemark (1997) emphasize the effectiveness of the "empty chair" for addressing unfinished business with someone who is no longer there.

Session 6

Purpose. The purpose of this session remains the same as that described in session 4—to support group members in grieving their loss.

Theme. Group members continue to focus on identifying and owning their feelings and issues. By now they may see their inner process with new eyes due to awarenesses gained in the group and through self-reflection. They may also have broadened their acceptance and understanding of the grief process. The theme of this session and the next is: "Going deeper."

Activities. This session opens with a brief segment on the gifts inherent in the grief process. Ask group members to identify what they may have gained as a result of both their loss and their grief. This discussion—or the memory of it—may help members to rebalance, now or in the future.

During check-in, members are asked to state how they are feeling as well as how they are progressing with their journal writing and with their creative project symbolizing loss. A minute of silence and a call for unfinished business from the last session precedes the open process, as usual. At the end of the session, remind members to bring their finished project to the next meeting of the group.

Process. In all probability the group has entered the third stage of development, the group involvement or

working stage, and is both bonded and productive. Members are taking responsibility for their own movement and change. They are also able to set their personal issues aside in order to listen to others. The leader shares responsibility for the group and acts as a member at least part of the time. The leader has more time to focus on supporting members in deepening their exploration of personal issues and risk-taking (Capuzzi & Gross, 1998; Price et al., 1995).

One of the issues that commonly arises in loss/grief groups is the fact that family and friends are not open to discussing the loss. According to Price et al. (1995), group discussion of this issue generally leads to the group member taking the initiative in expressing his or her need to talk.

Session 7

Purpose. The purpose of this session remains the same as that described in session 4—to support group members in grieving their loss.

Theme. The theme from session 6 continues—"Going deeper."

Activities. This session opens with a brief presentation on rituals and their usefulness in assisting with the resolution of grief. The leader emphasizes that ritual, when meaningful to the person who grieves, can provide a way of directing and externalizing feelings and taking action that is extremely therapeutic (Rando, 1984). Examples should be offered and the discussion opened to members who want to explore this possibility.

Following the segment on rituals, group members will observe a minute of silence and do a brief check-in. They are asked to state how they are feeling and whether they have something that they need to work on during open processing. They also are asked if there is any unfinished business from the last session.

The next activity is sharing the creative projects that the members have brought with them. Ask members to take turns presenting their completed project, saving their comments and discussion until the last person has finished. At that point the leader invites feedback on what has been presented, then turns the group over to open processing.

Before closing, ask that group members return to the next and last session prepared to deal with yet another loss, that of the group. Ask members to think about what they and other members have gained and contributed and how they are impacted by the fact that the group is ending.

Process. The process for this session is essentially the same as for session 6 with the addition of the presentation of group projects. The latter symbolize work completed over time, the weaving together of feelings, thoughts, and memories—hopefully, a culmination of the grief work that has been done. Members are asked to share their creation with the group, a step that will be harder for some than for others. The leader may want to acknowledge the difficulty of what is being asked and stand ready to instill confidence and provide support.

In bringing the awareness that the group is ending to the forefront, the leader formally opens the termination process. Members will want to reflect on the meaning of their group experience and how it has helped them. They will also want to prepare for the group no longer being a part of their lives.

Session 8

Purpose. The purpose of this session is to support group members in gaining a sense of closure on their group experience and to help them prepare for what lies ahead.

Theme. "Looking back, looking forward, and saying good-bye" is the theme of the eighth session. Group members address unfinished business, affirm what each has gained and contributed to the group, and discuss what they anticipate for themselves over the coming days, weeks, and months.

Activities. The group leader opens with comments related to the fact that grief is cyclical and long lasting. It is important that members stay with the ebb and flow of their grief process. Saying good-bye to the group may re-ignite feelings associated with their original loss; this need not throw them. It is but another opportunity to do the work of grieving, leading them eventually to full recovery. The leader should remind members that he or she is available for follow-up by phone and/or a private session and can also make referrals should someone feel the need for additional help.

After a minute of silence, ask if anyone has unresolved issues from the last session or related to the group in general. It is important that the process of resolving unfinished business be as complete as possible and that the group as a whole be ready to move on.

The check-in serves as a primary task of the session: Each member is asked to share his or her feelings about the fact that the group is terminating. While each person speaks, the group remains silent, supporting the member nonverbally, through their attentiveness and their presence.

The main and final exercise for the session is conducted as follows: Members take turns expressing what they have gained through the group experience; other members may then offer feedback regarding a member's progress and contributions to the group. If well facilitated, this exercise should provide a sense of closure for all members, along with validation for their personal growth and their significance to the group.

During the last 15–20 minutes of the group, ask members to complete a written questionnaire for evaluation purposes and to take whatever time remains to say good-bye informally to other group members.

Process. Capuzzi and Gross (1998) point out that the last stage of a group, the enhancement and closure stage, is generally recognized as being both inspiring and sad. In terms of the former, the process of reviewing the progress that has been made and of exchanging information relevant to each person's significance and contributions is generally affirming. The reality of losing a group that has offered acceptance, understanding, and support for one's issues and growth is hard.

Yalom & Vinogradov (1988) address the fact that members of bereavement groups often make arrangements to stay in touch with one another and/or to plan reunions or meetings without a leader. For this particular kind of group, the results of ongoing social contact have proven beneficial and can generally be safely encouraged.

STRATEGIES TO EVALUATE THE GROUP

It is important to evaluate the effectiveness of the group in meeting its goals. It is also important to know whether the leader's role and the group design supported individual and group process and growth. Finally, it seems important to allow room for feelings and preferences not necessarily covered by those previously stated. The writer has developed the following questions, to be answered in written form (printed on both sides of an 8 1/2 × 11 sheet of paper) by group members at the end of the eighth session:

1. To what extent did you:
   a. Feel safe in expressing your feelings openly in the group?
   b. Feel supported in experiencing and sharing your grief?
   c. Receive helpful information about the grief process?
   d. Gain a sense of normalcy about your feelings and experience?
   e. Receive tools that will help you to support your own process after the group ends?
2. To what extent was the leader effective in:
   a. Ensuring individual and group safety?
   b. Providing support?
   c. Facilitating individual growth?
   d. Offering information that was relevant to the grief process?
3. To what extent did the group design support your process and growth through:
   a. Educational presentations and discussions?
   b. Group check-in?
   c. Structured group exercises?
   d. Open processing?
   e. Homework assignments?

4. I liked_____.
5. I didn't like_____.
6. I would have liked_____.

Through the collective responses of group members, the leader should get some idea of the overall effectiveness of what he or she has attempted. Follow-up evaluations might also be considered to determine the long-range impact and efficacy of the group.

REFERRAL PROCEDURES FOR FOLLOW-UP

The group leader needs to be prepared to make referrals for individual or group counseling should the need become apparent during follow-up contact with a group member. If the group has taken place through a mental health agency, there will in all likelihood be a referral procedure in place. If working privately, it will be important that the leader know available resources in the community or private counselors to whom he or she can refer.

REFERENCES

Capuzzi, D., & Gross, D. R. (1998). Group counseling: Elements of effective leadership. In D. Capuzzi & D. R. Gross (Eds.), *Introduction to group counseling* (2nd ed., pp. 47–73). Denver, CO: Love Publishing.

Glick, I. O., Weiss, R. S., & Parkes, C. M. (1974). *The first year of bereavement.* New York: John Wiley.

Jacobsen, F. W., Kindlen, M., & Shoemark, A. (1997). *Living through loss: A training guide for those supporting people facing loss.* London: Jessica Kingsley.

O'Conner, N. (1984). *Letting go with love: The grieving process.* Apache Junction, AZ: La Mariposa Press.

Price, G. E., Dinas, P., Dunn, C., & Winterowd, C. (1995). Group work with clients experiencing grieving: Moving from theory to practice. *The Journal for Specialists in Group Work, 20,* 159–167.

Rando, T. A. (1984). *Grief, dying and death: Clinical interventions for caregivers.* Champaign, IL: Research Press.

Tatelbaum, J. (1980). *The courage to grieve.* New York: Lippincott & Crowell.

Vernon, A. (1998). Group counseling: Loss. In D. Capuzzi & D. R. Gross (Eds.), *Introduction to group counseling* (2nd ed., pp 251–275). Denver, CO: Love Publishing.

Worden, J. W. (1982). *Grief counseling and grief therapy: A handbook for the mental health practitioner.* New York: Springer.

Yalom, I. D., & Vinogradov, S. (1988). Bereavement groups: Techniques and themes. *International Journal of Group Psychotherapy, 38,* 419–445.

CHAPTER 16

SIMPLIFY YOUR LIFE

Beth Hunter

PURPOSE

The purpose of this group is to create an environment of open communication, mutual support, and sharing of ideas and information, both from the resources and experiences of group members, and also through suggested readings. In addition, the end purpose would be to form an ongoing group of supportive individuals to continue exploring aspects of voluntary simplification and to become a force for change in society in general.

CONCEPTUAL FRAMEWORK

The concept of simplifying one's life is not a new one, but it has come to be defined in new ways as a response to the current dissatisfaction expressed by many, that "life no longer has the same meaning" as it did in the past. Duane Elgin, a spokesperson for the Voluntary Simplicity movement, describes the essence of the movement in terms of two elements. "To live more *voluntarily* is to live more deliberately, intentionally and purposefully—in short, it is to live more consciously" (Elgin, 1993). When distractions in life become overwhelming, we lose track of those things that are most important to both our inner and our outer lives. We are not able to act in an intentional and purposeful way, but are motivated by outside forces full of "have-to's" and "shoulds."

Living more simply involves establishing a different type of relationship with all aspects of our lives; including the things we consume, the jobs we do, the relationships with others, all of our connections to the rest of the universe, and much more (Elgin, 1993). The concept of living more simply does not mean living a life of poverty, but living intentionally with a balance that provides for greater satisfaction and fulfillment.

Simplicity is not just one thing or one path. There is no one perfect way to live simply (Luhrs, 1997). Finding a meaning for simplicity is a very unique process for each individual, depending on a wide array of factors such as values, culture, spirituality, and relationship to the natural world. It is learning to create a life that reflects your own particular passions, and energizes you. It is getting rid of the things (and people) that don't support you (Wieder, 1998). It is learning to say "no," and making a conscious choice when you say "yes." It is realizing that you *can* live your dreams, and actually have the time to pursue those dreams, while still enjoying good health, feeling calm and relaxed, and feeling competent to live your life according to your own set of values.

Some believe that the secret is in finding the best blueprint for balance, within the concept of "connection" (LoVerde, 1998). Within this framework, strengthening bonds or connections with family, friends, and colleagues helps to bring about the connection that reduces stress and brings a higher level of satisfaction. Becoming connected to the spiritual side of life is also emphasized, whether that be through prayer or meditation, or through a close connection with nature.

Although there is no one way to live more simply, Duane Elgin (1993) describes several common traits for those choosing this style of life. Among them are the following:

- Investing time and energy in simpler ways with family and friends (walking, playing music, camping, and so on), or volunteering time to help others in the community.
- Working on developing the full potential of the individual, in terms of their physical, mental, and spiritual attributes.
- Understanding and nurturing a respect for nature, and working to enhance the quality of life for future generations.
- Voluntarily lowering the level of personal consumption—buying less, and buying more wisely, with an awareness of qualities such as durability, energy efficiency, and functionality.
- Reducing clutter by selling or giving away those items that could be productively used by others.
- Working in a job that has meaning for the individual and which contributes to the well-being of others.
- Valuing and celebrating the wealth of diversity in the human race, and working to preserve the freedom that supports that diversity.

Although these characteristics may be common in those already living a life of voluntary simplicity, there are many differences in those who are seeking some form of simplicity and who are potential candidates for change through the group process.

GROUP GOALS

Again, it is important to emphasize that there is no one prescribed path to achieve simplicity in life. Therefore, the goals and the focus of the group may be determined more by the actual makeup and issues of interest to the members than a recommended list of specific goals. There are some very common complaints, however, that are voiced by those who are seeking assistance in simplifying their lives. These areas will form the outline, or suggestions, for group goals, with some leeway for group-decided goals.

1. To create an environment of openness and mutual support where personal issues of problems around the concept of voluntary simplicity in one's life can be discussed and suggestions for change offered.
2. To explore options for change in sessions that are introduced by group members and co-facilitated by group members.
3. To make positive lifestyle changes and to commit to continuing the exploration of the concept of voluntary simplicity.
4. To become more accountable and more committed to personal values and to enriching the lives of others.

5. To embrace and respect the diversity of opinions on simplification, and not to harshly judge others whose values are different.
6. To fully participate in the group process, offering personal gifts of positive experiences and proven methods of simplification.
7. To consciously respect the frailty and limits of our natural resources and to take steps to build a cleaner, safer, and more sustainable environment for the future generations.
8. To recognize that the roles we choose to live in life (jobs, relationships, and so on) will have a great impact on the satisfaction we find for ourselves.

PRE-GROUP SCREENING AND ORIENTATION

Since this is a group that is directed at issues faced by the general population, and not intended for those with personality disorders or those who have conditions such as severe anxiety, screening should be done to assure that those with more serious conditions are referred to other therapeutic settings. In addition, screening should be done for willingness to participate in the group process by performing homework assignments such as outside readings, and by willingness to co-facilitate one of the sessions.

OUTLINE FOR EIGHT GROUP SESSIONS

Session 1

Purpose. The purpose of the first session is to allow group members a chance to get to know one another, and to start to share the challenges that brought them to seek assistance through the group process. The facilitator introduces the duties and responsibilities required of each member in order to abide by the rules of confidentiality, and to promote a positive and rewarding group process.

Theme. The theme for the first session is to define, for each group member, what the term "simplifying your life" means to them. The most common complaints offered by group members center around the themes of time, money, work, relationships, meaning, identity, possessions, health, and fulfillment.

Activities. The first activity is the introduction of each group member, with a brief description of simplicity issues that the members would like to discuss further. The facilitator then introduces the concept of voluntary simplicity and presents some background information on the history of living simply. The facilitator presents a personal item that was selected because of its meaning in relationship to the struggles that the facilitator has had with simplification. For example, an item such as an alarm clock may represent the fact that the facilitator never has enough time to sleep. This item is used as an ice-breaker, in order to start the conversation. At the beginning of each session, one group member will introduce an item of significance that fits in with the theme for that week. The group members should each be assigned a specific date at the first meeting, so that they have time to consider which item to bring. After the introductory item is presented, there is a time for check-in, so that each member may offer information on the last week's activities and accomplishments.

Process. The fact that the facilitator solicits ideas and challenges from each group member helps set the tone for the following sessions. The importance of involvement by all members of the group is emphasized, and members are selected to help facilitate future sessions, so that they are even more committed to the idea of simplifying their lives. Using props as a check-in is helpful to get conversations started, and it requires that each group member think about the meaning of the object for the member displaying it. Insight into the challenges faced by others is gained, and it starts to become apparent that members can offer solutions to each other for specific problems.

Session 2

Purpose. The purpose of the second session is for group members to start understanding the power of the group process, and to begin to share specific challenges that members are facing in their lives.

Theme. The theme of the second session is the issue of time, or lack of time, that is the single biggest challenge for modern-day Americans. There is a lack of time for sleep, for exercise, for spending time with friends and family, and for doing things for ourselves. There are too many conflicting priorities, and not enough hours in the day to achieve them all.

Activities. The group member selected for this session introduces his or her object, gives the group the story behind the object, and explains the challenge or success associated with the object. After this initial presentation, the group goes through a circular check-in and members can either comment on the object of the day or discuss any other issue that came up during the preceding week. The facilitator should make sure that everyone has an opportunity to discuss the subject of time, and the group discusses some methods that have been used in order to find the time needed. Ask group members to write down the top five priorities in their lives, in order of importance. An assignment for the next week is to pay attention to everything that is requested of them that does not have a relationship to the top five priorities. The group is asked to prepare a short list of those requests that they answered with a "yes" when it could have been "no," without affecting the top five priorities. This will be a subject of discussion at the check-in during the next session.

Process. The second session is the real start of the "working" process of the group counseling agenda, as individuals begin to get clarification on the challenges faced by all group members, and understand the value of the group process to creatively solve problems.

Session 3

Purpose. The purpose of the third session is to continue finding helpful solutions to simplicity issues through the group process.

Theme. The theme for the third session is the problem of the abundance of material possessions that we find overflowing in our attics, basements, and storerooms. The question is asked of each member, "What would look different about your life if you had fewer possessions?" Most people would answer that life would be a lot more simple, and it would not necessarily result in a loss of lifestyle.

Activities. Each member is asked to review their list of requests for time that did not fit into the "top five" category, the assignment from the last session. The facilitator should allow group members to discuss how they might have been able to say "no" to some of those requests.

The group member selected for this session introduces his or her object, gives the group the story behind the object, and explains the challenge or success associated with the object. After this initial presentation, the group goes through a circular check-in, and members can either comment on the object of the day or discuss any other issue that came up during the preceding week. Ask group members to offer suggested methods of reducing the number of possessions that have accumulated in their homes. Typical suggestions are garage sales, giving to charity, and getting rid of clothing that no longer fits or is outdated. The last activity is to think about the subject of money and what it means to each person, as the topic for the next session.

Process. The exercises in this session really begin to offer concrete suggestions for people to use in their daily life. They are becoming more aware of positive solutions and may begin to make commitments to change the way they look at time limitations and the abundance of material possessions that most Americans have hidden in the closets.

Session 4

Purpose. The purpose of the fourth session is to continue finding helpful solutions to simplicity issues through the group process.

Theme. The theme for the fourth session is the subject of money, which could include topics such as: What does money mean to you ? How much money is enough? Do you really know how you spend your money? and What is it worth to you to give up some of your money?

Activities. The individual selected to bring an object for opening gives the presentation and asks for comments. Again, each group member is asked to make comments about the preceding week, or express views on the topic of the day. Ask group members to offer information and personal success stories around the topic of money. Some common suggestions are: (1) Make a list of all expenditures for just one day; (2) bring your lunch one day per week; (3) take a walk instead of going out to eat; (4) make a financial plan and stick with it; (5) get out of debt and stay there; and (6) rethink your definition of success.

Process. The exercises in this session continue to offer concrete suggestions for people to use in their daily life. They continue to become more aware of positive solutions around the issue of having enough money to live simply, and according to individual values.

Session 5

Purpose. The purpose of the fifth session is to continue finding helpful solutions to simplicity issues through the group process.

Theme. The theme of the fifth session is finding work that you love, and getting paid for it. Some members of the group may choose to get involved in some career counseling activities that include testing for interests and skills. Becoming acutely aware of the true passions in our lives allows for an openness to see how we can live those passions through the work we do.

Activities. The individual selected to bring an object for opening gives the presentation and asks for comments. Again, each group member is asked to make comments about the preceding week, or express views on the topic of the day. Group members discuss the topic of how to find work that is meaningful. Some typical suggestions are: (1) Start your own business; (2) take a sabbatical from your job to explore options; (3) consider working part-time or job sharing; (4) try telecommuting or consulting; and (5) try temporary work while you are looking at new career options.

Process. The exercises in this session continue to offer concrete suggestions for people to use in their daily life. The group members continue to become more aware of positive solutions around the issue of finding work that fuels the individual's passions.

Session 6

Purpose. The purpose of the sixth session is to continue finding helpful solutions to simplicity issues through the group process.

Theme. The theme of the sixth session is the problem of relating to the environment in a positive way, and exploring options for recycling, reusing, and renewing. This theme is closely tied to all of the others, in the sense that it has a global approach to how we live our lives. To live more simply is to live with fewer "things," and to practice responsibility with those things we need to have to support our lifestyle according to our individual value system.

Activities. The individual selected to bring an object for opening gives the presentation and asks for comments. Again, each group member is asked to make comments about the preceding week, or express views on the topic of the day. Group members offer personal stories about successes and failures with clearing out the clutter in their lives. Typical suggestions are: (1) Have a garage sale; (2) buy used products instead of new; (3) repair and reuse whenever possible; (4) contact recycling centers to find out how to dispose of toxic or unusual items; and (5) read labels, and purchase products that have been made of recycled materials.

Process. The exercises in this session continue to offer concrete suggestions for people to use in their daily life. The group members continue to become more aware of positive solutions around the issue of respecting the environment and cutting down on material possessions.

Session 7

Purpose. The purpose of the seventh session is to continue finding helpful solutions to simplicity issues through the group process.

Theme. The theme for the seventh session is to examine the area of shopping habits and a reaction to the consumerism of this country.

Activities. The individual selected to bring an object for opening gives the presentation and asks for comments. Again, each group member is asked to make comments about the preceding week, or express views on the topic of the day. Group members offer suggestions on the theme of changing shopping habits and rejecting consumerism. Typical suggestions are: (1) Don't buy anything, unless you can also give two things away or recycle them; (2) turn off the TV and read a book; (3) don't eat and watch TV; and (4) proudly be different!

Process. The exercises in this session continue to offer concrete suggestions for people to use in their daily life. The group members continue to become more aware of positive solutions around the issue of reviewing the way people shop, and how they react to the media blitz on buying things. During this session, the facilitator begins the wrap-up activities, and asks group members to develop a list of goals for change that will be discussed in the last session.

Session 8

Purpose. The purpose of the eighth and final session is to do some general wrap-up activities of summarizing the previous seven sessions, reviewing all the categories of simplification that have been covered. In addition, group members are given the opportunity to discuss the possibility of continuing to meet in a group called a "simplicity circle." This title basically describes a group that chooses to continue meeting and working toward the goals of voluntary simplicity.

Theme. The theme of this session is review, wrap-up, and final goal-setting for all areas of voluntary simplicity. All group members are invited to contribute information as to how their lives have changed since the beginning of the eight sessions, and what changes they plan to make in the future.

Activities. After an initial check-in to review the previous week, each group member is given a period of time to list changes that have been made to this point, as well as changes that they expect to make, in line with voluntary simplicity. These changes are celebrated, and group members congratulate each other for the positive differences that have been accomplished. The facilitator polls the group to see if anyone would like to continue meeting in a simplicity circle, and then makes arrangements for the continued meetings.

Process. This session is meant to be not an ending, but a beginning to a new and simpler way of life. The group and the facilitator have become bonded, and there is a natural desire to continue the friendships and the mutually helpful atmosphere that appears at this stage of group development. The process can be continued for those who choose to continue meeting through the simplicity circle.

STRATEGIES TO EVALUATE THE GROUP

Several methods may be used to evaluate this group, including the following:

- **Individual evaluation forms** that ask the same questions that were addressed in the first session, but reflect the benefit of the knowledge that was passed along during the course of the eight sessions. These questions cover the areas expressed by each individual as most important, and as the cause of most concern at the beginning of the group meetings.

- **Group feedback** that is solicited during the last session, with requests for positive changes or new commitments that each member of the group has made during the process of the eight sessions. Special acknowledgments for unique and helpful suggestions that were offered during the sessions is empowering for all participants and is particularly appreciated by the individual who "helped" someone else.

- **Invitation to form a simplicity circle** confirms that changes in thinking, as well as acting, have been achieved and that commitments to a new approach to life have been made.

REFERRAL PROCEDURES FOR FOLLOW-UP

Since this group is not actually a therapy-based group, the procedures for referral or follow-up look somewhat different. As previously stated, there is an option for the group members to continue their study and practice of voluntary simplicity through an informal group setting which has been referred to as a simplicity circle. Within this group setting, there is no designated leader or facilitator, but instead there is a cohesiveness built upon likemindedness and commitment to mutual support and education. In reality, many of these circles have been formed, and each one is unique because of the values and interests of the individuals involved. For those group members who do not choose to join a simplicity circle, there are numerous opportunities available to become involved in community-based activities, in environmental causes, in the spiritual community, and in personal enrichment activities.

REFERENCES

Elgin, D. (1993). *Voluntary simplicity*. New York: William Morrow.

LoVerde, M. (1998). *Stop screaming at the microwave! How to connect your disconnected life*. New York: Simon & Schuster.

Luhrs, J. (1997). *The simple living guide: A sourcebook for less stressful, more joyful living*. New York: Broadway Books.

Wieder, M. (1998). *Doing less and having more: Five easy steps for discovering what you really want — and getting it*. New York: William Morrow.

CHAPTER 17

THE TRANSITION INTO PARENTHOOD: A GROUP FOR EXPECTING COUPLES

Christie L. Carlson

*"Making the decision to have a child—it's momentous.
It is to decide forever to have your heart
go walking around outside your body."*

Elizabeth Stone

PURPOSE

Why would couples take measures to prepare themselves for parenthood? A better question is, why wouldn't they? Many life transitions are now prompting proactive measures. For example, most churches now require engaged couples to go through premarital counseling before their wedding to prepare the transition into marriage. It is also common for couples to enroll in birthing classes to plan for the one- or two-day event of labor and childbirth. Despite the current trend of emotional and physical preparation, it is surprisingly uncommon for couples to engage in counseling to prepare them for the psychological transition into their lifelong new roles as parents.

Parenting could be the most rewarding experience people go through; yet, it indeed challenges the psychological well-being of individuals and couples. While there is a plethora of information about pregnancy, mountains of books about parenting, and a new surge in parenting classes for problematic circumstances, literature addressing the emotional and psychological preparation for parenthood is noticeably scarce. In fact, planning strategies for parenthood are remarkably absent in most marriage counseling books. Given this, counseling groups for expectant couples serve as a welcome preventative measure against the potential for psychological ills in couples entering parenthood. By providing information, fostering discussions, and inspiring a positive and confident approach to parenting, many unhealthy disruptions are circumvented. Accordingly, the general purpose of this group for expecting couples is to provide a safe and comfortable forum in which cou-

ples can learn about, consider, and discuss various aspects of the parenting experience.

Central to the philosophy of this group is that human beings inherently possess certain positive qualities. Therefore, the main purpose of the transition into parenthood group is to help individuals acknowledge and nurture the growth of innate characteristics that will enhance their parental roles. The second, and equally important, purpose of the group is to facilitate discussion between each couple about important issues such as role expectations and family of origin experiences. Many, if not most, couples expend a lot of energy planning the nursery and preparing for the birth. It is not as common, however, that time and energy is spent in conversations about inherited or assumed parenting styles.

The third purpose of the transition into parenthood group is to foster an appreciation of the honorable and hence trustworthy spirit of a newborn infant and young child. Children come into the world with a fresh and pure psychological delicacy; parental respect for and acknowledgment of a child's inherent goodness would, hopefully, create a positive, supportive, and nurturing perspective for parents.

An additional purpose of this Transition Into Parenthood Group is to present expecting parents with current information about infant temperaments, parenting styles, developmental stages, and marital health, and to consider their effects on parental effectiveness. Considerable research has been conducted in the past 30 years regarding infants, children, and parenting. This information is unquestionably valuable to new parents, and numerous interviews with parents conducted for the purpose of this publication revealed regret for their lack of knowledge about infant temperaments, effective parenting styles, and development issues. "I wish I had known" resonated in those conversations.

Planning for the adjustment into parenthood should involve both parents; therefore, another important aim of this group experience is to engage and inspire the father as well as the mother in the process. For many couples, the mother-to-be is the parent who reads the books, watches the videos, and generally prepares herself and the home for the new baby. In such circumstances, the father-to-be may miss the anticipatory joy and emotional comfort that comes with such preparation. Further, when fathers are involved in the process from the very beginning, they are more likely to feel invested in parenthood and immersed in their children.

A further intention of this group process is to create a sense of shared experience with others in the same pre-parental transition stage. Couples are given the opportunity to share personal experiences and discuss both the excitement and the fears they have about their impending parenthood. Like other groups, a sense of universality is a valuable component in the expectant couples group.

It is important to clarify that the purpose of these group sessions is *not* to tell anyone how to be a parent, nor is it to present specific techniques. Rather, it is to foster contemplation and discussion of our individual attitudes, expectations, and beliefs about parenting, and to inspire hope and confidence. The rationale behind the selected topics favors gaining insight over learning specific techniques because insight yields us the opportunity to make choices about our parenting approaches. Making an informed and positive choice about our approach to parenting can have benefits that carry parents through the entire process of raising children. Accordingly, the overall purpose is to get couples talking about things they may not have considered and to contemplate their fundamental parenting assumptions so they might choose to be proactive and positive in their parenting.

CONCEPTUAL FRAMEWORK

Research indicates that marital satisfaction follows a curvilinear pattern (Anderson, Russell, & Schumm, 1983; Rollins & Feldman, 1970; Rollins & Galligan, 1978), with very high satisfaction early in a marriage, dropping during the time couples generally have children, and rising again during the empty-nest stage. The demands and stresses of parenthood certainly contribute to this pattern, most especially when couples are not prepared for their new roles. Premarital counseling has a positive impact on the transition into marriage and it is asserted here that in that same way, pre-*parental* counseling would positively affect the transition into parenthood.

The fundamental assumption underlying this expectant couples group is that people come into the world with certain humanitarian capacities: specifically, to love and be loved (Sullivan, 1953), to nurture and be nurtured, to protect and be protected, to be compassionate and trustworthy (Rogers, 1959), and finally, that we are compelled to express these benevolent aspects of our character at some level. While some people's behavior suggests otherwise, others exhibit these humanitarian qualities habitually, which indicates that individual personality potentials are possessed on a continuum, meaning that each of us enter the world with a unique level of these qualities. The environment interacts with these inherent benevolent potentials producing our feelings, thoughts, and behaviors at any given time. These inborn capacities for love, nurturing, protection, compassion, and trust are fundamental to our parenting experience. Therefore, if we come to acknowledge them within ourselves and consider the effect that our personal experiences have had on the expression of these qualities, we can foster their growth.

Equally important as the positive attitude we possess about ourselves as people and as parents is the attitude we have about our children. A profound influence on our ability to function as effective parents is the degree to which we believe that our child is *also* a capable and trustworthy soul. Awareness of the benevolent qualities that our children possess inherently enhances our ability to function as effective, thoughtful, and loving parents.

The manner in which we parent is a choice, regardless of how we were raised. We can choose to perpetuate unhealthy parenting practices, or arrest them and incorporate new, healthy practices. All of our family-related experiences cause us to develop expectations about our partner, our child, others, and ourselves. If we acknowledge and analyze our experiences and the resulting expectations, we can adapt them if we choose.

Of further conceptual relevance to this group work is an individual's confidence in his or her parental aptitude. It is asserted here that a positive attitude about our ability to be effective parents gives rise to effective parenting. Further, that by augmenting and incorporating productive attitudes and behaviors, unproductive attitudes and behaviors will diminish naturally. An underlying assumption of these counseling sessions is that increasing healthy attitudes and practices will displace unhealthy ones.

GROUP GOALS

The goals for this group are:

1. To generate a positive perception of our parental aptitude.
2. To foster expression of our inherent benevolent parenting characteristics.

3. To develop a more accurate and healthy set of expectations about those around us and ourselves as we enter parenthood.

4. To contemplate the effects of our family of origin experiences on our potential parenting style.

5. To encourage and recognize the value of a trusting and faithful attitude about children.

6. To engage *both* parents in the process of preparing for parenthood.

7. To develop an appreciation for parental-relevant knowledge, such as infant temperaments, marital health, parenting styles, and developmental stages.

8. To encourage parental joy.

9. To come to understand that the effective parenting practices early in children's lives have tremendous payoffs later.

10. To accept that our attitude about parenting and children is a choice and our attitude underscores all of our parental decisions and behaviors.

11. To develop a parenting mission statement, which helps to guide us as we encounter new or challenging situations.

Note: It is important to mention the value of creating an accepting, nonthreatening, warm and supportive atmosphere in the first session, which is carried through the subsequent sessions. As in all group work, it is fundamental to the process of the group and attainment of the goals.

PRE-GROUP SCREENING AND ORIENTATION

The group is intended for couples that are expecting a child, though couples that are not yet pregnant but are interested in preparing themselves for parenthood should not be excluded. Measures should be taken to select group members whose goals are compatible with the goals of the group, who will not hinder the process, and who will not be psychologically harmed by the group experience (Capuzzi & Gross, 1998). Same-gender or cross-culture couples should not be excluded unless the group composition jeopardizes the well-being of, or inhibits the beneficial properties for, any parties.

The preventative, educational nature of this group approach implies that existing pathological issues of participating individuals or couples are not to be processed during the group sessions, but rather contemplated. Though these issues are not the intended focal points, they may be uncovered, and therefore potential members must be alerted to this risk before participation. It is suggested that orientation information and a questionnaire be prepared, distributed, and agreed to by potential group participants.

The orientation material would include the purposes, ground rules, expectations, topics, risks, and the format of the group sessions, as well as the qualifications and general philosophy of the leaders. Members must agree to abide by the ground rules and indicate an understanding of the purposes and potential risks by signing a consent form. The questionnaire should be designed to detect obvious individual psychological pathology or serious relationship issues, which may inhibit the group process or jeopardize individuals. In these cases, the couple should be excluded and a recommendation for appropriate counseling made.

Ideally, a male and female couple will lead the sessions. This type of leadership furnishes a couple model for the group and provides balance for both the members and the facilitators. Further, female or male group members may relate stronger to like-gender counselors, enhancing the potential for participation and learning gains. The weekly sessions should be at least 1 1/2 hours, preferably 2 hours, with a break near the midpoint.

OUTLINE FOR EIGHT GROUP SESSIONS

Session 1

Purpose. The purpose of the first session is to (1) become acquainted and to develop an atmosphere of comfort, safety, and trust; (2) foster a feeling of investment in the group and explain the rationale for conducting groups for expecting couples; (3) acknowledge the limitations of having eight sessions to address the monumental task of parenting and to discuss the reasoning behind the topics selected; and (4) proclaim the leader's belief in the innate and personally unique parenting qualities already present in every group member.

Theme. Let us get comfortable and acquainted.

Activities. The session opens with an unusual type of introduction, explained by the facilitators. Each leader demonstrates the introduction by introducing himself or herself as if he or she were the other leaders. A lighthearted comment about personality should be included. The male leaders might say:

> I'm Mary. I am a very fussy eater and often take an enormous amount of time giving my very specific food order in a restaurant. I adore my cats and always talk to them as though they are human, but they just gaze at me totally bewildered and confused. I am outgoing, but prefer small gatherings to large ones. I tend to be sensitive and can easily cry over commercials. I am also known to obsess over details and planning, often driving John crazy, though he is usually patient and accepting of my little quirks. I love to be outdoors and spend some of my leisure time golfing or gardening. I love kids, have two grown children of my own, and I am expecting my first grandchild soon.

Mary would follow by introducing herself as though she were John, making sure to, lightheartedly, incorporate certain of John's less positive character traits. Each group member is then asked to introduce himself or herself in the same manner. For example, Sally and Dan are a couple. Sally introduces Dan as though she was he, and Dan introduces Sally as if he were she.

After introductions, the leaders present the intended goals, general philosophy, and basic group rules. Leaders should submit their professional and personal qualifications, as well as their reasons for facilitating a group for expecting couples. Included in this segment should be the leaders' fundamental assumptions about human beings as they relate to parenting (see Conceptual Framework). The leaders should acknowledge the vast array of potential parenting topics and explain the rationale behind those selected. Group members should be encouraged to suggest additions or changes to the goals and rules, and to get necessary clarification before accepting them. Especially important is a discussion about consistent attendance and confidentiality.

The second activity requires dividing into foursomes; two couples each. In these smaller groups, the couples share with one another the first positive thing they remember thinking when they found out a child was going to enter their lives. After giving each foursome ample time to be acquainted and exchange stories, the larger group reconvenes and the couple's alternate introducing their new acquaintances to the entire group along with the positive parent-to-be thoughts they heard from one another. It is suggested that one man share another man's thoughts and one woman share another woman's thoughts. Closing would involve members stating what they gained from the first session, as well as the homework assignment.

Process. The leaders model effective and respectful communication in order to promote the same from group members and to create an atmosphere of safety. This, along with the discussion of rules, helps relieve some anxiety about the manner in which dialogue will be exchanged. The various introductions and personal statements help alleviate apprehension about the qualifications of the group leaders and uneasiness around the other couples, and foster a feeling of universality. Having couples introduce their partner as if they were that person is intended to bring a little levity to the session. Positive traits shared about partners build confidence. The intent is for personal awareness and public acknowledgement of character strengths, fostering their development and reducing fears about personal parenting inadequacy.

By having couples interact in foursomes and share about one another instead of themselves, they can develop a more intimate appreciation of other group members as well as enhance the potential for supportive relationships outside the sessions. This activity also requires attentive listening, careful interpretation, and accurate recounting, three important communication skills. Sharing the first positive thought that each person had when they found out they were expecting fills the room with many joys of impending parenthood. It also causes couples to consider the positive aspects of expecting a child mentioned by other couples that had not yet occurred to them.

Discussing the rationale behind the selection of topics serves a maintenance purpose; parenting involves an extraordinary array of issues, all of which cannot be fully explored in an eight-session format. Supporting the intended topics is an attempt to keep discussions closer to parenting attitudes, less about specific techniques, and assists in keeping sessions on track. This will also alleviate members' apprehension about what they stand to gain from their attendance and participation.

Involving the members in the creation of the goals and rules gives rise to a personal feeling of power and investment in the group experience. It also serves to ease concerns about expected behavior. To suppress fears about judgment from others and to promote the philosophy of the facilitators, helpful leaders comments might include:

> We see before us ten future parents with valuable and unique qualities. We do not know how much faith you have or do not have in yourself, but we can tell you that without ever having met you, we have unwavering faith in each of you as future parents.

Homework for next week.   Members are asked to imagine that the child they are expecting is now 5 years old and to put themselves in the mind and body of that child. They are instructed to write down three things that they love most about being their partners' child and three specific things that that parent has taught them. For example, Mark and Jenny are a couple. Mark would write as though he was Jenny's child and Jenny would write as though she was Mark's child. Individuals are asked to complete this exercise without discussing it with their partner.

Session 2

This session, and subsequent sessions, opens with comments, questions, or concerns that may have arisen after the prior session(s). Further, each session closes with the leaders asking if anyone feels unfinished or has comments or questions about the session.

Purpose. The purpose of the second session is to discuss the innate qualities that will enhance the effectiveness of our parenting and provoke a discriminating posture toward parenting advice, tips, research findings, and other external information. The intention here is to promote the value of primal intuition (not necessarily experiential). An additional purpose of this session is to consider our *expectations* and the potential impact they have on our parental effectiveness. Finally, this elevates individual confidence in parental aptitude and enhances couple cohesiveness.

Theme. Are we innately "parental"? In addition, what expectations do we have about parenthood?

Activities. The first part of the session is reserved for discussion about the inherent characteristics we possess that will enhance our parental effectiveness. As presented in the Conceptual Framework section of this chapter, the leaders address the inborn humanitarian characteristics of love, nurturing, protection, compassion, and trust, emphasizing that everyone has these qualities. The facilitators should open discussion by presenting this scenario:

> If you and your partner found yourself stranded on a desert island, how could you possibly raise your children? Childbirth is a process that proceeds naturally, is the same thing true about caring for and raising a child. What would our instincts have us do for our children? What would be important for them?

Members are asked to suggest answers to the last question and discussion follows.

Process (First Activity). Members usually report that if they were stranded on a desert island they would naturally be compelled to provide their children with shelter and food, make them feel safe, give them love, protect them, teach them skills, play with them, prepare them to take care of themselves, and so on. These natural compulsions arise from innate humanitarian characteristics that exist in all human beings. Without books, advice, experts, computers, TV, and nearly without thinking, we have the fundamental qualities most important in raising children. Raising children using only our benevolent qualities would produce secure, productive, confident, and happy children resilient to the many negative influences this fast-paced, pressure-ridden society may present to them. That we live in the information age should not be a reason to abandon these instincts. Rather, these instincts should be the force driving our parenting practices, and we should filter outside information through them more than ever before.

The second activity relates to the homework assigned in the first session. Each individual shares what he or she wrote about being his or her partner's child. After this sharing, ask each member how their partner's comments made them feel.

Process (Second Activity). As individuals share about being the child of their partner, expectations will surface giving the leaders and group members the opportunity to discuss them specifically. In addition, the laudatory nature of the exercise promotes an awareness of the strengths each person brings to the parenting experience, helping to elevate personal confidence and enhance couple cohesiveness. This exercise serves as a "jumping off point" for couples to discuss expectations in general. Encouraging couples to discuss expectations before a child is born circumvents the possibility of disruptions that could occur if problematic issues are forced into consideration as they arise. This process could also abate the development of resentment arising from unrealized expectations

Homework. Distribute a list with specific expectation topics for couples to consider and discuss at home. Suggestions for the list are: direct care of the child, parenting/household roles, job-related issues, spiritual beliefs, and holiday activities.

For next session. Ask each person to bring a personal story about his or her favorite childhood holiday experience.

Session 3

Purpose. The main purpose of stories about favorite holidays is to promote consideration of family traditions and the other family of origin practices that will influence our parenting, and to foster contemplation of alternative practices if necessary. In addition, the purpose is to develop an understanding that our parenting practices are **a choice**.

Theme. The influence of our families of origin.

Activities. Group members share the story they brought about a favorite holiday experience from their childhood. The leaders should elaborate on the vast array of influences our family has on us, and promote specific discussion about how our parenting practices and decisions are affected by our family of origin. Discipline is an important topic and should be included amongst the many other influences.

Process. Experiences from our upbringing cause us to develop assumptions about many things, including how holidays are celebrated, how to discipline, gender roles, how to resolve disputes, and generally how to interact in a family. This exercise, too, is a "jumping off point" for thought and discussion about the effects of our family of origin. Couples who address, before having children, the influences of their family of origin may avert confusion or disagreements in the future.

Homework for next session. Distribute a checklist that includes specific family of origin influences. Couples are instructed to consider and discuss the items on the checklist at home.

Session 4

Purpose. The purpose of this educational session is to acquaint expectant parents with infant temperaments and parenting styles, and to discuss how this knowledge may be helpful to them as future parents. Further, this session should instil in members an appreciation for proactively acquiring knowledge about their child's developmental journey.

Theme. Goodness of fit.

Activities. The leaders present information about infant temperaments such as easy, difficult, and slow-to-warm; and parenting styles including authoritarian, authoritative, permissive, and restrictive. The pros and cons of each are considered. Full details of these topics are not included here, but they are available from a variety of sources and described in *Life Span Human Development* by Sigelman and Shaffer (1995).

Process. Research has illuminated the parent roles but often neglects the infant's contribution to the parent-child relationship (Hetherington & Parke, 1993). An understanding of *infant temperaments* prepares expectant parents for the potential of having a child with an easy, difficult, or slow-to-warm-up tendency. This knowledge can help them provide an environment that best suits their child, which will enhance the possibility of a secure infant/caregiver attachment. Should an infant have a difficult temperament, parents may feel that they are doing something wrong because their baby seems irritable. However, some infants simply are born with this tendency and an awareness of this disposition can prompt parents to investigate the most effective parenting practices. Awareness that prompts adjustment alleviates the parental frustration that can arise when raising a child with a difficult temperament.

Knowledge about *parenting styles* provides mothers- and fathers-to-be parenting options from which they can make an informed choice as to how they will approach their new roles. We may have been raised in a family with either strict or lenient tendencies; this session promotes consideration of the parenting tendencies we might have inherited from our parents. This information empowers individuals to consider which of their inherited practices they want to incorporate into their forthcoming parenting roles, and it gives them options if they want to alter any of their tendencies.

A child's healthy personality development depends on the "goodness of fit" between the child and parent (Chess & Thomas, 1984)—that is, how well the infant's temperament and the parent's style create healthy growth potential. This educational session supports the assertion that our children are unique and that we need to fully understand and appreciate them as individuals in order to provide them with what they need. What may be beneficial to one child may not work best for another and it is the parent's responsibility to adjust to the temperament of the child to assist in healthy development.

Homework for next session. Ask members to bring with them a story from their childhood when someone important to them demonstrated unwavering, unconditional trust and faith in them. This could have been a mother, father, grandparent, aunt, uncle, teacher, coach, neighbor, and so on.

Session 5

Purpose. The purpose of this session is to stimulate couples to take an empathetic stance with their children. Further, to consider the importance of maintaining positive expectations about their children and to invite couples to hold a posture of genuine faith and trust in them. Helpful to parents interested in an empathetic, trustful relationship is knowledge about children's developmental stages. Examples of developmental stage issues are presented, and parents are encouraged to pursue information of this kind.

Theme. Surrounded by a positive environment, including encouragement, security, and approval, children learn to develop positive outlooks thus learning to like themselves. This is portrayed in Dorothy Nolte's (1998) poem, *Children Learn What They Live*, excerpted below.

> *If children live with encouragement, they learn confidence. . . .*
> Excerpt from D. Nolte's poem *Children Learn What They Live*

Activities. The first activity relates to the homework from last session. Members tell of a specific childhood experience in which they felt unwaveringly trusted. The stories should be followed with questions such as: How did that make you feel? and Is that what you want for your child?

For the second activity, the leaders present this scenario:

> Johnny is 2½ years old. As the family is getting ready to go out, Dad says, "Johnny, put your coat on." Little Johnny replies with a firm "NO!" This reply from Johnny has become routine.

Group members are asked to suggest some empathetic responses to this situation.

For the third activity, the leaders present another scenario:

> Brittany is 14 years old. She is getting ready for a school dance and notices that she has a pimple on her nose. Brittany becomes extremely upset and declares that she is not going to the dance.

Members are asked to suggest empathetic responses to Brittany's dilemma.

Process (First Activity). Consideration of an experience in which we have been fully trusted prompts us to recapture the feelings of the occurrence. People can be *told* about the value of feeling trusted; however, reliving the feeling is more impactful. After group members recount their story, they are asked how the unwavering trust made them feel and, further, how they behaved. Probably, the feelings were of belief in oneself and the actions taken from this stance were likely positive. Parents-to-be might be asked, "How do want *your* child to feel?" The goal is for expecting parents to appreciate that when we authentically believe in our children, we demonstrate, overtly and covertly, that they are trustworthy. Further, that children can sense if we are genuine; if we are, they are more likely to live up to our positive expectations.

Process (Second Activity). This exercise prompts expecting parents to consider how they might react in an actual toddler situation. To respond to Johnny empathetically, a parent must think like Johnny. What might cause him to react so defiantly to a simple request? Although Johnny's response may appear impudent, it is probably an attempt to assert his will. Erik Erickson (1963) asserts that, between the ages of 1 and 3 years, children *must* learn to be autonomous. If they do not, they will feel shame and doubt their abilities. Our perception of Johnny's "NO!" is different when it is viewed in the context of his developing independence. An example of teen maturation follows.

Process (Third Activity). Again through this activity, expecting parents have an opportunity to consider supportive, healthy, and understanding responses to a developing child. To react to Brittany empathetically, parents must understand her. In this adolescent stage of development, young people tend to be egocentric and many encounter the *imaginary audience* phenomenon (Elkind, 1967). Brittany probably believes that everyone at the dance would be looking at her and the pimple. Her self-consciousness and egocentrism may seem extreme but are quite natural. Yet, they might prevent her from grasping the idea that other teenagers at the dance are likely so preoccupied with *themselves* that they would not even notice her blemish.

Parents who make themselves aware of these types of developmental issues can better understand and feel trusting of the behavior of their children. They can also worry less that their child is "bad" or "unreasonable." Importantly, awareness that certain childhood behaviors may have functional or developmental purposes allows parents to interpret their child's actions from a more positive, trusting perspective.

Homework for next session. Come to next week's session prepared to take off your shoes and socks.

Session 6

Purpose. The purpose of this session is to discuss the importance of marital health to healthy child development

and, further, to encourage couples to actively pursue, marital *and* parental happiness and to seek help if needed. A final purpose of this session is to present couples with an example activity by which they can express, through tactile senses, the care and love they have for their partner. It is critical to the effectiveness of this activity that the leaders are comfortable with and confident about the value of openly expressed love and respect.

Theme. Embracing our relationship.

Activities. The leaders discuss the impact of the marital relationship on children by asserting that: "A positive, affectionate marital relationship predicts low levels of child and adolescent conduct problems, and provides a buffer for adults and children against a variety of stressors" (Sanders, Nicholson, & Floyd, 1997, p. 234). Underpinning the discussion activity is the attitude that marital happiness incites parental happiness and vice versa and that to seek couples counseling when needed is as proactive and healthy as going to the doctor when you are injured.

Topics for discussion can be gleaned from a variety of sources such as the reference cited above. It is suggested that in keeping with the conceptual framework of this group proposal, topics should focus on the positive aspects of the marital relationship that presumably pre-exist in couples (affection, support, trust, unconditional love, and so on).

The second activity for session 6 involves foot washing. Supplies needed include

Plastic containers about 15" × 15" × 6" (one per couple)

Washcloths (two per couple)

Dry, soft towels (two per couple)

Powder or lotion (two bottles each, shared by group)

Mild, allergy-free liquid soap

The interactive exercise requires that, before group members arrive, the leaders set up one foot-washing "station" per couple. Each *isolated* station has a chair, a plastic container filled with about 3 inches of warm, soapy water, two washcloths, two towels, and powder or lotion. One partner, the washee, sits in a chair with his or her feet flat on floor. The other partner, the washer, sits on the floor at the feet of their partner. This is a gentle and unhurried activity; the couples are told that they are conveying, through their hands and fingers, the love and respect they have for their partner. There is no verbal exchange during the foot washing, although the washee may make sounds. The washer is instructed to tenderly and lovingly pick up one foot, gently and slowly wash it, carefully pat it dry, and finally powder it (or put on lotion), then proceed to the other foot. After both feet are washed, the washer would carefully put on the washee's socks and shoes. It is appropriate for the washee to express gratitude, nonverbally, to the washer before the partners change roles and positions.

Process (First Activity). The presentation and discussion of marital health and its effect on children promotes couple's contemplation about the current state of their relationships and what aspects might need attention. The aim is to draw attention to the efficacy of healthy and happy relationships on children and to encourage couples to seek and incorporate practices that enhance their alliance.

Process (Second Activity). Foot washing, considered in some cultures to be a supreme display of honor for another person, stimulates closeness and a warm, loving, and appreciative attitude. It serves to promote intimacy and advance (or rekindle) the bond between couples. The nature of the exercise could challenge the comfort of some members, giving them an opportunity to break through any intimacy-inhibiting attitudes. A show of gratitude promotes expressions of appreciation. Though foot washing is the preferred activity because it incorporates some vulnerability, a sock-covered foot massage could be substituted if leaders feel, or participants display, a strong aversion to the washing.

Session 7

Purpose. The main purpose of this session is to incite a belief that our attitude about parenting is a choice and, further, that to choose an enthusiastic, trusting, empathetic, nurturing, supportive, and generally positive attitude about parenting and children pays off in tremendously rewarding ways later. Unconditional love is central to a positive parental attitude; this concept is defined, explored, and discussed.

Theme. The big pay-off.

Activities. The first activity is to discuss attitudes as choices. The second activity is watching the video *I am your Child* from The First Years Last Forever series by The Reiner Foundation. Discussion follows the video. The last activity involves the definition of unconditional love. A dictionary definition is presented. (Unconditional = absolute, without conditions or reservations. Love = a deep and tender feeling of affection for, or attachment or devotion to, a person or persons.) Couples give their interpretation of what unconditional love is, and why they think it might be critical to effective parenting.

Process. Discussing attitudes as choices will prompt individuals to consider the attitudes they maintain, and empowers them to make changes in their attitudes if they so desire. If we have, or can develop, an unselfish, loving, fundamental assumption about children and the roles of parents, this attitude will guide us through the

many difficult circumstances in which we are required to make tough decisions. The video promotes a proactive attitude and the long-term benefits of such an attitude. Providing very young children with all their physical and emotional needs, teaching them to act autonomously, allowing them to make decisions and mistakes, and constantly supporting them makes the parenting job easier as these secure, responsible children get older. Finally, discussing the definition and value of unconditional love strengthens the potential for consistent expression of it with our children and others.

Homework for next session. With their partner, members prepare a personal parenting mission statement. The statement should be concise and incorporate their foremost intent and confirmed values about their personal parenthood experience. As with business mission statements, the statement will provide members with guidance and remind them of their primary goals.

Session 8

Purpose. The purpose of the final group session is to inspire couples to examine what is truly important to them as parents, and to provide closure and propel confidence.

Theme. Our mission as parents.

Activities. Each couple is asked to share their mission statement and discuss the process of preparing it. Following this, members are asked to share individually how they feel about this being the last session. Next, members are asked to share what they believe is the most important thing they have gained by the group experience. Finally, a questionnaire is completed by individuals about their experience in the group, privately and anonymously.

Process. Preparation of a mission statement prompts couples to think about what is most important to them in their new roles as parents. They will take with them something they can refer to on their parenting journey when confronted with a challenging or new situation. The mission statement can also serve as a daily reminder.

Expressing their feelings about this being the final group session allows couples to experience a sense of closure. Further, stating what they have gained from the process, and hearing what other couples share about it, reinforces what has been learned and will bolster parental confidence.

STRATEGIES TO EVALUATE THE GROUP

At the end of the last group session, members complete a questionnaire relating to the quality of leadership and addressing if, and how, they benefited from the experience, and whether they would recommend it to others. Information is solicited as to what they believe would improve the group sessions. Questions are derived from the proposed group purposes and goals. The first part of the questionnaire should incorporate a Likert scale format and the second part should be short answer. Members are instructed to complete the questionnaires individually without consulting their partner.

REFERRAL PROCEDURES FOR FOLLOW-UP

Referrals for couples counseling should be recommended, and extended to any couple if the group encounters reveal it would be beneficial. Readings relevant to the various topics should be offered, as well as sources covering specific questions that might arise during the sessions. The leaders must be abreast of literature and local resources that address specific parenting issues so they can offer further information not covered in the sessions, or that elaborate on session topics.

Each of the members should be contacted via mail 6 months after the last session to gain follow-up information and to address the applicability of the subject matter. Have they applied any of what they learned? How so? The members should also be encouraged to form a network of support, possibly including the couples with whom they shared the group experience.

REFERENCES

Anderson, A., Russell, C., & Schumm, W. (1983). Perceived marital quality and family life cycle categories: A further analysis. *Journal of Marriage and the Family, 45,* 127–139.

Capuzzi, D., & Gross, D. (Eds.). (1998) *Introduction to group counseling* (2nd ed.). Denver, CO: Love Publishing.

Chess, S., & Thomas, A. (1984). *Origins and evolution of behavior disorders: From infancy to early adult life.* New York: Brunner/Mazel.

Elkind, D. (1967). Egocentrism is adolescence. *Child Development, 38,* 1025–1034.

Erikson, E. H. (1963). *Childhood and society* (2nd ed.). New York: Norton.

Hetherington, E., & Parke, R. (1993). *Child psychology: A contemporary viewpoint* (4th ed.). New York: McGraw-Hill.

Nolte, D. (1998). Children learn what they live: Parenting to inspire values (p. 224). New York: Workman Publishing.

Rogers, C. (1959). A theory of therapy, personality, and interpersonal relationships, as developed in the client-centered framework. In S. Koch (Ed.), *Psychology: A study of a science, 3* (pp. 184–256). New York: McGraw-Hill.

Rollins, B. C., & Feldman, H. (1970). Marital satisfaction over the life cycle. *Journal of Marriage and the Family, 32,* 20–28.

Rollins, B. C., & Galligan, R. (1978). The developing child and marital satisfaction of parents. In R. Lerner & G. Spanier (Eds), *Child influences on marital and family interaction: A life-span perspective* (pp. 71–105). New York: Academic Press.

Sanders, M., Nicholson, J., & Floyd, F. (1997). Clinical handbook of marriage and couples interventions. In W. Halford & H. Markman (Eds.), *Couples' relationships and children* (p. 234). Great Britain: Bookcraft (Bath) Ltd.

Sigelman, C., & Shaffer, D. (1995). *Life span human development.* Belmont, CA: Wadsworth.

Sullivan, H. S. (1953). *The interpersonal theory of psychiatry.* New York: Norton.

CHAPTER 18

USING THE WHEEL OF SELF-DISCOVERY: A CAREER TRANSITION TOOL

Colleen Baurassa

PURPOSE

The purpose of this group is to provide an environment conducive to career redesign or in developing the choice of a new career field through introspective examination within an atmosphere of support and creative learning. The group is for women currently employed but seeking more job stimulation, challenge, accomplishment, and opportunities for advancement.

CONCEPTUAL FRAMEWORK

One of the ten truths of job/career transition, according to Gross and Paskill (1999), is that "until you take yourself seriously and come to know your skills, values, and interests—the essence of who you are—it is unlikely that you will find enjoyable and satisfying work."

The group uses a "wheel" modeled after concepts found in Bolles (2000), who uses a flower, and Gross and Paskill (1999), who use a compass. Bolles (2000) has found that people need a clear picture of an ideal job in order to pursue the goals of being as happy as a person can be in a job, while at the same time doing effective work. The wheel is used to record the outcome of insights gained in each session, and later, to measure whether or not a job/career under consideration is a good match to the skills, values, and interests identified by the participant.

Any time individuals face change, the unknown, they experience to a greater or lesser degree heightened anxiety. Many resist change simply to avoid the anxiety

(Bridges, 1980). The prospect of initiating change, even for the "better," involves work, which often overwhelms them. Additionally, many often do not know where to begin. They do not know where to go to gather information so they can make informed choices (Bolles, 2000).

As counseling has advanced, we have discovered that group settings, when directed by skilled facilitators, can assist individuals to make desired changes by providing support and encouragement. This support and encouragement comes not only from the facilitator, but also from their peers (Boldt, 1999). Because they expect support from the facilitator, they do not prize that as much as they do the support of their peers, who have no perceived obligation to offer it. Individuals may perceive peer support and encouragement as more valuable or sincere, thus reinforcing self-confidence and esteem.

Also, the group setting provides individuals with a cost effective way to obtain professional guidance by not paying for one-on-one professional services (Miars, 1998).

Women not only face choices about what occupations they will choose to pursue, but also how multiple life roles will be integrated into a life plan (Phillips & Imhoff, 1997). This group is restricted to women participants so discussion can focus on women's various multiple roles that must be integrated with career choice.

Research has been done to establish the usefulness of thinking about one's occupational future in the context of possible selves (Meara, Day, Chalk, & Phelps, 1995). Results show the beneficial aspects of personalization of career-related choices (Matzedeer & Krieshok, 1995). Other research has documented that women participating in a six-week treatment career group designed to increase career-related self-efficacy made gains on career decision-making self-efficacy and vocational exploration and commitment compared with women in a non-treatment control group. The treatment group was shown to have maintained those gains at a six-week follow-up (Sullivan & Mahalik, 2000).

GROUP GOALS

This group will be focused on self-discovery and self-definition and how one's values provide a foundation for career choices. The goal is not to arrive at a specific, desired job title, but rather to:

1. Facilitate individuals getting in touch with who they really are and what they really want by identifying their interests, abilities, and values.
2. Assist individuals to select career fields based on these insights for further research.
3. Provide individuals with a plan for researching and evaluating different career options in light of their self-discoveries.
4. Establish an ongoing support group through the use of an Internet bulletin board in which members of this group and other graduates can network and further develop newly acquired skills. This could prevent loss of momentum and encourage continued exploration.

PRE-GROUP SCREENING AND ORIENTATION

The pre-group screening and orientation should be conducted through individual interviews to assess the readiness and appropriateness of the individual for group work. These personal interviews allow the group leader to identify those prospective participants who like structure and are willing to share openly with a group.

The pre-screening interview should last from 20 to 30 minutes during which time the group leader can determine if the individual is willing to help others and to be influenced by the group, ruling out those with iron-clad predispositions. The pre-screening process also orients prospective members to what is involved in group counseling. The group leader wants to ensure group compatibility in terms of interests and personalities. The group is limited to a maximum of eight persons so that all will have ample opportunity to participate.

The pre-orientation process provides the prospective members with enough information about fees, payment options, and their rights as members of the group for them to make informed choices. At this time, the group leader identifies their expectations of group members. Both the group leader and the prospective member should be evaluating each other to determine the feasibility of working together. At this time, if the group

leader feels the prospective member is ready, appropriate, and has realistic expectations, the leader would make a commitment to the prospective member and provide the client with a contract that states the group leader's qualifications and the specific nature of services to be provided for the stated fee. If the prospective member feels the group leader is qualified to provide the counseling and has confidence in the group leader's ability to meet her expectations, the prospective member would make a commitment to the group leader by signing the contract and paying the fee.

OUTLINE FOR EIGHT GROUP SESSIONS

Session 1

Purpose. The purpose of the first session is to introduce the group leader and his or her role, make group introductions, present and discuss ground rules, provide a suggested reading list, present the "wheel" concept, identify group goals, and discuss the first spoke of the wheel: interest.

Theme. Turning the Wheel of Self-Discovery: An Introduction.

Activities. The group members introduce themselves and share their reasons for participating in this group. The group leader begins the process of fostering group trust and promoting group cohesion by presenting suggested ground rules. The leader opens a group discussion of the ground rules that would be expected in a professional environment and facilitates agreement within the group to abide by the selected ground rules. At this time, members could write down their expectations and goals regarding this group experience.

The group leader distributes a suggested reading list to be used concurrently during the course as well as for future reference. Members begin to explore their personal interests to be completed in a homework assignment. This assignment is to review snapshots from different periods of their lives to stimulate their memories of interests and activities, which they enjoyed. The group members then write down their interests and enjoyable activities and share them in session 2.

The group leader closes the session by pointing out that members are no longer alone in their searches for career fields and by asking members to share any pertinent thoughts regarding comfort and support gained in their searches through the group experience.

Process. The process of discussing and then selecting agreed upon ground rules empowers the members, ensuring that they will be more willing to abide by the rules since they established them. The rules help to define and connect the group, making each member feel that it is safe to disclose personal information. This session give members a sense of purpose and direction. This session should clarify individual expectations creating anticipation of future sessions.

The group leader is modeling verbal and nonverbal behaviors to encourage and support group members open sharing and interaction. It is most important in these first sessions that members receive positive reinforcement for their willingness to share personal experiences and feel safe in sharing. Members of the group learn appropriate responses to sharing through the modeling of the group leader.

Session 2

Purpose. The purpose of the second session is to have a group discussion of the homework assignment from the first session and then to explore the second spoke of the wheel: Abilities.

Theme. Turning the Wheel of Self-Discovery: Interests.

Activities. Members of the group share insights and comments on the previous week's assignment regarding individual interests and determine if they are now or have in the past worked in fields that validate their interests. The group leader asks members how they felt about their work in relationship to the interests they have now defined. The group leader introduces the second spoke of the Wheel of Self-Discovery: Abilities. Homework for the next week is for the members to write stories from different time periods about their achievements in the work place, at home, and during leisure time to be shared in the next session. Members are encouraged to ask questions clarifying their assignment.

The group leader closes this session by asking members for positive feedback, on 3 × 5 cards, to give to others about the messages heard in their presentations. The group leader builds anticipation for the third session by sharing a short, personal experience that illustrates how the process of identifying interests within a group setting (i.e., sessions 1 and 2) assist in making a career redesign or change.

Process. The group identification has become stronger as members share the homework assignment, with trust within the group now beginning to develop. Members are becoming more open in sharing their personal interests from their pasts. Compliance with the ground rules is the key to members trusting and being trustworthy as the group leader reminds them to phrase questions to each other in terms of supporting interests without judging the worth or practicality of the interest.

Session 3

Purpose. The purpose of the third session is to identify the members' personal abilities, and then to introduce the fourth spoke of the Wheel of Self-Discovery: Work Values.

Theme. Turning the Wheel of Self-Discovery: Abilities.

Activities. Group members share their stories, insights, and comments about the process of identifying their abilities and share their homework assignment, a story of a past accomplishment. The group enters into a discussion of how their abilities have been used in current or past jobs and how the use or lack of use of their abilities made them feel about their jobs.

The group leader introduces the fourth spoke on the Wheel of Self-Discovery: Work Values. Work values encompass such issues as communication, responsibility, accountability, structure, creativity, flexibility, learning opportunities, time, freedom, humor, advancement, physical and/or mental challenges, diversity, independence, co-workers, and company support. The homework assignment for next week is to list personal work values and then to prioritize them. Members should come to the next class prepared to share their personal "top five" work values and to describe a perfect workday as it relates to their top five.

The members are invited to close the session by sharing in an open format something they admire or respect about the person next to them that they heard in the members' presentation of past accomplishments.

The group leader should have established the Internet bulletin board by this session and should encourage group members to locate and use this tool. To indicate that they have been successful, they should leave a message for the group leader.

Process. The group members are developing self-confidence and self-esteem as they identify their interests, rehearse their abilities in the group setting, and receive positive feedback from others. The process of their active and personal involvement in the group builds trust as the group leader encourages expression while maintaining safety for the participants.

Session 4

Purpose. The purpose of the fourth session is for members to share their personal top five work values and to describe a perfect workday as it relates to their identified work values. The group leader introduces the fifth spoke of the Wheel of Self-Discovery: Life Values.

Theme. Turning the Wheel of Self-Discovery: Work Values.

Activities. Group members share their stories of their perfect workdays. Other members of the group then identify which values appear to be important to the presenter as illustrated in her story. The members of the group can then brainstorm to suggest possible career fields for further research for each presenter.

The group leader then introduces the sixth spoke on the Wheel of Self-Discovery: Life Values. Life values include the prioritization of spiritual, familial, and work activities, adventure, physical and emotional health, self-growth, achievement, personal freedom, leadership, and service. The members are encouraged to add any other life value that is important to them. The homework assignment for the next week is to list their five most important life values to share with other members and to list personal activities that mirror those values.

The members close the session by sharing what the exercise of creating a perfect "workday" has meant to them personally.

Process. At this point the group as a whole has reached the Group Involvement stage in which members are more supportive of each other in what members have identified as their interests, abilities, and work values. Members feel included as integral members of a unit and begin to assume the role of peer counselor to each other as the group leader continues to provide direction and focus. The increasing reliance of the group members on each other in performing the functions of the group, as opposed to dependence on the group leader, promotes group solidarity.

Session 5

Purpose. The purpose of the fifth session is for members to share their five most important life values and personal activities, which mirror those values. The group leader introduces the sixth spoke of the Wheel of Self-Discovery: Lifestyle.

Theme. Turning the Wheel of Self-Discovery: Life Values.

Activities. Group members share their five most important life values and personal activities that mirror those values with other members. The group leader asks members what other activities they might enter into which would further express their commitment to those values.

The group leader then introduces the fifth spoke of the Wheel of Self-Discovery: Lifestyle. Lifestyle includes not only salary or wages but also benefits such as sick leave, vacation pay, tuition reimbursement, health and disability insurance, profit sharing, retirement plans, sabbaticals, where they live, what they live in, and transportation. The homework assignment for next week is to make two poster-sized collages of pictures from magazines to illustrate their current lifestyle and the lifestyle they're seeking through career transitions.

The members close the session by answering the question, "Were you surprised by any of the life values you selected? Why or why not?"

Process. As the group experiences increasing solidarity, individual members acquire greater helping skills. Members feel safe taking on other roles such as leadership, maintenance, and facilitation within the bound-

aries of the ground rules. These rules allow members to feel safe while they take greater risks in self-disclosure within the group setting.

Session 6

Purpose. The purpose of the sixth session is for members to present their collages to the group. The group leader facilitates discussion about what kind of career opportunities might offer the benefits identified.

Theme. Turning the Wheel of Self-Discovery: Lifestyle.

Activities. The group members present their collages to the group. The group offers suggestions to the presenter about possible career fields that would support the illustrated ideal lifestyle, keeping in mind information gained about the presenter's interests, abilities, and values as expressed in previous sessions. A discussion would explore issues of possible conflict between desired lifestyles and chosen life values.

The group leader then introduces the sixth spoke on the Wheel of Self-Discovery: Character. Character here is used to define specific individual characteristics such as intelligence, adaptability, precision, achievement-oriented, adventuresome, assertive, aggressive, passive, flexible, innovative, loyal, diplomatic, resourceful, poised, tactful, realistic, fanciful, dynamic, energetic, calm, influential, outgoing, introverted, peaceful, focused, scattered, and humorous. The homework assignment for group members next week is to write one paragraph each about two persons whom they admire and respect.

The members close the session with discussion about how members feel about the group experience so far. The group leader introduces opportunities for continuing development at the end of the eight sessions. This will begin the process of closure for the group.

Process. Adherence to the ground rules are especially important during this session to ensure that members feel safe. The group leader monitors the ground rules and blocks any judgmental or advisory behaviors that might occur if the members do not take steps to do the blocking themselves.

Session 7

Purpose. The purpose of the seventh session is for group members to share their stories of people they admire and respect and what they identified as desirable characteristics. The other members of the group should be invited to comment on how they see the presenter representing those same characteristics. The group leader introduces the plan for career research. The homework assignment for the next week is for members to interview two individuals currently working in a field of interest to them and to plan to share the results of one of the interviews in a discussion in session 8.

Theme. Turning the Wheel of Self-Discovery: Character.

Activities. Group members share their stories and identify the characteristics most valued by them. Other members then comment about the ways in which they see the presenter embodying those characteristics. The group leader opens the discussion to encourage members to share ways they envision fostering and nurturing the development of these valued characteristics in themselves and others with specific emphasis on career fields. At this point all "wheels" should be completed.

The group leader continues discussion of closure of the group experience and encourages members to share their emotions. Members are encouraged to begin plans to continue their research on an individual basis. If members voice apprehension about the group experience ending, they should be encouraged to exchange phone and e-mail information with each other. The online bulletin board can also be used as a source of communication between participants.

The group leader discusses career research and explains where and how to use the suggested reading list for specific ideas. The group leader also provides the members with questions to use in a research interview. The group leader and members role play the interview in preparation for the assignment for next week. The assignment is for each member to interview two persons currently working in a field of interest and to discuss the results of one interview in session 8. The group leader should also emphasize the importance of networking in career redesign by referencing the suggested reading list.

An important piece of networking is having business cards made with one's name, address, phone number, and e-mail address. There should be no title or company name on these cards. This prevents others from labeling you with an occupation or title that would keep them from visualizing your possibilities in other career fields.

In addition, members are asked to consider what ways the group has helped them. In preparation for answering this question, members should review their initial expectations and goals, which members wrote down in session 1.

The members close the session by discussing two questions: "In light of your discoveries, do you feel it's possible to 'have it all' in a career?" If the answer is "No," then, "In what area are you willing to compromise?"

Process. The atmosphere of safety and trust is now further enhanced as members begin affirming their growth and development stemming from the group experience. Members recognize their greater interdependence on each other. This interdependence makes them aware of impending loss with the end of the group in session 8.

Session 8

Purpose. The purpose of the eighth session is for group members to summarize one career research interview

and to comment on the interview process. The networking concept is discussed in greater depth.

Theme. Closure and evaluation of the group.

Activities. The members present a summary of one interview and the insights they gained. The interview not discussed should be published on the bulletin board for feedback from the group.

Members are encouraged to comment on the effectiveness of the ideas from the suggested reading list, or other sources, which helped them to gain information and to establish networks. A small party could be held to celebrate the completion and closure of the group.

The group leader distributes course surveys to be completed by the group members. Members share the results by comparing their initial expectations and goals with current feelings in the survey. Course surveys should be completed by the members and turned in to the group leader. The group leader posts the course survey results on the bulletin board.

The group leader checks the bulletin board on a weekly basis for a period of 30 days following course completion for those interested in continued use of the bulletin board. A list of other private career planning professionals should be provided to participants.

The group leader facilitates closure of the group experience by asking members to share their feelings regarding the ending of the group experience. Members should also be asked to describe how another member has been significant to group solidarity and to individual members' growth on 3×5 cards. Members are encouraged to share feelings verbally about how they will continue personal growth and development without the direct encouragement and support of the group.

Process. Group members have identified and refined themselves in terms of their interests, abilities, work and life values, lifestyle, and character. To chart their progress each member is given a small version of the wheel so they carry it with them and refer to it often. Comfort with this new knowledge is solidified and enhanced by the positive reinforcement they have received from other members of the group, especially in session 8. In this session their importance and significance to the group as a unit and to each individual in the group has been affirmed, as affirmations given by peers are usually accepted and highly valued.

STRATEGIES TO EVALUATE THE GROUP

The group leader should develop a group survey for distribution in session 8. As described above, members complete the survey anonymously. It should include statements generated from the goals of the group and statements about the group process and ratings on a Likert Scale format. Survey results should be furnished to group members by e-mail within one week.

Strategies for group evaluation include:

- Comparing initial expectations and goals from session 1 with actual realizations in session 8
- Rating of activities
- Rating of homework assignments
- Rating of individual safety within the group
- Rating of the facilitator
- Rating the group experience
- Rating the recommended reading list
- Other comments or suggestions

REFERRAL PROCEDURES FOR FOLLOW-UP

An online bulletin board (for instructions on how to set one up, see **http://amazingforums.com**) should be set up by session 3 and used in post-group follow-up with a scheduled time for the group leader to be available for ongoing support for a period of 30 days. The group can then decide if and how long the bulletin board will continue after the first 30 days. Members may also choose to proceed with further career counseling by choosing a professional counselor from the list provided during the last class.

REFERENCES

Boldt, L. G. (1999). *Zen and the art of making a living* (Revised ed). New York: Penguin/Arkana.

Bolles, R. N. (2000). *What color is your parachute? 2000.* Berkeley, CA: Ten Speed Press.

Bridges, W. (1980). *Making sense of life's transitions.* Reading, MA: Addison-Wesley.

Gross, P., & Paskill, P. (1999). *Want a new, better fantastic job?* Portland, OR: Spirit Press.

Matzedeer, M., & Krieshok, T. (1995). Career and self-efficacy and the predition of work and home role salience. *Journal of Career Assessment, 3,* 331–340.

Meara, N., Day, D., Chalk, L., & Phelps, R. (1995). Possible selves: Applications for career counseling. *Journal of Career Assessment, 3,* 259–277.

Miars, R. (1998). Group counseling: career and lifestyle issues In D. Cappuzzi & D. R. Gross (Eds.), *Introduction to group counseling,* 231–247. Denver, CO: Love Publishing.

Phillips, S., & Imhoff, A. (1997). Women and career development: A decade of research. *Annual Review of Psychology, 48,* 31–59.

Sullivan, K., & Mahalik, J. (2000). Increasing career self-efficacy for women: Evaluating a group intervention. *Journal of Counseling & Development, 78,* 54–62.

QUESTIONS TO USE IN THE RESEARCH INTERVIEW

1. How did you get to where you are now?

2. What was your path to this job?

3. What is your educational background?

4. What is the purpose of your job/department?

5. What do you like/dislike most about your job?

6. What challenges or issues will you or your department be facing in the next six months?

7. What publications should I be reading?

8. Who else would you suggest I talk with about this career field? May I use your name as a reference when calling the suggested person?

9. Who are your competitors?

10. What didn't I ask that I should have?

11. May I call you if I think of any more questions?

QUESTIONS TO ASK YOURSELF FOLLOWING THE INTERVIEW

1. What did I learn about the industry, company, or job?

2. How excited am I by the prospect of working in this industry, company, or job?

3. How does what I learned fit with the values I have identified as core values on my wheel?

4. What steps should I take next?

QUESTIONNAIRE FOR EVALUATION OF THE GROUP: USING THE WHEEL OF SELF-DISCOVERY

1. Were your expectations and goals met by the group experience?
   a. Yes
   b. No

2. Please rate the Activities on a scale of 1 to 5, with 1 as poor and 5 as excellent.

       1   2   3   4   5   (Circle one)

3. Please rate the Homework on a scale of 1 to 5, with 1 as poor and 5 as excellent.

       1   2   3   4   5   (Circle one)

4. Please rate your feeling of Personal Safety on a scale of 1 to 5, with 1 as poor and 5 as excellent.

       1   2   3   4   5   (Circle one)

5. Please rate the performance of the facilitator on a scale of 1 to 5, with 1 as poor and 5 as excellent.

       1   2   3   4   5   (Circle one)

6. Please rate how you feel about the Group Experience on a scale of 1 to 5, with 1 as poor and 5 as excellent.

       1   2   3   4   5   (Circle one)

7. Please rate the Recommended Reading List on a scale of 1 to 5, with 1 as poor and 5 as excellent.

       1   2   3   4   5   (Circle one)

8. What could have been done to make the group experience better for you? Please comment and/or give suggestions:

   _____

   _____

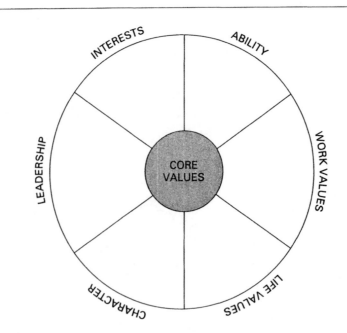

CHAPTER 19

RETURNING WOMEN STUDENTS: A TRANSITION GROUP

Virjeana A. Chambers

PURPOSE

The purpose of this group is to provide a safe, support- ive environment for returning women students. These women may need to explore, modify, adapt to new and/or different roles, or need help with the issues ac- companying the transition facing returning students. The group process empowers women by creating solidarity and bonding and provides the knowledge that they are not unique in feeling alone, anxious, and uninformed about options and alternatives at the university level. Group members are able to share resources and network information. They will learn techniques for dealing with stress and/or negative self-feedback. Additionally, mem- bers will learn to identify for themselves other cognitive tasks that may need restructuring. Members will then have the opportunity to work on these during the group sessions. This group could be offered as a service of the university counseling and psychological center or as an adjunct group/class in the women studies department.

CONCEPTUAL FRAMEWORK

Although we see life as a series of transitions or changes, Schlossberg (1984) asserts that we are not prepared or properly trained to deal with these effectively when they arise. Returning to school is a transition, which brings with it attending losses, both economic and supportive. There may be an accompanying identity shift and, there- fore, role restructuring might be necessary to maintain forward movement and growth potential. Managing an emotional and cognitive equilibrium while in this process can, at times, become both exciting and overwhelming.

To ensure a successful transition, certain psychosocial and cognitive tasks need to be accomplished. According to Golan (1981), these tasks include: the identification of, and understanding the need for, changes; the activity as- sociated with looking for options; and the search for al- ternatives and/or formulation of solutions. Once these re- spective tasks are accomplished, a person will need to make a choice and implement the associated changes. As a result of this process, a person will be able to function in a healthier manner under these new and different premises. This means a person will have the ability to cope with frustration, anxiety, ambivalence, or handle the shifts in status or circumstances, which may involve feelings of lack of self-worth and lessened confidence. There will be learning that takes place in order to adjust to the new stan- dards and different levels of satisfaction.

Some of these changes, losses, and regrouping can be facilitated in a healthy constructive way through a group setting. Regardless of the particular situation and issues that arise from this venue, those in transition can benefit from interactions with others going through the same process. A sense of universality is created through the group members' interactions with each other and serves as a common bond while members are minimally directed toward learning, which might include sharing techniques of stress and anxiety reduction and/or cop- ing mechanisms. This group is facilitated by a caring and congruent counselor anchored in the "here and now."

Transitions are about choices, new beginnings and endings, and positive and negative changes, all of which are accompanied by those feelings intrinsic to the process. Groups can play a vital role in the leavening process by providing a supportive, nurturing, and non-judgmental environment in which members can learn new coping skills and be shown how to network resources. This promotes a sense of cohesion with other group members in the same situation as returning women students.

GROUP GOALS

The goals for this group are as follows:

1. To provide a safe environment where conflictive issues can be dealt with in a productive manner.
2. To furnish an arena for members to examine old coping mechanisms; to aid members in the recognition of those coping mechanisms that are adaptive and to help them modify or discard those that are no longer appropriate; and to aid members in the learning of new coping skills. Group members will also be able to practice new skills by engaging in role-playing and by receiving positive feedback from other members regarding what works and what does not work.
3. To make available a space for support, sharing of feelings, and personal development for those struggling to define their sense of self during transition.
4. To establish a space that is reflective, nurturing, and caring for women who have not had the opportunity to bond with other women. These women will realize what strength can be found in common bonds.
5. A nexus whereby the group members and facilitator can come together to network resources and information at both the university and community levels that can provide needed options or alternatives for the members when needed.
6. To enable a respectful gathering of women who can teach and be taught personal skills of survival within the context of universal equality.

PRE-GROUP SCREENING AND ORIENTATION

A list of prospective clients can be obtained from referrals and word-of-mouth for those interested in the group process and how it can benefit them during transition. Prescreening interviews are necessary for prospective members to ensure safety and progress within a group format. Golden, Corazzini, and Grady (1993) stipulate that inclusion criteria such as ego strength, verbal skills, and motivation are important attributes to bring to group. Friedman (1989) states that clients who identify their problems as being interpersonal have a willingness to be influenced by the group, are realistic in their endeavors to change, and are willing to help others within the group.

This is a good and potentially useful set of criteria to be included when prescreening. During this prescreening interview, Corey and Corey (1987) suggest that time also be given the prospective member to interview the facilitator to inquire about the counselor's background in group work. Questions might also be raised about techniques that might be used, or any other aspect the prospective group member does not understand at that time.

Those clients who exhibit severe psychopathy, or seem to have impaired capacity for empathy, present suicidal ideation, or evidence a poor fit with other group members should be excluded because the probability that the individual will benefit from group is extremely low to nonexistent. If an individual is not accepted for a group, an explanation should be given as to why this group might not be appropriate and what other options may be available for that individual. This explanation needs to be made in an honest, direct, sensitive manner so that the rejection will not alienate the person from seeking appropriate alternatives.

Once the group has been formed it might be prudent to have a pre-group session. Corey and Corey (1987) strongly advocate a very short pre-group session. That way, the facilitator can outline the reason for the group and what topics might be explored. Also, the members can briefly meet each other and be given (1) a copy of the ground rules (see Appendix A) concerning confidentiality, common courtesies, and respectful listening; (2) time and place schedules; and (3) fee schedules, including sliding scales and other miscellaneous paperwork needed for that particular group. It should be explained that there will be eight weekly sessions that will run for 1 1/4 hours each.

The physical setting could be any private area, clear of distractions and interruptions, where 6 to 8 women could comfortably sit, either around a conference table or in a circle. A circle is more effective for observing body language, which can be utilized as part of the bonding and trust issues. In later sessions, the members themselves may tend to take an active part in forming the circle and thus adding cohesion to the overall framework of the group.

OUTLINE FOR EIGHT GROUP SESSIONS

Session 1

Purpose. The purpose of the first session will be to discuss the ground rules and courtesies, get acquainted with others and with the facilitator and his or her background, and establish a sense of what everyone would like to get out of the group experience by focusing on obtainable goals.

Theme. Start at the beginning.

Activities. The counselor should begin by introducing herself to the group. At this time, the counselor should give a brief biography, both personal and professional. The counselor should then extend the invitation to everyone and instruct the members to tell the rest of the group something about themselves that they are comfortable sharing. The counselor can look at the group and tell by body language and/or eye contact who would be a good candidate to start the introductions. Then the counselor should have the group continue going around the circle until the introductions are done.

A laminated copy of the ground rules, which were given to each member at the pre-group session, could be handed out. The counselor should instruct each person to read a rule and invite comments, questions, and discussion from the others until a general consensus is reached about what the rule means. In this manner, all members will arrive at an agreement regarding all of the rules. Then the counselor (counselor and facilitator will be used interchangeably) can ask group members what they want and expect from the group experience. The facilitator also needs to explain to the members what he or she expects to gain as well.

Opening and closing procedures need to be discussed. A dialogue should be focused on the idea that when beginning, or checking in each week, a general question is asked in order to garner information regarding a group member's state of mind, or general individual atmosphere, for that day and time. For example, the counselor could ask group members to pick a color that most represents how they feel at that particular moment, or for that particular day, and then have them explain why.

During later sessions, after group members feel more comfortable, it might be possible to work on some intense issues that are brought about in this manner. If this facilitation does occur, then the counselor needs to make sure that each person is emotionally stable enough to leave at the end of the session. If someone is not, then steps need to be taken to ensure the emotional safety of that individual before she departs. Check-in and checkout are routine most of the time, but occasionally an answer can be an indication that something more is going on with that member on that particular day. The counselor should be aware of underlying emotional currents and act as a stabilizing influence before departure.

Homework assignments (if any), miscellaneous questions or comments, or clarification of information are appropriate at this time. Just before the checkout, time should be given for one last comment or statement of appreciation from each member regarding the session. At the end of this first session, the checkout question might be: "How comfortable did you feel within this group setting and was it different from what you expected?" This is especially revealing if the members have not been in a group before.

Homework assignment #1. After each weekly session, each person should journal in a small tablet or theme book for 5–10 minutes. Themes can include hopes, likes, dislikes, or comments and private thoughts about the group. The journal is private and personal and only read by its author.

Homework assignment #2. The counselor should make a list of the different types of questions (and answers if known) about resources and services (both in the university and community settings) that he or she feels might be needed by group members to meet everyday needs and emergencies. This list should be brought to the group.

Process. When the counselor begins with his or her own brief, low-risk self-disclosure, an atmosphere of comfort is created. By inviting others to share, the counselor encourages a group norm that establishes self-disclosure, which is one of the therapeutic factors in the group process. By having the ground rules reviewed, discussed, and agreed upon by each group member, the rules become collectively owned by the group and validated as being important and necessary to the maintenance of a safe and trusting environment. The explanations regarding the opening and closing rituals and homework assignments, as well as allowing time for last minute comments, provides a structured framework that allows for a sense of stability through routine.

Session 2

Purpose. The purpose of this session is to open up a discussion on the difficulties of returning students, both in the university arena and from a personal standpoint as well. By sharing the problems, there is an excellent chance that someone has already faced that particular dilemma and found a solution, and if not an answer then at the very least, a workable coping mechanism in the interim. By having an open discussion, problems can be targeted so that goals can be formulated, inherent strengths and weaknesses can be evaluated, and the counselor can introduce some options available such as learning how to reduce stress, lower anxiety levels, role-playing, assertiveness, and self-empowerment.

Theme. Tap dancing on the problems.

Activities. Session 2 begins with a three-part check-in. One part could be, on a scale of 1 to 10, how do you physically feel today and why? Second, if you could define this last week in terms of a mood (e.g., serene, tearful), what would it be and why? It would be pertinent for the counselor at this point to make sure in this meeting, and in every meeting, to reiterate that if anyone needs time to speak, she should make that known.

Although each session may have a different theme, that does not mean that members should forego time needed for individual venting. Sharing with others is intrinsic to the group because that is the one place where everyone can learn from others while being provided a safe, caring environment and the opportunity to receive positive feedback, if wanted. This would also be the time to bring up any old business that had not been finished at the prior session.

Next, the first homework assigned from last week should be discussed. The counselor should explain that at a later session each member will be asked to reread her journal to ascertain growth and development progress, both personal and group, and (if comfortable), make comments about it to the group.

The second homework assignment can be discussed briefly, with the counselor advocating that if anyone has the answers or options to questions raised, to please bring the information back to the group the following week. In this manner, a resource folder can be created for every member to use if needed. This can segue into an exercise taught by the counselor that would address a particular problem, which may have been mentioned in the group the prior week. An example could be teaching group members the ability to reduce anxiety to an acceptable level through sensory counting.

The counselor can ask for a volunteer to help demonstrate this technique. This is a brief step-by-step procedure that can be self-applied when an individual needs it. The counselor asks the volunteer to think of a really anxious time in her life and to remember what it felt like, then:

- *Step 1.* The counselor instructs the volunteer to think of two things that she hears in the room and identify them out loud.
- *Step 2.* The counselor instructs the volunteer to look for two different colors and again verbalize those out loud.
- *Step 3.* The counselor instructs the volunteer to smell two different odors, and again, identify and verbalize out loud.

During this exercise, the counselor can have the volunteer work up to lists of four items in each category. After this exercise the counselor should as the volunteer ask herself if the anxiety level is still as high as it was in the beginning. It will not be. An individual cannot remain anxious *and* do cognitive work, such as sensory counting, at the same time. The result is a lowering of the anxiety level.

The counselor should invite comments about the exercise from the volunteer. Then it should be time for homework assignments, checking out, and one last positive comment or appreciation of someone or something. This kind of a statement leaves a feeling of positivity upon departing.

Homework assignment #1. Using the exercise learned in this session, group members should practice the technique and then journal about the results and be ready to

comment about their experience in the next session, if comfortable in doing so.

Homework assignment #2. Fill out the questionnaire (see Appendix B) and bring it to the next session. It will be done again toward the end of group and then compared.

Purpose. In this session, with the routine of checking in and checking out, comes a sense of continuity that the group environment is stable and supportive. Gross & Capuzzi (1998) discuss the first four stages of a group as being characterized by a need to discover where individuals fit into the group and how acceptable individuals feel they are to others. As the individual seeks some level of approval, these explorations are shrouded in different levels of anxiety, some more and others less.

This session should start alleviating some of this anxiety as the group moves into acceptance of each other by seeing the universality of common problems encountered. A sense of altruism may also be formed as group members come up with different solutions that may work for others as well as themselves.

Session 3

Purpose. The purpose of this session is to facilitate more self-disclosure regarding group issues and to help generate questions and promote positive feedback from others regarding the safety and nonjudgmental attitudes within group. The counselor should be somewhat more directive than usual and model correct boundaries if needed, which might include the use of "I" messages as opposed to "you" messages.

Theme. Put your little foot here—and here—and here.

Activities. Check in with a two-part scenario. The counselor should ask, "If you had to define your week in terms of an animal, what would it be and what would it be doing?" The counselor should also ask if anyone needs time. After this, the facilitator proceeds with some recapping strategies about the goals agreed on in the beginning, both personal and group goals, and see if group members still feel these are relevant or if they should be revamped. This session is a little like reviewing the dance steps (the group process) that the group decided to learn at the beginning. If these steps are not working, then the group may need to revamp the "footwork." The counselor might ask such questions as: "Is it easier to speak up or not and why?" or "What can be done to ease the way?" The counselor guides the flow of information exchange while being aware of the need to model congruent, genuine concern in a supportive, sensitive manner. Also at this time, the questionnaire from last week can be handed in for safekeeping.

Checkout and last comments should be started by the facilitator, who can perhaps make some positive comments inclusive of the whole group. These comments may center on observations that group members are acting in a respectful manner to each other. The counselor might even comment that it feels as though some bonding is beginning to take place, if this were the case. No homework assignment is given other then having group members think about what kinds of problems they are encountering, at this point, in the school term. The counselor should make sure everyone is emotionally stable enough to leave.

Process. This session is meant to be a reaffirmation of the first two sessions. By this third meeting, group member apprehensions regarding group work and issues such as confidentiality and safety ought to be recognized as a given, and individuals should be comfortable enough to input suggestions for recapping the goals if necessary. In doing so, group members should come to realize that each of them are an integral part of the group.

Session 4

Purpose. This session will be structured around identifying stressors and coping mechanisms. It will be identified which type(s) of stressors group members are experiencing at this point in their transition and for which they might need assistance. If a group member has found a workable solution, she can share with others.

Theme. Learning the dance steps.

Activities. For the check-in, the counselor can ask, on a scale of 1 to 10, for group members to rate how smoothly this week has or has not been and why. After the check-in and time given to any member who needs it, the counselor asks if any group member had time, since last week's request, to think about stressors and/or coping mechanisms. The counselor should actively guide the discussion by soliciting different stressful situations that have occurred for individual members. The group can brainstorm solutions or possible stress-reducing exercises that would address these stressors. At this stage, members should feel secure enough to start getting personally involved through self-disclosure and actively participating in positive interaction with other members.

It is also at this time that the facilitator should be able to spot those members that seem silent or subdued and begin to gently encourage their participation in the group. Before closing, the counselor can ask if members feel comfortable enough to receive or give feedback about themselves or others in a positive constructive way, regarding how they feel about other members of the group or to solicit feedback regarding how they might appear to others. If this is acceptable, the counselor should go around the circle and ask members if they would like the opportunity to give or seek feedback. Each member will have the opportunity to decline if that individual is not comfortable with this excercise.

If no one volunteers to start, the counselor can model the appropriate behavior by making comments to the members that are comfortable with this; the counselor should do this in a positive, reaffirming voice. This can be used as part of the closing process and can end with the question: "Are you emotionally stable enough to leave?"

Process. At this point, whenever anyone needs time to speak, the counselor can actively contribute by modeling different skills. One example would be interpreting what members say in a way that acts as a catalyst to help members want to explore their motivations and reactions. Paraphrasing or asking questions for further clarification of the situation can do this. By modeling nonjudgmental support and caring, the group becomes a space of nurturing and safety that can help activate self-empowerment and reaffirmation of self-worth.

Session 5

Purpose. The purpose of this session is to continue going over stressors and stressful situations. However, for this meeting, the main focus is on identifying individual strengths and applicable solutions and interacting with other group members in order to grasp the semantics and incorporate new and viable skills.

Theme. Finding the right rhythm for you.

Activities. The counselor should check in with group members and find out if any member needs time. After this task is accomplished, the counselor can bring up for discussion the past week's format of stressors and stressful situations, and explain that they should continue with this venue. However, this session will concentrate on strengths and solutions.

The facilitator can encourage positive interaction by using role-playing scenarios that depict stressful situations with adaptive basic solutions that can perhaps be applied to other similar issues. This will promote interpersonal communication and a sense of group connectedness. One stress-reducing exercise that can be utilized by anyone who becomes noticeably anxious or nervous before a test or presentation is called centering and grounding. This exercise (see Appendix C) can be led by the counselor by using a short handout and group participation. The handout can be used as a guide for future use by the individual.

Involving the whole group in this exercise enables it to be used later as a beginning point for other collective sharing of leadership roles within the group. Encouraging members to share strengths and solutions enables more bonding and can begin to create a sense of group identity. Sharing common experiences is a powerful tool. This exercise can be emotionally draining; because of this, it is especially important that everyone check out and verbalize that they are able to leave the group safely at closing.

Homework assignment. Make a list of at least three things that you want to work on to boost your sense of confidence.

Process. By interacting with each other, the group is moving more into the group involvement stage. Capuzzi and Gross (1998) show this to be characterized by individuals identifying with other group members' problems and solutions and finding these relevant to their own. Members working together to obtain answers also characterize this stage. The paradigm of member goals and needs becomes, in turn, the group goals and purposes. This builds on the universality and altruism already evident, as well as everyone becoming aware of the dynamics of group empowerment.

Session 6

Purpose. The purpose of session 6 is to further develop a sense of group identity by the counselor providing encouragement in participation, and where appropriate, lend support toward sharing leadership responsibilities within the group. This session also targets negative thinking and possible techniques to overcome it.

Theme. Practicing group dancing.

Activities. The check-in can be two parts. Questions that can be asked include: "What kind of music would represent you today (e.g., blues, classical) and why?" and "Does anyone need time or is there any unfinished business?" After the check-in is concluded, the counselor should ask the members to bring out their homework. By going around the group, the facilitator will likely find a recurrent theme of negative thought production intruding into the confidence building area being looked at. The counselor should encourage exploration and participation by the group in bringing up personal instances and how resolution was obtained. The counselor should be very aware at this point that because of the bonding and trust that has been established within the group, self-disclosure could be of an extremely emotional nature. Care needs to be taken that the exploration of multiple solutions does not become overwhelming to the recipient of the feedback. The facilitator needs to intervene so that a few options can be considered and discarded if necessary or adopted if applicable.

After this discussion has gone on for a while, the counselor can shift the focus onto the topic of positive affirmation and how and why this can be effective as well as a counter deterrent to negative thoughts. The counselor can explain that just as a person learns through repetition, so too does that person's inner consciousness respond to repetition. A list of positive affirmations (see Appendix D) can be handed out. At this point the group should be informed that this will be their final homework assignment and that there are only two sessions left.

This will facilitate a discussion regarding closing, and possible expression by members regarding their desire to find the kind of cohesiveness and cooperation found within the group within their everyday lives. The counselor should encourage this kind of discussion, but will need to help the members understand that what they have achieved within the group will probably not be the norm outside of the group. The counselor should remind members that they will be able to take with them a great many skills that will foster good interactions when needed. The session closing is done as usual, making sure everyone is emotionally stable enough to leave.

Homework assignment #1. The counselor should instruct members to pick one affirmation from the list handed out or to create one that fits better individually. Members should be told to write the affirmation on post-its and put these in different places within their homes (e.g., on the mirror, the refrigerator, the inside of the bedroom door, the dash of the car) or any other place where these will most likely be seen. The counselor should instruct members that whenever they see the note, they should repeat it to themselves and when they are doing something repetitious, they should repeat the affirmation to themselves over and over again. Members can do this while exercising, driving, or doing the dishes. Members should be instructed to make a habit of doing this two or three times daily. This is a long-term task so it is important that members understand to regard it as a routine that will be ongoing. Members should be told that they can change affirmations or add to them if they wish. This homework assignment is designed to enable members to practice and learn a useful skill.

Homework assignment #2. Group members should be instructed to reread their journals and be ready to comment on any progress they feel they have made. These may be changes, added skills, the extinction of a maladaptive behavior, or anything else that is relevant to an individual member.

Process. In this session several therapeutic factors important to the group process are facilitated and encouraged by the counselor. These factors, as indicated by Bloch & Crouch (1985), include: member acceptance of others, the universality of sharing similar problems in transition, individual recognition of having personal information that is of value to helping others solve problems, the development or enhancement regarding the ability to interact with others in a positive manner, and members having the ability to ventilate in a safe and nonjudgmental environment. These are all examples of good healing processes that are found in group work.

Session 7

Purpose. The purpose of this session is to resolve unfinished business from previous sessions, make plans for the ending session, and review individual journaling.

Theme. Cleaning up the choreography.

Activities. Check-in is as usual with the counselor reminding everyone that this will be the next-to-the-last session. In essence, this is getting ready for the "dress rehearsal," and the counselor might ask group members the question, "How does your costume (changing persona) look and feel?" This is the time for reviewing and closure of old business, shifting from affective to intellectual mode, and evaluating progress and changes made, both personal and through the group process. The counselor can initiate discussion on what members discovered by asking them to reread their journal. This can include positive changes, elimination of maladaptive habits, or learning new skills. It is a good idea to end this session with some generalized comments from everyone about the efficacy of group work. The counselor should remind everyone that the last session will be somewhat shorter than usual.

Homework assignment.   At this time the questionnaire (see Appendix B) that was handed out in the first session can be handed out again. Group members should be instructed to complete and return it during the last session.

Process. By resolving unfinished business and generally commenting on group work and its efficacy, the stage is set to end the group at the next and last session. Members should attain a sense of positive empowerment as they review their progress through rereading their journal and discussing those changes that have been wrought.

Session 8

Purpose. The purpose of this last session is to finalize the work of this group and say goodbye. It is also the time for future plans to be made, if wanted or needed, and an opportunity for each member to provide some final feedback to other members and/or to the counselor as well.

Theme. The Last Waltz.

Activities. For this last session, check-in is somewhat nostalgic and should begin on a positive note. The tone should be light, positive, and forward moving, which can be modeled by the counselor's behavior and attitude. The group members may want to make the rounds one last time with positive comments and affirmations directed toward group work, the counselor, or other members. Arrangements can be made for post-interviews; perhaps a future group reunion can be planned, in order to give members a chance to reconnect and update each other. The questionnaire from last week can be handed in as well.

As a way of saying good-bye on a positive note, the counselor can end the group by addressing each member individually while handing each a small token of remembrance. The counselor can wish for them some kind of positive affirmation that is unique to each person. It is also at this time that each group member can say a few words to the facilitator, toward the group in general, or something reaffirming to another member. This is a time for appreciation and celebration for all concerned because it is directed in looking and moving toward positive goals.

Process. It is the process of ending one phase and beginning another for each individual. This is a reaffirming and empowering time for all, a time of changes and shifts ever forward, and for each a learning and growing experience.

REFERRAL PROCEDURES FOR FOLLOW-UP

The questionnaire handed out in session 1 and again in session 7 can be compared and utilized as a measurement of group efficacy. It can also be used as a basis to identify which group members would benefit from additional counseling. Opportunities for post-interview appointments should be made available for those members wishing them in session 8. Follow-up can be planned either through a group reunion in 3 months or by sending out a simple questionnaire ascertaining how group members are faring emotionally and whether or not the coping skills learned in group are being utilized effectively.

REFERENCES

Bloch, S., & Crouch, E. (1985). *Therapeutic factors in group psychotherapy.* Oxford, England: Oxford University Press.

Capuzzi, D., & Gross, D. R. (1998). Group counseling: elements of effective leadership. In D. Capuzzi & D. R. Gross (Eds.), *Introduction to group counseling* pp. 47–74. Denver, CO: Love Publishing.

Corey, M. S., & Corey, G. (1987). *Groups: Process and practice.* Monterey, CA: Brooks/Cole Publishing.

Friedman, W. H. (1989). *Practical group therapy: A guide for clinicians.* San Francisco, CA: Jossey-Bass Publishers.

Golan, N. (1981). *Passing through transitions: A guide for practioners.* New York: Free Press.

Golden, B. R., Corazzini, J. G., & Grady, P. (1993). Current Practice of Group Therapy at University Counseling Centers: A National Survey. *Professional Psychology: Research and Practice.* vol. 34, no. 2, pp. 228–230.

Gross, D. R., & Capuzzi, D. (1998). Group counseling: stages and issues. In D. Capuzzi & D. R. Gross (Eds.), *Introduction to group counseling* pp. 31–46. Denver, CO: Love Publishing.

Schlossberg, N. K. (1984). *Counseling adults in transition.* New York: Springer Publishing.

GROUND RULES FOR GROUP FORMAT

- Be courteous about arriving on time.
- Be attentive and present in the "here and now" of the group.
- Know that what is said in group stays in group even to the extent that nothing is revealed to significant others in your life.
- Be respectful and accepting of other members in the group. This does not mean that you have to agree with them.
- Listen to others courteously and quietly without interruption.
- Do not volunteer feedback without asking permission first.
- Remember this is a group and, as such, decisions may be made by consensus.
- Know that if you do not wish to speak at a certain time, you may pass with or without an explanation.
- Speak in "I" language, not "you" language.
- Actively work at keeping the group environment nonjudgmental, nurturing, and safe.
- **Above all else, harm none.**

Evaluation Questionnaire

The following questionnaire is used as a measurement for group efficacy and group process. Please circle those appropriate at the present time.

1. Returning to school after a prolonged absence is:
   a. a great adventure.
   b. a difficult but necessary transition.
   c. something I had never thought possible.
   d. frightening and overwhelming.

2. Entering the classroom for the first time, I felt:
   a. prepared and alert.
   b. nervous but determined.
   c. awkward and stressed.
   d. ready to panic.

3. My stress level at this point in my transition is:
   a. non-existent.
   b. noticeable but controlled.
   c. shaky but still moving.
   d. "I'm a basket case."

4. My comfort level at this stage is:
   a. a walk in the park.
   b. a jog around the track.
   c. speed walking the campus.
   d. a mile run through rush-hour traffic barefoot.

5. My support network at present is:
   a. as strong and accepting as ever.
   b. somewhat puzzled about my shifting role but there for me.
   c. thinks I'm crazy.
   d. "My dogs still love me."

6. My coping skills are:
   a. strong and versatile.
   b. O.K., but I need additional ones.
   c. "I know I have some somewhere."
   d. "What are coping skills?"

7. As a returning woman student, I feel right now that:
   a. there are lots of us and I fit in fine.
   b. I am no different than any other student.
   c. I feel somewhat different but it's O.K.
   d. I feel isolated and devalued.

8. In reflecting on the group experience, I:
   a. highly recommend it.
   b. think it can be a learning experience.
   c. could do just as well on my own.
   d. Feel there is no way I will ever do it again.
   e. Not applicable at this time.

9. The facilitator of this group:
   a. created a safe, caring, nonjudgmental learning environment.
   b. allowed everyone to share equally in the experience.
   c. did not facilitate the group adequately.
   d. monopolized the group to where the members had no freedom to speak.
   e. Not applicable at this time.

10. This group accomplished what it set out to do:
    a. It was highly motivating and effective.
    b. It completed most of the tasks.
    c. Some of the goals were met.
    d. Were there goals?
    e. Not applicable at this time.

Thank you for your help in filling out this questionnaire.

APPENDIX C

CENTERING AND GROUNDING

- Find a quiet place to sit and calm yourself by closing your eyes and relaxing.
- Concentrate on your breathing, that is all you can hear, in—out—in—out—.
- Breathe in on a count of 4, breathe out on a count of 4. Do this until you can feel yourself settling, and continue to breathe slowly, establishing a rhythm that feels right to you.
- Still breathing rhythmically, visualize your feet on the earth, firmly placed, and visualize your center of mind (I find mine around my navel), and focus on that space. It should be there quiet, waiting.
- Now, still breathing slowly, see in your mind's eye tendrils that are the essence of you traveling gently down the length of your body, down through your legs and feet, now reaching into the rich earth still continuing downwards. Feel the richness of the soil, the structure of pebbles and rocks. It feels comforting and nurturing.
- Continue moving the tendrils of your essence deep into Mother Earth until you start feeling warmth and a sense of stillness. Feel how serenity and strength surround you, encompass you, support you.
- Take that feeling of stillness and strength, draw it into you, and wrap its calmness around you.
- Now take notice again of your breathing; it will still be slow and measured and allow that which is you to travel back to the surface and encompass into your center of being that gift of calmness and strength which has been given you.
- Sit for a minute or two, come back into the focus of here and now, feeling ready to do whatever it is that needs to be done.

With practice, this small exercise can make all the difference in the world when you need to have a sense of calmness and focus. It can be done anywhere and anytime that you need that additional balance.

POSITIVE AFFIRMATIONS

- I act with confidence in my ability.
- I am at peace and am focused.
- I believe in myself.
- I listen to my inner voice and know it is right.
- I like myself.
- I pay attention to my intuition.
- I am good at what I do.
- What I need to know is available when I need it.
- I love myself and therefore I can love others.
- I can let go of the old and enjoy the new in my life.
- I am willing to accept help when I need it.

CHAPTER 20

CODEPENDENCE RECOVERY FOR ADULTS ABUSED AS CHILDREN

Susan A. Kelsey

PURPOSE

The purpose of this educational-counseling group is to help individuals discover a lost sense of self. In this education-counseling group each individual will have an opportunity to learn about codependency and its many facets. The group members will talk about themselves and explore their own feelings and life experiences in a safe, productive, positive environment. The individuals that participate in this group will have an opportunity to learn, grow, and change.

Codependency and its link to various forms of child abuse is a complex subject (Mellody, Miller, & Miller, 1989). Because of dysfunctional childhood experiences, a codependent adult lacks the ability to be a mature person, capable of living a full and meaningful life (Mellody et al., 1989). The primary purpose of this educational-counseling group is to help the individual begin a journey toward recovery from codependence. A codependent individual must stop denying the fact of codependence and begin to take responsibility for facing it. As an individual begins to own and face his or her codependency, he or she will want to actively work toward healing from the devastating effects of childhood and from living as a codependent adult.

Group counseling is generally the treatment of choice for codependents. Because codependence tends to be triggered within relationships, group counseling is especially effective at eliciting symptomatic behavior, thus bringing a client's problems into the counseling session. The multiple relationships within a group and an environment reminiscent of the family setting helps to provide a situation resembling a family and the many relationships (Cermak, 1986). It is valuable for codependents to receive support and validation from peers, not just from the counselor. The group experience becomes a corrective emotional experience for clients to be part of a healthy, recovering "family system," one in which positive feedback is given for breaking denial and speaking the truth about one's feelings and needs (Cermak, 1986).

The purpose of this group is to help codependent individuals become aware that codependence exists in their lives, what the symptoms are, where they come from, and how they sabotage their lives. Through this process individuals can learn to recover from codependence and lead more fulfilling lives.

CONCEPTUAL FRAMEWORK

The conceptual framework for this education-counseling group is from a book by Pia Mellody, Andrea Wells Miller, and J. Keith Miller, *Facing Codependence* (1989) and the practical group work that Sue Cooper, M.S., from Vancouver, WA, uses with adults abused as children in her counseling practice.

In *Facing Codependence*, Mellody et al. trace the origins of codependence back to childhood, describing a whole range of emotional, spiritual, intellectual, physical, and sexual abuses. Because of these earlier experiences, codependent adults often lack the skills necessary to lead mature lives and have satisfying relationships. Mellody et al.

believe that recovery from codependence is achieved by learning to re-parent oneself. Central to the book's concept is the idea of the "precious child" that needs healing within each adult. There are two key areas of a person's life that reflect codependence: the relationship with the self and relationships with others. Mellody et al. believe that the relationship with one's self is the most important, because when people have a respectful, affirming relationship with themselves, relationships with others automatically become less dysfunctional and more respectful and affirming (Mellody et al., 1989).

The codependent's self-concept has developed around the needs of others instead of developing in its own right. As children, most codependents felt responsible for other family members' feelings or behavior. If a family member was unhappy or in trouble, the codependent child came to believe that it was his or her job to "fix it." Later as an adult, others came to depend upon this person for help, especially in crisis. This person, who was and is always so good at helping others, is the codependent.

Codependence is a disease of lost selfhood. It can mimic, be associated with, aggravate, and even lead to many of the physical, mental, emotional, or spiritual conditions that befall people in daily life. People become codependent when they turn the responsibility of their life and happiness over to their ego (false self) and to other people. Codependent people become so preoccupied with others that they neglect their True Self—who they really are.

Codependence is the most common of all addictions: the addiction to looking elsewhere. People believe that something outside of their self—that is, outside of their True Self—can give them happiness and fulfillment. The "elsewhere" may be people, places, things, behaviors, or experiences. Whatever it is, people may neglect their own selves for it. Codependence is about giving away power over one's own self-esteem.

Counselors who want to conduct group sessions about codependence should become familiar with the subject matter. There are many good books on the subject. Most of these sessions are based on work by several authors: Pia Mellody, Sue Cooper, James Kitchens, Timmen L. Cermak, Laura P. Webb, and James Leehan. It is recommended that counselors conducting this group experience should become familiar and knowledgeable with the information contained in books written by the above authors.

These sessions are designed to last approximately 1 1/2 to 2 hours, meeting once per week. The subject matter can bring up many emotional issues for each client, and they may not get resolved each week. The counselor may need to progress at a pace that the group is ready for; each group will move at their own pace. The group leader may want to only present a new topic every other week, depending on the members of the group and how many members are a part of the group. It is recommended to keep the group on the small side, four to six participants. Less than four participants does not provide an adequate group experience, and a group larger than six may not be conducive to meet the needs of all members. Keeping the group with only four to six members allows each participant time to process information with the group and allow for other group members to respond and interact with members. This is very beneficial to group members so they can learn to relate and interact with others in a supportive and safe environment.

The individual topics covered in the eight sessions include: The Disease of Codependence, The Five Core Symptoms of Codependence, Boundaries, The Precious Child, Family and the Origins of Codependence, Abuse, and Recovery and Personal Empowerment from Codependence. How well group members process the information presented and interact with the group activities determines how quickly a group leader can move from topic to topic. It may be necessary to adjust the sessions to meet the needs of group members as they progress. Group leaders should assess how their group is proceeding and determine if they are ready to move on to the next topic.

GROUP GOALS

The primary goal of this educational-counseling group is to help individuals toward a journey of recovery from codependence in a safe and therapeutic environment. Other group goals include:

1. Help the codependent person understand what codependence is and that he or she can begin to change some of the thinking, emotions, and behaviors that have sabotaged his or her life.
2. Help the codependent person actively work toward healing from the devastating effects of his or her childhood and living as an adult codependent.
3. Help the codependent person understand his or her history of abuse and move beyond denial.
4. Help the codependent person confront his or her core symptoms of codependence.
5. Provide a safe and therapeutic environment for personal change and growth.
6. Help increase self-awareness and develop a sense of identity.
7. Provide encouragement to help members embrace their own history, look at it, become aware of it, and experience their feelings about the less-than-nurturing events in their past.

PRE-GROUP SCREENING AND ORIENTATION

When forming a small (four to six members) therapy group, screening each participant is very important to protect the safety of each member and to ensure that the group process can flow and the goals of the group can be achieved. The leader of this group must screen prospective members to select individuals whose needs and goals are congruent with the group goals, who will not be detrimental to the group, and whose well-being will not be jeopardized by the group experience (Association for Specialists in Group Work, 1989).

Members for this type of group work could be found through recommendations from other counselors or mental health agencies that think their client would benefit from the group experience. Advertisements can also be placed in the community, or individuals from one's own private practice could be placed in this type of group.

It would be beneficial for the leader of this type of group to conduct private meetings with each prospective group member. During this session the leader should assess if *this* particular candidate should be included in *this* particular group at *this* time with *this* group leader (Corey & Corey, 1987). Members selected to participate in this group should be willing to learn, disclose, share, and listen to others. It is important to select individuals who are ready to face their past and embrace new discoveries about themselves.

Group selection is a subjective process and the leader of this group should invite possible members that are willing to be cooperative, want to participate in a group experience, want to make changes in their life, and be willing to interact with other members in listening, sharing feedback, and communicating with non-judgmental understanding and caring.

Participants who are chosen for this group should be free of any major personal or family crises, not have had a recent death of a loved one, currently not be using any illegal drugs, and not be a practicing alcoholic. Participants in this group should be free of any major problems that would interfere with their concentrating on working toward recovery from codependence.

A pre-group orientation should be held before the actual formal sessions begin. This pre-group orientation would include an opportunity for the group leader to go over what topics will be taught and explored at each session, what the purpose of the group is, what the group process is about, the ground rules, the policies, what confidentiality means, and to begin the getting-acquainted process (Corey, 1990).

During the pre-group orientation, members of the group have an opportunity to explore his or her concerns, expectations, fears, goals, and misconceptions about group work. The prospective member can also use this time to question the group leader about his or her concerns. The pre-group orientation should be a two-way process so that potential members can form an opinion about the group and the leader (Corey & Corey, 1987). Given enough information about the group, a member can make a better informed decision about whether to en-

ter it or not. This pre-group orientation should cover the basic rules and guidelines for participating in a group and the first introduction of members to each other.

During this pre-group orientation each member should be informed that he or she will have the option after completing the eight-week sessions of continuing on with the group, continue working on codependence with an individual counselor, or joining a support group. Recovery from codependence takes time, and work, and each group member should be encouraged to continue with a recovery program after the eight sessions are completed.

OUTLINE FOR EIGHT GROUP SESSIONS

Session 1

Purpose. The purpose of the first session is to bring the group together; get acquainted; discuss the group rules, goals, and behavior for group participation; and begin the educational portion of this particular group.

Theme. The theme for the first session is "The Disease of Codependence." This beginning session introduces the concept of codependence and gives group members an opportunity to assess their own life and how codependence is impacting their life. The first session covers broad generalizations about codependence, and members can talk about codependence in their lives in a broad spectrum, giving members an opportunity to disclose as much as they want during this initial phase.

Activities. At the beginning of this session, every member is given an opportunity to volunteer information about themselves, who they are, what they do, what brought them to this group, and so on. After each member has introduced himself or herself, the leader asks members how they have been feeling and coping with life during the last week. This information should give the leader an opportunity to assess if anyone in the group needs particular or extra attention during the session.

After the initial orientation and exploration, the leader gives a short lecture about what codependence is and how it impacts a person's life. Some of the topics that can be covered are: what codependency is; how codependency arises in a pathological family of origin; describing the faces of codependency and its origins, types, and attributes; signs of codependence; primary symptoms of codependence; the development of codependence; and a codependent's belief system.

When the educational portion of the group session is over, the leader can lead a discussion with the group members about what they heard, and if the information applies to them. The leader can help members to disclose and talk about how codependence is impacting their life at this time. The activities during this first session should be structured to establish a climate of supportive growth, introduce participants to self-disclosure in a nonthreatening way, and help members feel they are each a valuable member of the group.

Process. During this first session, it is very important for the group leader to develop trust, a sense of safety, and cohesiveness with the group members. During the first part of the group session, members have an opportunity to *volunteer* information about themselves. No one is forced to speak. Basic introductions are fairly safe for everyone to volunteer. After the lecture, members can either choose to comment on the material presented in a nonpersonal way, or they can apply the information to their situation and share how it has impacted their life. During this first session it will be helpful for the leader to encourage each member to contribute to the discussion.

Session 2

Purpose. The second session's purpose is to continue the educational process about codependence and help group members to feel safe to explore and share their past history and current issues regarding codependence.

Theme. The five core symptoms of codependence.

Activity. The group session begins with a check-in with members to find out how their past week has been, and if there have been any problems or issues they need to discuss during the session. After the check-in, the leader gives a short lecture about the five core symptoms of codependence. The five core symptoms of codependence are: difficulty experiencing appropriate levels of self-esteem, difficulty setting functional boundaries, difficulty owning your own reality, difficulty acknowledging and meeting your own needs and wants, and difficulty experiencing and expressing your reality moderately (not acting at one extreme or the other) (Mellody et al., 1989).

Process. After the lecture, participants are asked to think about and discuss with the group how these five core symptoms are impacting their life today. The group leader can ask the group if anyone has any thoughts about what has been presented, and if the information is clear and understood. After a discussion of the general concepts of the five core symptoms of codependence, the leader can ask members how these symptoms play a part in each of their lives. When members discuss their own symptoms of codependency, other members may be able to get in touch with codependency symptoms that they had not thought about before. As each member gets in touch with ways he or she is codependent, the leader should look for what feelings are being felt and how it is affecting each individual as well as the group as a whole.

Session 3

Purpose. The purpose of the third session is to have group participants think about what it means to have boundaries, and the different kinds of boundaries. Another purpose is to have group members assess and analyze their own boundaries and if they are effective.

Theme. Boundaries protect and contain a person's reality. Having boundaries means that one is not the extension of the other. Boundaries do not represent unavailability. Rather, when there are clear boundaries, open communication may flow in both directions (Kitchens, 1991).

Activity. This session begins with a check-in with members about how their past week was and to see if there are any issues left over from the previous week that need to be discussed. After check-in, the group leader presents a short lecture about boundaries. Topics that can be discussed are: what boundaries mean, the purpose of boundaries, the benefits of boundaries, the types of boundaries (external, internal, sexual, spiritual), boundary fitness (no boundaries, damaged boundaries, walls, intact boundaries), difficulty setting functional boundaries, why boundaries must be taught, and where dysfunctional boundaries come from (Cooper, 1997; Mellody et al., 1989).

Process. After the lecture, the group leader can ask the group if they understand what it means to have boundaries and if there are any questions about boundaries. There are a variety of exercises that can be done to help individuals understand boundaries and clarify if their boundaries have been abused or if they abuse other people's boundaries. Some questions to ask the group members about external boundaries are: Who is respectful and courteous regarding your space? Who is respectful about touching you? Who is disrespectful and discourteous with regard to your space? Whose space do you invade? Who do you touch without permission? These questions can be discussed verbally, or group members can write answers down on paper and then share verbally if they choose. Questions for internal boundaries can include: Who violated your feeling boundary today? Who violated your thinking boundary today? Who violated your behavior boundary today? Whom did you harm by telling them what they felt or did not feel? Whom did you harm by telling them what to think or not to think? Whom did you harm by telling them how to behave or not to behave? Ask group participants to keep a log or journal during the next week and assess their external and internal boundaries, who has violated their boundaries, and how they have intruded upon other people's boundaries.

Session 4

Purpose. The purpose of this session is to help the group participant understand how a less-than-nurturing environment during childhood is at the root of codependence.

Theme. "The Precious Child" (Mellody et al., 1989). It is important to understand how a dysfunctional, less-than-nurturing, abusive system prevents an individual family member from successfully maturing into adulthood.

Activity. As with the other sessions, begin this session by checking in with members and asking them how their week was and if there are any concerns or issues from the past week or other sessions that need to be discussed or processed. When finished with the check-in, the group leader can present a short lecture about "The Precious Child" (Mellody et al., 1989). This lecture should include topics such as: the five natural characteristics that make children authentic human beings (i.e., that children are valuable, vulnerable, imperfect, dependent, and immature), the importance that all children are born with these five attributes, and that functional parents help their children to develop each separate characteristic properly, so that they arrive in adulthood as mature, functional adults who feel good about themselves (Mellody et al., 1989). Other topics to include are: how a functional family supports children's value, protects a child's vulnerability, supports a child's imperfection, meets a child's needs and wants, supports a child's immaturity, the precious child in a dysfunctional family and how the five natural characteristics are sabotaged, and what the adult characteristics look like in the codependent adult.

Process.   When the lecture is finished, ask for questions and ask if anyone needs clarification about what was presented. Then ask participants to think back about their childhood and look for ways that their family was less than nurturing. Ask participants to think about how they developed survival traits and attributes to survive in a dysfunctional family. The group can spend time writing their answers in their journal or just spend time thinking about the answers and sharing verbally with the group. To continue the process of trying to understand the less-than-nurturing behavior each person received, ask them to work on a log at home during the next week. This log would include the type of less-than-nurturing behavior, who did it, the age it occurred, what happened, how it affected them then, and how it affects them now.

Session 5

Purpose. The purpose of this session is to provide an overview of how the family of origin is a critical factor in how a child comes to know others, their self, and the world. It is also the intent of this session to provide an understanding of how important it is to face our own codependence and not pass down from generation to generation the behaviors that perpetuate codependency.

Theme. Family: how it is the root of codependence and how to break the cycle.

Activity. During this session, continue doing a check-in with participants to find out how their week was and if any issues surfaced that they may need to process. The

group leader can ask for volunteers to share the logs they kept during the week about any less-than-nurturing behavior they encountered when they were a child. Next, do a check to see if, while doing these logs, there has been any emotions or disturbing thoughts that individuals might want to discuss and process. A short lecture would then be presented about "Family" and how poor parenting can lead to the development of false self, low self-esteem, poor boundary management skills, and fears of engulfment and abandonment. The lecture should also include: how the roots of codependence are in the childhood experiences of abuse, and that it is the shame core that perpetuates the disease of codependency from generation to generation; what is the shame core and how it perpetuates codependency; how family secrets are repeated and abuse not dealt with and how secrets are unconsciously transmitted to the next generation; what constitutes less-than-nurturing family experiences; codependent survival traits condoned by society; how to tell the difference between shame and healthy guilt; and the cycle of shame.

Process. After the lecture, ask the group if members would like to share how these concepts help them understand their childhood. During this intervention, try to help the individual discover and reveal both past and present feelings and to interpret their meanings. Group members can begin to explore how their childhood has impacted their life today and how the feelings generated from the way they interpret their past events are affecting them today. At this time, the group leader can examine how these interpretations lead the codependent into trouble because their thinking is skewed and the conclusions they draw are often inaccurate, all unbeknownst to the codependent.

Session 6

Purpose. The purpose of this session is to provide an understanding of the different types of abuse and the effects that abuse in a family system has on a person as an adult. A second purpose is to help each group member look at the different types of abuse that happened to each one of them during their childhood.

Theme. The focus is on abuse within the family system and how its long-term effects are debilitating to the adult child of such behaviors.

Activity. Since this session has the possibility of being very emotional and difficult for members of the group, start the session with a check-in of each person; as in the other sessions, make sure there is no unfinished business that needs to be discussed and that everyone is in a position to look at childhood abuse. If the group is ready to proceed, present a lecture about abuse, the different types (physical, emotional, sexual, intellectual, spiritual) (Cooper, 1997), and the two major forms of abuse, overt and covert. The five principles that guide us through the process of understanding abuse should be presented: (1) the child is always innocent, (2) each form of abuse has an overt and covert behavior associated with it, (3) abuse is usually intergenerational, (4) there are special, sneaky abuses that deserve attention (manipulation, being in control, psychological abuse, implied threats, verbal attack, unrelenting criticism, denial, re-writing history, shifting blame), and (5) children have two major needs, a need for structure and a need for nurture (if children did not receive these, they were abused) (Cooper, 1997). Abuse is not always the product of malicious intent; a parent may be physically or emotionally incapable of providing care and safety for his or her child, despite the parent's best intentions (Webb & Leehan, 1996). Even though all forms of abuse are harmful, it is important to acknowledge that there are differential effects. Each form of abuse creates different personality and behavior dynamics. Other aspects of abuse include the relationship of the abuser to the victim, the age of the victim, and forms of assistance and support available to the victim (Webb & Leehan, 1996). The last part of the lecture should provide some guidelines to help each member evaluate his or her own history of abuse and help each member to understand that getting his or her history straight is a vital step in the process of recovery from codependence. Discussing the process of healing and what it is like is of importance at this stage and should be emphasized.

Process.   After the lecture, ask if the material was understood and if there are any questions or concerns. Have members answer some questions in their journal; these questions would include (Cooper, 1997):

1. How many generations of abusers can you count in your family?
2. Did you receive the structure you needed?
3. Did you receive the nurture you deserved?
4. Were you manipulated?
5. Were you battered?
6. Were you enmeshed with one or both parents, grandparents?
7. Did you become your parent's partner or buddy?
8. What didn't you get that you truly deserved?

After the group members have had time to write answers to these questions, ask if anyone would like to share the information with the group. The discussion during this session can be very powerful and emotional; the group leader needs to be very aware of what is happening during this session to make sure that each participant is doing okay. At the end of this session do another check-in with each member to make sure that there is no unfinished business and that each person is emotionally stable. This session is very critical to helping members face their roots of codependency and may actually take more than one session to finish all the business necessary to help each client.

Homework would be assigned to help facilitate members to face their own history. The guidelines to assist in the process of helping members get their history straight are (Mellody et al., 1989):

1. Have each participant look at each year of his or her life from birth to age 17.
2. Have each member recall his or her history and have him or her identify what the shaming acts were and who did them.
3. Hold the abusers accountable, but do not blame them, just acknowledge what really happened.
4. Do not compare your history to someone else's.
5. Do not use judgmental words (good, bad, right, wrong, and so on) to describe what happened to you.
6. Focus on what your caregivers did not do, not what you are doing today.

There are three reasons why looking at the past is very necessary for recovery, and failure to do so inhibits recovery. The first reason is as a person brings up these childhood incidents and remembers them, you can begin to see specifically how the parenting a person received affected them. Another reason is that to recover, a person must purge from his or her body the childhood feelings of reality he or she had about being abused. The third reason to uncover our past is that there is evidence that people who were raised in dysfunctional families, as adults, often choose to relate to people who create the same emotional atmosphere they had in their family of origin and that dysfunction needs to be stopped (Mellody et al., 1989).

The group leader may find that this topic, abuse, needs more than one session for the group members to help them to face their abusive past history. If this is necessary, the leader may want to eliminate another topic, extend to more sessions, or present this topic during an earlier session.

During session 6, remind group members that the last session is session 8 and begin to prepare them for termination of the group. The group leader should also discuss with the group members about continuing with the group therapy process, or individual therapy, or joining a support group. Clients should begin to reflect if they received everything they wanted or needed from this group experience. Reminding the group that the last session is near will give each member time to think about the group ending and bring up any leftover issues during the last two sessions.

Session 7

Purpose.   The purpose of session 7 is to help group members understand what recovery looks like and how members are able to empower themselves to make positive changes. It is also the purpose of session 7 to prepare to end the group therapy work.

Theme. "Recovery and Personal Empowerment" from codependence (Mellody et al., 1989).

Activity. This session again begins with a check-in with each group member to see if anyone has issues or left-over issues, thoughts, or concerns from the past sessions and would process them. Then ask for any volunteers who might want to share their history of abuse with the group and find out how members handled looking at their past history of abuse. This session could be very emotional and there may need to be a lot of processing with group members. Looking at past abuse may bring up some very strong feelings, and it is suggested that the group should stay with the process until everyone is comfortable and ready to move on to the lecture about recovery.

If the group is ready to move on, a short lecture would be presented about what recovery means and looks like. Recovery for most codependents feels like an abnormal life pattern. The codependent feels more comfortable with old patterns. Being functional (acting in one's own best interest) feels awful and shameful, as if they are doing something wrong. But as the codependent enters into recovery they begin to see what they thought was normal is actually dysfunctional. Becoming aware of what is dysfunctional and what is normal is part of the recovery process. The recovery process is about not being in denial, delusion, or minimization regarding one's own recovery and reminding each member recovery takes time and it is not easy. Recovery for the codependent is about learning to empower themselves. Facing codependence is the first step to beginning recovery. Recovery feels extreme because functional behavior feels so unfamiliar. Recovery begins with pain, it usually does not occur to the codependent that he or she needs to change unless there has been painful consequences resulting from the dysfunctional behaviors. During the process of recovery there will be unexpected fears and uncertainties. Just understanding and knowing about codependence will not make it go away by itself; each person must do his or her own work towards recovery.

Process. After the lecture, ask if the information was clear and if there were any questions. The discussion can then turn to how members are going to make their recovery work for them and what recovery will feel like. Members can offer solutions and possibilities that will help them to overcome codependence. These solutions and possibilities could also be written in their journal for future reference.

Session 8

Purpose. The purpose of session 8 is to help group members prepare for termination of the group and continue to look at what their life will look like with recovery from codependence.

Theme. Termination of the group and continuation of recovery from codependence.

Activity. This last session should be focused on finishing up loose ends, old business, and concerns about termination of the group. This last session again begins with a check-in with group members to see if anyone has issues or concerns from the past week and are willing to share their concerns. At this time, the leader can check in for any concerns or issues that may need to be discussed from past lectures or group experiences. When the group has finished with unfinished issues and questions the group will need to move on to termination of the group and closure.

Process. The last part of this session needs to focus on closure of the group. Group members are asked if they would like to share what it has meant to them to be a part of this group and what they have received from being a member of this group. The leader can also point out to each client what positive behaviors and changes he or she has noticed that makes the client ready to leave the group, and reminding members of their accomplishments. At this point the leader could use a "stemming" exercise (Kitchens, 1991). The leader gives the group members a few words of a sentence (the stem) and they finish it. The leader goes around the room to each person and then gives another stem and the group completes the sentence. Some examples of sentence stems include:

- Codependence means _____.
- One thing that is changing about me is _____.
- The most important thing I am learning about me is _____.
- Recovery from codependence for me will mean _____.
- The thing I have enjoyed most about this group is _____.

After the group has finished the stemming exercise, ask if anyone wants to say anything else to the group and then remind the group that this is not an ending but a beginning to a more fulfilling life. At this time, also remind group members that they should continue to practice the things they have learned in group and continue to support each other. The group could also discuss at this point if they wanted to stay together as a group and continue working at facing their codependence and building strength for continued recovery.

STRATEGIES TO EVALUATE THE GROUP

In a follow-up session with the group, the leader can help members to evaluate their experience with the group and help the leader evaluate what was beneficial and effective in the material and activities that were presented.

An evaluation form can ask members to assess their degree of satisfaction with the group and the level of investment they had in it. It can ask members to recall highlights or significant events. It can ask them to specify actions they took during the group to make desired changes. It can ask them to state what techniques were most and least helpful and to give suggestion for changing the format. A structured checklist might be devised or an open-ended letter might be asked for, or a combination of a rating scale and essay questions might be used. This evaluation procedure is a valuable tool for the leader to measure the effectiveness of the group and it also helps the members to focus their thinking on what they did during the group and what they received from the experience (Corey, Corey, Callanan, & Russell, 1988). Some questions that might be used are:

1. Did you learn what codependence was and how it affects your life?
2. What were the highlights of the group experience for you? What was most meaningful to you?
3. What specific things did you become aware of about yourself and your relationship with your family members?
4. What changes have you made in your life that you can attribute at least partially to your group experience?
5. Which lecture had the most impact on you? Which lecture had the least impact on you?
6. What kinds of problems did you encounter in the outside world when you tried to implement some of the changes you made during your group experience?
7. Did the group experience have any negative effects on you?
8. How did your participation in this group affect significant people in your life?
9. If you had to say in a sentence or two what the group meant to you, how would you respond?
10. What are some of your perceptions of the group leader and the style she or he used?
11. What would you change about the eight sessions?
12. Has the information you learned in this group inspired you to continue work on your codependency issues?

REFERRAL PROCEDURES FOR FOLLOW-UP

Working with adults abused as children can be a very powerful and rewarding experience for each member. When these eight sessions are completed the recovery process for each individual should continue. It is important as a group leader to help direct those individuals who want to, and will, continue their process of recovery from codependence. Individuals also need to know where to go if some of the issues they uncovered during the eight sessions have left them feeling unsettled or

are causing them anxiety. There are some things the group leader can do to help each individual find the support he or she may need or desire. Some of the possibilities are:

1. Offering private consultations if any member should need this service at least on a limited basis to discuss a member's reactions to the group experience.
2. Providing for a follow-up group session to assess the impact of the group.
3. Offering several specific referral resources for members who want, or need, further consultation.
4. Encouraging members to find some avenues of continued support and challenge so that the ending of the group can mark the beginning of a search for self-understanding.
5. Assisting members to develop contracts that will enable them to make use of support systems among the group members and outside the group.
6. Offering an opportunity to have a group reunion. This will offer members an opportunity to reconnect, share, and provide support and encouragement.
7. The leader can also suggest reading material on the subject matter or organizations that support recovery from codependence. Providing a printed list of reading material and resources available in the community will be a valuable resource for each member.

It is important to offer each member of the group a variety of options that they may avail themselves to, for continued support and recovery of their codependence.

REFERENCES

Association for Specialists in Group Work. (1989). *Ethical guidelines for group counselors*. Alexandria, VA: Author.

Cermak, T. L. (1986). *Diagnosing and treating co-dependence*. North Minneapolis, MN: Johnson Institute Books.

Cooper, S. (1997). *Resources one; adults abused as children handbook for phase one*. Vancouver, WA: S. Cooper.

Corey, G. (1990). *Theory and practice of group counseling* (3rd ed.). Pacific Grove, CA: Brooks/Cole.

Corey, G., Corey, M. S., Callanan, P., & Russell, J. M. (1988). *Group techniques*. Pacific Grove, CA: Brooks/Cole.

Corey, M. S., & Corey, G. (1987). *Groups process and practice* (3rd ed.). Pacific Grove, CA: Brooks/Cole.

Kitchens, J. A. (1991). *Understanding and treating codependence*. Englewood Cliffs, NJ: Prentice-Hall.

Mellody, P., Miller, A. W., & Miller, J. K. (1989). *Facing codependence*. San Francisco, CA: Harper & Row.

Webb, L. P., & Leehan, J. (1996). *Group treatment for adult survivors of abuse: A manual for practitioners*. Thousand Oaks, CA: SAGE.

CHAPTER 21

A Positive Approach to Disciplining Your School-Aged Child

Kelly Peterson

PURPOSE

How many times have parents just felt like screaming with frustration over how their children were behaving? And how often have those parents felt guilty because of the choices they made when disciplining them? Most parents would probably respond with the answer, many! Parenting is a hard and extremely difficult task. It comes with practically no training and requires numerous skills that tax the most from you. However, the component that appears to create the greatest anxiety for all members of the family is discipline. Discipline is defined as the instruction and training of the mind, body, and/or moral faculties which exhibit self-control (Gibson, 1983). In other words, discipline is about teaching. One role of parents and adults is to teach children so they cannot only move from parental discipline to self-discipline, but also learn from us and to achieve the following:

1. To teach the child how to achieve for himself or herself.
2. To teach the child self-discipline, so he or she can function independently later in life.
3. To have the child develop a sense of pride in doing what is right (May, 1979).

The group focus will be to help parents learn the skills needed to create a positive environment for their school-aged child, and then learn to integrate these three goals. The sessions will also include areas beyond techniques. Time will be spent during the first two sessions on understanding of the parent-child relationship and how it affects discipline. An important aspect of the parent-child relationship is the need for each to know the other. Parents need to understand themselves by examining their own experiences and realize how these experiences have impacted their own expectations as a parent. Once accomplished, the parent then needs to examine who the child is, what the child's personality is *really* like, and how the child fits in with *the parent's* expectations. With this new insight parents can determine the patterns they have fallen into that are not working because of these factors and look for a new and, hopefully, more effective approach for both the parent and the child. Each person is a unique individual with different response sets, coping skills, and needs. It is all about finding the right balance between the two individuals when disciplining. This is where the group leads into the discussions about new positive parenting/discipline skills and then ends with how to maintain support for them.

CONCEPTUAL FRAMEWORK

Why is good discipline so important? There are many reasons and theories about the importance of childhood and how one was raised. Some of these go back to Sigmund Freud. He was the first to conclude that the events or environment of a person's childhood affects and creates the adult we see later in life (Hoffman, 1994). But it was Alfred Adler that was the first to address the *quality* of the child's environment and its effects on a child's development. In 1904, Adler wrote an article entitled "The Physician as Educator" (Hoffman, 1994). He suggested that physicians take on the roles of educators to parents and school teachers about the prevention of emotional problems in children (Hoffman, 1994). Some of those specific recommendations included: warmth, affection, promotion of confidence and choices, praise, and reward. He also emphasized the concept that parents should not punish without an explanation that encourages alternative behavior choices (Hoffman, 1994). These are the same concepts found in research and self-help literature today regarding the discipline of children.

After compiling all the data, there were six common components in positive disciplining that reflect the same ideas Adler initiated: understanding, modeling, prevention, redirection, consequences, and alternative disciplining techniques (e.g., Boyd, 1994; Gibson, 1983; Lighter, 1995; May, 1979). The alternative discipline techniques, such as corporal punishment, are rarely effective by themselves, but done in a particular manner and combined with other more positive techniques it can, if used occasionally, be effective (Gibson, 1983). These six components are the underlying concepts to this group proposal and consist of what is covered in the eight group sessions.

GROUP GOALS

Depending on the group and their own experiences, needs, and expectations, the following goals for a parenting group can guide the eight sessions:

1. For members to experience support and validation from other parents in similar situations.
2. To help each other deal with guilt over parenting/discipline choices by their sharing of experiences.
3. To help members realize and understand their own issues left over from their parents' choices and how it effects them today.
4. To help parents by giving them a greater number of discipline choices and skills so that they can help their own children achieve the three target goals of discipline.

PRE-GROUP SCREENING AND ORIENTATION

Pre-group screening and preparation are vital to protect the safety of the group members and ensure the success of the group and its process. During screening interviews the counselor should select clients that display signs of cooperativeness and seem to have a commitment to interpersonal change (Sieber & Lewis, 1998). The counselor should also screen out those with any serious mental disorders, especially considering

the cognitive content of this group and the time allotted. This includes those parents with children who are behaviorally challenged. This is because, although some of the methods covered in this group would work well with that population, the time allotted is too small to cover all of the needs of those parents and their children. Counselors need to create a smaller, lengthier, more homogeneous group in order to more effectively meet the needs of group members with behaviorally challenged children. The counselor will also have to exclude any children that have more complicated underlying issues, such as children who have been abused or are differently abled. Even though these children may have a strong need for a group similar to this one, this group could not address all or enough of these issues and still be effective. It is vital to ensure that counselors are giving the parents *all* the tools they need to meet success. It is also important to note that this psychoeducational group only addresses discipline concerns for the school-aged child (ages 5 to 12) and it is assumed that the child possesses the ability to reason. Last, it is important that parents selected for this group are open to new ideas and are able to respect others. A good approach would be to ask the client during pre-group orientation what discipline method he or she uses and its effectiveness. Most parents will probably respond by saying that their current method has not been working and that is why they have taken this next step. The counselor should then ask potential group members if they have any intolerance about parenting styles and, if so, what these are. Not only can counselors use this information to match the clients to this group, but it will also let the counselor know which group members will respond the most positively to each other, thus creating a more successful and cooperative group.

OUTLINE FOR EIGHT GROUP SESSIONS

Session 1

Purpose. The purpose of the first session is for group members to introduce themselves and to build a foundation for open communication. It will also be necessary to cover the basic format of each session so that each member knows what to expect, the ground rules, and concerns about confidentiality. The facilitator would want to know each member's reason for joining the group and the expectations concerning the group experience. The counselor should be flexible and try and meet each member's needs.

Theme. In order for the group to progress successfully, the counselor should start with a theme of *comfort and acceptance*. It is not only a time for introductions and ground rules, but more importantly, a time for each group member to learn from the others, start to make connections, and develop safe boundaries.

Activities. Expectations are the key component to the success of the group process. If members do not feel they are getting their needs met, then the group has not accomplished its goal. Although this group cannot solve everyone's problems, each member should be able to have at least one need or goal met. Since each person is different with unique issues, the group needs to be flexible. Therefore, during the beginning of the first session, the facilitator should propose to discuss this concept with the group and have them share their ideas and goals. The group would also go over the pre-set goals for the group; the ground rules, including confidentiality; and introduce the idea of termination for the eighth session. Some good basic ground rules to start with would be:

1. Start and stop on time, be respectful of other's time commitments.
2. Respect and accept one another at all times, we are NOT here to judge, we all make mistakes.
3. Remain silent while another is talking, no cross talk.
4. Be "present" and participate constructively.
5. Communicate with "I" sentences. You can only speak for yourself.
6. Maintain confidentiality. Nothing said goes outside the group. If this is an issue, it needs to be discussed with the group.
7. Set your own boundaries. You can provide as much or as little information as you are comfortable sharing. Keep yourself safe and don't disrupt others' safety. This is *everyone's* group.
8. No advice giving is allowed during session. Ask the member if they would like advice later. If receptive to it, members may share with them *after* group.

The reason for the last rule is to try to eliminate feelings of inadequacy in their parenting and judgment. It is important to keep in mind that not all children respond in the same way. So, although the advice a member may give was done with all the right intentions, he or she may essentially be adding to the other's feelings of failure and inadequacy. Parenting is a very personal and sensitive issue. If a member has something to share, perhaps tell his or her own personal story as a way to display a connection. That way members can take from the story what they feel is safe to receive. During this time the facilitator is also establishing his or her position in the group. It is important that the facilitator is able to communicate trust within the group. The group members rely on the facilitator to keep the group safe by supporting the ground rules and modeling respect.

Next, the facilitator should start with an activity that would both introduce the members and invite them to share a little about their children. The activity would be to pick a color from the crayon box that most reminds the parents of one or more of their children and explain why. This way the group gets a little background on group members' family dynamics. If members are reluctant to go around and discuss it, the facilitator should pair up people into like color groups and have them share with each other what they have to say. Then they can come back to the circle and introduce their partner instead of themselves. This is an opportunity for the parents to talk amongst each other and create a little more personal connection.

To close the session, the facilitator should ask the members if they made any connections or heard any stories in which they could relate and what that connection was like for them. The facilitator could again touch upon the personal goals of each member. This would enable group members to feel ownership and that this is their group. It will be up to them what will be accomplished. Once members decide, then they can work together to meet each others' needs.

Process. The objective of the first session is for the members to make connections and take ownership in the group and its process—all while staying safe. By breaking up into small groups, the members were able to share information and make connections with others in a safe manner. The rules helped define the group and lay down the first of expectations. After the rules, the members were able to express their goals and needs for the group and further established commitment to the process and ownership.

The facilitator's role during the first session sets the tone for the group throughout the eight sessions. Therefore, it is important that the facilitator try to create an environment where the group members can be safe by supporting the ground rules and modeling respect. The facilitator should try to keep the group focused and allow for most of the interactions to come from group members themselves.

Sessions 2 and 3

Purpose. During the next two sessions the facilitator will want the members to start doing some introspection of themselves about the issues around how their parents raised them and how that affects them today. Time should also be spent in having parents look objectively at their children and how they blend in with the parent's own experiences. This is a very personal place to start, but it is a critical component to effective discipline.

Theme. The theme is "Understanding who I am and who my child really is." Often parents do not really see their children for who they are. Their vision is clouded with their own expectations of their children and their disappointment when the children do not live up to the parents ideals. Sometimes parents will compensate, through their children, for things that were lacking in their own childhood. For example, parents who always did poor in school as children may want their own children to read a lot so they do better. However, it may be the child's natural temperament to want to run and play and do more large motor activities. This would not be fitting the parent's idea of how the child should behave, even though the child is not actually doing anything wrong or disobeying the rules. So what is the parent teaching the child? That the child is not okay or that he or she is not making good choices. This could be interpreted as setting the child up for failure because the parent is going against the child's natural inclination to play. Children will probably have a difficult time measuring up to that expectation and consequently start a cycle of failure. Not only will children feel like they are failing their parents, but parents will feel like they are doing something wrong when disciplining their children. Therefore, it is important to know your expectations as a parent and where they come from. Are they realistic? Or do parents need to reassess them? Then look at the child. Does the child's personality conflict with the parent's expectations? Is this the source of the discomfort with each other? Has the cycle of failure started yet? All of these questions need to be addressed during these two sessions so the group can move on to skills acquisition.

Activities.   After the check-in and dealing with any old business or conflicts that arose over the week that needs to be discussed, the group begins the session with the facilitator introducing and explaining the topic and then opens discussion with the following story:

> *Once there was a woman named Samantha, who was brought up in a neglectful house with only her mother raising her. Her mother had serious mental health issues that never were addressed. For example, she would do awful things to people and never show remorse. The mother would always pronounce that they owed her these things. Later, when Samantha became a parent and had a young two-year-old daughter, Ann, of her own, she started running into some disciplining problems. Every time Samantha would get mad at Ann, Ann would ignore Samantha and space out. This just made Samantha even more mad, and she would punish her daughter more severely then she had originally planned. Later, Samantha would feel extremely guilty and hate herself for it and feel like an awful parent.*
>
> *One day she was talking to a friend about her guilt, and her friend, who has known her since they were children, commented that Ann's reaction reminded her a little of how Samantha's mother would react, nothing. Samantha went home reflecting on what her friend had said. After a couple of days, she came to the conclusion that she was hurt by her daughter's reaction to her anger because it reminded her of the way her own mother hurt her by*

> *reacting without remorse. That is why Samantha acted so irrationally. With even more reflection, she realized that if she was going to yell whenever she was angry, then it was her daughter's right to withdraw. Young children often do not understand anger and withdraw to cope. Maybe if she changed her tactic when she was angry, she'd get another response. Samantha decided that it was more important for her to have her daughter respond to her when she was upset then for her to express her anger so blatantly and have Ann withdraw. So, Samantha mellowed her response and pleasantly discovered that her daughter started reacting to her and showing remorse. They had broken the cycle.*

The objective of the story is to stimulate group members into reflecting upon their own relationships within the family and how their past and expectations have come into play. Although initially it is not to be expected that the group members will be able to share any of these insights, the group can begin discussion about the story itself, how it felt, and what thoughts they have about what they heard. It may be necessary for the facilitator to promote further discussion if the members seem to not respond by switching the discussion from a personal perspective to a conceptual perspective. For example: What do you think of the notion that past events can influence how people perceive things today? This type of questioning should reveal where the group members are currently at. The facilitator may need to adjust the pace according to what is most beneficial for the group members. It is important not to rush members beyond where they are ready to be.

The session would wrap up with the facilitator asking group members to think about the story they heard and to try to notice any connections in their own lives throughout this next week.

Process.   The success of these two sessions depends upon two main factors: the ability of the facilitator to provide a safe environment to disclose very personal and difficult issues and the willingness of the members to be open to that level of introspection. This is one of the reasons that the screening needs to be done carefully. In order for the members to have any success in the group, they need to be open to new ideas and be at a point in their life where they have the resources to analyze themselves. But it is also important for the facilitator to let the members set their own boundaries. Members need not disclose a very personal issue in order to walk away with any useful knowledge. It is enough that each can recognize and be *aware* of the possibilities of the pattern.

This is also where the group members start to connect more and validate each other's feelings and frustrations through their own experiences. In effect, this could facilitate that safe environment just recently discussed.

Session 4

Purpose. For the fourth session, the facilitator starts to introduce the skills portion of the group. During the skills section, the facilitator explains the disciplining concepts and starts role-playing these techniques. This will enable the members to feel more confident about integrating them into their discipline routine. For a check-in each week, after this session, members tell the group about how their experience was using the new discipline technique. This gives the group an opportunity to decide if there needs to be additional time spent on old material, to double check the members' confidence using it, and to decide if it is working for them.

Theme. The session starts with the discipline concept called *prevention*. Prevention, when referring to discipline, is simply defined as creating an environment so the parent or provider is not stuck in a trap of always saying "no" or providing the child enough opportunities so they are less inclined to display negative behavior (Lighter, 1995). There are many ways to accomplish this and the group will only have time to touch upon the main ideas: warmth, affection, provide choices, and set clear and firm boundaries (safety issues).

Activities. After checking in by completing old business and discussing the past week, members are split into groups of two to discuss their homes and their physical environment regarding child safety. This can include anything from outlet protectors to household rules for the child. Next, the small group members help each other think of ways to enhance the environment provided and draw a picture or make a collage about those ideas. Members are asked to share their ideas and creation with the rest of the group. The purpose of this exercise is to think of simple ways parents can rearrange their house so they are not forcing their child and themselves into a cycle of always saying "no." Again this is a matter of prioritizing parents' expectations by choosing battles and focusing most of the rules around the concept of safety and respect of others. This provides parents with a solid reasoning behind their choice of rules.

Process. At this stage, the group is focusing on skills acquisition, modeling, and redirection. The facilitator encourages group members to work together developing new skills to help them in this specialized area, discipline. By working in teams, members can obtain a clearer perspective and be able to brainstorm ideas with each other. The group starts working together cohesively now that each has established themselves in the group and has set their individual boundaries. The facilitator should start backing off from individual interactions and letting the group members seek the support each needs from other members rather than the facilitator. The facilitator should still ensure and support the

boundaries while at the same time being available for any questions about the new skills introduced.

Session 5

Purpose. Session 5 starts with skills acquisition, this time focusing on modeling and redirection in connection with discipline techniques. The facilitator should also ask members to try to use these techniques little by little with their children at home and provide feedback during the check-in about how it is progressing for them. At this point the group should discuss any problems or concerns they have about implementing them and start doing problem resolution around those issues.

Theme. The fifth session combines two techniques, modeling and redirection. The first is slightly introspective because it requires taking a look at the double-bind messages parents send their children by modeling behaviors they do not want their children to emulate. Next, the group will spend time on learning how to redirect the child's behavior instead of immediately moving to a consequence or punishment. Concepts included in the discussion on redirection are: distraction, substitution, and the offering of choices. Some members may bring up techniques such as corporal punishment. The facilitator should let the members know that the group will be discussing it later on in session 7.

Activities. After the check-in, the facilitator asks members to think about and then write down one positive thing that they have taught their child through modeling alone. After sharing this with the group, members are then asked to think of a behavior that they perceive as a negative behavior that the child has learned from the parent through modeling. During this activity the facilitator is looking for examples where the parent has verbally told the child one expectation, but preceded to model the opposite. Did the child chose to follow the behavior that was modeled or the rule given? Why does the group think this is? Why are double-bind messages unfair and confusing to children? Again, this is an introspection activity, therefore, it is important not to push and to let the member absorb the information given. There is plenty of time next week, during check-in, to share the member's individual discoveries.

Most of the session time is taken up with modeling, so the portion on redirection is mainly informative, using clear examples as a means for promoting discussion and sharing about member's experiences, such as when a child starts to misbehave, parents could walk up to the child and suggest a new activity.

Process. The process of session 5 mimics session 4's process goals. Again it's about skills acquisition, rehearsal, and learning to interact and support each other as a group.

Session 6

Purpose. The purpose of sessions 6 and 7 is to mirror the previous two sessions: skills acquisition, rehearsal, and the sharing of how the new methods are working for each of the members at home.

Theme. This session's focus is the technique used most often in disciplining school-aged children today: *consequences.* There are two types of consequences: natural and logical. A natural consequence happens without the parent's/provider's involvement. An example of this would be if a child decides that he or she does not have to wear his or her coat outside in the winter. The natural consequence would then be that the child gets sick. A logical consequence requires parental intervention, but it is also fair and related to the negative behavior. For example, if a child throws food on the floor, then the logical consequence is that he or she has to clean it up. When deciding on an appropriate logical consequence it is important to remember that parents are trying to *teach* their child something about that behavior. Parents not only want children to understand what the wrong behavior was, but how to fix it and what would have been a better choice. Choice is a strong component here. Parents should let their children know that they *always* have choices. Children may not like the choices but they do have them; they also need to learn *why* it is necessary to behave in certain ways. In order for children to internalize it, parents need to consistently communicate with them the reasons and consequences. Then they should eventually understand that for every action there is a comparable reaction.

Activities. A very effective rehearsal technique for this discipline skill is role-playing. Instead of choosing the situations for the parents, the facilitator asks members to think of one situation that they have been recently dealing with that has given them difficulty. Then break off into pairs and try dealing with these situations using this new technique, role-playing. Afterwards, the group will all reassemble and talk about the role-playing experience and how it went. If there were any difficulties, now would be the time to give input and problem solve within the group.

Process. During this process the group continues to focus on skills, group involvement, and support. But because of the role-playing activity, the facilitator needs to watch carefully and redirect any attempts at judgment or advice giving. By this stage, group members should be able to communicate their ideas and support without interfering with each other's safety.

Session 7

Purpose. There are two purposes for this group session. The first is finishing up the skills acquisition portion by talking about alternative discipline choices, such as corporal punishment. Punishment is not a very effective form of discipline on its own; however, used infrequently and properly it can work. In the second part of this session, the group will discuss goals and concerns about the techniques and revelations they have learned concerning discipline. It is also time to start to look at the termination of the group and what it will personally mean to each of the members and the group as a whole.

Theme. Again the theme is *alternative disciplining techniques and goal setting.* The facilitator wants the members to start focusing and thinking about their success in being able to implement these new techniques.

Activities. During the beginning of this session, members open discusssion by asking the group to define punishment. Punishment is doing something unpleasant in order to get rid of a behavior; that is, corporal punishment/spanking (Gibson, 1983). But why doesn't it work all of the time? Punishment does not teach the child self-discipline. All it does is show the child what to do to escape punishment. It does not teach the child the appropriate behavior or why. Therefore, the child will never internalize it. Punishment also cannot be effective without an enforcer. Some of the other discipline techniques, however, work without the parent needing to be physically present. However, when nothing else works, used sparingly, and combined with an alternate technique, (such as explaining positive choices), punishment can be a viable alternative. After the facilitator introduces this topic, it should be opened up for discussion among the group members.

For the last half of the session, the facilitator talks about the members' goals and their expectations regarding their ability to successfully implement these techniques into their lives. The facilitator wants the members to feel comfortable and knowledgeable about using the new discipline techniques and to feel they can do so with consistency, which is the key to disciplining. Again, this is a time to problem solve and support each other. The facilitator should start discussing the termination of the group and what that means to each memeber.

Process. The same group process that has worked for sessions 4 through 6 should work for session 7 also. Members should feel a shift during the last half of the session when the group starts discussing the termination of the group. Here the members should start reflecting on what they got from the group, whether or not it met their expectations, and how well each feels they will be able to cope without the support of the whole group. This is an important part for the facilitator because it lets members focus on which of them needs to have additional support later on and how well they will maintain what they have learned.

Session 8

Purpose. The last session should conclude with any issues or concerns about old business and the things the group has learned. It is a time for reflection and support. Members have an opportunity to express whether or not the group met their individual goals, expectations, and whether they have grown from the experience. Of course, each member should have some type of group closure.

Theme. The theme for this session is *assessing the group experience*: ourselves, other group members, and the facilitator. This includes seeing how members impacted each other in both positive and negative ways.

Activities. Most of the session is group members openly discussing how they feel they've grown from this experience and how effective they feel about continuing to use these new skills. This is a great time for both the facilitator and group members to share their strengths and support members in their assessment of how well they accomplished their goals. It is also an advantage to look ahead and determine the member's support system around this topic and how to develop it. Some of the members may choose to network; if not, the facilitator should recommend some appropriate resources and referrals. To conclude the session, the facilitator asks the group members to fill out a short survey and return it in a month by mail. That way the members have more of an opportunity to use and practice new discipline skills before being asked how helpful and useful the class was for each of them.

Process. It is important during this session to tie up loose ends and make sure the members are leaving with what each needs, concerning both skills and support. Part of this support includes the comments and affirmations of other group members. Trying something new, especially something new that affects the development of their families, requires a lot of confidence, and it is important during the last stage for the group members to build each other's self-esteem by positively affirming each other and recognizing each member's strengths.

STRATEGIES TO EVALUATE THE GROUP

At the end of the final session the facilitator should pass out the survey explaining to group members that they are to take it home and fill it out after approximately four weeks, and then mail it back. The reasoning behind this is to give each member time to adjust more fully and objectively to the new discipline styles at home. It is often very difficult to change interaction styles with other family members, because it also means a shift in the family dynamics.

The survey reflects upon the quality of the class by evaluating the information, the facilitator, and the group environment (see Appendix A). Each item uses a Lickert scale, rating the overall satisfaction. Also there is a short answer space provided so the members are encouraged to write about what they specifically liked and did not like and about how well each is doing with the skills he or she learned. The survey should ask if parents are getting the support they need right now. At the end of the survey there is a place for them to request if they would like to be contacted for any additional help or support. This includes referrals needed or additional groups.

REFERRAL PROCEDURES FOR FOLLOW-UP

For this type of psycho-educational group class, the facilitator will probably not have members requesting additional support during the last session. That is why the survey form (Appendix A) is to be mailed back four weeks later and includes requests on support, help, and referrals. This lets the members realistically see what they are having issues with. And if they do come in on a referral, then they can talk specifically about what is not working for them. This method should enable the facilitator to meet the needs of the members most effectively.

REFERENCES

Boyd, C. F. (1994). *Different children, different needs: The art of adjustable parenting*. Sisters, OR: Multnomah Books.

Gibson, J. T. (1983). *Discipline is not a dirty word: A positive learning approach*. Brattleboro, VT: Lewis Publishing.

Hoffman, E. (1994). *The drive for self: Alfred Adler and the founding of Individual Psychology*. Massachusetts: Addison-Wesley Publishing.

Lighter, D. (1995). *Gentle Discipline: 50 effective techniques for teaching your children good behavior*. New York: Meadowbrook Press.

May, G. (1979). *Child discipline; Guidelines for parents*. Chicago: National Committee for Prevention of Child Abuse.

Sieber, C., & Lewis, R. E. (1998). Group work in specific settings. In D. Capuzzi & D. R. Gross (Eds.), *Introduction to group work* (2nd ed., pp. 131–158). Denver, CO: Love Publishing.

A Survey Form for the Group Proposal

Please take the time to fill out the following questionnaire about your experience in the Disciplining your School-Aged Child group class. It would be helpful to both the facilitator and yourself to take the time to make additional comments below each rating scale. This will let your facilitator know if you need additional help and in what area you are having difficulties. The facilitator will respond to each request of additional support and information within thirty days. Thank you for participating!

Each question will use the following responses. Circle the response that most applies: 1—not at all, 2—slightly, 3—pretty much, 4—almost completely, 5—definitely.

1. How well did you feel you accomplished your goal for the group?

    1   2   3   4   5

2. How helpful was the facilitator in helping you meet that goal?

    1   2   3   4   5

3. How helpful were the other group members in meeting your goal?

    1   2   3   4   5

4. How helpful and realistic was the information given?

    1   2   3   4   5

5. Do you feel able to integrate these techniques into your life? (If not, please make a note at the bottom of the survey commenting on what and how you would like support with.)

    1   2   3   4   5

CHAPTER 22

TRANSITIONING INTO SINGLE PARENTHOOD

Melinda Haley

PURPOSE

The purpose of this group is for newly single parents to have a safe, secure environment to work out their feelings of anger, guilt, grief, or loss and be supported in finding a new identity as a single parent. In this manner, intense feelings can be normalized and feelings of isolation can be minimized. During emotional stress, many of us feel our experiences are unique and perhaps see our own reaction to these experiences as abnormal. This group would give comfort and solidarity to these newly single parents. Group members would share resource information, ideas, and conceptual frameworks for helping each other through this transition.

CONCEPTUAL FRAMEWORK

When recognizing single parents and their families, what is often overlooked by the greater society is the pain and psychological trauma that the actual birth of these families entail. Each single parent family, regardless of its origin or circumstances, began with the loss of one parent and the "normative" concept of family. Depending upon the actual circumstances of this loss, whether through death, divorce, desertion, or choice, a myriad of emotions such as grief, anger, despair, depression, stress, and/or unworthiness may be present. If the losses of single parent families are not recognized and mitigated, psychopathology and dysfunction can follow (Morawetz & Walker, 1984).

Unresolved loss and grief may cause psychological disequilibria within single parent families (Hansen & Lindblad-Goldberg, 1987; Hill, 1986). This group therapy experience would focus on the accompanying feelings, fears, and stressors surrounding single parenthood.

The feelings and emotions that can be experienced by the "death" of a relationship, which is ultimately the basis for the formation of a single parent household, can be explained by a model that Elizabeth Kubler-Ross developed to explain the emotional needs of those dying or dealing with the death of a loved one (Benokraitis, 1999; Sigelman & Shaffer, 1995). An emotional passage must occur before mourning can be completed. This emotional journey includes denial, isolation, anger, bargaining, depression, acceptance, and finally, hope. Although this is frequently listed as occurring in stages, often it does not, but is instead a fluid process with overlapping emotions or symptoms of progression and regression. Worden (1991) also identified four basic tasks that must be completed in the mourning process: acceptance of the loss, working through the accompanying pain and grief, adjusting to new circumstances, and withdrawing from the lost relationship and investing oneself elsewhere.

Inability to complete the mourning process can lead to depression in the parent and symptomatic behavior in the child(ren). The problems this can cause can become reciprocal between parent and child; the stress and anxiety of one can fuel the other in a continuous cycle of grief, despair, and possible psychopathology (Charlton & Fleming, 1998; Cheung & Suk-Ching Liu, 1997). The method the parent uses to cope with the loss will have a significant impact on his or her child(ren). Good mental health in the parent is positively correlated to good health in the child(ren). If the parent is unable to cope, or copes maladaptively, it will most likely cause emotional problems in the child. Mourning reactions must be acknowledged and supported so they can run their course and not continue to affect the family (Hanson, 1986; Ladd & Zvonkovic, 1995). Group therapy with these newly single parents can help direct them to resources and coping methods so they can deal effectively with these issues.

Single parent families have not only lost a parent but many of them have also lost a great portion of their social network. The mourning process itself can lead to self-isolation. Loss of social supports can be detrimental to the grieving and coping process. These parents have also lost a sense of validation from their spouse or significant other and may become unable or unwilling to find it in someone else. These parents may therefore remain silent and their grief and loss goes unassuaged. When social networks are maintained or rebuilt, it helps mitigate the loss of the other parent and facilitates increased mental health within the family (Achille, Lachance, & Saintonge, 1998). Psychological adjustment of the family is greater when they are involved in social networks and social support is affirmatively correlated with positive health outcomes (Abbott, Meredith, Self-Kelly, and Davis, 1997; Gass-Sternas, 1995; Hanson, 1986; Turner & Scherman, 1996).

Another important aspect of this group, then, is that the support experienced within the group can help mitigate these feelings of isolation and desertion. Group therapy can also provide social opportunity among compatriots. The group members, even though their individual stories may differ, all share one commonality: They are all now single parents. They are all experiencing some level of pain and stress.

GROUP GOALS

The goals of the group would be for the sessions to facilitate the following:

1. Group members should understand that it is normal and acceptable to grieve for what they have lost regardless of the manner that this loss occurred. The Kubler-Ross and Worden models are helpful in assisting each member to identify the associated feelings that may occur as the single parent faces his or her new life.
2. These models also assist in helping members feel that individual responses are normal. Group members should understand that anger or rage, grief, denial, isolation, and depression are all common emotional reactions and through the group experience

should be able to accept these feelings and work through them.
3. Coping mechanisms are examined and each individual will do a self-analysis of what is adaptive and therefore working and/or what is not working or is actively hindering progress. Group members decide for themselves what is maladaptive or needs to be changed in order for them to cope more effectively with their own unique situation.
4. Group members should understand the benefit of a social network and can examine theirs and identify if improvement is needed. Members can share resource information as well as be directed to community resources by the counselor.
5. The group members can work out their new identity as a single parent within the safety of the group. The members should benefit from the solidarity that comes from people experiencing a similar circumstance.

PRE-GROUP SCREENING AND ORIENTATION

Pre-group screening is always important in any group counseling format. For this group, it may be beneficial to ensure that both genders are represented. This will help ensure that gender bashing does not occur and may help members to cope, or gain understanding, by having the oppositional view represented. If both genders are represented it may be helpful to consider having co-facilitators representing both genders so that all members feel comfortable and safe within the group. This group can also be done with only one gender represented both in facilitation and/or group membership.

The goals of the group should be explained to each potential member. This is a support and educational group for those who are in the process of working through the stated issues, and therefore a potential member should be actively working through some part of the grieving process or need help in dealing with the stress of his or her new life. However, it would be prudent to select members who are experiencing differing emotions or "stages" of grief. For example, if each group member's primary or current emotional response is anger, the group experience may turn into a grievance session, which probably will not be effective in helping members cope with this life transition. Having members in different emotional places, points, or "stages" can help other members recognize and deal with these emotions when they arise and see them as normal responses to circumstances and the grieving process.

Potential members should be willing to be open about their own circumstances (within reason and within their comfort zone) and their accompanying problems, emotions, or experiences. This ensures that not only will members receive the greatest benefit from the group but also will contribute maximally for the benefit of others. Potential members should be willing to look at their feelings and beliefs and express a desire to move past the experience of loss and grief, learn from it, and grow as individuals. If the only activity the potential member wants is to complain about the ex-partner, then this person probably would not facilitate growth within the group.

After the group is chosen, members should be notified and asked to bring a photo album, mementos of the lost relationship, or make a collage that represents the aspects of the story that each member would like to share with the group. This will facilitate discussion and introductions for session 1.

OUTLINE FOR EIGHT GROUP SESSIONS

Session 1

Purpose. The purpose of the first session is to discuss group goals, rules, confidentiality, and its exceptions. Members also discuss and agree on the ground rules that will govern the group, introduce themselves to the group, and share their personal stories of their lost relationship or how they came to be a single parent.

Theme. The theme for session 1 is "exploration and identification."

Activities. Session 1 is the opportunity for members to explore their own feelings in regards to the grieving process, their own feelings of safety and acceptance within the group, and what each individual wants to achieve from this counseling experience.

The counselor should have members introduce themselves to the group. After this is accomplished a handout is given to each person listing member's rights, responsibilities, and rules of confidentiality. This handout should come from the clinic in which the group is being held. If one is not provided then one can be obtained from the following sources: Sharon Johnson's *The 1-2-3s of Treatment Planning*, page 354, or Edward Zuckerman's *The Clinicians' Thesaurus*, page 78. At this time, group rules of conduct should be discussed and each point should either be agreed to or amended by group consensus. This empowers the group and helps facilitate cohesiveness. By developing rules for the group, the members will come to know that this is their group and not the facilitator's.

One point that should be made clear to all members is the time limitation of this group, as it is only held for eight sessions. Termination, and what it means to each member, should be discussed. It should be noted that this will be one more form of loss for each member and time should be given for members to process this with the help of the facilitator. Additional time can be used in other sessions should members need the time as termination draws closer.

After these points of business have been taken care of, the group can then proceed in the sharing of background history by using the photo albums, mementos, or collages that each member was asked to bring. This enables the members to talk about their own situation and how they came to be, or the process by which they are becoming, single parents. It should be emphasized that the purpose of the group is not to work out old relationships, devise strategies to rectify mistakes, devise strategies to develop new relationships, or vilify the ex-partner.

In addition, it should be underscored that members should only share what they are comfortable sharing and can set their own boundaries in disclosure. This is the only session where members will dwell on individual stories of how they came to be a single parent. The rest of the sessions focus on the grieving process and material that enables members to progress, grow, deal with stress, and accept the changes this new transition has brought to them.

The counselor should ask group members to pick a flower that identifies for them most closely how they are feeling about themselves in this stage of single parenthood. Members should state the flower and why it was chosen to represent them at this particular time. The counselor should note these answers for comparison to answers given to the same questions in other sessions.

Because these discussions are apt to evoke a lot of emotion, a checkout should be done to make sure each member is emotionally stable enough to leave. Any member that feels in need of assistance in the process of achieving emotional equilibrium should receive that help before being sent home. One way to deal with the emotionality that members are experiencing, either in-session or elsewhere, is for the group leader to teach the group various relaxation techniques. There are many excellent references that can be utilized that teach these techniques. One in particular is Sharon Johnson's *Therapist's Guide to Clinical Intervention*, pages 151–158.

Another technique that can be used to handle emotionality is a containment exercise. The counselor can lead the group or group member who is being emotionally overwhelmed in the technique of sensory counting. Have the member verbally state: (1) One item she or he can see in the room; (2) one sound she or he can hear in the room; and (3) one thing she or he can touch in the room. Then ask the group member to state two things she or he can see, hear, or touch in the room and proceed by asking the member to list additional things she or he can see, hear, or touch until that group member becomes calm.

Another emotional containment exercise is affective shrinking. Have the group member close his or her eyes and breath deeply and slowly while concentrating on each breath. Then have him or her visualize that there is a container (e.g., a box, Tupperware container, or zip lock baggie) and have him or her imagine putting his or her feelings into the container and shutting the lid. Then have the member imagine digging a hole in the yard and burying the container or throwing the container into a river and letting it float away.

Once all members have reached emotional equilibrium, a closing exercise can be done. The group leader should lead the group in a chosen relaxation exercise and then ask the checkout question, "If you were a color what color would you be and why?" This is an excellent way for the group leader, as well as the group members, to ascertain what progress was made in this session.

Homework assignment #1. The counselor should ask members to think about their own circumstances and prepare to share with the group which emotions are most prominent for them (anger, denial, grief, depression, and so on) and why they believe they are experiencing that one emotion or combination of emotions at this particular time. Again, collages made from personal photographs or magazines, drawings, poems, or any other form of expression can be used to help members share and facilitate discussion.

Additionally, the form found in the section entitled "Strategies to Evaluate the Group" should be given to each member to be filled out at the end of session 1. The facilitator should keep it for comparison. It will be given again at the end of the group experience to evaluate efficacy and determine which members may need additional counseling.

Process. What makes this first session work is the sharing of personal stories. Members should realize that they are not alone and that their own pain is shared in similar ways. "Telling their story" is an important part of the grieving and healing process and is cathartic for individual members. Having both sexes represented in the group helps members overcome any negative feelings for the opposite sex they may be experiencing as a residual effect from their own personal breakup. Sharing common themes of loss and grief, becoming single parents, lost hopes and dreams, or fears help build cohesiveness and solidarity between group members and facilitate bonding and sharing.

It is important that the counselor facilitates group safety and emphasizes that members only have to share the parts of their personal stories that they feel comfortable sharing with the group. The emphasis is on the reconciliation of the grief process, and the foundation for the healing process, and not the intimate details of each breakup. A time limit should be set ahead of time to limit discussion of each breakup so that each individual group member can share and the group will not run out of time. At this time, feedback should not be given. The goal is that members feel heard, that they are able to verbalize their pain, and let other members understand why

they may be experiencing different emotions than others in the group. Each member's story is unique and so too is his or her grieving process.

Session 2

Purpose. The purpose of this session is to identify more concretely where members are in the context of the grieving process, and to identify personal goals in what the members want to achieve in relation to their own personal growth. This session also begins to identify strengths and weaknesses that are helping or hindering each member's progress.

Theme. The theme for session 2 is "lost and found." Members discuss individual responses and emotions surrounding their personal loss and grief.

Activities. Time should be given at the start of this session for anyone who feels there is unfinished business from the last session. After this is satisfied the counselor can ask members to bring out their collages, poems, drawings, or whatever medium of expression was chosen to convey an individual member's emotional state within the grieving process.

The purpose of using different mediums rather than just verbal expression is that it more clearly defines what that particular emotion means to that particular individual. What represents anger to one person may represent annoyance to another and anxiety to a third. Using this format will help the particular group member who is sharing to be better understood by the group, and should also foster discussion among other group members.

The emphasis should be on the individual strengths exhibited by members. During the initial stages of the grieving process, some members may be self-pitying, self-blaming, or focusing on their own weaknesses. While weaknesses should be discussed, it should be in the context of turning them into strengths or using them to facilitate growth and not as a means of self-degradation. The focus should be on identification of response and emotion, saving a more in-depth discussion on individual strengths and weaknesses for sessions 3, 4, and 5.

The counselor can talk about the general theories surrounding the grief process using the Kubler-Ross, Worden, or other models. The emphasis should be on the normalizing of all the possible responses such as anger, guilt, grief, or depression. The counselor can accomplish this by describing the grief process as a transition explaining the possible effects of unresolved grief and loss on single parents and their family. Furthermore, the counselor should explicate that each "stage" may or may not be experienced by each individual, may be experienced many times within the process, or that after reaching emotional equilibrium an event may occur that causes a person to regress. In other words, the counselor should make clear that there is not a typical grief process and each response is individualized, yet shares common elements with all others. A handout with the pertinent information regarding grief and loss and how it applies in particular to the single parent process can be given out at this time (see Appendix A).

After group members have shared their unique grieving process with the group, they should also state what personal goals they would like to get out of the group experience. This will help ensure that the facilitator can mold future sessions to respond to group needs. It might also be therapeutic for the facilitator to note any transference that may be occurring within the group process if this is a mixed gender group. Some group members may identify a trait within another member that reminds them of their ex-partner. Exploring these feelings and the issues surrounding them can facilitate healing. It might be helpful for the member, who is transferring, to say to the group or the individual upon whom she or he is transferring the emotion what it is the member wished he or she had the chance to say to their ex-partner. The facilitator must ensure at all times the safety of the group and make sure it is acceptable with the group members that an individual member does this. At the end of the session, there should be a checkout as described in session 1.

At the end of the session the counselor should lead the group in a relaxation exercise and/or containment of emotion if necessary. A checkout should be done: "If you were a dog, what kind of dog would you be and why?"

Homework assignment #2. Members are sent home with a questionnaire to facilitate identification of their own particular stressors and their responses to the stressors for the next session (see Appendix B). Additionally, in order to facilitate discussion for the next three sessions, distribute to all group members a notebook sized, blank piece of paper that is divided by a graph into four sections. Instruct members to list in section one what they perceive is causing them stress as a single parent. In section two, have them list the solutions they have tried and whether these were successful or unsuccessful in solving the problem(s). In section three, have them list what they perceive to be the strengths that are helping them and their children during this transitional process. In section four, have them list what they feel is hindering their ability to deal successfully with their stressors or situations (i.e., parent is fatigued and therefore gets cranky when dealing with upset or misbehaving children, which is exacerbating family stress).

Process. What makes this session work is the sharing of everyone's concept of their own emotional pathway and recognizing the similarities that each member shares with others. This helps absolve the feelings of hopelessness and isolation. Each member can recognize through the stories of others that this is a process and a transition. Additionally, they will recognize that each person

faced with the loss of a relationship goes through some form of what they are experiencing, and this is or should be a temporary state. In addition, through the sharing, members can learn what has worked well for others in the same or similar situations. The facilitator should be careful to keep the discussion on the grieving process and not on bashing the ex-partner. What happened is less important to the group then the process by which members are dealing with their pain and loss.

Session 3

Purpose. The purpose of session 3 is to be supportive and educational. During this session, the therapist should discuss anger, stress, depression, and grief management. Members should use this session as a forum to identify what their stressors are and learn effective ways of coping with them.

Theme. "Exorcizing the demon."

Activities. Time should be given to deal with any unfinished business left over from the last session. Using the questionnaire group members brought home from the last session, this session should revolve around the discussion and identification of particular stressors individual members are experiencing. The counselor can ask members to rate their stress level on a scale from 0 to 10 with 0 being equivalent to the absence of stress and 10 being equivalent to unbearable stress. This will enable the counselor to identify which group members need attention first, and which members are either dealing with the stress adequately (or are in denial). Members can then share individual strategies on how they are dealing with particular stressors (i.e., solutions to daycare problems, finding time for one's self, dealing with financial problems, role overload, burnout, dealing with the ex-partner and his or her family, and so on). Members can also collectively brainstorm (with counselor facilitation) additional or alternative courses of action to deal with stressors. At the end of this session, the counselor should do a checkout. One example would be, "If you were a car, what kind of car would you be and why?" The counselor should handle any stress or excessive emotionality with relaxation and containment exercises.

Process. What works in this session is the sharing of common problems and solutions. It is therapeutic for individuals who are struggling to know that they are not alone in their conflict. Members who have successfully dealt with a stressor and found a solution that works can share their success with others. Understanding that solutions can be found to problems can help these single parents feel back in control over their life and situation. They will begin to feel hope again instead of hopelessness. Their outlook will begin to become more positive as they realize that these are temporary problems and will not be lifelong tribulations.

This session is also helpful to those single parents who are feeling overwhelmed and haven't identified what their particular stressors are or haven't begun to resolve these issues. Solidarity with others in the same situation helps mitigate feelings of loneliness and isolation that often plagues newly single parents as they withdraw from others to keep from being further damaged emotionally.

Session 4

Purpose. The purpose of session 4 is to continue what was started in session 3. Now that group members have identified their stressors and talked about possible solutions, it is time to discuss what their strengths are in order to build upon them. Coinciding with this is the other side of the coin, which are weaknesses. While these weaknesses should be addressed, the focus for this session is on strengths, saving a more in-depth discussion on weaknesses or ineffective coping mechanisms for session 5.

Theme. "Accentuate the positive."

Activities. Using the graph from Homework Assignment #2, discussion in this session centers on what these single parents have accomplished and not on what they have had problems coping with or what is still left unresolved. Before weaknesses are discussed in session 5, it is imperative that members feel a sense of accomplishment. This is a difficult transition and these parents are within the midst of loss, grief, and emotional trauma. Mistakes are made but these parents have also done a lot of things right. Often, during the midst of a divorce or separation of a family, the parents experience a lot of guilt, worthlessness, and sense of personal failure. They will tend to dwell on the negative and what they perceive they did wrong. It is therapeutic for them to dwell on what they did right. Recognizing their strengths and positive coping mechanisms helps them to overcome their weaknesses and helps them to recognize maladaptive or ineffective coping mechanisms that are hindering their progress to grow and heal, not only within themselves, but as a family unit.

Therefore, members should share what they think are their own strengths. This can be utilized to identify what sources can be drawn from during this transition. In turn, this will enable members to begin to think about what areas they would like to strengthen. Each member's graph can help facilitate this sharing. The important consideration is to get group members recognizing the area where they are coping well and using that as a springboard to improve self-esteem. It is also helpful to group members to identify areas that may be hindering their progress or behaviors they are exhibiting that are preventing them from getting what they want.

Sharing strengths can also generate ideas between members. Coping mechanisms can therefore be examined within the group. Since members are apt to be experiencing many similar crises, it would then seem reasonable that similar coping mechanisms could be shared. For example, one member might cope with his or her stress by engaging in vigorous exercise, while this strategy might not have occurred to other members. Another might cope by engaging in alcohol consumption, which, while self-medicating, is ineffective at solving the problem. While this particular member might not share this with the group, she or he is exposed to other members' successful coping strategies and therefore should have an increased arsenal with which to work and should be able to identify that the coping strategy of alcohol consumption is maladaptive and is hindering his or her progress. At the end of the session, the counselor should do a checkout and relaxation or containment exercises as previously described.

Process. Having group members focus on the positive aspects of this transition and their strengths, again, instills the feelings of hope and control. It is common for people to focus on the negative aspects of separation and divorce, but it is important and therapeutic for members to recognize the positive aspects that came out of this experience. Not everything is negative. Through this process, group members realize that they have the resources to cope with this difficult transition and this leads to self-empowerment. Once empowered in this way, the group generates more solutions to the problems being faced individually by members.

Session 5

Purpose. The purpose of session 5 is to recognize maladaptive coping mechanisms, negative thoughts or self-talk, or self-defeatism. The focus is on finding adaptive methods of coping and positive self-reinforcement.

Theme. "Eliminate the negative."

Activities. The graph from Homework Assignment #2 can again be utilized to facilitate discussion. At this point, as a result of the discussion from session 4, members should have some ideas about what is not working well for them. They should also have garnered ideas from what other members have shared regarding what changes they might need to make to help find solutions to their problems and deal with stress. They are now armed with information regarding what they are doing well and how they can use their strengths to overcome the areas in which they might be having difficulty.

The activity for this session is a continuation of the previous session, but the focus is on what each group member would like to improve. Members should self-analyze what is not working for them and share this with the group. Discussion should center on turning these "weaknesses" into strengths as the group suggests new solutions. Members can then apply what they think will work in their own situation or may generate new ideas based upon group suggestions. At the end of the session, the counselor should do a checkout and relaxation or containment exercises as previously described.

Process. What works for session 5 is keeping members focused on small changes that they can make *now* that will make a difference in their lives. Linking their weaknesses to their strengths can help relieve their feelings of helplessness, frustration, or anger over their situation.

Session 6

Purpose. The purpose of session 6 is to help group members understand the importance of support networks and how it relates to improved mental health. The goal of this session is to get group members to identify the people in their lives who can be a source of support for themselves as parents, and for their children.

Theme. "Building bridges."

Activities. During this session the counselor can give members a list of local State and County agencies that can be used as a source of support (e.g., the local chapter of Parents Without Partners, local crisis hotline numbers, and State organization numbers such as Families With Dependent Children).

To facilitate discussion about how connected each group member feels to his or her family of origin, the absent parent's family, extended family, or the greater community, the counselor can ask members to pick an animal that would represent themselves and how they feel regarding this issue and why they picked this particular animal. For example, if a group member picked a hamster and proceeded to describe the reason for this choice as he or she knows hamsters prefer solitude and only seek others of their own species during mating season, it might indicate to the group that this group member was indeed feeling isolated. However, if a member picked the gorilla and described his or her reason as gorillas like to live in close familial groups, it might be indicative of a person who was feeling connected and had a strong support system in place.

The important aspect of this session is to foster support for members. It is common for newly single parents to feel lonely and isolated. In a divorce, many of the friends shared by the couple withdraw so as not to "take sides," and the single parent may feel abandoned. The newly single parent can feel overwhelmed by the new role as a single parent and the intensified work load and responsibilities that were previously shared between two parents. This can hinder the parent's social functioning. The parent may withdraw and the family may become isolated. Psychological adjustment of the family is greater when they are involved in social networks and social support is affirmatively correlated with positive health outcomes (Abbott et al., 1997; Gass-Sternas, 1995; Hanson, 1986; Turner & Scherman, 1996). At the end of the session, the counselor should do a checkout and relaxation or containment exercises as previously described.

Homework assignment #3. The counselor should have the group members reflect on, and prepare to discuss during session 8, what their personal goals were during this group process and whether or not these goals have been met.

Process. What makes this session work is the support group itself. The comradery and sharing exhibited by the members during these last six sessions should emphasize most explicitly how healing a support network can be. Members can talk about how they felt before they joined the group and how being in the group has helped them deal with their transition, their healing process, and the stress of being a single parent. Discussing this issue should make it clear to members the importance of not isolating themselves and strengthening and expanding their support network.

Session 7

Purpose. The purpose of this session is to identify any issues that were not addressed by the previous six sessions, which may still need to be attended to by any individual member or by the group as a whole.

Theme. "Reflections."

Activities. Discussion should center on the homework assignment given regarding personal goals and what each member wanted to get out of the group experience. Time should be given to any member who has a need that was not addressed during the previous six sessions.

The counselor can start the discussion by asking each group member to pick a flower or a plant that most closely resembles how each member is feeling about being a single parent at this point in the group therapy experience. Discussion about the progress individual members have made can be facilitated by comparing the answers given during session 1. This will also help identify any areas that an individual did not feel were covered by the other sessions. This session is not as structured as the other six because the course of discussion will be member-led by what the group needs to discuss.

The counselor should also remind and prepare members for the transition out of the group that will occur during the last session and get members thinking about this new aspect of separation and loss in their lives. Time should be given for members who would like to process what this transition means to them. At the end of the session, the counselor should do a checkout and relaxation or containment exercises as previously described.

Process. What works for this session is that the process facilitates the realization that members can identify for themselves what areas of their lives need attention. Members can apply what they have learned from the group process and can be motivated to meet and fulfill their own needs. They have learned to identify their own strengths and weaknesses and how to tell if their coping mechanisms are working for them or not.

Session 8

Purpose. The purpose of session 8 is to clear up any unfinished business left over from the previous sessions and to say goodbye to the group.

Theme. "Out with the old and in with the new."

Activities. Time should be given for each member to process feelings of sadness and loss associated with the ending of the group. This session should be reflective of what the group has learned about loss and the stresses associated with loss. Members can tell the group what they will take with them from the group experience and what was most helpful to them in dealing with this life transition.

Each ending is also a new beginning and this should be emphasized. The counselor should note to the group that life is a series of transitions and with each loss comes some gain and new opportunity for personal growth. This will also be the last group session, and goodbyes need to be made, feelings processed, and referrals made for additional counseling if requested. At the end of the session, the counselor should do a checkout and relaxation or containment exercises as previously described.

Process. What will make this session work is emphasizing the skills and tools the group has acquired in dealing with personal loss. Support that has been garnered by the members need not end just because the formal group is ending. This is also a support group and members can continue to informally support one another outside of group therapy. This is a time for goodbyes but also a time to look back and reflect on the growth and personal gains made by each member during the group process.

STRATEGIES TO EVALUATE THE GROUP

The following questionnaire helps determine efficacy of this group and its process. The first seven questions are the same as the ones given during session 1. The answers can be compared to ascertain for the facilitator and each individual member how much progress each member has made during the group experience. Efficacy can be determined by evaluating the degree of improvement shown. It can also help the counselor determine which group members need follow-up counseling:

1. The statement or description that best represents my ability to cope with my transition as a single parent at this stage is:
   a. Self-assured and in control.
   b. Self-doubting and not sure what to do next.
   c. Stressed out and feeling hopeless.
   d. Depressed and feeling like giving up.

2. The statement or description that best represents how I feel about the stress in my life is:
   a. I am either not bothered by stress or I have the tools to cope with it and know what to do about future stressors.
   b. I am overwhelmed by the stress and not sure what to do about it.
   c. I am managing so far. What I am doing seems to work but I do not know why.
   d. I am not sure of what the stress is or how to deal with it.

3. The statement or description that best represents how I feel about the support I am receiving from my family, co-workers, and friends (support network) is:
   a. I feel very supported and know the people or agencies I can rely on for help.
   b. I do not know whom I can or cannot count on for help if I need it or where to go to find it.
   c. I am feeling very unsupported and feel blamed by others for my situation.
   d. There is nowhere to turn for help. I do not know how to ask for help.

4. The statement or description that best represents how I feel about my own strengths is:
   a. I have clearly identified my strengths.
   b. I only minimally know what my strengths are.
   c. I am not sure what my strengths are.
   d. I do not have any strengths.

5. The statement or description that best represents how I feel about my own weaknesses is:
   a. I do not have any weaknesses.
   b. I have identified my weaknesses and know what to do to either turn them into strengths or cope with them, as they exist.
   c. I have identified my weaknesses but I do not know how to turn them into strengths nor do I know how to cope with them.
   d. I have too many weaknesses to know what to do or where to start.

6. The statement or description that best represents how I feel about my role as a single parent is:
   a. I feel lost, depressed, and hopeless.
   b. I am feeling overwhelmed in my role as a single parent but I feel things will eventually get better because it can't get any worse than this.
   c. I feel overwhelmed but have the tools to make my situation better.
   d. I am feeling in control and know what to do to make things work and for me to succeed in my role as a single parent.

7. The statement or description that best represents how I feel about where I am in the grief process is:
   a. I do not feel I will ever get over my feelings of grief and loss but I am coping.
   b. My feelings of grief and loss are overwhelming and I feel suicidal.

c. I have no feelings of grief and loss.

d. I know that my feelings of grief and loss are normal and are part of my life during this transition.

The following three questions should be given at the end of the group counseling experience to evaluate leadership effectiveness and overall success of the group.

8. The statement or description that best represents how I feel regarding how well the group leader(s) facilitated this group experience is (pick more than one if more than one description applies):

a. The leader allowed me to feel safe, heard, and able to share equally in this experience.

b. The leader did not allow me to feel safe, heard, or able to share equally in this experience.

c. I feel the leader was inadequate and did not facilitate the group.

d. I feel the leader totally monopolized the group and did not allow the group the freedom to get our needs met.

9. The statement or description that best describes how I feel regarding the effectiveness of this group in meeting my needs is:

a. Very effective. The group was tailored to fit group needs and individual members' needs.

b. Somewhat effective. Some things were addressed but some were not.

c. Very poor. Some members' needs were met but mine were not.

d. Terrible. The group therapy was set up with preconceived notions that were not changed even though group needs were not being met.

10. The statement or description that best describes my feelings of this group overall is:

a. It was the best thing that could have happened to me at this stage of my life and I highly recommend it to others in the same situation.

b. It was a good experience. It helped me somewhat.

c. It was better than nothing.

d. It was one of the worst experiences of my life.

REFERRAL PROCEDURES FOR FOLLOW-UP

Using the answers from the above questionnaire, the counselor should be able to identify which group members would benefit in having additional counseling. In addendum, any member who requests additional counseling should also be referred. Follow-up can be as simple as sending out a questionnaire to discover how well members are utilizing the skills they learned in group and how they are maintaining their emotional equilibrium or it can consist of a follow-up group session three

months after the official end of the group to assess this in more detail.

REFERENCES

Abbott, D. A., Meredith, W. H., Self-Kelly, R., & Davis, E. M. (1997). The influence of a big brothers program on the adjustment of boys in single-parent families. *The Journal of Psychology, 131*(2), 143–157.

Achille, P. A., Lachance, L., & Saintonge, S. (1998). The influence of big brothers on the separation-individuation of adolescents from single-parent families. *Adolescence, 33*(130), 343–354.

Beaman, J., Conger, R. D., Johnson, C., Simons, R. L., & Whitbeck, L. B. (1996). Parents and peer group as mediators of the effect of community structure on adolescent problem behavior. *American Journal of Community Psychology, 24*(1), 145–172.

Benokraitis, N. V. (1999). *Marriages and families: Changes, choices and constraints* (3rd ed., p. 495). Upper Saddle River, NJ: Prentice-Hall.

Brown, J. C., Hagan, M. S., & Linder, M. S. (1992). In G. W. Clingempeel & E. M. Hetherington (Eds.), *Coping with marital transitions: A family systems perspective.* Monographs of the society for research in child development. Serial no. 227. *57*(2–3), 35–72.

Charlton, J. R. H., & Fleming, D. M. (1998). Morbidity and healthcare utilization of children in households with one adult: Comparative observational study. *British Medical Journal, 316*(7144), 1572–1577.

Cheung, C., & Suk-Ching Liu, E. (1997). Parental distress and children's problems among single-parent families in China. *Journal of Genetic Psychology, 158*(3), 245–261.

Gass-Sternas, K. A. (1995). Single parent widows: Stressors, appraisal coping, resources, grieving responses and health. In S. Hanson, M. Heims, D. Julian, & M. Sussman (Eds.), *Single parent families: Diversity, myths and realities* (pp. 411–446). Binghamton, NY: The Haworth Press, Inc.

Hansen, J. C., & Lindblad-Goldberg, M. (Eds.). (1987). *Clinical issues in single-parent households.* Rockville, MD: Aspen Publishers.

Hanson, S. (1986). Healthy single parent families. *Family Relations, 35,* 125–132.

Hill, R. (1986). Life cycle stages for types of single parent families: Of family development theory. *Family Relations, 35,* 19–29.

Holloway, R. L., Meurer, J. R., & Meurer, L. N. (1996). Clinical problems and counseling for single-parent families. *American Family Physician, 54*(3), 864–868.

Johnson, S. L. (1997). *Therapist's guide to clinical intervention: The 1-2-3's of treatment planning.* San Diego, CA: Academic Press.

Ladd, L., & Zvonkovic, A. (1995). Single mothers with custody following divorce. In S. Hanson, M. Heims, D. Julian, & M. Sussman (Eds.), *Single parent families: Diversity, myths and realities* (pp. 189–212). Binghamton, NY: The Haworth Press, Inc.

Morawetz, A., & Walker, G. (1984). *Brief therapy with single-parent families*. New York: Brunner/Mazel.

Sigelman, C. K., & Shaffer, D. R. (1995). *Life-span human development* (2nd ed., pp. 489–490). Pacific Grove, CA: Brooks/Cole.

Turner, S., & Scherman, A. (1996). Big brothers: Impact on little brothers' self-concepts and behaviors. *Adolescence, 31*(124), 875–883.

Worden, J. W. (1991). *Grief counseling and grief therapy: A handbook for the mental health practitioner.* New York: Springer Publishing.

Zuckerman, E. L. (1995). *Clinician's thesaurus* (4th ed.). New York: Guilford Press.

APPENDIX A

1. Loss can be used as a vehicle for change and growth but can also affect one's own self-esteem, relationships, and routines. It is important to recognize how the loss is affecting one's life in both positive and negative ways.

2. Each person will experience the mourning process in his or her unique way but will usually transition through similar common feelings during the healing process. These can include denial, isolation, anger, guilt, sadness, anxiety, helplessness, hopelessness, unworthiness, frustration, depression, acceptance, and hope. All of these are normal and accepted responses to loss and grief. The process also entails:
   a. Working through the pain and accepting the loss of the relationship.
   b. Adapting to the new circumstances and reality.
   c. Identifying and mitigating the stress associated with single parenthood.
   d. Working through withdrawal, the fear of being hurt again, and refocusing emotional energy.
   e. Forming a new identity as a single person and as a parent without a partner.

3. If the losses in single parent families are not recognized and mitigated, psychopathology and dysfunction can follow. It is important for single parents to work through their own loss experience in order to help their child(ren). Discussions within the family should be encouraged so that all family members can express their grief.

4. The grief of a child may not manifest itself directly but may appear as frequent illnesses, headaches or abdominal pain, eating disorders, sleeping disturbances, aggressive behavior, regression, restlessness, difficulty or truancy in school, separation anxiety, substance abuse, loneliness, depression, low self-esteem, and at its extreme psychosis or psychopathology (Gass-Sternas, 1995; Holloway, Meurer, & Meurer, 1996). The more disruption the child experiences in the process of the loss, the greater these symptoms may be. Often these children have little outlet for these feelings as the remaining parent is often preoccupied with his or her own problems (Gass-Sternas, 1995).

5. Feelings of abandonment by the absent parent can also lead to feelings of shame, worthlessness, or inadequacy and can permeate all aspects of a child's life. If internalized, it can lead to a misguided foundation of identity and continue to plague the child for a lifetime (Brown, Hagan, & Linder, 1992). Frequently, because a child burdens the blame for the loss of the parent or feels caught in the middle of "warring" parents, the child will remain silent and not voice his or her distress. When families do not speak about or confront the loss, many of the feelings go unresolved, only to plague their victim later (Hansen & Lindblad-Goldberg, 1987).

6. Many aspects of the original family may change because often there are new rules, routines, patterns, roles, boundaries, and even perhaps a change of residence. In most families, these changes create a shockwave that can reverberate for months or years, particularly in cases where the accompanying emotions are unrecognized, ignored, or repressed (Hansen & Lindblad-Goldberg, 1987; Ladd & Zvonkovic, 1995). It is important as a parent to facilitate the healing process for your child. Expect residual fallout even after you think your child has adjusted to this loss.

7. Guilt may also cause the remaining parent to try to remedy things for the child. The parent may try to compensate for the child's loss by becoming lax in setting rules and boundaries or by not setting any limits for the child. However, this only adds confusion to a child's loss of the family (Achille, Lachance, & Saintonge, 1998; Cheung & Suk-Ching Liu, 1997; Hansen & Lindblad-Goldberg, 1987). It is important at this time to keep routines the same and keep stability and structure in the child's life. There is strong evidence that poor parenting increases a child's psychological distress following a death or divorce (Beaman, Conger, Johnson, Simons, & Whitbeck, 1996).

1. What things about your current situation do you find stressful?

2. What do you notice about yourself when you are under stress? Do you become nervous? Upset? Angry? How does your body respond? Do you begin to sweat? Breathe hard or heavy? Does your heart race or palpitate?

3. What stress can you eliminate from your life? Can you delegate some chores to others? Can you identify any area of your life where you can cut back either temporarily or permanently? Can you let the house go or hire a housekeeper once a week to do the heavy work? Can you change anything in your routine or environment that would eliminate this stress or stressors?

4. What do you do right now to cope with these particular stressors? Are your coping methods helping you? Are you finding relief by using these methods or are using these methods ineffective or making your situation worse?

5. Can you reduce the intensity of your emotional response to this stressor? Have you tried deep breathing or relaxation techniques? Sensory counting? Containment of your emotions?

6. Are you viewing this stressor realistically or are you subconsciously exaggerating it because of negative connotations (thinking) associated with your particular situation? Are you viewing things that could wait as being critical or urgent? Are you trying to please *everyone!*

7. Do you take any time during your day for just you?

8. In what things do you find pleasure? Could you increase or find time to do something enjoyable just for you?

CHAPTER 23

SYSTEMATIC DESENSITIZATION FOR SPECIFIED PHOBIAS

Jonathan W. Carrier

PURPOSE

As this is purely a behavior therapy group for individuals suffering from specified phobias, its singular purpose is to alleviate or lessen the intense anxiety response an individual may feel when faced with a feared stimulus. Peripheral effects of a behavior therapy group may include an increased social network, peer acceptance to unique stressors, and an enhanced sense of self-efficacy. This group format is intended for use with most animal, natural environment, blood-injection-injury, and situational subtypes of specific phobia.

CONCEPTUAL FRAMEWORK

Behavior therapy may be defined as the application of experimentally established principles of learning to the purpose of overcoming maladaptive habits (Wolpe, 1976). Systematic Desensitization and other modern behavioral interventions arose from the early classical conditioning work of Ivan Pavlov and John Watson. Although Pavlov (1927) formulated the principles of classical conditioning and conditioned reflex through his experimentation with dogs, Watson was the first to apply these principles to human behavior. Watson (1913) argued that all behavior could be reduced to stimulus-response units, although this description may be deceptively simplistic. To Watson, a response may be something as simple as a knee jerk, but can also be as complex as eating, writing a book,

building a house, or, in this case, internalizing fear (Schultz & Schultz, 1996). Watson's classic experiment, conditioning 11-month-old Little Albert to fear white rats, became one of the most influential studies in psychology and demonstrated his theory of conditioned emotional responses (Watson & Rayner, 1920). This early experiment is often cited as being the prototypical example of phobia formation through classical conditioning. It must be stated, however, that in a contemporary view, such cognitive elements as vicarious learning, overestimation, and pre-interpretation of the feared stimulus should be taken into account when working with phobic individuals (Davey, 1997).

Although Watson did not have the opportunity to decondition Little Albert's fear, Mary Cover Jones, a student of Watson, began a series of studies with another child who displayed a similar phobia to discover if fear could be unlearned. Her deconditioning experiments with Peter, a 3-year-old child who showed a fear of rabbits, paired the feared stimulus with something pleasurable, in this case food (Jones, 1924). While Peter was eating, the rabbit was brought into the room, at first at some distance to avoid eliciting a fear response. Over several trials, the rabbit was brought progressively closer until Peter could touch the rabbit without fear. Jones's work has been described as the precursor to behavior therapy, some 50 years before the technique became popular (Schultz & Schultz, 1996).

Systematic desensitization, then, was born out of these early experiments that paired pleasurable or inhibitory stimuli with the feared stimulus. In systematic desensitization, a physiological state that is, by nature, inhibitory of anxiety is induced in the client by means of deep muscle relaxation (Wolpe, 1982). The client is then exposed to low levels of the anxiety-provoking stimulus for a short period of time. As the exposure is repeated, the stimulus progressively loses its anxiety-inducing effect (Wolpe, 1982). Successively stronger stimuli are then inserted until the fear is extinguished.

Systematic desensitization is built upon Sherrington's (1906/1961) physiological observations leading to the concept of reciprocal inhibition. He observed that the excitation of a singular muscle group automatically sets off the inhibition of other antagonistic muscle groups (Wolpe, 1995). The most commonly used example of this is the knee-jerk reaction. A tap on the patellar tendon causes a reflex extension of the leg with concurrent relaxation (inhibition) of the leg's flexor muscles (Wolpe, 1995).

Wolpe (1954) generalized these physiological concepts to therapeutic use with deep muscle relaxation in systematic desensitization. Deep muscle relaxation has been shown to have autonomic attributes that are directly opposed to those of anxiety (Jacobson, 1938; Paul, 1969; Wolpe, 1976). As in the knee-jerk reaction (the flexor muscles cannot be excited while the leg is extended), anxiety may not be felt during a physiological state of relaxation. While a client is in a state of deep muscle relaxation, the counselor asks him or her to imagine the anxiety-provoking stimuli at low levels for a few seconds, then returns the client to a relaxed state. Through hierarchical repetition, the fear response to the stimulus is reconditioned and thus extinguished.

Systematic desensitization has been proven to be highly effective in the treatment of phobias, anxiety, and a myriad of psychological difficulties. Cary and Dua (1999) evaluated the efficacy of systematic desensitization in reducing perceived stress of family and community caregivers for individuals with disabilities. All subjects in the study showed a decrease in perceived stress. Desensitization procedures can have far-reaching effects even after a single session. Sturges and Sturges (1998) attempted single session treatment of an 11-year-old girl's elevator phobia. After establishing a behavioral hierarchy and an individualized desensitization program, they were able to aid the girl in resuming elevator use without detectable fear. At a one-year follow-up, no reoccurrence of the fear was reported. Systematic desensitization has also been proven to be a multiculturally relevant treatment method. Systematic desensitization procedures were used in a Chinese study by Wang and Chen (2000) on the efficacy of behavior therapy in nine subjects with phobia. Results showed that six of the subjects recovered fully while the other three exhibited vast improvement.

GROUP GOALS

The following goals are provided for the individuals participating in this group and should serve as facilitative guidelines:

1. Members recognize that fear is a natural and healthy response to threatening or traumatizing environmental stimuli.
2. Members understand that they are not deviant, aberrant, or less able because they experience a unique stressor.
3. Members respect and provide emotional support to each other as each individual deals with his or her fear on a subjective level.
4. Members learn relaxation techniques that will aid them in overcoming their fear.
5. Members learn to manage or overcome their fear.

PRE-GROUP SCREENING AND ORIENTATION

When working with individuals who are experiencing a strong emotional state like fear, special care must be applied to screening procedures. For this reason, the addition of a co-therapist or trained observer may be warranted throughout the screening process and during each or several of the group sessions. In the screening process for this group, clients should first be assessed as to their level of anxiety during the imagination of feared stimuli. Wolpe (1976) states that in 15 percent of subjects, this imagine-based technique will not work, as they do not experience fear or anxiety when they imagine the situations or stimuli that in reality cause them anxiety. These clients, obviously, will not benefit from a group of this type. Some clients, however, may exhibit such an overwhelming fear response at the mere thought of the feared stimulus that they lose consciousness (this is more common with those suffering from blood-injection-injury type phobia). These individuals are more likely to benefit from individual counseling and would likely block group process.

Attention must also be paid to whether the phobia is actually bound to surrounding trauma as in Post Traumatic Stress Disorder. For example, someone who seems to suffer from claustrophobia may actually have been raped, assaulted, or otherwise traumatized in an enclosed area from which he or she could not escape. Generalization may have occurred; therefore, these clients are better suited to dealing with the loss of control issues in one-to-one counseling before desensitization can take place. For this reason, questions as to the origin of the phobia are a necessity in a screening interview.

A further consideration in screening clients for group participation is comorbidity of mental illness.

Some states of psychosis may contain episode-bound specified types of phobia. Obsessive-compulsive and other nonspecified phobia anxiety disorders must also be screened for, as some preoccupations may mimic specified phobias (preoccupation with germs in some obsessive-compulsive disorders).

Finally, a discussion of the general purpose and goals of the group must be discussed with prospective members, along with an overview of desensitization procedures. Prospective group members should be motivated to change and should be willing to support others in their efforts to change.

OUTLINE FOR EIGHT GROUP SESSIONS

Session 1

Purpose. The purpose of this session is typical of most initial group meetings. Introductions, group goals, and confidentiality issues are all covered in this first session. The concept of systematic desensitization and the manner in which it affects change also is introduced.

Theme. The theme for this session may best be described as one of "introduction and education," as clients get to know each other, the counselor, and the therapeutic procedure.

Activities. At the beginning of the first session, the counselor introduces himself or herself and the purpose, goals, and rules of the group. The rules of this group are open to those preferred by the counselor, provided they revolve around basic group confidentiality, client safety, and respect for each individual's subjective experience of fear.

After this, the clients introduce themselves, rate their level of anxiety on a scale of 0 to 100, with 0 being the least anxiety they have ever felt and 100 the most (counselors should make queries about high numbers), state the phobia they suffer from, and what they hope to accomplish in the group. Although each client will naturally suffer from the same phobia, this activity is affirming and adds to group cohesiveness. Clients should not go into great detail about their phobia, so that anxiety levels stay at a minimum. Because any group of clients dealing with fear are especially prone to anxiety, counselors working with this population must remain extremely vigilant and monitor each client carefully as the sessions develop.

Next, the counselor gives a description of the technique of systematic desensitization and its usefulness with specified phobias, after which the counselor opens the floor to questions about the procedure, the group, the type of phobia the group will be dealing with, or any other concerns the clients may have. The counselor should stress that the desensitization procedure will progress at a very slow and safe level so that very little anxiety will be felt at any one time. This segment is crucial, as clients suffering from a phobia naturally require much stability and reassurance as they attempt to combat and overcome their fear.

At the close of the session, the counselor asks each individual to checkout by rating his or her level of anxiety on a scale of 0 to 100, something learned about the group, and repeat what he or she hopes to accomplish in the group. The latter is important because repetition of the goal of counseling keeps individuals mindful of their motivation to change and continues to promote group cohesiveness. After every client has checked out, the counselor states the topic of the next session and dismisses the group.

Process. As the theme of this session is one of introduction and education, the process of this session involves allowing the clients to become acclimated to and "feel out" each other, the counselor, and the subject matter of the group. This is extremely important, especially with individuals suffering from anxiety. Individuals who do not feel safe and do not know what to expect from each group session will likely experience even greater levels of anxiety, which can only hinder the group process. Along these lines, the question and answer time toward the end of this initial session is a must for counselors working with this population because of their inherent need for safety and structure. This gives clients a chance to clarify and become comfortable with any issues that may have been a point of concern.

Although counselors working with individuals suffering from phobias must always exhibit confidence and control, so as to alleviate any fears of a nonstructured environment in the clients, no session is more important to demonstrate this than the first. The part of this session where the counselor shares information with the clients as to the nature of the specific phobia the group will be dealing with and the procedure of systematic desensitization is designed to allow the counselor to demonstrate his or her knowledge and ability in working with this disorder. If the clients believe they are working with an able and knowledgeable professional, their ability to manage or overcome their fear can only be bolstered. For this reason, any counselor facilitating this group should be well acquainted with the specific phobia and the procedure of systematic desensitization.

Session 2

Purpose. The purpose of this session is for clients to continue the "feeling out" process and begin to learn the technique of deep muscle relaxation. A crucial part of this is for clients to learn to closely monitor their level of anxiety at any given time.

Theme. The theme of the second session is one of "relaxation and gauging anxiety." Members begin to learn to relax on a deep physiological level and learn to gauge this relaxation.

Activities. At the beginning of this session, each client checks in by rating his or her anxiety on a scale of 0 to 100 (again, high numbers should result in counselor queries) and stating something he or she accomplished or overcame during the week. Accomplishments do not have to be extremely personal or extravagant like climbing Mt. Everest; they can be as simple and as impersonal as each client feels is necessary for personal safety. After this, the counselor introduces the topic of deep muscle relaxation by giving a short account of what it entails and its opposing physiological state to anxiety. It must be stated before the description of relaxation techniques that these techniques are similar in nature to those of Jacobson (1938) and further adaptations of Jacobson's techniques by Wolpe (1982). Counselors looking for more in-depth information on the nature of these techniques should refer to these sources.

After the brief description of deep muscle relaxation, clients should be asked to close their eyes and take a deep breath, which will be exhaled over a slow count of five. This should take place five successive times to allow clients to get used to the feeling of being relaxed and focused on relaxation. The counselor should not be making any verbal suggestions besides counting down from five, as clients are only being relaxed, not hypnotized. After this, each client will rate their anxiety level from 0 to 100. This is so clients will become used to quantifying their anxiety and will thus allow them to gauge differences between altering states of stress.

After this, clients are told to grip the sides or seats of their chairs tightly and are asked to pay close attention to the muscle tension in their forearms. The counselor should ask clients to note the difference between the tension felt in their fingers and the tension in their forearms, as the tension in their fingers is pressure from gripping the chair and not the same type of muscle tension as can be felt in the forearms. After 20 to 25 seconds, the counselor should ask the clients to slowly release their grip on the chair, all the while noting the changing tension in their forearms as their grip decreases. While clients are relinquishing their grips on the chairs, the counselor should urge them to breathe deeper and slower and to exhale longer. The counselor should encourage clients to continue letting go even after their hands no longer grip the sides or seat of the chair and hang limply at their sides. The counselor should continue to urge clients to keep on letting go, until they feel as though their arms belong to someone else or are no longer attached to their bodies. The counselor should let the client's arms hang limply at their sides for 15 to 30 seconds, continually asking them to note how relaxed their arms feel. After the clients are finished relaxing their forearms, they should each report their level of anxiety on a scale of 0 to 100.

After this, the counselor should ask clients to replace their hands however it is most comfortable for them and then to tense their facial muscles by raising their eyebrows as high as they can. The clients must hold this for 20 to 25 seconds and then be urged to slowly relax and to continue letting go after they seem totally relaxed in the same manner outlined above. Again, it is important that, after each tension period, clients begin to breathe deeper and slower as they relax the tensed muscle group. The other facial muscles should also be tensed and relaxed in this manner by asking clients to scowl (frown), wrinkle their noses, and clench their teeth.

These relaxation exercises should be continued to the other major muscle groups (neck and shoulders, abdomen and back, and legs and feet) in the same manner of tensing and then slow relaxation accompanied by concurrent relaxation of the respiratory muscles (characterized by slowed breathing). It is imperative that before and after each relaxation clients report back their anxiety level from 0 to 100, so that they have an objective manner with which to note the difference in tension and so the counselor may ensure the relaxation is working. The counselor should ensure that enough time is allowed for checkout and client questions at the end of the session. Half of the third session will be dedicated to further relaxation practice, and uncovered muscle groups may be addressed during that time.

At the end of the session, the counselor should take a few minutes for questions or concerns about deep muscle relaxation, its use with phobias, or any other concerns clients may have. As a checkout, clients must rate their level of anxiety from 0 to 100, state something they learned during this session, and what they hope to accomplish by attending the group. Before the session ends, the counselor should assign the "homework" of practicing the newly learned relaxation methods for 10 to 15 minutes everyday (more if possible) and state what the next session will cover.

Process. This group session is a continued effort at helping the clients to feel they are part of a structured and safe environment. It is also a session for teaching them the tools they need to combat their fear. The check-in exercise of clients stating something they accomplished during the previous week is intended to empower the clients and to provide them the realization that they can affect change in their lives and that they do it more often than they think. It is also a method of vicarious empowerment to other group members and may aid them in realizing the range of accomplishments that can occur on a day-to-day basis. Counselors should make every effort to "build up" and empower the ability of these clients at every opportunity, as they will require an increased sense of self-efficacy as they attempt to affect change and overcome their fear.

Session 3

Purpose. The purpose of the third session is to continue relaxation exercises and to build a "hierarchy of fear" which the counselor will use during desensitization.

Theme. The theme of this session revolves around relaxation and a discussion of what situations or stimuli cause the least and greatest anxiety.

Activities. At the beginning of the session, each client checks in by stating something he or she hopes to be able to do or accomplish after the end of the group sessions. This can range from a hope to be able to ride in an elevator for a client suffering from claustrophobia to someone suffering from a spider or insect phobia hoping to be able to go camping. After this the counselor asks clients to breathe in and exhale out slowly for 5 seconds and repeat this 5 times in the same manner outlined in session 2. Clients are then asked to rate their anxiety on the scale from 0 to 100. This exercise is especially important because the next exercise may cause some anxiety in the clients as they will be establishing a hierarchy of fear by outlining situations or stimuli from least anxiety-provoking to most anxiety-provoking. Counselors may consider having a co-therapist or trained observer present during this or even the rest of the sessions in the unlikely event that one or more of the members experiences extreme anxiety or even a panic attack. Because of the sensitivity of this population, if one member manifests a panic attack, there is a definitive risk that this could create a "domino" or "landslide" effect leading to panic attacks among other members. The presence of a co-therapist or trained observer, whose role is mainly of a monitoring nature, greatly reduces the risk of this type of situation occurring and increases the safety of the group and its process.

Normally, when working with an individual client, the counselor would establish a baseline level of anxiety by asking the client to rate a specified situation or stimulus on its anxiety-provoking power on a scale of 0 to 100 and then adjust it accordingly. For example, when working with a claustrophobic person, a counselor might ask the client to rate how anxious the thought of being in an elevator makes him or her feel. If the client responds that the thought of being in an elevator gives him or her an anxiety level of 45, the counselor will mark this down and work down from this to establish the lowest registered level of anxiety without reaching 0. The next question might be: How anxious does the thought of a crowded square make you feel? and so on.

This is the same manner that should be employed in a group setting with the exception that a consensus for each situation should be reached. Using our claustrophobia example, group members would be asked to rate how anxious being in an elevator would make them feel. If the scores are fairly similar, then an average should be computed and the next question should be

posed. However, if there is a wide range of variance or several outliers surrounding a specific question, the question should be thrown out and another posed. This should continue until there is a hierarchy ranging from 5 or 10 to about 80 or 85. For claustrophobics, a crowded square may rate at 10 or 15, a crowded room may rate at 45 or 50, and a stuck elevator or a small room with a locked door may rate at 75 or 80. There should be about 20 items on the hierarchy so the counselor has plenty of material for desensitization.

During the discussion of hierarchical feared stimuli or situations, the counselor should remain vigilant of anxiety levels and periodically stop to undertake the breathing relaxation exercise outlined in session 2. This should be done as much as needed to ensure the comfort and safety of group members.

After the hierarchy has been established, the counselor should continue the muscle relaxation exercises introduced in session 2. This should be done until just before the end of the session, when the counselor answers questions and addresses concerns that may have arisen as a result of the discussion of the fear hierarchy or any other items clients wish to discuss. For checkout, clients rate their level of anxiety and restate something they hope to be able to do after completing the group. Before ending the session, the counselor briefly states what will be covered in the next session and reassigns the homework from session 2.

Process. This session is a preparatory session for the beginning of desensitization in session 4. The establishment of the hierarchy of fear is an important step for the clients, as it gets them thinking about the battle they are about to undertake in attempting to overcome their fear. The check-in and checkout exercise of stating something they hope to be able to do once the group has ended is important because it keeps the goal of counseling fresh in their minds and keeps them hopeful that it will be realized.

Session 4

Purpose. The purpose of the fourth session is for clients to undertake the struggle of overcoming their fear. In this session they are exposed to very light anxiety-provoking stimuli and begin to understand how the procedure of systematic desensitization works.

Theme. The theme of the fourth session is one of "taking on fear."

Activities. At the beginning of the session, the clients check in by rating their level of anxiety and then rating their ability to (confidence in) overcome their fear on the same scale of 0 to 100. After this, the counselor asks clients to undertake the same breathing exercise in session 2. After this, as outlined by Wolpe (1982), the counselor states his or her intention of having the clients relax while they are asked to imagine several scenes. The counselor further states that when each scene is clear in the client's minds, they should raise their index fingers one inch. This is necessary so the counselor knows to continue with the next step. The counselor then asks the clients to isolate and relax each muscle group as outlined in session 2 and ends with a final statement of the clients being wholly relaxed, at ease, and extremely comfortable.

The first scene the clients imagine is a control scene in that the patient is not expected to have an anxious re-action to it (Wolpe, 1982). An example might be having the clients imagine they are sitting at home reading a book or newspaper (Wolpe, 1982). Once every group member's fingers are raised for 5 to 10 seconds, the counselor tells the clients to stop the scene and asks them to rate on a scale of 0 to 100 how much anxiety they experienced while imagining the scene (it should be 0 for the control scene). Once this has been done, the counselor should have the clients return their attention to relaxing. The clients then should imagine the lowest item on the fear hierarchy. Again, after all fingers have been raised a few seconds, the counselor stops the scene and asks for anxiety reports. After receiving these reports, the clients are returned to relaxation and asked to imagine *the same scene* again. This process should continue until all anxiety levels are at 0 for that scene. Once each client has reached a 0 anxiety level for the first scene on the fear hierarchy, the counselor may move to the next item. This should go on until checkout time near the end of the session.

At the end of the session, the clients are made to re-lax once more before answering questions and address-ing concerns. After taking questions, for checkout, clients rate their level of anxiety and re-rate their ability to (confidence in) overcome their fear on the same scale of 0 to 100. Before dismissing the group, the counselor should briefly state the topic of the next session and re-assign the homework from session 2.

Process. As this was the initial desensitization session, the process involved was one of exploration and acclimation. This session should progress very slowly, as clients are being subjected to thoughts of anxiety-provoking stimuli within the bounds of counseling for the first time. As for each session, comfort and safety should remain as pri-mary concerns for counselors working with this popula-tion. The check-in and checkout exercise is intended to boost self-efficacy, as there should be a rise in the ex-pected ability to overcome fear from the beginning to the end of the session as clients begin to become desensitized to their fears. Again, counselors should remain aware of every possibility to raise self-efficacy in this population.

Session 5

Purpose. The purpose of session 5 is to continue desen-sitization procedures and continue to bolster client self-efficacy.

Theme. The theme of this session is "continuing the battle."

Activities. The activities of sessions 5, 6, and 7 are very similar as clients continue to become desensitized to their fear. For check-in, clients are asked to rate their level of anxiety and as in session 4, clients are once again asked to rate their ability to overcome their fear. After this, clients are asked to relax using the deep mus-cle relaxation method, and the fear hierarchy once again is started. For this and subsequent sessions, the first scene to be presented should be the last scene on the hierarchy that aroused 0 anxiety (Wolpe, 1982). Desensitization procedures should continue until ques-tion and concern and checkout time.

Exposure to hierarchically high level or especially disturbing scenes can dramatically increase phobic sen-sitivity (Wolpe, 1982). Because of this, after an especially fear-provoking scene, counselors may wish to move two to three extra levels down the fear hierarchy and work back up so that clients remain calm and safe. As with every session and especially toward the latter sessions, counselors should remain ever vigilant of client safety.

Near the end of the session, the counselor should stop the hierarchy, once again relax the clients, and take questions and concerns. For checkout, clients rate their anxiety levels and reiterate their rating of personal abil-ity to overcome their fear. At the end of the session, the counselor states the topic of the next session and con-tinues the homework assignment from session 2.

Process. The process of session 5 is a continuation of that of session 4 in that clients continue to learn to manage and extinguish their fear through the vehicle of desensitization. The check-in and checkout from session 4 was carried to this session in order to further promote self-efficacy. By the end of session 5, clients should be displaying high self-ratings of ability to overcome their fear.

Session 6

Purpose. The purpose of session 6 is continued desensi-tization and client empowerment.

Theme. The theme of session 6 is "turning the tide."

Activities. Clients check in by stating how they might use their relaxation techniques in other areas of their life and with their usual self-rating of anxiety. After this, the counselor induces relaxation and continues up the fear hierarchy. By this point, the group should be operating fairly high up or even at the top of the hierarchy, so counselors should remain mindful of the anxiety levels these stimuli once evoked and could again if the hierar-chy increases too rapidly. Again, the safety of this pop-ulation cannot be stressed enough.

Once again, toward the end of the session, the counselor should stop the hierarchy, relax the clients, and take questions and concerns. For checkout, clients rate their anxiety levels and restate something they could use their relaxation training with outside of the group sessions. At the end of the session, the counselor states the topic of the next session, continues the homework assignment from session 2, and assigns additional homework consisting of clients attempting to utilize their relaxation training for purposes other than those for counseling sometime during the upcoming week.

Process. The process in this session is a continuation of that of sessions 4 and 5. The check-in and checkout and the extra homework assignment of using relaxation in everyday life are attempts to help the clients realize they now are empowered with new tools to help them cope with life stressors. An enhanced sense of personal power may accompany this knowledge, which the clients may find useful as they approach the second-to-last group session.

Session 7

Purpose. The purpose of session 7 is to continue the desensitization efforts of sessions 4, 5, and 6 and to continue to increase self-efficacy.

Theme. The theme for session 7 will be "conquering fear."

Activities. For check-in, clients report something they used their relaxation training for during the week and report their level of anxiety. After this, the counselor once again asks the clients to relax and continue with desensitization procedures. During this session, counselors should change the wording of items on the hierarchy to ensure that desensitization generalization to like situations and stimuli is occurring. Care should be taken to not deviate from the central theme of each item, however, or its position on the hierarchy could become confused. Items should be very close to or at the top of the hierarchy during session 7, so counselors should continue to be vigilant of possible increased anxiety, especially since the wording is being changed slightly.

The same procedures for pre-dismissal as in previous sessions should occur after the counselor relaxes the clients for the final time. For checkout, clients rate their level of anxiety and rate how close they feel, on a scale of 0 to 100, to conquering or managing their fear. Before dismissal, the counselor should state the topic of the final session and reassign the relaxation homework from session 2.

Process. The process is virtually the same as sessions 4, 5, and 6 except that by varying the wording of some of the items of the fear hierarchy, the counselor is, in essence, feeling out the level of client's desensitization. The checkout of clients' self-ratings of how close they feel to conquering or managing their fear is also a vehicle for this. The varying of wording of hierarchical items and the checkout question are both imperative as it allows the counselor to not only gauge clients' progress, but also allows for some planning of the final session's subject matter.

Session 8

Purpose. The purpose of the final session is to ensure a structured close to the group and to provide members with any additional information or support that may be needed.

Theme. The theme of the final session is "victory."

Activities. At check-in, clients provide a self-rating of anxiety and, as in session 7, state on the same scale of 0 to 100 how close they feel to conquering or managing their fear. Counselors should take note of especially low ratings on the latter scale, as this indicates the need for referral or follow-up procedures for these clients. After check-in, counselors should induce relaxation in the clients and proceed at the highest levels on the fear hierarchy the group has attained until the session is half to three-quarters over. At this point, the counselor asks the clients to relax one final time and asks each client to state one thing he or she hopes to accomplish as a result of being in the group and one thing he or she actually has accomplished as a result of being involved in the group.

Just before the end of the session, the counselor should ask each member to checkout by rating their level, on the same scale of 0 to 100, in the hope of maintaining the gains made in the group. Before the counselor dismisses the group for the final time, he or she should provide any information the clients may need for referrals and follow-up procedures.

Process. The process of this final session involves bolstering the desensitization progress made in sessions 4, 5, 6, and 7, providing referral and follow-up information, and ending the session on a hopeful note. By providing time for the clients to share something they hope to accomplish as a result of being in the group and something they have accomplished as a result of being in the group, the counselor is sending the group out into the world with a sense of cohesion, hope, and accomplishment. This continues to increase client's self-esteem (in knowing they were a part of something beneficial), which they will need when they attempt to utilize their new skills as they face real world situations and stimuli. It is also important that counselors ask the clients to rate their hope for maintaining gains in the future. This ends the group on a positive and hopeful note, which should provide clients with a sense of accomplishment as they look back over the last eight sessions and forward to the rest of their lives.

STRATEGIES TO EVALUATE THE GROUP

Unfortunately, as there is a wide array of possible phobias that may fit into a group desensitization format, it would be implausible to list a survey here that would be inclusive of items that could cover every type of phobia. Although, in lieu of this, counselors may wish to develop their own surveys with which to evaluate the group, there are a plethora of established surveys in the literature by which counselors can gauge the efficacy of a desensitization group. A prime example would be the Wolpe-Lang Fear Survey Schedule (Wolpe & Lang, 1969), which presents items that refer to stimuli and experiences that may cause fear or anxiety to be answered through ratings of (this stimulus causes me to feel disturbed) not at all, a little, a fair amount, much, and very much. Counselors also may find it useful to adapt previous group's fear hierarchies into evaluation tools.

REFERRAL PROCEDURES FOR FOLLOW-UP

In some cases, there may be clients who, for whatever reason, prove unamenable to group desensitization procedures. As these clients still have issues surrounding fear of one form or another, it is the ethical duty of the counselor working with the client to provide individual counseling or refer the client to another professional for further assessment. It is recommended that all clients involved in this group be given a 3- to 6-month follow-up session to assess whether the desensitization procedure has held up in real world situations. If some or all fear has returned, the counselor should have the client return for further assessment and possible individual counseling or referral.

REFERENCES

Cary, M., & Dua, J. (1999). Cognitive-behavioral and systematic desensitization procedures in reducing stress and anger in caregivers for the disabled. *International Journal of Stress Management, 6*, 75–87.

Davey, G. (1997). A conditioning model of phobias. In G. Davey (Ed.), *Phobias: A handbook of theory, research and treatment*. New York: John Wiley.

Jacobson, E. (1938). *Progressive relaxation*. Chicago, IL: University of Chicago Press.

Jones, M. C. (1924). A laboratory study of fear: The case of Peter. *Pedagogical Seminary, 31*, 308–315.

Paul, G. L. (1969). Outcome of systematic desensitization. II: Controlled investigations of individual treatment, technique variations, and current status. In C. M. Franks (Ed.), *Behavior therapy: Appraisal and status*. New York: McGraw-Hill.

Pavlov, I. P. (1927). *Conditioned reflexes*. New York: Oxford University Press.

Schultz, D. P., & Schultz, S. E. (1996). *A history of modern psychology*, (6th ed.). New York: Harcourt Brace.

Sherrington, C. S. (1961). *Integrative action of the nervous system*. New Haven, CT: Yale University Press. (Original work published 1906).

Sturges, J. W., & Sturges, L. V. (1998). In vivo systematic desensitization in a single session treatment of an 11-year-old girl's elevator phobia. *Child & Behavior Family Therapy, 20*, 55–62.

Wang, C., & Chen, W. (2000). The efficacy of behavior therapy in 9 patients with phobia. *Chinese Mental Health Journal, 14*, 351–352.

Watson, J. B. (1913). Psychology as the behaviorist views it. *Psychological Review, 20*, 158–177.

Watson, J. B., & Rayner, R. (1920). Conditioned emotional reactions. *Journal of Experimental Psychology, 3*, 1–14.

Wolpe, J. (1954). Reciprocal inhibition as the main basis of psychotherapeutic effects. *Archives of Neurological Psychiatry, 72*, 205–226.

Wolpe, J. (1976). *Theme and variations: A behavior therapy casebook*. New York: Pergamon Press.

Wolpe, J. (1982). *The practice of behavior therapy* (3rd ed.). New York: Pergamon Press.

Wolpe, J. (1995). Reciprocal inhibition: Major agent of behavior change. In W. O'Donohue & L. Krasner (Eds.), *Theories of behavior therapy*. Washington, DC: American Psychological Association.

Wolpe, J., & Lang, P. J. (1969). *Fear survey schedule*. San Diego, CA: Educational and Industrial Testing Service.